FRIDAY 243 320

I Test

II test Wed ! 12-16

42

4

COLLEGE LAW

Fifth Edition

By

A. Aldo Charles, LL.B., D.Ed.

Virginia Bar

Professor of Business Law

University of Georgia

Published by

SOUTH-WESTERN PUBLISHING COMPANY

Cincinnati 27 Chicago 5 San Francisco 3 Dallas 2 New Rochelle, N. Y.

L87

Library of Congress Catalog Card Number: 57-6103

H560

Printed in the United States of America

PREFACE

This is the Fifth Edition of COLLEGE LAW, a textbook that was first published in 1933.

Laws are relatively stable. Changes in the law, either by legislative enactment or by judicial decision, are slow and gradual. For that reason, a revision of a textbook on business law need not be revolutionary. The primary need is to bring it up to date in the light of the changes that have been made. But writing a good textbook is like painting a good picture. The job is never complete. There is always the need to add a touch here and there to bring it as near as possible to perfection.

A clear exposition of the law that has not changed is as good today as it was in 1933. But it takes more than a clear exposition of the law to make a good textbook. The average student who studies business law has had little or no business experience. He has difficulty in visualizing the business transaction in which the application of a particular law occurred. As far as our ingenuity permits, we must create a business setting wherein the student can easily visualize himself as one of the participants, and then demonstrate how a knowledge of law will aid him in making the correct decision.

This Fifth Edition makes a noticeable advance in this method of presentation. The case problems at the end of each chapter, which constitute a new feature of this edition, do more than apply a principle of business law. For the most part each student can easily imagine that he is one of the contracting parties. This makes the teacher's task much easier because the student is motivated out of self-interest to learn the law.

The author acknowledges a debt of gratitude to all teachers who have written to share with him their experiences with the Fourth Edition of COLLEGE LAW. These suggestions and comments have made possible a number of the improvements in the Fifth Edition.

A. A. C.

TABLE OF CONTENTS

PART I. LAW AND ITS ENFORCEMENT

PART VI. AGENCY AND EMPLOYMENT

PART VII. PARTNERSHIPS

PART VIII. CORPORATIONS

PART IX. RISK-BEARING DEVICES

PART X. PROPERTY

Part I
LAW AND ITS ENFORCEMENT

Chapter 1

Law—Its Nature, Sources, and Classes

What Is Law? The word "law" has several uses. There are natural laws, moral laws, and the laws of governments. As used here, *law* includes those rules of conduct that can be enforced in courts if necessary. In this text we are concerned with the laws enacted by governmental bodies, particularly those for regulating man's business relationships.

The ledger of life might be said to consist of rights, privileges, and prerogatives on the debit side; and duties, obligations, and responsibilities on the credit side. Courts have been set up to referee disputes between their citizens concerning these debits and credits as such differences arise. In each case, the court will enforce rights when they are wrongfully withheld but only on condition that the parties perform their duties which arise in the particular controversy. A knowledge of law, then, is necessary to enable us to know not only our rights, but also our legal duties and obligations.

Sources of Law. There are four important sources of law in the United States:

1. Constitutions, federal and state
2. Statutes, federal and state
3. Law by judicial decision
4. Common law

(1) CONSTITUTIONS. A constitution is to a state what a foundation is to a house; the foundation fixes, within narrow limits, the nature of the superstructure. The federal Constitution is often called "the supreme law of

the land" because the whole legal superstructure in America must conform to its provisions.

Actually, a *constitution* is not a law but rather a written instrument which defines and limits the powers of the legislative body of a state to make laws. When the constitution says that "the state shall have the power to prohibit contracts in restraint of trade," that is not a law. It only empowers the state through the legislature to pass a law prohibiting contracts in restraint of trade. Constitutions as a rule contain for the most part an enumeration of the acts which the state cannot prohibit.

- The federal Constitution differs from the state constitutions because the federal government is one of delegated power. It has only the power granted to it by the states. All other powers are reserved to the states. The federal government, then, has only the powers enumerated in the federal Constitution. Each state, on the other hand, has the power to pass any law not prohibited by either the federal or the state constitution.

(2) STATUTES. Within the limitations fixed by the Constitution, lawmaking bodies may pass any law they deem desirable. These *statutes* constitute the most important source of law. Constitutions are difficult to amend and, for this reason, are not so responsive to the changing demands of the people. Statutory laws may be enacted, repealed, or amended at any regular or special session of the lawmaking body.

The three chief lawmaking bodies in the United States are the federal Congress, the state legislatures, and the city councils. The laws of the city councils are called *ordinances*, but an ordinance is properly called a statutory law. In the United States, if any law, whether federal or state, is in conflict with the federal Constitution, it is unconstitutional. If there is a conflict between a state law and a law of the United States passed by the United States Congress in accordance with the federal Constitution, the latter prevails.

H. Armstrong Roberts

The Capitol Building.

(3) LAW BY JUDICIAL DECISION. The federal Constitution divides the federal government into three departments: (a) the legislative department, to make laws; (b) the judicial department, to interpret the laws; and (c) the executive department, to execute the laws. This same division into departments exists in the states.

Congress has the power under the Constitution to make laws regulating interstate commerce. The complex interrelationships between the productive and the distributive processes frequently make it difficult to determine what activities are interstate commerce. For example, in 1933 Congress passed the Agricultural Adjustment Act, which among other things provided a measure of regulation of the production of wheat. The Supreme Court held that the Act was unconstitutional on the ground that the production of wheat was not interstate commerce. This judicial decision stands as the law of the land unless it is reversed by a later decision of the Supreme Court.

It is evident that the Constitution is the primary source of the law, but the judicial decisions make the general provisions of the Constitution and of statutes enforceable in a particular case. These judicial decisions in both the federal and the state courts comprise as large a body of law as do the statutory laws. Whenever an author uses the expression, "The law is . . . ," he is just as likely referring to one of these decisions as he is to some statutory law. For this reason judicial decisions are referred to as a source of law even though the courts cannot originate laws.

(4) COMMON LAW. The term *common law* refers to that system of law which developed in England purely as a result of court decisions in which the judges applied principles, rules, and customs reflecting the people's ideas of what was just and the customary thing to do. There were in most cases no written or statutory laws to guide them. These court decisions were later put into written form in Blackstone's Commentaries. Judges were then able to ascertain how judges decided in the past cases involving the same or similar fact situations. The judges were expected to follow these precedents unless it could be shown that the law had been misinterpreted or misapplied. In this way uniformity gradually developed in the court decisions, resulting in a well-established set of legal principles called the common law.

The colonists brought this system to America. Today many of the legal principles of the common law have been enacted into statutory law. But in American courts today judges continue to develop common law principles to aid them in rendering a decision in a situation where there is no statute to govern it and to meet the problems of a changing social order.

Other Laws. There are many laws other than those derived from the four sources listed above. There is, for example, *ecclesiastical law* which deals with religious matters, such as marriages, divorces, and disputes involving clergymen. Also there is the *admiralty law* dealing with maritime trade, and the *mercantile law* dealing with disputes between and with merchants. In America these branches of the law are incorporated into our system of jurisprudence so that they have lost their special characteristics.

There are three branches of our law as it exists today which deserve analysis:

1. Equity law
2. Administrative law
3. Criminal law

(1) EQUITY LAW. *Equity* simply defined means justice. A judge must interpret a statute literally. This does not always give justice. For example, the owner of an adjoining lot may be digging a basement pit so close to the house on the next lot that the house is in danger of toppling over. The law, provided the house does topple over, will allow the injured party monetary damages. Justice demands, however, that some remedy be provided whereby the man can save his house. A court of equity has the power to issue an injunction to prevent the adjoining property owner from endangering his neighbor's house.

Hundreds of similar situations developed in the early days of the common law. Judges tended to interpret the common law so strictly that many wrongs were left without a remedy. Equity law developed in a fashion similar to the early common law to give relief where the common law was inadequate. Judges decided cases according to their concept of justice. These court decisions became *precedents*, and these precedents now constitute equity law.

Equity law, then, was intended to grant relief where the law courts could or would not give an adequate remedy to litigants. This law by judicial precedent

Harold M. Lambert

Business Law Deals with the Transactions of Producers and Manufacturers.

differs from other law by judicial decisions in that the latter arises from the court's interpretation of a Constitutional or a statutory law, while equity decisions are interpretations of principles of justice. Equity rules became in time as well settled as the rules of the common law courts.

(2) ADMINISTRATIVE LAW. Many of our governmental functions today are carried on by means of administrative agencies set up by our legislative bodies. These boards and commissions, because of the complex nature of our economic order, must be given wide latitude in setting up rules of procedure. They are semijudicial bodies even though they are an arm of the executive branch of the government. They issue orders and decrees which have the force of law. For example, the National Labor Relations Board is empowered to issue a "cease and desist" order against an employer who is committing an unfair labor practice. This order is as binding upon the employer as a statutory law.

(3) CRIMINAL LAW. *Criminal law* is that branch of the law which has to do with crimes and the punishment of wrongdoers. A *crime* is an offense of a serious nature

H. Armstrong Roberts

Business Law is Also Concerned with the Transactions of Merchants and Individuals.

that tends to injure society as a whole. Business law has to do with crimes only incidentally. There are, however, certain criminal offenses, such as arson, forgery, fraudulent conveyances, embezzlement, and the like, that are closely related to business activities.

Crimes are usually classified according to the nature of the punishment as felonies and misdemeanors. Generally speaking, *felonies* are the more serious crimes and are usually punishable by death or by imprisonment in a penitentiary. *Misdemeanors* are offenses of a less serious character, which are punishable by a fine, or by imprisonment in a county jail, or by both. Committing a forgery is a felony, but driving an automobile in excess of the prescribed speed limits is a misdemeanor. The criminal statutes define acts that are felonies and those that are misdemeanors.

Business Law. The term "business law" does not imply that there is a system of business law comparable, for example, to the common law or criminal law. *Business law* consists of all the laws of every source which govern and regulate business transactions. This law is as applicable to two individuals who trade horses as it is to two giant corporations that buy and sell raw materials to each other. When Jones hires Smith to mow his lawn, he is engaging in a business transaction as surely as the Ford Motor Company is when it hires 300,000 workers.

Business law, then, is also personal law, as necessary for the farmer and the housewife as it is for the secretary or the accountant. Every purchase of merchandise, every contract of employment, every purchase of insurance, and every check written in a business transaction is governed by some phase of law. This book on business law, then, deals with contracts, sales, agencies, insurance, and all other types of business transactions carried on by both individuals and business concerns.

Questions

1. Why is the federal Constitution called the supreme law of the land? ✔

2. Wherein do statutory laws differ from constitutional laws?

3. If there is a conflict between a state law and one passed by the United States Congress in accordance with the federal Constitution, which prevails?

4. Why are we justified in classifying law by judicial decision as a source of law?

5. If a common law and a statutory law are in conflict, which one prevails?

6. Define equity law and show wherein it differs from common law.

7. If one party announces an intention to perform some act that will unlawfully deny another party his legal rights, what remedy does the innocent party have if he wishes to prevent the injury?

8. What is the legal effect of an order issued by an administrative agency?

9. Classify the following crimes into felonies and misdemeanors: murder, theft of 10 cents, drunkenness, robbery, overtime parking, and forgery.

10. What is business law?

Chapter 2

Courts and Court Procedure

Functions of the Courts. The function of a court is to declare and apply the common law and to enforce the laws passed by the legislative arm of the government. This is not the whole story, however. Constitutions by their very nature must be couched in generalities. The statutes passed by the lawmaking bodies are less general than constitutions but still must be made specific to apply to a particular court case. It is one of the chief functions of the courts to interpret and apply the law of whatever source in a given situation. For example, the federal Constitution gives the federal Congress power to pass "all laws to promote the general welfare." In conformity with this constitutional provision Congress passes a law to regulate interstate commerce. This is more specific than the term "general welfare," but is still general.

A specific case involves the regulation of wage rates in a sawmill located in a rural section of the country. The court must decide whether or not this sawmill owner is engaged in interstate commerce. The court's decision may become a judicial precedent that will be followed in the future until the court changes its decision.

Jurisdiction of Courts. A corporation's officials consist of a president, a vice-president, and many subordinate officials. Each individual has very definite authority in his limited field, with the authority broadening as one goes from the foreman up the scale to the president. To a certain extent our courts follow a similar pattern, starting with the justice-of-the-peace courts and extending up to the Supreme Court of the United States.

The power or authority which each court has to hear cases is called its *jurisdiction.* This jurisdiction may involve the subject matter of the case before the court. If the claim is for damages due to an automobile accident, a probate court will not have jurisdiction since this court deals with wills and the distribution of property of deceased persons to the heirs. A court may have jurisdiction over the subject matter but not over the person. If a resident of Buchanan County is charged with trespassing on his neighbor's property in the same county, the judge in adjoining Tazewell County does not have jurisdiction over the person of the accused. Nor does the judge in Buchanan County have jurisdiction over the person of the accused if the accused has not been properly served with notice of the trial.

Before any court can try a case, it must first be established that it has jurisdiction over both the subject matter and the person in the case at issue. This is just as logical and necessary as it is, for example, to say that the advertising manager has no control, that is, jurisdiction, over an accountant in the accounting department.

Classification of Courts. Courts are classified for the purpose of determining their jurisdiction. This classification can be made in a variety of ways. One classification can be made according to the governmental unit setting up the court. In this sense they are classified as (1) federal courts, (2) state courts, and (3) municipal courts. The same courts may be classified according to the method of hearing cases. In this sense they are called trial courts and appellate courts. The *trial courts* conduct the original trial of the cases and render their decisions. The *appellate courts* review the cases appealed from the decisions of these trial courts.

The federal government and the states have a separate court structure and this structure is best understood by classifying first the federal courts and second, the state courts.

Federal Courts. The federal courts are classified as:

1. District courts
2. Courts of appeals
3. United States Supreme Court
4. Special federal courts

(1) FEDERAL DISTRICT COURTS. By far the largest class of federal courts consists of the district courts. These courts are strictly trial courts in which are tried all criminal cases involving a violation of the federal law. The federal courts also have jurisdiction of civil suits which are brought (a) by the United States; (b) by citizens of the same state where the amount in controversy exceeds $3,000 and arises under the constitution, and federal laws and treaties; (c) between citizens of different states; and (d) between citizens of one of the states and a foreign nation or one of its citizens or subjects.

(2) FEDERAL COURTS OF APPEALS. The federal courts of appeals hear only appeals from a federal district court or from a state supreme court decision if the case involves a federal constitutional question. If one is convicted in a state court for "Unlawfully distributing pamphlets," he may appeal to the state supreme court. If he loses in the state supreme court, he may next appeal to the federal court of appeals since the federal Constitution guarantees freedom of speech. If only the state constitution is involved, no right of appeal to a federal court exists.

(3) UNITED STATES SUPREME COURT. For the most part, the United States Supreme Court hears only appealed cases from the federal courts of appeals. Under certain circumstances a decision of a federal district court may be appealed directly to the Supreme Court. The Supreme Court is the highest tribunal in the land, and its decision is final until the Court reverses its own

Harris & Ewing

United States Supreme Court Building.

decision or until the Congress changes the effect of a given decision by a constitutional amendment or by a legislative enactment. A decision of a federal court of appeals is binding upon all lower courts within the jurisdiction of that circuit court unless the Supreme Court reverses that decision.

(4) SPECIAL FEDERAL COURTS. The special federal courts are limited in their jurisdiction by the laws of Congress creating them. For example, the Customs Court hears only cases involving the rates of duty on various classes of imported goods, the collection of the revenues, and similar controversies. The decisions of the Customs Court may be appealed to the Court of Customs Appeals. There is also a Claims Court to hear cases involving claims against the United States Government. The Government, being supreme, cannot be sued without its consent, but this consent is seldom withheld.

Control of Appeal Courts over Lower Courts. All federal courts derive their authority from the people, either through the Constitution or the Congress, but the appellate courts exercise considerable authority over the courts under them. A judicial trial calls for a verdict; and the basis for this verdict in all cases is the trial court's authority as set out by the Congress and the appellate courts. Rules for the admissibility of evidence, trial procedure, the manner of selecting the jury, and many other important matters are determined by the appellate courts. The district court must adhere strictly to these rules as well as those laid down by the Congress. Furthermore, the district court, which is the trial court, is bound in its decision by the decisions of the federal courts of appeals and the Supreme Court in cases where the facts are substantially the same.

One can say that the Constitution gave the Supreme Court authority to exercise authority over any inferior courts which Congress might establish and that the Supreme Court gave the federal courts of appeals the power to exercise authority over the federal district courts, subject to review by the Supreme Court.

Classification of State Courts. State courts can best be classified into the following groups:

1. Inferior courts
2. Courts of original general jurisdiction
3. State supreme courts
4. Special courts

(1) INFERIOR COURTS. The inferior courts of the states hear only minor disputes between citizens and minor criminal offenses. In the counties and smaller towns the most common inferior court is the justice-of-the-peace court. A justice of the peace hears all claims between citizens up to the maximum fixed by the state, usually $500 or less. In addition, he may try all criminal cases involving misdemeanors. In the cities the function

of the justice of the peace may be performed by the mayor, small claims courts, and police courts. The loser in any of these courts may appeal to the court of original general jurisdiction.

(2) COURTS OF ORIGINAL GENERAL JURISDICTION. Courts of original general jurisdiction are for the average citizen the most important courts of the state. These courts have broad general jurisdiction involving disputes between two or more parties as well as criminal offenses against the state. They are called *courts of original jurisdiction* because it is in them that the case is first instituted. They hear appeals from inferior courts, but this does not make them appellate courts since the trial is conducted *de novo*, that is, as though it had never been instituted in the inferior courts. An official, permanent record is kept of the trial showing the judgment and the findings of the court. For this reason these courts are often referred to as trial courts and courts of record. The official name of such a court in most states is Circuit Court.

Circuit court, then, is the official name given to a court of record, a trial court, or a court of original general jurisdiction.

If the defendant in a criminal case, or both parties in a civil suit, are satisfied that the decision of the trial court is in accordance with the law and the evidence, the controversy ends here.

(3) STATE SUPREME COURTS. In all states provision is made for an appeal to an appellate court by the party dissatisfied with the final judgment of the trial court, or any of its rulings and instructions. Only a court which hears appeals from a trial court is an appellate court. Usually the official name is State Supreme Court.

(4) SPECIAL COURTS. Many states have special courts, such as *probate courts* to probate wills; *juvenile courts* to try cases when children, usually under fourteen years

of age, are charged with a crime; and *domestic relations courts* to hear cases involving disputes between husbands and wives. These are not courts of general jurisdiction, but of special jurisdiction. In many states these courts are of the same level as the trial courts. When this is the case, they too are properly called trial courts and courts of record. In other states they are on the same level as the inferior courts and are not courts of record.

If a case that is tried in a trial court involves a federal constitutional issue, then it may after reaching the state supreme court be appealed to a federal court of appeals. It may in turn be further appealed to the United States Supreme Court. For example, if a man is tried and convicted in a circuit court for illegally distributing printed leaflets, he may appeal to the state supreme court on the ground that this violates his freedom of speech as guaranteed by the federal Constitution. If the state supreme court rejects his appeal, he is then permitted to take an appeal to a federal court of appeals, and finally to the United States Supreme Court. If only a state law or the state constitution is involved, however, he cannot appeal to a federal court.

Court Officers. The chief officer of an inferior court is the *justice of the peace,* trial justice, or similar officer; while the executive officer is the *constable.* In a state court of record the chief officer is the *judge,* the executive officer is the *sheriff,* and the recorder is the *clerk of the court.* This is also true of the federal courts except that the executive officer is called a *marshal.*

Persons who are educated in the profession of the law and who are legally qualified to practice law are known as *lawyers* or *attorneys.* They are officers of the court and are subject to punishment for a breach of duty. Lawyers ordinarily represent the parties in a civil or a criminal action, although many states permit the parties to a case to conduct their own trial. The practice of conducting one's own trial, however, is not advisable.

Procedure in Filing Suit. Courts with but few exceptions are powerless to settle disputes between individuals unless one of the parties petitions the court. This petition or complaint is the beginning of a civil suit. The one who institutes the action is called the *plaintiff*, and the one against whom action is brought is called the *defendant*. The order of events in bringing an action is as follows:

(1) The complaint or petition is filed with the clerk of the court. This petition sets forth the nature of the claim and the remedy sought.

(2) As soon as the petition is filed, the clerk issues a *summons* or, as it is sometimes called, a *process*. This merely summons the defendant to appear in court and file his answer to the petition. The complaint and the answer constitute the first pleadings or attempts to join issue. Before the case can be placed before a jury, the issue or issues of the suit must be clearly specified through these preliminary pleadings, answers, and motions.

(3) The jury is impaneled and the trial opens.

Trial Procedure. The trial proceeds in the following order:

(1) The attorney for the plaintiff makes an opening statement to the jury indicating the nature of the action and what he expects to prove. This is followed by the opening statement of the defendant's attorney.

(2) The plaintiff presents his evidence in the form of witnesses and documents. This is followed by the defendant's evidence.

(3) The attorney for each side summarizes the evidence and argues his points in an attempt to win the jury to his version of the case.

(4) The judge instructs the jury as to the points of law which govern the case. The judge has the sole power

Ewing Galloway

A Court Scene.

to determine the points of law, and the jury decides what weight is to be given to each point of evidence except that it cannot disregard undisputed evidence.

(5) The jury adjourns to the jury room and in secret arrives at its *verdict*. This verdict may be set aside by the court if it is contrary to the law and the evidence. Unless this is done, the judge renders judgment in accordance with the verdict.

Appeals. If either the plaintiff or the defendant is dissatisfied with the jury's verdict and the court's judgment, he may appeal to the state supreme court. When an appeal is taken, a complete transcript of the trial is printed and the state supreme court reviews the entire proceedings. The attorney for each side files a brief setting forth the reasons which warrant the supreme court in either affirming or disaffirming the judgment of the lower court. If this action is the first time that the legal issue involved has been passed upon by the supreme court, the decision of this court becomes a *judicial precedent* and is binding upon all lower courts in the state. The supreme court may, however, reverse itself in a future case. This is seldom done unless the personnel of the court changes, and even then, reversals seldom occur.

Questions

1. What is the function of a court?

2. Which is the most specific—a constitution, a statutory law, or a court decision?

3. A corporation located in Alabama commits an act in Alabama that is illegal in Georgia. Does a Georgia court have jurisdiction over the Alabama corporation?

4. (a) Name the largest class of federal courts.
(b) Name two special federal courts.

5. If the Supreme Court of the United States declares a law unconstitutional, how may that decision be changed?

6. Is a decision of a state supreme court binding upon all the lower courts in that state?

7. Name the court in which the following disputes would be settled: (a) a dispute over the interpretation of a will; (b) a claim for an unpaid bill of $10; (c) the claim of a wife that her husband refuses to support her; (d) a damage suit for $2,500; (e) an appeal from the decision in the preceding suit; and (f) a claim against the federal government.

8. Who are the officers of a court?

9. (a) What is the first step in bringing a civil suit?
(b) What is the first step in a civil suit after the jury is impaneled and the trial opens?

10. Smith sues Jones for $5,000 and the jury renders a verdict for $3,000. May either or both of these parties appeal this decision?

Part II

CONTRACTS

Chapter 3

Contracts— Nature and Classes

Definition of a Contract. A *contract* is an agreement between two or more persons that is enforceable at law.

Business transactions are the result of agreements. Every time a person makes a purchase, buys a theater ticket, or boards a bus, an agreement is made. Each party to the agreement obtains certain rights and assumes certain duties and obligations. When such an agreement meets all the legal requirements of a contract, the law recognizes it as binding upon all the parties. If one of the parties to the contract breaks it, the law allows the other party an appropriate action for obtaining damages or enforcing performance by the party breaching the contract. It is evident, then, that contracts form the very foundation upon which all modern business rests.

Contracts Contrasted with Agreements. A contract must be an agreement, but an agreement is not necessarily a contract. Whenever two or more persons' minds meet upon any subject, no matter how trivial, there is an agreement. It is only when the parties intend to be obligated by the terms of the agreement that a contract comes into existence. In addition, the subject matter of the contract must involve a business transaction as distinguished from a social transaction.

- Mary and John promise to meet at a certain place at six o'clock and have dinner together. This is an agreement, not a contract, since neither is legally bound to carry out the terms of the agreement.

  If John says to Mary, "I will pay you $10 to type this manuscript for me," and Mary replies, "I accept your offer," the agreement results in a contract. Mary is legally obligated to type the manuscript, and John is legally bound to pay the $10.

Classifications of Contracts. Contracts may be classified in a number of ways. The following classifications will be helpful at this time:

1. Express and implied contracts
2. Void, voidable, and valid contracts
3. Formal and simple contracts
4. Executory and executed contracts

(1) EXPRESS AND IMPLIED CONTRACTS. If contracts are classified according to the manner of their formation, they fall into two groups—express and implied contracts. An *express contract* is one in which the parties express their intentions definitely, whether in writing or orally (by word of mouth), at the time they make the agreement. Both their intention to contract and the terms of the agreement are expressly stated. Nothing is left to implication.

- If John, by word of mouth or in writing, expressly agrees to pay $90 a month as rental for a house, and the Jones Realty Corporation expressly agrees to give possession of the house for $90 a month, this is an express contract.

An *implied contract* is one in which the duties and the obligations which the parties assume are not expressed, but are implied by their acts or conduct. The adage "a man's actions speak louder than his words" very appropriately describes this class of contract. The parties may indicate so clearly by their conduct what they intend to do that there is no need to express the agreement by words in order to make the agreement binding.

- If Jones walks into Smith's place of business, sees an article marked $12, picks it up and, with Smith's knowledge and consent, carries it away as he has done several times before, there is an implied contract that Jones will pay Smith $12. There is no doubt about what his conduct implies or what his intentions are. Likewise, Smith by his silence implies that he agrees to sell the article for $12.

Seldom are contracts implied in their entirety. They are usually partly expressed and partly implied. For example, if Randolph said to Haley, "I will give you $100 for that power mower," and Haley replied, "I will accept your offer," a contract was formed but many parts of the contract would be implied. Was the sale for cash or on credit? When was delivery to be made? It would be implied that the sale was to be for cash and delivery was to be made immediately. The theory is that if they had intended otherwise, they would have indicated their intentions.

(2) VOID, VOIDABLE, AND VALID CONTRACTS. If contracts are classified according to their enforceability, they fall into three groups—void, voidable, and valid.

An agreement that is seriously intended by all parties to be a binding contract but is without any legal effect is a *void contract*. If the agreement involves an illegal act, such as stealing a car, it is a void contract. It is not enforceable by any party to it, and thus is a complete nullity.

A *voidable contract* is one that may be avoided by at least one of the parties. The test of a voidable contract is the existence of a choice by one party to abide by or to reject the contract. A contract made by an adult with a person not of lawful age (legally known as a minor or infant) is often voidable so far as the minor is concerned. It is enforceable against the adult but not against the minor. If both parties to an agreement are minors, either one may avoid the agreement. Until the party having the choice to avoid the contract exercises this right, the contract remains in full force and effect.

A *valid contract* is one that will be enforced by the courts upon a plea by one of the parties. In order to be enforceable, that is, valid, a contract must fulfill the following definite requirements:

(a) It must be based upon a mutual agreement by the parties to do or not to do a specific thing.

minds must meet

(b) It must be made by parties who are, according to law, able and competent to enter into a contract that will be enforceable against both parties.

(c) It must include consideration (such as the payment of money, the delivery of goods, or the promise to do or refrain from doing some future act) given by each party to the contract.

(d) It must be for a lawful purpose; that is, the purpose of the contract must not be illegal, such as the unauthorized buying and selling of narcotics.

(e) It must, if it falls into a class of contracts required by law to be in a special form, meet the requirements of the law as to that form.

These five requirements are the criteria by which one may test the validity of any contract. If the agreement fails to meet one or more of these requirements, the contract may be void, or voidable, but never valid. A layman can, in most instances, analyze all business transactions in the light of these five requirements to ascertain their enforceability.

(3) FORMAL AND SIMPLE CONTRACTS. A contract under seal is a *formal contract.* In olden days when very few men could write, contracts were signed by means of an impression in wax. As time passed, a small wafer pasted on the contract replaced the use of wax. The wafer seal was in addition to the written signature. This practice is still used occasionally, but the more common practice is to sign formal contracts in one of these ways:

John Doe (Seal) ; John Doe [L. S.] ; John Doe (SEAL)

In jurisdictions where the use of the seal has not been abolished, the seal implies consideration and gives validity to the contract. However, in most states today only a few types of contracts require the use of the seal, the most common being a corporate contract.

Today many contracts are made formal by the parties to them even though their enforceability does not depend upon their being formal. Bonds and deeds are virtually the only contracts required by most states to be formal. But in many states if any contract is made formal, even though the law does not require it to be formal, some added significance is attached to it. For example, in Virginia a note under seal has a longer life than a note not under seal. A person has five years from the date of the note in which to sue for its collection if the note is not under seal; he has ten years in which to sue if the note is under seal. Other states make no distinction between contracts under seal and other written contracts.

All contracts other than formal contracts are informal and are called *simple contracts*. A few of these, such as an agreement to sell land or to be responsible for the debt of another, must be in writing in order to be enforceable; otherwise they need not be prepared in any particular form. Generally speaking, informal or simple contracts may be in writing, may be oral, or may be implied from the conduct of the parties.

A *written contract* is one in which the terms are set forth in writing rather than expressed orally. The law requires some contracts not only to be in writing, but to be in a particular form. (The most important contracts of this nature are negotiable instruments discussed in Chapter 19.) Some writers classify these as formal contracts because of their required form. The more common practice is to restrict the definition of formal contracts to those under seal.

An *oral contract* is one in which the terms are stated in spoken, not written, words. Such a contract is usually enforceable, but it is not so satisfactory as a written contract. When a contract is oral, disputes may arise between the parties as to the terms of the agreement. No such disputes need arise about the terms of a written contract if the wording is clear, explicit, and complete.

For this reason most businessmen avoid making oral contracts involving matters of considerable consequence.

(4) EXECUTORY AND EXECUTED CONTRACTS. Contracts are classified to indicate the stage of performance as executory contracts and executed contracts. An *executory contract* is one the terms of which have not been fully carried out by all parties. If a man agrees to work for another for one year in return for a salary of $300 a month, the contract is executory from its inception until the twelve months expire. Even if the employer should prepay the salary, it would still be an executory contract because the other party has not yet worked the entire year, that is, executed his part of the contract.

An *executed contract* is one that has been fully performed by all parties to the contract. The Young Men's Shop sells and delivers a suit to Hale for $60, and Hale pays the purchase price at the time of the sale. This is an executed contract because nothing remains to be done on either side.

Questions

1. Give a definition of a contract.

2. "All contracts are agreements, but all agreements are not contracts." Explain.

3. Relative to the manner of their formation, how may contracts be classified? Define and give an example of each class.

4. May a contract be partly implied?

5. Relative to the enforceability of contracts, name the three groups into which they are classified. Define and give an example of each group.

6. Name the five requirements of a valid contract.

7. (a) Illustrate three ways by which one may indicate that a contract is under seal.

(b) Does a seal add anything of importance to a contract?

8. Is an oral contract usually just as valid as a written contract?

9. If one has ten witnesses to an oral contract, can he enforce it if the contract is required by law to be in writing to be enforceable?

10. (a) Define an executory contract.

(b) If one party to a contract has executed his part but the other party has not, is this an executed or an executory contract?

Case Problems

1. Endicott and Brownell orally agree to invest $10,000 each in a retail shoe store and to operate it as a partnership. Nothing was included in the contract other than the amount to be invested. List several matters about which a disagreement may arise as to what they contracted to do?

2. Isabella was invited to a formal dance. Her mother engaged Mrs. Schwartz to make an evening dress for Isabella for $150. After the dress was finished but before it was delivered, Isabella's boy friend canceled the invitation. Her mother then refused to accept and pay for the dress, claiming the transaction was a social obligation, not a business transaction. Do you agree with this interpretation?

3. In a certain state all executory contracts made on Sunday are void. James purchased a pair of shoes from David on Sunday, had them wrapped, and paid for them but asked David to hold them until Tuesday for him. On Tuesday he refused to take the shoes and demanded a return of his money. To determine their rights it was necessary to classify this contract. Was it an executed contract or an executory contract?

4. All states require contracts to sell land to be in writing. Anderson wrote Flemming, offering to sell his home for $18,000. Flemming wired immediately, "I accept your offer." Anderson later tried to avoid this contract because it was not in writing. Could he do so?

5. Garrard wrote to Ruark as follows: "I will pay you $4,200 a year to serve as our bookkeeper." Ruark called Garrard on the telephone and said, "I received your offer this morning and have decided to accept it." Classify this contract as express or implied; valid, voidable, or void; formal or simple; and executed or executory.

Chapter 4

Offer and Acceptance

Mutual Agreements. Usually there can be no valid contract unless the minds of the contracting parties are in complete accord. This accord is achieved by means of an acceptable offer and an unqualified acceptance of this offer. In other words, there must be a meeting of minds before a contract can come into existence.

The parties may expressly state, either orally or in writing, what they agree to do, or they may indicate their intentions by their actions. The innermost thoughts of a person's mind can be known only to himself. If his conduct reasonably leads another person to believe that the party intends to enter into a binding contract, then that party is bound as effectively as if he had expressed his intentions. In business, seldom does one indicate his full intentions solely by his acts. In most cases he expressly states a part of the contract and implies the other part.

The two essential elements of a contract are: (1) an offer, either expressed or implied; and (2) an acceptance, either expressed or implied.

● Hardin wrote Smith as follows: "I will sell you my Plymouth for $1,500." Smith replied immediately, "I accept your offer and will come to get the car at ten a.m. tomorrow." When Smith came to get the car, he tendered Hardin in payment $500 cash and a note for $1,000. Neither Hardin in his offer nor Smith in his acceptance expressed the terms of the sale. Since Hardin in his offer did not say anything about selling on credit, however, he implied that the terms were cash. Smith, in turn, implied in his acceptance a willingness to pay cash by his failure to indicate otherwise. There was a contract for a cash sale because their minds had met as indicated both by their words and their acts.

Harold M. Lambert

Either the Offer or the Acceptance or Both May Usually Be Made by Telephone.

The Offer. The beginning of a contract is the offer made by the offeror. There are three tests of an offer:

1. The offer must be definite.
2. It must be seriously intended.
3. It must be communicated to the offeree.

(1) THE OFFER MUST BE DEFINITE. A contract will not be enforced unless the court can ascertain the intentions of the parties. The offeror's intentions are ascertained from the offer, and this cannot be done unless the offer is definite.

• Sailors wrote Dince as follows: "I am prepared to pay you about $200 a month and a fair commission on all sales made in the southern half of the state." This offer is not an acceptable offer because it is not definite. The minds of the parties cannot meet until the parties agree as to what is a "fair" commission and the exact line that separates the northern half of the state from the southern half. Furthermore, "I am prepared to pay" may or may not mean "I will pay," and "about $200" may mean $199.75 or it may mean $180.

(2) THE OFFER MUST BE SERIOUSLY INTENDED. One may make an offer in jest, banter, fear, or extreme anger; and if this fact is known or should be known by the offeree because of the surrounding circumstances, no contract is formed. A business transaction is ordinarily not entered into in jest or because of extreme fear or anger, and the offeree has no right to think that the offer is seriously intended when it is made under these circumstances. There are times, however, when the offer is not seriously intended, but the offeree has no way of knowing this. In that event such an offer may be accepted. This is the exception, however, not the general rule. In the two examples below these points are illustrated from actual business transactions:

- Gates's house was aflame. His dog was trapped on the second floor. Its barking could be heard in the street. Gates said, "I will give $5,000 to anyone who will rescue my dog." A young man scaled the walls and, at great risk to his own life, rescued the dog. He later demanded that Gates pay him the $5,000; and upon Gates's refusal, he brought suit to recover this amount. The court would probably hold there was no contract since the offer was made under highly emotional circumstances, and the offeree should have taken that into consideration before responding to the offer.

As previously noted, the innermost thoughts of the parties are not the controlling factors. If the offeree with reason thinks that the offer is made in earnest and accepts it, a binding contract will result even though the offer is made in jest.

- Hendler in a serious manner offered Knapp a painting worth $250 for $10. Knapp, being a poor judge of the value of paintings, accepted the offer. Hendler contended that he had made the offer just as a prank to see if Knapp appreciated the value of the painting. Since there was no circumstance or act on Hendler's part to indicate that the offer was made in jest, Knapp was reasonable in believing that the offer was seriously made.

(3) THE OFFER MUST BE COMMUNICATED TO THE OFFEREE. Even if the offer is definite and is seriously intended, it is still not an acceptable offer until it has been communicated to the offeree. If one writes out an offer and the offer falls into the hands of the offeree without the knowledge or consent of the offeror, it cannot be accepted. Furthermore, an oral offer directed to a specific individual or firm cannot be accepted by anyone else. This is true because one has a right to choose the people with whom he deals.

- Arnold wrote a definite offer to Barber offering to buy his house. He intended to deliver the offer to Barber at a later date. Barber saw the offer lying on Arnold's desk and attempted to accept it by delivering to Arnold a written acceptance of the exact terms of the offer. No contract resulted because the offer had not been communicated to Barber.

- Stevenson orally offered to sell his Buick to Harold for $2,000 cash. Harold refused the offer but Dukes, a bystander who had overheard the offer, said, "I accept your offer." No contract was formed because the offer was never legally communicated to Dukes.

Invitations to Make Offers. In business many apparent offers are not true offers. They are instead treated as invitations to the public to make offers at certain terms and prices. If the invitation is accepted by a member of the public and an offer is submitted embodying all the terms set out in the invitation, the offer may be rejected. The most common types of general invitations are advertisements, window displays, catalogs, price lists, and circular sales letters. If a merchant displays in his store window a suit for $45, he is not bound to sell at this price. Most businessmen consider this a very poor business policy, but it is nevertheless the law.

- Lanier, a clothing merchant, inserted this advertisement in the Banner Herald: "All suits reduced 35% in price." Through an error, the discount was listed as 35% when Lanier intended it to be 25%. Since this was not an offer, he was not bound.

The general rule is that a circular sales letter is not an offer but an invitation to the recipient to make an offer. It is often difficult, however, to distinguish between a general sales letter and a personal sales letter. The fact that the letter is addressed to a particular individual does not make it a personal sales letter.

• Smith wrote the Twin City Typewriter Company as follows: "What are the price and terms on the new Excello typewriter?" The company replied: "We will sell you a new Excello typewriter for $175 cash, or $185 with 20% down and the balance at the rate of $10 a month." This was a personal sales letter written in response to an inquiry and was an acceptable offer. Had the same letter been sent to several prospective buyers who had made no inquiry, the letter would have been only an invitation to them to make an offer.

Under special circumstances advertisements may also be offers. This is primarily true with advertisements that offer rewards.

• Foster placed the following ad in the newspaper: "I will pay $1,000 to anyone giving information leading to the arrest and conviction of the person who set fire to my property." Brewer saw the ad and set out to find the guilty party. As a result of Brewer's information, Dunnaway was arrested and tried. There was strong circumstantial evidence of his guilt, but the jury acquitted him. Brewer demanded his $1,000. Foster did not have to pay because his ad laid down two conditions, namely, that the guilty party be "arrested" and "convicted." Since Dunnaway was not convicted, Foster did not have to pay.

Duration of the Offer. An offer may be revoked, that is, withdrawn, at any time before its acceptance. An agreement to hold the offer open for a definite length of time is not binding unless this agreement is supported by a consideration. Such a contract is known as an *option.*

With reference to time, offers are divided into two classes: those made for a stipulated period of time, and those that have no definite length of time to remain open.

Ewing Galloway

At an Auction Each Bid Is an Offer.

In the first class, the offer automatically terminates at the end of the time designated in the offer, although it may be withdrawn before that time unless it is an option contract or has previously been accepted. In the second class, the offer remains open for a reasonable length of time or until withdrawn. The withdrawal, however, must be actually communicated to the offeree or his agent. A mere intention to withdraw the offer is not sufficient.

● On Monday, March 10, Hicks offered by letter to sell Moorehouse his library for $1,000, the offer to remain open for six months. Moorehouse accepted by letter Wednesday, June 12, but the letter did not reach Hicks for one month as he was on an extended vacation. In the meantime, he sold the library to Walker and wrote Moorehouse he was withdrawing his offer. This revocation never reached Moorehouse. Hicks was liable to Moorehouse for breach of contract. The revocation actually had to be communicated to the offeree before his acceptance.

The death or the insanity of the offeror automatically revokes an offer by operation of law even though the offeree has no knowledge of the death or the insanity. Both parties must be capable of contracting at the moment the contract comes into existence.

The law, then, dealing with the duration of offers can be summarized as follows: (1) An offer may be revoked at any time prior to acceptance unless some consideration has been given to the offeror by the offeree to hold the offer open for a definite period of time. (2) If the offeror fixes a definite time limitation on the offer, the lapse of this time automatically revokes the offer. (3) If no time is fixed by the offeror as to how long the offer is good, the lapse of a reasonable length of time revokes the offer. (4) Death or insanity of the offeror before acceptance revokes the offer.

The Acceptance. When an offer has been properly communicated to the party for whom it is intended, and that party, or someone authorized to act for him, accepts, a binding contract is formed. The minds of the parties have met. No formal procedure is required for this acceptance. The acceptance may be made by words, oral or written, or by some act which clearly shows an intention to accept. Silence does not, except in rare cases, constitute an acceptance; nor is a mental intention to accept sufficient. The acceptance must be made in the manner, at the place, and within the time limit stipulated in the offer.

Counteroffers. An offer must be accepted without any deviation in the terms of the offer. If the intended acceptance varies or qualifies the offer, this is a counteroffer and is a rejection of the original offer. This counteroffer may be accepted or rejected by the original offeror.

- Dean offered by letter to sell Burke 1,000 shares of stock in the Blank Corporation for $10,000 cash. Burke replied immediately by letter:

  "I accept your offer but can pay only $5,000 now. Will pay the balance in thirty days." This was a counteroffer and rejected the original offer. Burke could not later accept the original offer unless Dean restated it.

The offeree may make an inquiry without rejecting the offer. For example, if the offer is for 1,000 shares of stock for $10,000 cash, the offeree may inquire as follows: "Would you be willing to wait thirty days for $5,000 and hold the stock as collateral security?" This is a mere inquiry and is not a rejection of the offer. If the inquiry is answered in the negative, the original offer may still be accepted, provided it has not been revoked in the meantime. This is not true of counteroffers.

If the general price level is either rising or falling rapidly, or if the price of the particular item is subject to a rapid fluctuation in price, the lapse of a relatively short period of time before an offer is accepted may constitute a rejection of the offer. A good example of this is found in the sale of stocks. An offer to sell U. S. Steel common stock today at a certain price does not imply that the offer will be good tomorrow. Not much time is allowed for inquiries or investigations in situations of this kind.

Offers and Acceptances by Correspondence. When a person makes an offer by mail, he may, if he wishes, state that the acceptance will not be valid until it is actually received. In that case the agreement is not completed until the acceptance is actually delivered to the offeror. If, however, a person sends an offer by mail but does not specify that the acceptance is not to be valid until it is received, he is considered to have authorized the acceptance to be sent in the same manner as the offer was sent. In this case the agreement is completed when the acceptance is mailed, not when it is delivered.

It must not be presumed, however, that if the offeree adopts an unauthorized method of sending the acceptance, he has rejected the offer. If an offeree who receives an offer through the mail sends his acceptance in the form of a telegram or a personally delivered message, the agreement is completed when the acceptance is delivered.

Similarly when an offer is received in a telegram, the delivery of an acceptance to the telegraph company completes the agreement. If in such a case the acceptance is sent by mail, the agreement is not completed until the acceptance is received by the offeror.

Because of the hazards involved, careful and prudent persons can avoid most of these difficulties by stipulating in the offer how it must be accepted and when the acceptance is to become effective. If this stipulation is ignored, the offeror is not bound. For example, the offer may state, "The acceptance must be sent by wire and be received by me in Chicago before the contract is complete." If the acceptance is mailed, the offeror is not bound. The acceptance is not effective unless it is by wire and is actually received by the offeror in Chicago.

• Dillingham wrote Froelson as follows: "I agree to employ you for twelve months beginning June 1, at $500 a month. If acceptable, wire me collect by May 15, at the Riggs Hotel, New York, acceptance not binding on me unless telegram actually received by me."

Froelson wired Dillingham immediately but the telegram was, for some reason, not delivered. There was no contract even though Froelson used the same agency in communicating his acceptance to the offeror as the offeree used.

Questions

1. How may one know when the minds of the parties have met?

2. Give an illustration of an offer that is not definite enough to form the basis of a contract.

3. Name the three tests of an acceptable offer.

4. Is a window display of a suit for $60 an offer that can be accepted by a prospective customer?

5. Under what conditions may one accept an offer that is made in the form of a newspaper advertisement?

6. (a) When may an offer be revoked?

(b) What is the effect of death or insanity of the offeror on an offer?

7. What is the effect of a counteroffer?

8. How may an offer by mail be accepted?

9. When one makes an offer by correspondence, how is it possible that he can be bound on a contract and not be aware of it?

10. If an offer is made by telegram and the acceptance is sent by letter, when is the contract formed?

Case Problems

1. Davis and Harrell were pulpwood workers. In attempting to contract with Harrison relative to a tract of pulpwood, they made Harrison this offer: "We will cut, haul, and ship the pulpwood for $8 a cord provided we can earn expenses and daily wages of $6 a day at this rate." Harrison accepted the offer. Was a contract formed?

2. A local corporation formed for the purpose of drilling for oil was defunct. The stock was considered by all the townspeople to be absolutely worthless. Hipps, the owner of 1,000 shares of this stock, offered to sell them to Hurley for 10 cents a share. Hurley accepted. A few minutes later a radio report stated that oil had been discovered on a tract of land adjoining the property of the defunct corporation. Hipps refused to sell Hurley the stock, claiming that the offer was made in jest. Was there a contract?

3. Joel wrote Brcadnax a letter, offering to sell him a tract of real estate owned by Joel. Twenty-four hours later Joel sold the land to Ledbetter without waiting to hear from Broadnax. As soon as Broadnax received Joel's offer, he accepted. Joel contended that his selling the land to Ledbetter was a revocation of his offer to Broadnax. Do you agree?

4. Harrison offered to sell Duff his automobile for $1,200 cash and stated that he would give Duff ten days to decide whether or not he would accept the offer. Duff paid Harrison $10 for his agreement to hold the offer open. Four days later Harrison revoked his offer and offered to return the $10. Did Harrison have the right to revoke the offer before the expiration of the ten days?

5. Cullison wired O'Mary, offering to sell O'Mary 100 shares of stock in the Bank of Omar at $150 a share. One hour later Cullison died of a heart attack. O'Mary, not

knowing of Cullison's death, accepted the offer. Was a contract formed?

6. Reece mailed some mimeographed sales letters, offering to sell office desks for $120 each. Kittle received one of these letters and immediately wrote Reece asking for further details about the desks. Reece replied immediately. Kittle, based upon the information included in the original letter plus the additional information in the answer to his letter, accepted Reece's offer. Reece refused to sell the desks. Was a contract formed by Kittle's acceptance?

7. Park ran the following ad in the local paper: "I will pay $10 to anyone who will return my dog, Tala." Carson, a boy of ten years old, read the ad and decided it was not right to keep a dog that did not belong to him. He returned the dog and demanded the $10. Park refused to pay it, claiming Carson knew it was his and should have returned it for nothing. Was there a contract?

8. Adrian Publishing Company wrote the Davis Office Supply Company a personal sales letter offering to sell it some typing paper of a certain weight and quality for 90 cents a ream in lots of 5,000 reams. The Davis Office Supply Company wrote immediately as follows: "Are you willing to supply this paper at the quoted price and ship the 5,000 reams at the rate of 1,000 reams a month?" The Adrian Publishing Company made no reply to this inquiry. The Davis Office Supply Company waited sixty days and then accepted the offer for 5,000 reams at the terms and price originally quoted. The order was rejected. Discuss the legal rights of the parties.

9. The Athens Lumber Company offered to sell the Rowe Construction Company a quantity of oak flooring of a given grade at $200 a thousand feet. The offeree wrote: "I accept your offer on the assumption that we will receive the usual contractor's discount of 10%." Was a contract formed?

10. At 9 a.m. Potts wired Lemly as follows: "I will sell you 1,000 bales of cotton 1-inch middling at 35 cents a pound." At 3 p.m. Lemly sent an acceptance in writing by a messenger boy. Before the boy reached Potts' office, Lemly received a telephone call from Potts stating the offer was revoked. While still talking to Lemly on the phone, the messenger boy delivered the acceptance. Was a contract formed?

Chapter 5

Defective Agreements

Mistakes That Make Agreements Defective. As a general rule, a mistake made by one party without the knowledge of the other has no effect on the validity of the contract. There are, however, certain mistakes that make agreements defective. Such mistakes are:

1. Mistakes as to the nature of the transaction
2. Mistakes as to the identity of the party
3. Mutual mistakes as to the identity of the subject matter
4. Mutual mistakes as to the existence of the subject matter

(1) MISTAKES AS TO THE NATURE OF THE TRANSACTION. A mistake as to the nature of the transaction renders the contract void. If, through trickery, a man is induced to sign a deed under the impression it is a note, he is not bound by his signature. But to avoid the contract on the ground of mistake, he must not have been negligent. Thus, one unable to read will not be excused on the ground of mistake if he fails to have some disinterested party read the contract.

- Black bought an automobile, paying $500 down and signing three notes of $500 each for the balance. While Black's attention was diverted, the seller substituted for one of the notes a ten-year lease on Black's business property. The contract was void because of Black's mistake as to the nature of the transaction.

(2) MISTAKES AS TO THE IDENTITY OF THE PARTY. Freedom of contract includes among other things the freedom to choose the parties with whom one contracts.

With but rare exceptions, the law does not compel one to contract with a person who is objectionable to him for any reason. If one is mistaken as to the identity of the party with whom he is contracting, then the contract is void. Naturally such a contract would have to be negotiated by mail, telegram, or telephone.

If a person contracts with another in a face-to-face relationship, he is presumed to have intended to contract with this particular individual even though he thought it was someone else. Even if the other party said, "I am John Smith," when in fact he was Henry Holden, the contract would be valid if the party was mistaken only as to the man's name, not his real identity. If he deals with him at a distance, however, and the other party falsely represents himself to be someone who he is not, the contract is void. Under these circumstances he has no way of ascertaining through reasonable diligence that he was mistaken.

If the mistake as to the identity of the party involves an executory contract, then the remedy consists merely of refusing to perform the contract. If it is executed, then the innocent party may rescind the contract by returning anything of value which he received and demanding that the other party do likewise. As far as possible, the law provides that in the rescission of a contract both parties be restored to their prior positions.

• A salesman, knowing that Janet Fortson would not deal with the Ward Company, claimed that he represented Kenmore Washing Machine Company. He sold Fortson a Kenmore Washing Machine, but as an agent of the Ward Company, not the manufacturer of the Kenmore Washing Machine. Fortson was under no obligation to accept the washing machine after she learned of the mistake. If the contract had been executed before she discovered the mistake, she still could rescind the contract by returning the machine and demanding the return of her money.

(3) Mutual Mistakes as to the Identity of the Subject Matter. Unlike the mistakes described in the

two preceding sections, mistakes as to the identity of the subject matter of a contract must be mutual. If both parties do not have in mind the same subject matter, their minds can never meet and thus there can be no contract. For example, if *A* offers to sell and *B* agrees to buy "all the pulpwood on my Barnett Shoals Road farm" and *A* has two farms on that road, the parties may not have the same farm in mind. This cannot become a binding contract until the farm described in the offer is clearly identified.

Often the parties correctly identify the subject matter of the contract but are mistaken about some other aspect of the transaction. For example, John has two stacks of lumber. One is high grade and the other is low grade. John, pointing to the high-grade lumber says, "I will sell you this lumber for $5,000." Henry, the offeree, accepts. They both thought the particular stack of lumber identified was the low-quality lumber. The contract is valid, however, since the offeror pointed to, that is, identified, this particular stack of lumber. They were not mistaken as to which stack was meant.

- Roger Hurley sold Lydia Lester for $2,000 "the lot 'fernenth' my house at 237 Springdale Avenue." Hurley owned one lot beside his house and one in front of it directly across the street. Huriey thought "fernenth" meant "beside of" and Lester thought it meant "in front of." This was a mutual mistake as to the identity of the subject matter.

(4) Mutual Mistakes as to the Existence of the Subject Matter. If two parties enter into a contract relative to a specific subject matter, but at the moment of the contract this specific subject matter does not exist, the contract is void. Again the mistake must be a mutual mistake, not a unilateral one. Such a mistake most often arises when the subject matter of the contract has been destroyed by flood, fire, tornado, or other means, but its destruction is unknown to either party when the contract is formed.

- Smith sold the Missouri Pacific Railroad 5,000 railroad ties for $1.50 each. Prior to the contract but unknown to either party, the ties had been destroyed by a forest fire. The contract was void since the mistake involved 5,000 specific railroad ties, not just any ties of a designated grade.

It is evident from these four classes of mistakes that it is not the function of the law to save us from the consequences of our mistakes. These four classes of mistakes cover a very small percentage of those made in business transactions. Knowledge and diligence, not law, are the chief bulwarks against losses due to mistakes.

Mistakes That Do Not Make Agreements Defective. Some of the most common mistakes in business transactions do not affect the validity of the contract. Two of these classes of mistakes need special emphasis.

1. Mistakes as to value, quality, or price
2. Mistakes as to the terms of the contract

(1) MISTAKES AS TO VALUE, QUALITY, OR PRICE. When two parties deal face to face, the law will not intervene to protect either of them simply because one was mistaken as to the value, quality, or price of the subject matter of the contract. If the buyer does not trust his judgment, he has the right to demand of the seller a warranty as to the quality, quantity, or the value of the article he is buying. His ability to contract wisely is his chief protection against a bad bargain. If Dean sells Thompson a television set for $350, Thompson cannot rescind the contract merely because the set proved to be worth only $100. This is a mistake as to value and quality. He should obtain as a part of the contract an express warranty as to the set's quality. Conversely, if the seller parts with a jewel for $5, thinking it is a cheap stone, he cannot later complain if the jewel proves to be worth $5,000.

Mistakes as to value, quality, and sometimes quantity are mistakes, as a rule, of judgment. Mistakes as to price, however, may be the result of errors in typing or in misunderstanding of an oral quotation of the price. But again the wheels of commerce could not run smoothly if either party could avoid the contract merely because he was mistaken as to price. If the E&S Tire Company offers by letter to sell 1,000 tires at $14 each, it cannot avoid the contract on the basis that the secretary incorrectly typed the price $14 instead of $16, the price dictated. The seller is bound on the contract for $14.

- Hardigree offered by letter to sell auto batteries of a given grade for $7.75 each. The stenographer erroneously typed the offer to read $7.05. The offeree immediately accepted the offer for 1,000 batteries. This error in price does not render the contract void.

It is the purpose of the law to promote equity, not inequity. If these laws as to value, quality, and price were enforced to the letter, the result would often be very inequitable. For that reason, we find one basic exception to these rules. This exception is that one cannot knowingly take advantage of another's mistake as to value, quality, or price.

- Hoover offered by letter to sell Harrell a new Plymouth automobile for $209. Harrell accepted by letter immediately. The true price was $2,009, but the typist erred in writing up the offer. The error was so gross and apparent to Harrell that he could not in good conscience hold Hoover to the offer.

- The Vaugh Lumber Company sold the Hope Construction Company 10,925 feet of lumber at $187.75 per thousand board feet. The bookkeeper, because of his lack of knowledge of business arithmetic, prepared an invoice showing the total price to be $205.11. The correct amount was $2,051.17. After the purchaser had paid the $205.11, he received a bill for an additional $1,846.06. He must pay it because here there was no error in the unit price, of $187.75. The error in calculation on the invoice should have been evident to the purchaser.

(2) Mistakes as to the Terms of the Contract. One of the most common mistakes relates to the terms of the contract. Such a mistake is usually the result of a failure to read the contract if it is written or a failure to understand its meaning or significance. If the contract is oral, either of the parties may be mistaken as to the terms of the contract without the other party's being aware of it. Such mistakes in both written and oral contracts do not affect their validity; otherwise anyone could avoid his contract merely by claiming that he was mistaken as to its terms.

● Roman subscribed for hospitalization insurance with the Chicago Insurance Company. The policy contained this clause: "The underwriter is not liable for illness caused by communicable diseases." After he had paid his $50 annual premium and received his policy, he wished to cancel and receive a return of his money on the ground that he did not understand the meaning of "communicable diseases." It is an almost universal rule that such mistakes do not afford grounds for abrogating the contract.

Frequently contracts are entered into orally and then reduced to writing. If, through a typographical error, the written terms vary from the oral terms, and the mistake is evident to the other party, such a mistake may be the ground for reformation.

● Walker orally agreed to sell and Smith agreed to buy 1,000 reams of a specified grade of typing paper at one dollar a ream. A sales invoice was immediately prepared and through error fifty cents was typed instead of one dollar. Smith would not be allowed to enforce a sale for fifty cents.

Fraud. One who induces another to enter into a contract as a result of a false statement of a material fact, is guilty of *fraud.* A contract so induced is voidable, not void, since the party defrauded intended to make the contract, but was induced to do so through fraud.

Fraud may be perpetrated by three methods:

1. Express misrepresentation
2. Concealment of material facts
3. Silence when it is one's duty to speak

(1) EXPRESS MISREPRESENTATION. Fraud, as a result of express misrepresentation, consists of four elements, each one of which must be present to constitute fraud:

(a) A false statement of a material fact must be made.

(b) The false statement must be made by one who knew it to be false, or by one who made it in reckless disregard of its truth or falsity.

(c) There must be an intent to induce the party to act by reason of the false statement.

(d) The false statement must be relied upon by the innocent party.

If these four elements are present, the injured party may, at his option, rescind the contract. If he has been damaged by reason of the fraud, he may, in addition to rescinding the contract, sue for damages.

• Simpson falsified his financial statements to induce a bank to make him a loan of $5,000 for ninety days. After the loan was made and the discounted value of the note was deposited to his account, the bank learned of the fraud. The bank was entitled to rescind the contract and demand immediate repayment. Had the bank acted to its detriment, it could have also sued for damages.

Statements of opinion, as contrasted with statements of fact, do not, as a rule, constitute fraud. The dividing line between fact and opinion is often obscure, but close analysis will usually enable even a layman to distinguish between the two.

(2) CONCEALMENT OF MATERIAL FACTS. If one actively conceals material facts for the purpose of preventing the other contracting party from discovering them, such

concealment is fraud even though there are no false statements.

Merely refraining from disclosing pertinent facts unknown to the other party is not fraud as a rule. There must be an active concealment.

- A coal company had been prospecting for coal on *A*'s land and found none. Later *A* filled up the excavations to keep *B*, a prospective purchaser, from discovering the failure to find coal. This active concealment was fraud if *B*, to the knowledge of *A*, thought there was coal on the land.

(3) SILENCE WHEN IT IS ONE'S DUTY TO SPEAK. If one's relationship with another is that of trust and confidence, then silence may constitute fraud. Such relationship exists between partners in a business firm, an agent and his principal, a lawyer and his client, a guardian and his ward, and in many other trust relationships.

- Gates appointed Greiner, his agent, to sell his real estate. Greiner later learned that a new factory was soon to be built that would cause real estate values to increase considerably. This fact was not known to Gates. Greiner bought the property himself, expecting to hold it until the price increased and then sell it at a profit. Failure of Greiner to disclose this information to his principal was fraud, and Gates could rescind the contract.

Duress. For a contract to be valid, all parties must enter into it of their free will. *Duress* is a means of destroying another's free will by obtaining his consent to a contract by means of a threat to do him, or members of his family, some harm. The threat may relate to one's property, or to his earning power. Regardless of the nature of the threat, it is duress if it is serious enough to destroy one's free will.

- Harold purchased a used car from Jarvis. He gave a check for $300 in payment. The check was a bad check, and Jarvis threatened to prosecute Harold. Later he said to Harold: "If you will buy a new car for $2,200 cash, I will refrain from prosecuting you."

Harold accepted the offer but later wished to avoid the contract. He could do so because the contract was voidable on his part because of duress. His guilt was irrelevant. The threat destroyed his free will to contract.

Undue Influence. Undue influence may destroy one's free will even though there is no duress. If a party in a confidential or fiduciary relationship to another induces him against his free will to enter into a contract, the agreement is voidable because of *undue influence*. If, under any relationship, one is in a position to take undue advantage of another, undue influence may render the contract voidable. Undue influence may result also from sickness, infirmity, or serious distress. Examples of such relationships are family relationships, a guardian and his ward, an attorney and his client, and physician and his patient, and any other relationship where confidence reposed on one side results in domination by the other.

• An unmarried daughter lived with her aged and infirm father. The father was obsessed with the fear of being left alone. The daughter played upon this fear, threatening to leave him alone unless he conveyed to her all his real estate. The contract was rescinded on the ground of undue influence.

Remedies for Breach of Contract Because of Fraud, Duress, or Undue Influence. Since fraud, duress, and undue influence render contracts voidable, not void, one must know what to do when he is a victim of one of these acts. If he does nothing, the contract is ratified. The contract may also be ratified by some act or word indicating an intention to be bound. After the contract is affirmed or ratified, one is as fully bound on it as if there had been no fraud, duress, or undue influence. But still the innocent party may sue for whatever damages he has sustained.

If instead of affirming the contract, one elects to rescind it, he must first return or offer to return any consideration he received under the contract. After this is done, he is in a position to take one of three actions depending upon the circumstances:

(1) He may sue to recover any money, goods, or other things of value he has parted with, plus damages.

(2) If the contract is executory on the part of the innocent party, he can refuse to perform. If the other party sues, he can then interpose fraud, duress, or undue influence as a complete defense.

(3) He may bring a suit in equity to have the suit judicially declared void and ask for damages.

- Darter, a shoe merchant, was induced through fraud to purchase some shoes for $6,500. The shoes were purchased on 90 days' credit. Darter's best remedy in this case is to affirm the contract but to refrain from paying for the shoes. When the seller sues him, he can set up the fraud as a counterclaim. If he could prove that he was damaged to the extent of $3,000 by reason of the fraud, then he would pay the balance of the account, or $3,500.

Questions

1. How is a contract affected by a mistake as to the nature of the transaction?

2. What is the effect of negligence on the part of a person who attempts to avoid a contract on the ground of mistake as to the nature of the transaction?

3. (a) If one is mistaken as to the identity of the party with whom he contracts, may he avoid a contract in which the dealings were face to face?

(b) Can the minds of the parties be in mutual agreement when they are honestly mistaken as to the identity of the subject matter of the contract?

4. If the subject matter of the contract did not exist at the time the contract was formed and both parties were unaware of this fact, is the contract valid or void?

5. (a) May either party avoid the contract on the grounds of a mistake as to quality by both parties?

(b) May one party who knows the true value of an article take advantage of the other party's ignorance of the value of it?

6. What are the tests of fraud?

7. (a) Can there be fraud by concealment when there is no active act of concealment?

(b) Under what circumstances may one commit fraud by silence?

8. Define and give an example of duress.

9. Give an example of a relationship in which undue influence may exist.

10. What are the remedies for breach of contract because of fraud, duress, or undue influence?

Case Problems

1. Mary Jones was a secretary in the Hope Furniture Company's office. Gowen wished to purchase $10,000 worth of furniture. He inquired of Miss Jones, since her employer was out, what were the terms of sale. She replied, "2 per cent discount for cash." Thereupon Gowen bought the merchandise and paid cash for it. The invoice read "$10,000, less 2% discount, or $8,000." Later the Hope Furniture Company learned of the error and attempted to collect the difference between the $2,000 discount given by Miss Jones and the correct discount of $200. Could it collect?

2. The Lapp Jewelry Company had a diamond necklace for sale. The price was $7,500. McLean, a prospective purchaser, inquired of the salesman as to the price. The salesman looked up the price and said "$750," thinking that was the price shown on the price list. Neither the salesman nor the buyer knew the true value of the necklace. McLean agreed to purchase it. Was the Lapp Jewelry Company bound on this contract?

3. Harris Bibb was office manager for the Griffin Wholesale Company. In this capacity he signed a contract with the Atlanta Collecting Agency to collect $50,000 of delinquent accounts receivable. The written contract with the agency contained this clause: "The Griffin Wholesale Company agrees to pay the Atlanta Collecting Agency 25% of the aggregate listing as its collection fee." Bibb thought this meant that for each $1,000 collected, the agency would take $250 and remit $750 to the Griffin Wholesale Company. The true meaning was that the agency kept the first $12,500 collected and remitted all over that. Was the Griffin Wholesale Company bound on this contract?

4. Dince offered to sell Roman his fishing boat for $300. Roman accepted the offer and paid the $300. At the time of the contract, the boat had been destroyed by flood waters but neither party knew this fact. Was there a contract?

5. Hardin offered to sell Jones his automobile for $1,200. The speedometer showed the car had been driven 28,000 miles. Hardin knew the true mileage was 38,000 miles. Jones asked him: "Is this the correct mileage?" Hardin evaded the question by pointing to the whitewall tires on the car. After Jones agreed to buy the car, he learned of the true mileage of the car. Was he bound on the contract?

6. Michael, in an attempt to sell his home to Lance for $15,000, assured him that the house "is absolutely free of termites." Michael did not know that termites were in the house but had recently seen them swarming about the foundation. The house was in fact badly infested with termites. Lance wished to rescind the contract. Could he do so?

7. Bramlett, an accountant, had for several years audited the books and made all tax returns for John West, a lumber merchant. On many occasions West had concealed facts so as to avoid paying income taxes. Bramlett knew of these acts. He never threatened to report West, but almost daily he would remind West that he was in position to do him great harm. After he had thoroughly alarmed West by hints, not threats, he offered to buy a half interest in West's business at about one fourth of its true value. West accepted the offer but the next day attempted to rescind it. Could he do so?

Chapter 6

Competency of Parties

Capacity to Contract. In order that an agreement may be enforceable at law, all parties must have the legal and mental capacity to contract. The general rule is that all parties are presumed to have this capacity. Some parties, however, in the eyes of the law, lack such capacity because of age, physical condition, or public policy. Among those whom the law considers to be incompetent in some degree are minors, insane persons, and drunken persons.

Minors. The common-law rule that persons under twenty-one years of age are *minors* has been retained by most of the states. In about fifteen states laws have been passed making girls competent to contract at eighteen years of age. In a few other states all minors who are married are fully competent to contract. In still other states minors who are in business for themselves are bound on all their business contracts.

CONTRACTS OF MINORS. A minor may make contracts freely, and many of these contracts are fully as valid and enforceable as those of an adult. A few of his contracts are void, but most of them are merely voidable at the minor's option. If a minor wishes to treat a contract made with an adult as valid, the adult is bound by it.

Business firms that carry on business transactions in all the states must know the law dealing with minors in each of the forty-eight states. Mail order houses and correspondence schools are particularly susceptible to losses when dealing with minors. The significance of the law is that, with but few exceptions, you deal with a minor at your own risk. The purpose of the law is to protect minors from unscrupulous adults, but in general the law affords the other party no more rights in scrupulous contracts than in unscrupulous ones. The minor is the sole judge as to whether or not he wishes to be bound.

CONTRACTS OF MINORS FOR NECESSARIES. A minor is liable for the reasonable value of necessaries actually supplied him or his family if he is married. His contracts for necessaries are voidable, but he is liable on an implied contract to pay what is reasonable. It is an obligation imposed by law, not by contract. If a minor is already fully supplied with necessaries, then he is not liable for the purchase of an additional quantity. Also, even though he needs the merchandise, he may avoid his executory contracts for necessaries.

There are a large number of court cases in all states defining necessaries. The dividing line between necessaries and comforts is often a fine one; but, for the most part, there exists a well-defined group of goods and services which can be classed as necessaries. These are food, clothes, and shelter, necessary medical services including surgery, dental work, and medicine, education through high school or trade school, and in a few states through college, working tools for his trade, and other goods which are luxuries to some people, but necessaries to others because of peculiar circumstances.

DISAFFIRMANCE. The term *disaffirmance* means the repudiation of a contract, that is, the election to avoid it. A minor has the legal right to disaffirm a voidable contract at any time during his minority or within a reasonable time after becoming of age. An adult does not, however, have the right to avoid a contract because the other party is a minor.

If the contract is wholly executory, that is, neither party has performed his part of the contract, a disaffirmance completely nullifies the contract.

If the contract is executed by one of the parties but not by the other party, it is still classed as an executory contract. Here, however, the minor, upon electing to disaffirm the contract, must return whatever he may have received under the contract, provided he is still in possession of it. The fact that the minor is not in possession of the property, however, regardless of the reason, does not prevent him from exercising his right to disaffirm the contract. The same rule generally applies if the contract is wholly executed.

● Carpenter, a minor eighteen years of age, bought a horse from Moore. The horse became so disabled that an agent of the Society for the Prevention of Cruelty to Animals ordered it to be shot. Carpenter disaffirmed the contract and sued for the amount of money paid to Moore. Although Carpenter was unable to restore the property, he was nevertheless permitted to disaffirm the contract and recover the cash that he had paid on the purchase price.

In many states a contract conveying real estate can be disaffirmed by a minor only after he is of age. In the case of personal property, however, he may avoid his contract before he becomes of age, or within a reasonable time after he becomes of age. There is no particularly sound reason why a distinction should be made between a minor's contracts involving real estate and those involving personal property. The reason generally given by the courts is that the minor may suffer irreparable loss in the case of personal property because it can be consumed or easily disposed of. The courts reason that this danger is less likely to exist in the case of real estate. Under the rule *stare decisis,* that is, "stand by the decisions," courts generally follow the decisions of former courts under similar circumstances. The early courts made the distinction between real estate contracts and personalty contracts, and the precedent has generally been followed down to the present time. In several states the courts have ceased to make this distinction.

Ratification. A minor may ratify a voidable contract only after he has attained his majority. By *ratification* is meant a restatement of one's willingness to be bound by his promises made during minority. It is in substance a new promise and may be oral, written, or merely implied by his conduct. He cannot ratify a part and disaffirm a part; he must ratify all or none of it.

It should be noted that there is a difference between a minor's executed contracts and his executory contracts. After he reaches majority, his silence ratifies an executed contract while it disaffirms an executory contract.

• Boyden sold an automobile to Rowland, a minor. Rowland kept the car, used it for about a year after attaining his majority, and then exchanged it for another automobile. The court held, when Rowland attempted to disaffirm the contract, that his conduct amounted to a ratification of the contract and that he could not thereafter disaffirm the agreement.

Minor's Business Contracts. Many states, by special statutory provision, have made a minor's contract relative to the business in which he is engaged fully binding on him. The minor's liability on these contracts is limited to the assets of the business that he is operating.

• Sanders, a minor, owned and operated a filling station. In this capacity he purchased gasoline, tires, and other merchandise amounting to $3,000. He was sued on this account, and his filling station was sold to satisfy the debt. There still remained a balance of $350 after the proceeds of the sheriff's sale were applied on the debt. He is not obligated to pay this $350 since his liability is limited to the net worth of the business which he owns and operates.

How One May Contract Safely with Minors. Since in general one deals with minors at his own risk, every businessman must know how to protect himself when contracting with minors. The safest way is to have an adult guarantee in writing that the minor will abide by the terms of the contract. This does not bind the minor, but it does give the other party the right to sue the adult who guaranteed the contract. In addition, the adult should, if in doubt, ask the other party if he is twenty-one, or eighteen, as the case may be. If he answers "Yes," in a majority of the states this is a tort if false and will either bind him on the contract or subject him to a suit for damages. Thirdly, a merchant must run some risks when dealing with minors. If he sells to a minor, the contract may be avoided by the minor years later and a refund of the purchase price demanded. So few minors exercise this right, it is more profitable for a businessman to run this risk than to seek absolute protection against loss. The loss in profits in lost sales would exceed the refunds.

MINORS' TORTS. A *tort* is a legal wrong, such as negligently or willfully damaging another person's property. As a general rule, a minor is liable for his torts as fully as an adult. If a minor misrepresents his age and the adult relies upon this misrepresentation to his detriment, this is a tort. The law is not uniform throughout the United States as to whether or not a minor is bound on a contract induced by misrepresenting his age. If it is a face-to-face contract and the minor appears to be twenty-one, most courts will hold him bound on his contracts when he expressly states he is twenty-one.

Insane Persons. In determining an insane person's capacity, the status of his insanity must be fixed. If he has been examined according to law and been formally adjudicated insane and a guardian has been appointed, then in most states his contracts are void. Whether or not the subject matter of the contract is a necessary, or whether undue advantage was taken of him, are wholly irrelevant questions. He is considered incapable of making a valid acceptance of an offer no matter how fair the offer is. If he is merely insane but has not been officially adjudicated insane, then his contracts are voidable, not void. Like a minor, he is liable for the reasonable value of necessaries that have been supplied to him. He may elect to avoid all other contracts. Upon disaffirmance, he must return anything of value received under the contract provided it is still in his possession.

In many types of insanity, a person has lucid or sane intervals. During these intervals he is as fully competent to contract as any adult except in those states where his contracts are void if he has been judicially declared insane. His guardian must be discharged before he regains full competency to contract. After one has regained sanity, he may affirm or disaffirm his voidable contracts. In general, the same rules governing affirmance and disaffirmance of minors' contracts apply to the contracts of insane persons. Most of the laws governing the contracts of insane persons are the result of state statutes. Although these laws are reasonably uniform, there are but few general statements that hold true in every state.

- Robert Stacey was judicially declared insane. A guardian was appointed for him. Later Stacey sold his car for $500, a fair price. His guardian sued for a return of the car. The court held that the buyer had to return the car because Stacey's contract was void. Stacey had to return any money which had not been lost or spent.

Drunken Persons. Contracts made by a person who has become so intoxicated that he cannot understand the meaning of his acts are voidable. Upon becoming sober, he may affirm or disaffirm his contracts made while he was drunk. Disaffirmance is contingent upon there being no innocent third party who would be injured thereby. In this sense, the drunkard's contracts differ from those of minors and insane persons.

Questions

1. Whom does the law consider to be incompetent in some degree to contract?

2. Why is it important for business firms to know the law dealing with minors in their own and other states?

3. If a minor wishes to treat a contract with an adult as binding, may the adult avoid it because the other party is a minor?

4. Name some necessaries for which a minor may be held liable for payments.

5. When may a minor disaffirm his contracts?

6. When a minor disaffirms a contract, must he return any benefit which he received from the contract?

7. When may a minor ratify a voidable contract?

8. (a) If a minor purchases two articles by the same contract, may he disaffirm the contract for one of the items and ratify it for the other one?

(b) How may a businessman protect himself when dealing with minors?

9. Is an insane person liable on his contracts for nonnecessaries made during a lucid interval?

10. If a person is under the influence of intoxicants but is fully aware of the nature of his acts, are his contracts void, voidable, or valid?

Case Problems

1. Harper, a minor, purchased a suit for $75 and an overcoat for $100 from the Young Men's Shop. As a part of the sales contract, the seller agreed to alter both the suit and the overcoat to fit the buyer's measurements. These alterations were rather extensive. Harper paid $10 at the time of the purchase and agreed to pay the balance when the articles were ready for delivery. After they were altered, Harper notified the seller that he had changed his mind and did not want the clothes. He also demanded a refund of the $10. Could Harper refuse to abide by the contract?

2. Graff, aged 20 years and nine months, agreed to purchase a used car from the Whitehall Sales Corporation. The cost of the car was $2,700, and the terms called for a cash sale. After all the details were arranged and the sales agreement was signed, the salesman asked Graff, "Are you 21 years old?" Graff said, "Yes." The salesman for the sales corporation became suspicious, checked with the registrar of the college Graff was attending, and learned that Graff was not yet 21 years old. He thereupon refused to deliver the car to Graff. Graff tendered the $2,700 and demanded the car. Upon refusal, he sued for breach of contract. Discuss the rights of the parties.

3. Tate, aged 20, owned and operated a sporting goods store. He incurred $4,000 in business debts. He could not pay these debts; consequently, his creditors sued him on these debts. He raised the defense that he was a minor and therefore not liable on these contracts. Was this a good defense?

4. John, a married minor, purchased groceries on credit for $200. He refused to pay for the groceries because he was a minor at the time they were purchased. The seller brought suit for $200. Was the seller entitled to judgment?

5. Frank Clark, aged 20 years and 10 months, became engaged and bought his fiancee an engagement ring costing $200. He paid $25 down and agreed to pay $2 a week on the balance. About three months after he reached his majority, his fiancee broke the engagement and returned his ring. Having no other prospects, he offered to return the ring to the jeweler and demanded the return of the $69 which he had paid and a cancellation of the balance of the debt.

(a) Did he have a legal right to do so? Discuss fully.

(b) Would your conclusion be different if he had paid cash in full at the time of the purchase and had demanded a return of his money within ten days after attaining his majority?

6. Short, when he was 18, signed a written contract to pay Martin $1,000 when he, Short, became 21. After Short reached 21, nothing was said about the contract although both men worked for the same firm and saw each other daily. About six months after Short became 21, Martin demanded payment and Short refused on the ground that he was a minor when he signed the contract. Was Short liable?

7. Dougherty became insane and his family was in desperate need of groceries. Campbell supplied groceries over a period of six months amounting to $500. Dougherty regained his sanity but refused to pay the $500. Was he liable for this amount?

Chapter 7

Consideration

Nature of Consideration. Courts will compel compliance with an agreement only when it is supported by consideration. The consideration is the line that divides mere agreements from binding obligations. *Consideration* may be something of value to the promisor, or something detrimental to the one who gives it. Consideration also may be another promise. It need not be money or money's worth, but it must be something which, in the eyes of the law, has value.

- John promised to give Mary, his girl friend, a watch for her birthday. He later changed his mind and did not carry out his promise. There was no consideration, legally speaking, to support the promise; therefore, the courts would not compel compliance. If the promise had been executed, the court would not compel a restitution. It will neither upset an executed gift nor enforce an executory promise unsupported by a valuable consideration.

A common form of consideration is an exchange of promises. Not every promise for a promise, however, constitutes a consideration. The subject matter of the promise must be a business transaction rather than a mere social obligation. Furthermore, the two promises must be concurrent in time to constitute a consideration. The promise of one party must induce the other party to make his promise.

For an exchange of promises to constitute consideration the promises must create mutual obligations. If one of the parties so words his promise that he is not bound to perform unless he chooses to do so, such a promise cannot constitute a consideration. The promise must impose a legal obligation upon the promisor.

- The Acme Office Supply Company agreed to buy a quantity of typing paper at a given price and the Macon Paper Company agreed to sell at that price provided it could see fit to do so after their cost records were completed. Here the promise of the Macon Paper Company was illusory. It could elect to sell or not to sell as it saw fit. Since such an illusory promise is not a legal consideration, there was no binding contract, even if the Macon Paper Company was now willing to sell at that price. The agreement was invalid *ab initio*, that is, from the very beginning.

Either of the promises may call for one of the parties to forego a right or do something that is detrimental to the promisor. If a grandfather promises to pay his grandson $5,000 when the latter reaches twenty-one and imposes upon the grandson the obligation to refrain from smoking until he is twenty-one, the grandson gives up a right in exchange for the promise to pay $5,000. Any forebearance, detriment, loss suffered, or responsibility assumed is sufficient to constitute a consideration.

Adequacy of Consideration. The law does not prohibit bargains, nor does it attempt to measure the value each party receives as his consideration. There need be no equality of value, only some value. This value may be no more than a detriment to the one who gives it. If a farmer deliberately chooses to sell a $10,000 farm for one dollar, the court will not decline to enforce the contract simply because of inequality of consideration.

Part Payment. A partial payment of a past due debt is not sufficient consideration to support the creditor's promise to cancel the balance of the debt.

The promise of a creditor to accept $800 in full settlement of a $1,000 debt, which is past due, is a new independent promise which is to be distinguished from his original promise for which the debtor agreed to pay the $1,000. This new promise must have a consideration entirely apart from the original promise. While the payment of $800 alone will not cancel the debt of $1,000,

Ewing Galloway

The Painter Gives Service and Material as Consideration in Exchange for the Owner's Promise to Pay.

yet this payment plus the delivery of a five-cent cigar will cancel the debt, if the cigar was bargained for and intended by the creditor as consideration for his promise to discharge the debt. The cigar is the consideration to support the new contract.

There are several exceptions to this rule:

(1) If the amount of the debt is in dispute, the acceptance in full settlement of a lesser sum than that claimed will cancel the debt.

(2) If there are several creditors, and each one agrees to accept in full settlement of his claim a percentage of the amount due, this agreement will cancel the debts owed to these creditors. This is known as a *composition of creditors*.

(3) If the debt is evidenced by a note or other written evidence of the debt, a cancellation and return of the written evidence cancels the debt.

(4) If the payment of the lesser sum is accompanied by a receipt in full and some indication that a gift is made of the balance, the debt may be canceled.

(5) If a secured note in a lesser amount is given and accepted in settlement of an unsecured debt, the entire unsecured debt is discharged. The security is the consideration to support the contract to settle for a lesser sum.

Insufficient or Invalid Consideration. Many apparent considerations lack the full force and effect necessary to make enforceable agreements. Sometimes the distinction is very narrow, and close scrutiny is required to determine whether or not the consideration is valuable. Consideration of the following classes is either insufficient or invalid:

1. Performing or promising to perform what one is already obligated to do
2. Refraining from doing or promising to refrain from doing what one has no right to do
3. Moral obligation
4. Past performance

(1) PERFORMING OR PROMISING TO PERFORM WHAT ONE IS ALREADY OBLIGATED TO DO. If the consideration in an agreement consists merely of a promise to do what one is already legally obligated to do anyway, there is no valid contract. Such a consideration is said to be invalid; and if the consideration is invalid, the contract is invalid. Such invalid promises usually consist of promising to do what the law requires one to do anyway, or promising to do what one is already obligated to do under a previous contract.

- Adams contracted with Barclay to build a house and to accept in part payment a specified bond and mortgage. Afterwards Adams refused to complete the building unless Barclay would guarantee the payment of the bond. Barclay did this. The court held that the guarantee could not be enforced for want of consideration. In building the house, Adams did only that which he had previously agreed to do. "The performance of an act which the party is under legal obligation to do cannot create or constitute a consideration for a new contract."

(2) REFRAINING FROM DOING OR PROMISING TO REFRAIN FROM DOING WHAT ONE HAS NO RIGHT TO DO. When one promises to refrain from doing something, such an act is called *forebearance.* If the promisor had a right to do the act, forebearance is a valid consideration. When the forebearance consists of a promise to refrain from doing something which one has no right to do, however, such a promise is an invalid consideration. This is particularly true where one promises to refrain from unlawful conduct.

- Simpson promised his tenant, Howard, not to raise the rent if Howard would make several enumerated repairs which Howard was under no obligation to make. Howard agreed to do this but failed to make them. Simpson sued Howard for the estimated cost of making repairs. The court held Simpson could not collect because at the time of the agreement the rent control laws prohibited Simpson from raising the rent. Simpson, therefore, was promising to refrain from doing what he had no right to do anyway.

(3) MORAL OBLIGATION. A moral obligation is one assumed not by law, but by one's sense of right or wrong. Smith was unemployed and destitute. Jones, purely as an act of charity but at a great sacrifice to himself, supplied Smith $150 worth of groceries. If Smith found employment and was able to repay Jones, he should do so. He had a moral obligation to do so, but he had no legal obligation.

(4) PAST PERFORMANCE. As a rule, an act performed prior to the promise does not constitute a detriment to the promisee. If a carpenter gratuitously helps a neighbor build his house with no promise of pay, he cannot enforce a promise to pay that is made after the house is completed. The promise to pay must induce the carpenter to do the work, and this cannot be done if the promise is made after the work is completed. There is no new benefit to the promisor or detriment to the promisee.

A debt that is discharged by bankruptcy may be revived under certain circumstances, usually by the debtor's agreeing in writing to pay it. Such promises are enforceable even though the creditor, the promisee, gives no new consideration to support the promise. The debtor is said to have waived his defense of past consideration under such circumstances. This is an exception to the general rule that past performance will not support a present promise.

- Parrish was seriously injured in an automobile accident. Dr. Davis, without being asked, gave expert first-aid treatment which saved Parrish's life. Sometime later Parrish's brother-in-law said to Davis: "I am going to pay you $50 for your services to Parrish." He later refused to do so. It was held that there was no consideration to support the promise and that there was no legal liability.

Questions

1. (a) What is consideration?
(b) Must every contract have consideration to make it valid?

2. How may the consideration in contracts be expressed?

3. (a) If two parties enter into a contract, the consideration of which is an exchange of promises, why must each of these promises have value?
(b) If a promise does not impose a legal obligation upon the promisor, can such a promise constitute a consideration?

4. If a boy promises his father that he will not own and operate an automobile until he is eighteen in exchange for his father's promise to pay him $2,000, is this a valid contract? What is the value of the boy's promise?

5. If one owes a note for $1,000 and the holder agrees to mark it "Paid in full" if the maker will pay $800 even though the note is past due, will such a payment cancel the note? Explain.

6. During Halloween night, two young men promised not to damage Day's car if Day would agree to pay them $50. Why cannot this contract be enforced?

7. Why cannot a moral obligation constitute the consideration for a contract?

8. A son gave up his job to care for his father during a serious illness. He lost $1,000 in wages during that time. The son's brother promised to reimburse him for $500 for this loss, but that promise had not induced him to quit his job. Was this agreement enforceable?

9. Why must a promise to induce an act be made before the act is performed?

10. Under what circumstances may one waive his defense of past consideration?

Case Problems

1. John, aged 22, lived in a distant city from his father and was not dependent on his father. He became seriously ill and incurred a large hospital and doctor bill which he was unable to pay. John's father wrote the doctor, who owned the hospital, and promised to pay both the hospital bill and the doctor bill. He failed to do so, and the hospital sued the father. Was the father liable?

2. The Pacific Ice Company offered Hancock its dealership for ice in a given area. The company agreed to furnish Hancock with ice at a stipulated price per pound if Hancock would purchase his own ice truck and would agree to solicit orders in his district and make deliveries and collections. Hancock wrote upon the offer the word "accepted" and mailed the offer back to the ice company. After Hancock bought his truck and had obtained about 300 orders for daily delivery of ice at a stipulated price, the ice company refused to sell him ice at the price quoted in the offer. Hancock sued for damages alleging breach of contract. Was Hancock entitled to damages?

3. Dave and Mary, newlyweds, purchased $1,000 worth of appliances from the Home Appliance Company. After they had paid $400, Dave became unemployed and was unable to keep up the payments. The contract had this clause in it: "In the event any one monthly payment becomes delinquent, the entire balance of the account becomes due and payable at once." The Home Appliance Company called attention to this clause and demanded $600 at once. The company offered, however, to settle for $400 if paid in two days.

Dave and Mary pledged their furniture to a loan company to raise the $400. As soon as they paid the $400, the Home Appliance Company immediately sued them for the other $200. Were Dave and Mary obligated to pay it?

4. Todd, an artist, promised to paint a portrait of Lowe's wife. Nothing was said about any charge. Two days later, and shortly after Todd began work on the portrait, Lowe, an architect, promised to draw for Todd a set of blueprints for his proposed new home. Nothing was said about any charge for this work. Todd completed the portrait and delivered it to Lowe, but Lowe never made the blueprints. Todd sued Lowe for $500, alleging a breach of contract. Was there a contract between Todd and Lowe?

5. Holliday, an attorney, agreed to represent Dodd in a legal proceeding if Dodd would landscape Holliday's lot. Holliday represented Dodd successfully but Dodd refused to landscape the lot, claiming there was no consideration to support the contract. Do you agree?

6. The Addison Construction Company entered into a contract with Olsen to construct a house for Olsen for $16,000. The house was to be constructed according to specifications and was to be completed as soon as possible. There was considerable delay in beginning the construction, and Olsen promised to pay an additional $500 if the Addison Construction Company would begin work on the house within one week. They did this and then demanded the $500. Were they entitled to it?

7. Baldwin agreed to help Murphy, his brother-in-law, who was unemployed, build a house with the understanding that Baldwin was to receive no pay. After the house was completed Murphy said to Baldwin, "When I go back to work, I am going to pay you $400 for the work you did for me." Later Baldwin attempted to enforce this agreement. Was Murphy liable for the $400?

8. Diamond was unemployed and had no place to live. His aunt, being sorry for him, allowed him to live with her until he could find work. Diamond lived with his aunt for four months and then obtained employment with an excellent salary. His aunt demanded that he pay a reasonable board bill for the four months and Diamond refused. Was the aunt entitled to collect?

Chapter 8

Illegal Agreements

Illegality. A contract, to be valid and enforceable, must among other things be for a lawful purpose, and this purpose must be achieved in a lawful manner. If this were not true, the court might be placed in the absurd position of compelling one party to a contract to commit a crime. Any act the commission of which would be a crime cannot be the subject of a contract. If the act itself is legal, but the proposed manner of committing the act is illegal, the contract is void. In other words, both the end and the means must be legal.

If the contract is entire and cannot be performed except as an entity, then illegality in one part renders the whole contract invalid. If the contract is divisible so that the legal parts can be performed separately, the contract is enforceable for these parts. For example, when one purchases several articles, each priced separately, and the sale of one or two of these articles is illegal for some reason, the whole contract will not fall because of these one or two articles.

Contracts Prohibited by Statute. Any act specifically prohibited by statute cannot constitute the subject matter of a valid contract. The number of such acts is legion, but some of them are of such general interest that they need to be given special emphasis.

These acts may be classified under the following four headings:

1. Gambling contracts
2. Sunday contracts
3. Usurious contracts
4. Contracts of an unlicensed operator

(1) GAMBLING CONTRACTS. A *gambling contract* is a transaction wherein the parties stand to win or to lose based on pure chance. What one gains, the other must lose. There is no exchange of values as with legitimate business transactions. Under the early common law wagering contracts were enforceable, but they are now generally prohibited in all states by statute. In recent years certain classes of gambling contracts, such as pari-mutuel systems of betting on horse races and dog races, have been legalized.

In general, the courts will leave the parties to a wagering contract where it finds them. The court will not redress the grievance of either party. But this rule cannot be applied to every phase of gambling contracts. Since gambling is contrary to public policy, the law should encourage men to desist. If the sums wagered are deposited with a stakeholder, one party may recover if he repents before the outcome of the wager is known. In a few states he may not only recover from the stakeholder after the outcome is known, but may even recover from the winner. In no state, however, can the winner compel the loser to pay. Furthermore, no state will permit a stakeholder to retain the winnings. This is based on the theory that the contract of the stakeholder is to account for money entrusted to him and that this is not illegal.

Trading on the stock exchange or the grain market represents legitimate business transactions. But the distinction between such trading and gambling contracts is sometimes very fine. These two sets of facts illustrate the distinction:

- Crane agrees to sell Finch 10,000 bushels of wheat at $1.70 a bushel, settlement to be made at the end of six months. The agreement does not contemplate any actual delivery of wheat, but merely that the seller or the buyer will pay the other the difference between the current price at the end of the six months and the contract price. Such a contract is a gambling contract that is illegal.

Harold M. Lambert

Trading on the New York Stock Exchange Represents Legitimate Business Transactions, Not Gambling Contracts.

- Arnold agrees to sell Bolde 10,000 bushels of wheat to be delivered six months later at $1.70 a bushel. Arnold does not own any wheat, but he expects to buy it for delivery. At the end of the six-month period, the seller may not actually deliver the wheat; but if the price of wheat has gone up, the seller may pay the buyer the difference between the current price and the contract, or if the price of wheat has gone down, the buyer may pay the seller the difference. Nevertheless the contract is legal because the original intention was to deliver.

The primary difference between the two situations is in the intention to deliver. In the second case Arnold intended at the time of the contract to deliver the wheat and Bolde intended to accept it. In the first case no such intention existed.

(2) SUNDAY CONTRACTS. The laws pertaining to Sunday contracts are the result of statutory legislation and judicial interpretation. These laws and interpretations vary considerably from state to state. Some of these laws prohibit all Sunday labor except work of necessity and charity. In others both labor and transactions of busi-

ness on Sunday are prohibited. If only labor is prohibited, a contract though made on Sunday is valid if it does not provide for labor on Sunday. Conversely, if the contract is made on a week day but calls for labor on Sunday, it is void. If business transactions on Sunday are prohibited, a contract made on Sunday is void because that is classed as a business transaction.

• In a certain case Justice Brewer said: "At common law a contract made on Sunday was valid. But in England and practically every state of the Union there have been enacted what are familiarly known as Sunday laws, for the prevention of labor and business upon that day. Most of these statutes prohibit both labor and business; and under the latter term the making of a contract has in many states been decided to be within the prohibition. But the Kansas statutes simply prohibit labor."

The performance of an act on Sunday which is prohibited by law is a misdemeanor but seldom are the violators prosecuted. For this reason the types of transactions one observes being carried on on Sunday are not a very good guide as to the restrictions contained in these laws.

(3) USURIOUS CONTRACTS. Nearly every state has enacted a law to limit the rate of interest which may be charged for the use of money. Frequently there are two rates, the contract rate and the legal rate. The *contract rate* is the maximum rate which may be charged; any rate above that is *usurious*. The *legal rate,* which is a rate somewhat lower than the contract rate, applies to all situations in which interest may be charged but in which the parties were silent as to the rate. If merchandise is sold on thirty days' credit, the seller may collect interest from the time the thirty days expire till the debt is paid. Since no rate is ordinarily agreed upon in a situation of this kind, the legal rate may be charged.

One cannot accomplish by subterfuge what is prohibited by law. If one borrows $1,000 for thirty days supposedly at 6 per cent interest, but the note is made out for $1,050, the contract is usurious in those states having a usury law. On the other hand, if a loan is made on real estate in a state where the maximum rate is 6 per cent, an additional 1 per cent may be charged as an appraisal fee without making the contract usurious. The additional charge must be a reasonable charge for a legitimate service.

● Davis loaned Crocket $5,000 for two years at 6% interest, the legal rate. In addition he charged a commission of 5% for making the loan. This was usurious if he was loaning his own money. Had Davis not loaned his own money, but had acted merely as a broker in bringing the lender and the borrower together, the 5% would have been a legitimate charge. In that case, the lender would receive only a legitimate interest.

Small loan companies, pawn brokers, and automobile finance companies operate under special statutes permitting them to charge rates as high as 42 per cent a year.

(4) CONTRACTS OF AN UNLICENSED OPERATOR. Many types of services can be legally performed only by a licensed operator. Doctors, lawyers, certified public accountants, real estate brokers, and many others can enforce a charge for their services only if they have previously been licensed to operate. This law protects the public from incompetent operators. The penalty imposed on an unlicensed operator is both civil and criminal. He cannot maintain a civil suit to collect for his services. In addition, he may be prosecuted for operating without a license.

Contracts Contrary to Public Policy. Many contracts are unenforceable because they are contrary to public policy. Many acts have been declared by statute to fall within this category; but, as a rule, the courts must determine from the very nature of the act whether or not it is contrary to public policy.

The most common types of contracts which are invalid because they are contrary to public policy are:

1. Contracts limiting the freedom of marriage
2. Contracts affecting the administration of justice
3. Contracts injuring the public service
4. Contracts in unreasonable restraint of trade

(1) CONTRACTS LIMITING THE FREEDOM OF MARRIAGE. It is contrary to public policy to enter into any contract the effect of which is to limit freedom of marriage. Such contracts are void.

The following provisions in contracts have been held to render the contract a nullity: (a) an agreement whereby one party promises never to marry; (b) an agreement to refrain from marrying for a definite period of time (An agreement not to marry during minority, however, is valid.); (c) an agreement not to marry certain named individuals; (d) an agreement to seek a divorce for a consideration.

(2) CONTRACTS AFFECTING THE ADMINISTRATION OF JUSTICE. The impartial administration of justice is the cornerstone of democracy. Any contract that may obstruct our legal processes is null and void. It is not necessary that justice be actually obstructed. If the contract has the tendency to do so, the courts will not enforce it.

The following provisions have been held to render contracts void: (a) an agreement to pay a witness a larger fee than that allowed by law, provided the promisor wins the case; (b) an agreement by a candidate for sheriff that he will appoint a certain individual deputy sheriff in return for his aid in bringing about the promisor's election; (c) an agreement to pay a prospective witness a sum of money to leave the state until the trial is over; (d) a contract not to prosecute a thief if he will return the stolen goods.

(3) CONTRACTS INJURING THE PUBLIC SERVICE. Any contract that may, from its very nature, injure public service is void. A person may contract as an attorney to appear before any public authority to obtain or oppose the passage of any bill. But a contract to use improper influence to obtain the desired result is void. Also an agreement to supplement a legislator's salary has been held to be void because it tends to injure public service.

Contracts to use one's influence in obtaining a public contract usually let to the lowest competent bidder, to obtain pardons and paroles, and to pay a public official more or less than the statutory salary are also void.

(4) CONTRACTS IN UNREASONABLE RESTRAINT OF TRADE. It is the policy of the government to encourage competition. Any contract, therefore, intended to restrain trade unreasonably is null and void. The dividing line between reasonable and unreasonable restraint of trade is often dim, but certain acts have by judicial decision become well established as unreasonable restraint of trade. The most common acts in this class are:

(a) Contracts not to compete
(b) Contracts to form a monopoly
(c) Contracts to fix the resale price
(d) Unfair trade practices

(*a*) *Contracts Not to Compete.* When one purchases a going business, he purchases not only the physical assets but also the goodwill, which is often the most valuable asset of the firm. If the seller should attempt to regain any of the physical assets without paying for them, he could be prosecuted for larceny, robbery, or burglary depending on the method used to regain them. In the absence of a contract prohibiting his attempt to retake the asset "goodwill," he may do so. It is customary and highly desirable when purchasing a business to include in the contract a provision prohibiting the seller from entering the same business again in the trade territory for a specified length of time. Such a contract not to compete is legal if the restriction is reasonable both as to time and space.

The time varies with the type of business, but five years is too long for most types of business. The court decides what is a reasonable time in each individual case, but three years tends to be the maximum safe limit. This gives the buyer time to establish his own goodwill.

The restriction as to territory should not go beyond the trade area of the business. For many types of businesses, such as hardware stores, grocery stores, shoe stores, and similar types of retail outlets, the trade area can be established with reasonable accuracy. But for such firms as motels, barbecue stands, filling stations, and other types of business the area may be very indefinite. The law simply states the restriction must be reasonable.

Closely allied to this type of contract is one whereby an employee, as a part of his employment contract, agrees not to work for a competing firm for a certain period of time after terminating his employment. These contracts also must be reasonable as to time. What is a competing firm is not always definite but must be determined in each case by the circumstances.

• Joiner was appointed Manager of the Elite Business College; and, as a condition of employment, Joiner agreed not to work for any other school in the state for ten years after terminating his employment with the Elite School. The time, ten years, was an unreasonable restraint. If the school drew students from all over the state, the territory was not too extensive, but the contract was nevertheless void because of the unreasonable time restriction.

• The Apex Jewelry Company owned by Cooper sold the stock of jewelry and goodwill to Walker. Cooper agreed never to enter the retail jewelry business again in the United States. This restraint was unreasonable, both as to time and territory.

(*b*) *Contracts to Form a Monopoly.* Contracts among businessmen to fix prices, divide up the trade territory, limit production so as to reduce the supply, or otherwise limit competition are void. Such contracts which affect interstate commerce and which are therefore subject to regulation by the federal government are specifically declared illegal by the Sherman Anti-Trust Act and the Clayton Act. Most of the states have similar laws applicable to intrastate commerce.

(*c*) *Contracts to Fix the Resale Price.* Under the Federal Sherman Act of 1890 it is illegal for a manufacturer to attempt to control the resale price of its manufactured goods unless the individual manufacturer has his own retail outlets. Several of the states passed legislation permitting resale price maintenance to apply to intrastate trade. In 1937, Congress passed the Miller-Tydings Act, which is in substance a modification of the Sherman Act of 1890 in that it permits manufacturers in one state to make contracts with merchants in other states having resale price maintenance laws without being guilty of restraint of trade. If a state does not have a resale price maintenance law, the Miller-Tydings Act does not permit resale price maintenance.

(*d*) *Unfair Trade Practices.* The Robinson-Patman Act attempted to eliminate certain unfair trade practices in interstate commerce. Under this act it is unlawful to discriminate in price between large and small buyers if the goods are of like grade and quality. Most states have passed similar laws for intrastate commerce. These state laws as a rule go further and prevent the resale of goods at a loss to attract customers. The purpose of these laws is to encourage competition and to prevent monopolies.

● The Black Canning Company entered into a contract with the Great Gulf Florida Company to sell canned tomatoes at a discount of 50 cents a case in quantities of 50,000 cases or more. Under the Robinson-Patman Act this contract was invalid because the difference in price was not justified by the difference in the cost of selling 50,000 cases and smaller quantities.

Questions

1. May a contract for a lawful purpose be enforced if it calls for performance by illegal methods? Explain.

2. What is the effect of a contract a part of which is illegal?

3. What are some of the types of contracts that are illegal?

4. What is the test of a gambling transaction?

5. What is the distinction between gambling and trading on the stock or grain exchanges?

6. If a law prohibits acts of labor on Sunday, what effect does it have on a contract?

7. What is the difference between the contract rate of interest and the legal rate of interest?

8. (a) John promised not to marry Miss Hayes if Henry, who also wanted to marry her, would pay him $5,000. Could this contract be enforced?

(b) Smith promised to pay Sheriff Puff $50 if he would arrest Towe for larceny. Puff arrested Towe and obtained a conviction. Could Sheriff Puff compel Smith to pay him the $50?

9. Give an example of a contract in unreasonable restraint of trade.

10. Hall was planning to open an accounting office in town. Dennis, another accountant, promised to pay Hall 5 per cent of his accounting fees if Hall would refrain from opening an office. Could this contract be enforced?

Case Problems

1. In a state where business transactions, with certain exceptions, are void if made on Sunday, Henry and Sally Brewer entered into a sales agreement with the Dixie Homefreezer Corporation to purchase a homefreezer for $650. As a part of the sales contract, there was a five-year guarantee on the freezer. The purchasers paid $150 down and executed a $500 note for the balance. The sale was completed on Saturday. The salesman dated all the papers on Sunday, but the Brewers did not notice this fact. The seller immediately discounted, that is, sold the note to a bank. The freezer was of poor quality and in few respects met the

qualities set out in the guarantee. The Brewers sued for breach of warranty and refused to make any further payments. Were they entitled to damages?

2. Adolphus contracted to pay his niece, Anna Bell, $5,000 if she would not marry until she finished college. Anna Bell finished college and never had a date during that time. She demanded the $5,000, and Adolphus refused to pay on the ground the contract was void because it restricted the freedom of marriage. Was this a good defense?

3. Griffin, who purchased the Dalton Insurance Agency, inserted this provision in the contract: "The seller hereby agrees not to own or operate another insurance agency in Canton for the next three years." About two weeks after Griffin purchased this agency, Mrs. Dalton, the wife of the seller, opened her agency and employed her husband as salesman. As a result they captured about half of the old customers of the Dalton Agency. What were Griffin's rights, if any?

4. Hargrove and Tanner entered into a wager as to the outcome of a football game. They deposited $100 each with McCarley, a stakeholder, with instructions to pay the $200 to the winner. At half-time Hargrove's team was losing, so he went to the stakeholder and demanded a return of his $100. Was he entitled to a return?

5. Hunnicutt and Boyd agree to buy and sell stock between themselves. The contract calls for them to meet each day as soon as the stock market closes and to settle on their contracts at the price quoted when the stock market closed. They did this for about two months, during which time Boyd lost $2,000. On October 29 his loss amounted to $800. He not only refused to pay this but demanded that Hunnicutt return his $2,000. Discuss the rights of the parties.

6. Hunt contracted with the Blank Manufacturing Company to use his influence with the proper government officials to obtain a $10,000,000 government contract for the Blank Company. Hunt was to receive 5 per cent of any contract he obtained, nothing if he was unsuccessful. His contract bound him to use all methods "fair or foul" to obtain the contract. Through bribery he obtained a $6,000,000 contract and then demanded a fee of $300,000. Was he entitled to collect?

7. Pearl Klug purchased and paid for a dress on Sunday in a state where executory contracts on Sunday were void. She asked the seller to hold the dress a few days, and said she would call for it later. Two days later she took the dress home. A week later Pearl returned the dress and demanded the return of her money. Was she entitled to its return?

8. Charles Munson loaned Carl Parrish $500 at 6 per cent interest, the contract rate in that state, even though Parrish was perfectly willing to pay 10 per cent interest. In order to keep within the 6 per cent limit, he agreed to do about $50 worth of work on Munson's car and to make no charge for it. Later Parrish sued to collect the $50. Was he entitled to collect?

9. Adams owned a hardware store in a town of about 10,000 population. Many of his customers were farmers who lived in the surrounding territory. The street on which the store was located was a state highway. Therefore he did a small amount of business with tourists and travelers. Adams sold the business, including the goodwill, to Baker. As a part of the selling price, Adams agreed not to engage in the hardware business in that particular county for five years. Three years later Adams again entered the hardware business in that county, and Baker brought suit to prevent his doing this. Discuss the legal rights of the parties and state your conclusion.

Chapter 9

Form of Contracts

Reasons for Written Contracts. All contracts of importance ought to be in writing, but only a few must be written in order to be enforceable. An oral contract, if its meaning can be ascertained, is just as effective and enforceable as a written contract unless it is one of the few types specifically required by statute to be in writing.

A written contract has several advantages over an oral contract provided it includes all the terms and provisions of the agreement. In the first place, the existence of a contract cannot be denied if it is in writing. If there were no witnesses when an oral contract was formed, one of the parties might successfully deny that any contract was formed. The party suing on a contract must establish the existence of that contract together with its contents by a preponderance of the evidence. In the second place, one of the parties may die or become insane. The administrator or executor of an estate in case of death, or the committee or guardian in case of insanity, is tremendously handicapped in enforcing an oral agreement made previously by the deceased or insane person. Even when there are witnesses present at the time an oral contract is formed, the testimony may vary considerably as to the actual terms of the contract. Written evidence, composed in clear and unambiguous language, is always better than oral evidence.

For these reasons most businessmen prefer to have contracts pertaining to matters of considerable importance reduced to writing even when this precaution is not required by law.

Parol Evidence Rule. *Parol evidence,* that is, oral testimony, cannot be introduced at a trial to modify, alter, or contradict the terms of a written contract that is clear in its language and complete. If the contract includes ambiguous terms or if it is clearly incomplete, however, oral testimony may be introduced to clarify the ambiguous terms or to prove the provisions of the oral contract not shown in the written part. For example, in a written contract to sell land nothing is said as to when the purchaser is to get possession. If there was an oral agreement prior to the signing of the written contract that the seller was to retain possession for 90 days after the sale, oral testimony may be introduced to prove this provision. If the written contract stipulates that possession is to be given to the buyer in 30 days, however, oral testimony cannot be introduced to vary or contradict this provision.

There are at least two important exceptions to the parol evidence rule. First, one may raise the question of mistake, fraud, or alteration as a defense to a written contract as freely as he can to an oral contract. If the written contract calls for payment in 30 days while the oral contract actually called for 90 days, one may introduce oral testimony to prove this was due either to a mutual mistake, fraud, or alteration. In a sense, this is not done for the purpose of altering the terms of the written contract but in reality is an attack upon the validity of the contract. If a written contract is materially altered, the entire contract is invalidated. In other words the entire contract as written is either valid or invalid. Secondly, for a valuable consideration a written contract may be replaced by a subsequent oral contract containing most of the terms of the written contract. This is in reality a new contract and not an attempt to vary the terms of a written contract.

Statute of Frauds. In the year 1676 the English Parliament enacted a statute, one of the chief provisions of

H. Armstrong Roberts

Important Contracts Should Be Written Even Though the Law Does Not Require Them to Be in That Form.

which was an attempt to prevent fraud and perjuries. This act was known as the Statute of Frauds. The statute listed certain classes of contracts which could not be enforced unless their terms were reduced to writing and unless they were signed by the parties to be bound. The fourth and the seventeenth sections of the Statute of Frauds contained a list of these contracts. Most of our states have adopted these two sections with but slight variations.

It is well to remember that in our country it is not the English Statute of Frauds but its American adaptation that determines which contracts must be in writing. The general provisions of the fourth section are given below while those in the seventeenth section will be discussed in Chapter 13.

Fourth Section of the Statute of Frauds. The fourth section of the Statute of Frauds provides that the following types of agreements must be in writing:

1. An agreement of an executor or administrator to pay debts of the estate from his personal funds

2. An agreement to become responsible for the debts, default, or miscarriage of another

3. An agreement in which the promise of one person is made in consideration of marriage

4. An agreement to sell, or a sale of, land or any interest in or concerning land

5. An agreement the terms of which do not call for performance within one year from the time it is made

(1) AN AGREEMENT OF AN EXECUTOR OR ADMINISTRATOR TO PAY THE DEBTS OF THE ESTATE. When a person dies, his executor (if he left a will), or his administrator (if he left no will), takes over all his assets and from these assets pays all the debts of the deceased before distributing the remainder to the heirs. Naturally, the executor or the administrator, is not expected to pay the debts of the deceased out of his personal funds. He may wish to do so under certain circumstances, however, in order to protect the estate. For this reason, his promise to pay the debts of the estate from his personal funds is in reality a contract to become responsible for the debts of another and must be in writing to be enforceable.

(2) AN AGREEMENT TO BECOME RESPONSIBLE FOR THE DEBTS, DEFAULT, OR MISCARRIAGE OF ANOTHER. The term "debt" here refers to an obligation to pay money; "default" refers to a breach of contractual obligations other than money, such as a contract to build a house; and a "miscarriage" refers to duties and obligations not based on a contract, such as a sheriff's obligation to perform the duties of his office in a creditable manner.

A man may obligate himself to pay the debts of another if he cares to do so even though he receives no benefit from it. To be enforceable, such a contract must be in writing. Contracts of this nature are generally referred to as "guaranty" and "suretyship," topics which are discussed in Chapter 40. It is important to note carefully the wording of a guaranty. One must actually stand for the debt of another. Taking upon oneself an original obligation, even though another receives the benefit, need not be in writing.

● Green wishes to buy an automobile from the Uptown Motors Company; but because of his poor credit rating, he is required to provide added security. Hasch, to enable Green to buy the car on credit said, "Let him have it and I will be responsible for the unpaid balance." Here Hasch is lending his credit by joining in the principal debtor's obligation. He thus makes himself primarily liable, and the contract need not be in writing.

If Hasch had said, "I will pay you if Green defaults in his payments," he would have been making only a collateral or secondary obligation. Green is liable primarily, Hasch, secondarily, that is, if Green defaults. This contract must be in writing.

This rule does not hold if the main purpose of the guaranty is to gain some advantage for the guarantor. This provision of the Statute of Frauds was designed especially for those situations where one guarantees the debt of another person purely as an accommodation to that person. There are situations where one person guarantees the debt or default of another because it is to the guarantor's personal financial interest to do so. When the guaranty is not gratuitous but is a calculated business proposition, the contract of guaranty need not be in writing.

● Ward owned and operated a farm. Robinson worked the crops on a share-crop basis. Ward said to a merchant, "Let my tenant, Robinson, have credit up to $50 a month during the crop season; and if he does not pay you in the fall, I will." This wording makes this clearly one of guaranty, but it need not be in writing. The main purpose was to gain some advantage for Ward himself.

(3) An Agreement in Which the Promise of One Person Is Made in Consideration of Marriage. Mutual promises to marry constitute an enforceable contract in most states. The consideration of each party is the

promise of the other party, and the contract need not be written. An agreement that is based upon marriage as the consideration for a promise to pay money to another or to settle property upon another must be in writing.

• If Hoffman promises to pay Alice Hansen $10,000 if she will marry him, the promise is unenforceable unless it is in writing. Hoffman's promise to pay $10,000 is made "in consideration of marriage." It is this feature which brings the agreement within the Statute of Frauds.

(4) AN AGREEMENT TO SELL, OR A SALE OF LAND, OR ANY INTEREST IN OR CONCERNING LAND. In a sale of land generally two contracts are involved. The first is a contract to sell. This contract should include all the terms agreed upon by the parties. At a later date, another contract is executed and title to the land is conveyed. There must be written evidence of both of these contracts to make them binding. The contract conveying real estate, called a *deed,* must not only be in writing but also must be notarized.

One may wish to sell, not the land itself, but only an interest in the land. The evidence of this contract also must be in writing. These sales usually involve right of ways, joint use of driveways, mineral rights, timber, and any other interest in land. A lease for more than one year must also be in writing.

• Youngblood orally agrees to sell his house and lot to Rasmussen for $10,000. There are four witnesses to this agreement. Later Moorehouse offers him $10,500 for the property. Youngblood wishes to rescind his agreement with Rasmussen. He can do so because the contract must be in writing no matter how many witnesses there may be.

Frequently oral contracts relative to land are performed before any question of their validity is raised. For example, one leases a building by oral contract for two years. He occupies the building for that period and then refuses to pay the rent, alleging that the contract is invalid because it is oral. The law will compel him to pay the rent. If one has paid money or performed a service under an oral contract, he may recover the money or the value of the service, even though he cannot enforce the executory part of the contract.

(5) AN AGREEMENT THE TERMS OF WHICH DO NOT CALL FOR PERFORMANCE WITHIN ONE YEAR FROM THE TIME IT IS MADE. The terms of a contract that cannot be performed in one year are likely to be forgotten. To minimize the need to resort to the courts to determine one's right, the law requires all contracts that cannot be performed within one year to be in writing.

- If Kromm orally employed Dennis to build a house for him costing $12,000, the contract would be enforceable even though Dennis might take fifteen months to perform his part of the agreement. The terms of the contract were silent on the time required to complete the house; but since it clearly could have been completed in one year, the contract did not need to be in writing. On the other hand, if Kromm had on February 26 employed Dennis to work for him for one year, beginning on March 1, the contract would be unenforceable unless it was reduced to writing because from its very terms it could not be performed within one year from the date it was made, February 26.

Note or Memorandum. The laws dealing with written contracts are concerned primarily with requiring written evidence of the contract rather than requiring the contract itself to be in writing. In the sale of land, the contract itself, that is the deed, must be in writing. In other cases the law is complied with if some written note or memorandum setting forth all the relevant facts is present. The memorandum must contain the names of the parties, the subject matter of the contract, the basic terms of the contract, including the price and the manner of delivery, and it must be signed by the one to be charged.

A written contract must be signed by both parties. This is not true of the note or memorandum. If suit is instituted on a contract that is evidenced by a memorandum, clearly one of the parties wishes to be bound. He need not sign it since he will abide by its terms anyway. If he sues, the other one is the party that is charged. If this party has signed the memorandum, the contract is enforceable against him.

The law states that the memorandum must contain all the essential terms of the contract; yet it differs materially from a written contract. Probably the chief difference is that one may introduce oral testimony to explain or complete the memorandum. Under the parol evidence rule this is not true of a contract. The court held the following receipt was an adequate memorandum: "Received of Sholowitz twenty-five dollars to bind the bargain for the sale of Noorigan's brick store and land at 46 Blackstone Street to Sholowitz. Balance due $1,975." The size of the lot, the type of deed, and other essentials could be established by oral evidence.

The memorandum need not be made at the time of the contract. It need be in existence only at the time suit is brought. The one who signs the memorandum need not sign with the intention of binding himself. If Jones writes Smith, "Since my agreement to buy your Buick for $1,200 was oral, I am not bound by it." This is a sufficient memorandum and makes the contract binding on Jones.

Other Written Contracts. The five classes of contracts that are listed by the Statute of Frauds are not the only contracts required by law to be in writing in order to be enforcable. Every state has a few additional requirements. The more common ones are insurance contracts, contracts reviving a debt that has been extinguished by bankruptcy or by a Statute of Limitations, and agreements that are not to be performed during the lifetime of the promisor, but only after his death.

● Hipps promised his niece, Nancy, that if she would care for Hipps' sister, Nancy would be paid $2,000 out of Hipps estate after he died. This contract in many states must be in writing.

Questions

1. As a general rule, an oral contract is just as enforceable as a written contract. Why, then, should all important contracts be in writing?

2. What is the parol evidence rule?

3. Give an example of oral testimony that may be introduced to explain the terms of a written contract.

4. Which contract of an administrator or an executor need not be in writing?

5. Under what circumstances would an administrator promise to pay the debts of the estate from his personal funds?

6. (a) If one takes upon himself an original obligation, even though the benefits go to another party, must the contract be in writing to be enforceable?

(b) If one contracts to be responsible for the debt of another in order to obtain some advantage for himself, must this contract be in writing?

7. What is the difference between a "contract of sale" of land and one "to sell"?

8. Give three illustrations of interests in land other than ownership of the land outright.

9. Who must sign the memorandum before the contract can be enforced?

10. Name some additional types of contracts that must be in writing.

Case Problems

1. The Reed Paper Company had for some time been negotiating with Downs on a business deal of the utmost importance to the company. The parties finally reached an agreement. Paul Chapman, secretary to the president of the Reed Paper Company, made a written memorandum of the contract, and Downs signed it. Chapman filed the memorandum. Later Downs refused to conform to his agreement.

The memorandum could not be found since Chapman could not remember how or where he had filed it. The contract involved the sale of several thousand acres of pulpwood and the processing of the wood into paper over a period of three years. Could this contract be enforced if the memorandum was not found?

2. Mosely was employed by the Crawford Company at $350 a month. A competing firm in a nearby city offered Mosely $400 a month. The contract was made on May 10 with the work to start on July 1 and was to last for at least twelve months from July. All the arrangements were made orally. Mosely resigned his position with the Crawford Company, sold his home, and had his furniture packed and ready to move when he was notified that the position was not available. What recourse did Mosely have?

3. John Barner was sales manager for the Patterson Motor Company. Billy Seabolt, a minor, agreed to purchase a secondhand car for $1,400. As a part of the contract Barner stipulated that an adult must "stand good" for the payment. Steedman, an uncle of Seabolt, said, "Let him have the car; and if he does not keep up the payments, I will." This was an oral promise. Barner interpreted this wording to meet the test of a contract of suretyship; consequently he did not require it to be in writing. Seabolt wrecked the car and then demanded a refund. Could Barner look to Steedman for the selling price?

4. Pat Snow owned and operated the Snow Barber Shop. He orally contracted with Buddy Broadnax to give Broadnax, a druggist, and his three boys all the haircuts and shaves they needed for the next two years for $300 cash. Broadnax was to pay the money the next day, but he changed his mind and refused to pay it. Snow wrote Broadnax a letter and demanded that "you pay me the $550 as you promised." Broadnax immediately replied by letter: "I never agreed to pay $550. It was $300. Anyway it is an oral contract, so try to collect it." Snow claimed this constituted a sufficient memorandum. Do you agree?

5. Beverly Hick and Myrna Mathis were secretaries. On October 8 they rented an efficiency apartment where they could prepare their meals. To tidy up the apartment, they repapered it, painted all woodwork, and did various other improvements. The total cost of the improvements amounted to $180. Their oral lease was to run to December 31, the following year. Three months later the landlord raised the rent $25 a month. Could he compel them to pay it?

6. Helen was private secretary to John, a wealthy widower, twenty years her senior. He proposed to Helen daily, but she declined. Finally he said, "Helen, if you will marry me, I will set up for you an irrevocable trust for $1,000,000. This trust and the income from it will be yours absolutely." After they were married, John's business failed and he refused to carry out his oral promise relative to the trust fund. Could Helen compel him to do so?

7. John and Mary Dennis entered into an oral agreement with George Carpenter, a contractor, to build a house for them. Many proposals and counterproposals were made. When the parties finally agreed to all the terms, they decided to reduce the terms to writing. Carpenter agreed to write the contract. When John and Mary Dennis read it, they contended that the price agreed upon included a terrace not shown on the blueprint. Carpenter then agreed to include the terrace, but he suggested that they sign the contract as it had been prepared. They signed the contract. When he built the house, Carpenter refused to include the terrace, and John and Mary Dennis withheld $100 from the final payment. Carpenter sued for the $100. Who was entitled to win? Why?

8. Rochester, a farmer, contracted with Harris to farm for him on a share crop basis. To enable Harris to buy groceries until the crops matured, Rochester said to Harrelson, a groceryman, "Let Harris have groceries up to $80 a month for five months and I will see that he pays you when his cotton is sold." This was an oral contract. Was it enforceable?

9. Horner, by letter, offered to employ Holmes as his accountant at $4,800 a year, work to begin January 1. Holmes on November 28 called in person at Horner's office and orally accepted the offer. Holmes resigned his job on December 1 to become effective December 31 so that he would be ready to start on his new job. After working for Horner one month, he was laid off and was not able to find another job for twelve months. He sued Horner for his loss of wages. Was he entitled to collect?

10. Darlington purchased a piano from Davey, Incorporated, for $560. A sales ticket was made out and signed by Darlington. The sales ticket contained a statement that delivery was to be made December 5, and payment was to be made on delivery. When the truck drivers brought the piano Darlington refused to receive and pay for it. Davey, Incorporated, sued him for breach of contract. Was he liable?

Chapter 10

Assignment of Contracts

Rights and Obligations. A contract grants both rights and obligations. Originally, one who is not a party to the contract has no right to the benefits to be derived from the contract, nor has he any of the duties or obligations. Third parties, however, may acquire these rights or assume these duties.

If a contract is executory, that is, if it has not been performed by either party or both parties, one of them may wish to transfer his rights or to delegate his duties under the contract, or to do both. Whether or not he may legally do so depends upon the nature and content of the contract.

Assignment of Rights. As a general rule, the rights under a contract may be assigned, but the duties and obligations under a contract may not be assigned. One's rights under a contract may be transferred almost as freely as his property rights. Such a transfer is referred to in law as an assignment. An *assignment* may therefore be defined as the means whereby one party conveys his rights or interest in a contract to another who is not a party to the original undertaking. The party making the assignment is known as the *assignor*; the one to whom the right is transferred is the *assignee*.

Restrictions on One's Right to Assign. Since an assignment is a voluntary act, it is not the purpose of the law to impose many restrictions upon one's liberty to assign his rights under contracts. About the only legal restriction of any significance is a law prohibiting the assignment of future pay by soldiers, sailors, and marines.

This is based on the theory it is contrary to public policy. Many states and cities also prohibit the assignment of the pay of public officials. Contractors on public works are in many states prohibited by law from assigning a certain minimum percentage of their wages. This is to protect the wage earner and his family from hard pressing creditors.

Often one's right under a contract is to receive the services of the other party, such as a bookkeeper, salesman, or other employee who contracts to work for a stipulated period of time. The right to this party's personal services cannot be assigned, but such a restriction is not the result of a statutory law. Courts merely refuse to honor and enforce the attempted assignment. This limitation applies to all employees. The law will not compel you to work for a man or firm against your will.

An assignment of a right is voidable if it imposes new conditions upon the party to the contract, whether the new conditions are favorable or unfavorable. For example, if you have the right under a contract to have 50,000 bricks delivered at a stipulated price to a certain town, you cannot assign that right to another person and have the bricks delivered to a different town even though it is nearer to the seller's place of business. If the assignment imposes a new condition that is material upon the other party, he is not bound to honor the assignment. This in reality constitutes a material alteration of the contract.

The parties to a contract may include a provision that prohibits the other party from assigning his rights. A limitation to this rule is that if the only right under the contract is to receive money, this right cannot be prohibited by contract.

Delegation of Duties. In most cases one cannot assign his duties under a contract. This is particularly true in cases where credit, skill, or confidence in one's ability to perform according to contract is present. This condition exists in all employment contracts involving skill, trust,

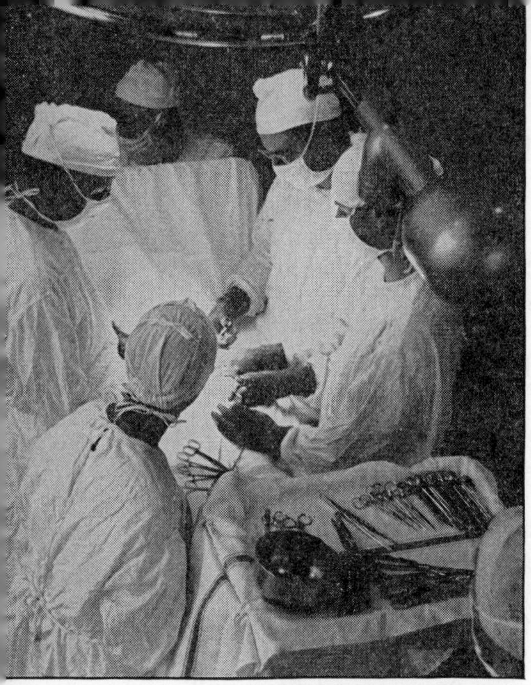

E. I. duPont de Nemours & Co.

Ordinarily Neither the Duty to Perform a Personal Service Nor the Right to That Service Can Be Assigned.

and confidence. Only when the performance is standardized or highly nontechnical, can one delegate its performance to another. In the construction industry there is a vast amount of delegation of duties because the correct performance can be easily ascertained. Contracts calling for unskilled work or labor may in most instances be delegated.

In all cases of delegation the delegating party remains fully liable under the contract. He may be sued for any breach of contract even though another party actually performed. In such an event he may in turn sue the party who performed inadequately.

Effect of an Assignment. The nonassigning party retains all his rights and defenses as though there had never been an assignment. For example, if the nonassigning party was incompetent to contract, or entered into the contract under duress, undue influence, fraud, or misrepresentation, he may offer these defenses against the assignee as effectively as he could have done against the assignor.

The assignee must take the contract as it exists at the time of the assignment. The effect of the assignment upon the assignor is not uniform throughout the various states. If Smith leases a house for two years from Hart, and then assigns the lease to Sebba, he (Smith), in most states, remains liable for the rent. He may avoid this liability by obtaining a release from Hart.

Most assignments involve claims for money. The Fair Deal Grocery Company assigned $10,000 worth of its accounts receivable to the First National Bank. The assignor warranted that the accounts were genuine. If a customer, therefore, refused to pay the bank because he did not owe the account, the grocery company would be liable. If he failed to pay merely because he was insolvent, most courts would hold that the assignor was not liable. If the bank took the assigned claims as security for a debt owed by the grocery company, and the claims were uncollectible due to insolvency of the customers, the bank could still collect the debt owed to it by the grocery company. Prudent businessmen avoid any difficulty in this regard by covering these points in the contract of assignment.

Form of the Assignment. An assignment may be made either by operation of law or by the act of the parties. In the event of death, the rights and duties (except for personal services) of the deceased are assigned by law to the administrator of the estate. In the event of bankruptcy, the rights and duties of the bankrupt are assigned by operation of law to the trustee in bankruptcy. No special form is necessary under this type of assignment.

> In consideration of one dollar and other good and valuable considerations, I, the undersigned, agree to assign unto John Meade all my rights in an oral contract existing between the undersigned and Adam Smith, of Athens, Georgia. These rights consist of a promise by Adam Smith to pay the undersigned within six months from June 1, the sum of $500 with interest at 4% from June 1 till paid.
>
> Given under my hand this second day of September, 1956.
>
> Ralph H. McGill.

When the assignment is made by act of the parties, it may be either in writing or oral. If the original contract is one which must be in writing, the assignment must be in writing; otherwise, it may be made orally. It is always preferable to make the assignment in writing. This may be done in the case of written contracts by writing the terms of the assignment on the original contract. Oral contracts may be assigned by executing an informal written assignment.

Notice of an Assignment. As a general rule no notice of an assignment need be given. Business prudence demands, however, that the original promisor be notified of the assignment. The promisor has a right to assume that the claim has not been assigned. For example, F. Dodd promised to pay Hodges $500 in thirty days. When the account came due, Dodd, since he had no notice of assignment, was safe in paying Hodges. But if Hodges had assigned the account to Wilson and Wilson had not given Dodd notice, then Wilson would not have been able to collect from Dodd. If Hodges was inclined to be dishonest, he could sell the account to several persons. The assignee who first notified Dodd of the assignment would have the first claim. A few states hold that the first assignee gets preference.

Novation. *Novation* is the substitution of a new obligation for an old one, which is thereby extinguished. In the assignment of duties and obligations, the assignor is not relieved of his duties. He becomes fully responsible for the proper performance of the duties by the assignee. It is very important, therefore, to distinguish between an assignment and novation.

If Goff owes Ratcliff $500, Goff cannot shift this obligation to Lester without Ratcliff's consent. Ratcliff, however, can consent to the release of Goff and the substitution of Lester. In this event there is not an assignment, but a novation; that is, a new contract is formed. Goff is fully discharged. An obligation may be shifted in this manner only with the consent of all the parties.

Questions

1. What is an assignment?

2. Name and identify the parties to an assignment.

3. In what ways may an assignment be made?

4. Why may rights to personal services not be assigned?

5. If one delegates his duties under a contract, what is his liability under the contract?

6. What is the effect of an assignment upon each party involved?

7. Whom should the assignee notify of the assignment?

8. In the event the assignor assigns the same contract to two different assignees, which assignee has priority?

9. How may the assignor be relieved of his duties under a contract that has been assigned?

10. Distinguish between a novation and an assignment.

Case Problems

1. Mary Keller was secretary and bookkeeper for the Dale Television Sales Corporation. A marine at the Quantico Marine Base purchased a television set for $400. After he had paid all but $100 on the set, he assigned $100 out of his military pay to make full settlement for the account since he wanted to sell it to John Davis and give him clear title to it. Miss Keller accepted the assignment, marked the account "paid in full," and gave the Marine a clear title. He immediately transferred title to Davis. As soon as Miss Keller notified the marine base of the assignment, they refused to honor it. The marine refused to pay the $100, and Davis refused to let the seller regain possession of the set. Discuss their rights.

2. Harper Lumber Company made all its employees sign a contract agreeing not to make any assignment of their wages. In spite of this, Stover, an employee, assigned $80 of his wages to the Ferguson Company. This company immediately notified Donahue, the bookkeeper of the Harper Lumber Company, of the assignment. Donahue refused to honor it and paid Stover the full amount due him. The Ferguson Company sued the Harper Lumber Company for the $80 since Stover never paid the account. Was the lumber company liable?

3. Eugene Black was credit manager for a furniture store. Stine purchased some furniture and in payment assigned to the furniture store $800 which was owed to him by the Clarke Engineering Corporation. Since the $800 was not due until ten days after the date of the assignment, Black held it until that date and presented it for payment. Payment was refused because Stine had offered the Clarke Engineering Corporation a 10 per cent discount if they would pay him before the account was due. This they did. Must the corporation also pay the furniture store?

4. The Holcomb Filling Station sold a lot of gasoline on credit to local business firms. One of these firms, The Apex Bakery, was in debt to the station for $450. The owner of the bakery offered to turn over to the station $500 of its accounts receivable if the station would not sue the bakery. The offer was accepted. The filling station was able to collect only $100 on the accounts receivable because the debtors were insolvent. The station sued the bakery later for $400, the uncollectible balance of the accounts receivable. Was it entitled to collect?

5. Delaney, who owned and operated the M & N Cafeteria, sold it to Harper for $30,000, with $10,000 cash and the balance paid by note. Sometime later Harper sold the cafeteria to Mitchell; and Mitchell, as a part of the purchase price, agreed to assume Harper's obligation to pay Delaney the $20,000. Mitchell operated the cafeteria profitably for several months during which time his net profits were $18,000, but he made no payment on the notes. He became ill and the business declined rapidly. Delaney demanded that Harper pay the balance due on the original selling price. Was Harper obligated to pay this?

6. Chambers, an artist of some note, contracted to paint a portrait of Dudley's wife for $1,500. Before the painting was begun Chambers became ill and assigned his rights and duties under the contract to Hughes, an artist of far greater renown than Chambers. Dudley refused to let Hughes paint the portrait. Was Dudley justified in this refusal?

7. Mathis contracted to build a house for Youngblood according to certain definite blueprints and specifications. Mathis sublet, that is, assigned, this contract to Saye, and Youngblood refused to let Saye proceed with the construction. Mathis sued Youngblood for damages for breach of contract. Was Mathis entitled to collect?

Chapter II

Termination of Contracts

Methods by Which Contracts Are Terminated. The preceding chapters have dealt with the law relative to the formation of contracts. It is equally important to know the law dealing with the termination of contracts. Some contracts, like marriage, are easy to enter into but often are difficult to terminate. There are five common methods by which contracts may be terminated. These are (1) performance of the contract, (2) voluntary agreement of the parties, (3) breach of the contract by one of the parties, (4) impossibility of performance, and (5) discharge by operation of the law.

Performance. When all the terms of a contract have been fulfilled, the contract is discharged by performance. Not all the parties, however, may be discharged simultaneously. Each party is discharged as soon as he has done all that he agreed to do. The other party or parties are not discharged if any material thing remains to be done.

It may seem to be a simple matter to determine when a contract has been discharged by performance. There are several factors to be considered, however. They are:

1. Substantial performance
2. Satisfactory performance
3. Tender of performance
4. Time of performance

(1) SUBSTANTIAL PERFORMANCE. Under the early common law, each party to a contract had to perform to the last letter of the contract before he was entitled to demand his rights under the contract. Such a rule was often extremely inequitable. If a contractor builds a

$50 million office building, it is well nigh impossible to avoid some slight deviation from the contract. It would be grossly unfair to say that he could collect none of the $50 million because of this slight breach of contract.

The law today can be stated as follows: If a contract is substantially performed, then the party performing may demand the full price under his contract. The other party then is entitled to file a counterclaim for the deficiency. In the case of the office building, if the cost of completing the building according to contract would be $3,000, the contractor could collect $50 million minus the $3,000. Suppose, however, that the contractor completed the excavation and then quit. He would be entitled to collect nothing. Just how far he must proceed toward full performance before he has substantially performed is often difficult to determine. The performance must be almost complete.

- The Acme Typing Service contracted with the Harrell Hatchery to address and mail 100,000 circulars for $6,000. They typed and mailed 98,000; the other 2,000 had been ruined by the typists. The Harrell Hatchery could not avoid paying for the work because the performance was substantial and the failure to perform to the extent of 100,000 copies was not willful. The Hatchery must pay $6,000 minus the damages. The damages might be more than $120, the proportional cost of addressing the 2,000.

(2) SATISFACTORY PERFORMANCE. It frequently happens that contracts specifically state that the contract must be "satisfactory to" or "to the satisfaction of" a certain person. What constitutes satisfactory performance is frequently a disputed question. Certainly one should not be permitted to avoid a contract on an arbitrary standard of satisfaction impossible to attain. The courts generally have adopted the rule that if the contract is performed in a manner that would satisfy an ordinary, reasonable person, the terms of the contract have been met sufficiently to discharge it. There is one

exception to this rule: If the performance involves the personal taste or fancy of one of the parties, he may arbitrarily reject it on the ground that it is not satisfactory to him.

- If Roy employs Farr to paint a portrait of his (Roy's) wife to his satisfaction, he personally must be satisfied regardless of how well Farr may have performed.

(3) TENDER OF PERFORMANCE. An offer to perform an obligation in satisfaction of the terms of a contract is called a *tender of performance.* If a contract calls for the performance of an act, a tender of performance will discharge the obligation of the one making the tender, so long as the tender conforms to the agreement, if the person to whom the obligation is owed will not accept the tender.

- Cook hired the Thomas Transfer Company to move his household furniture to Atlanta on Monday, June 6, at 8 a.m. On that day the Thomas Transfer Company sent a truck to Cook's residence to load the furniture. Cook told the driver he was not ready and asked him to return at 2 p.m. As far as the Thomas Transfer Company is concerned, the contract is terminated since it tendered performance at the time specified. The transfer company's rights are determined by the circumstances. If their truck was idle because of Cook's breach of contract, it can sue for damages, the profit it would have made. It is under no obligation to return at 2 p.m.

An offer to pay money in satisfaction of a debt or claim is a *tender of payment.* The debtor must offer the exact amount due, including interest, if any. He must also make an actual offer of the money. If he says, "I am now ready to pay you," he has not made a sufficient tender. It is required that the debtor must seek out the creditor and pay or tender to him the amount due.

A tender in the form of a check is not a proper tender. The payment must be tendered in *legal tender.* With but few minor exceptions, this is any form of United States money. If a check is accepted, the contract is performed as soon as the check is cashed or deposited. Some courts have held that if a check is tendered in payment and payment is refused for some other reason, later proved invalid, the party cannot later claim the check was an improper tender. If a check is marked, "In full payment," the tender may be refused because the amount is not correct. If, in a suit, the debtor proves that the amount was correct, the other party cannot then for the first time raise the objection that the check was an improper tender. He must raise this objection at the time of the tender.

If the tender is refused, the debt is not discharged. Although a proper tender does not pay the debt if the tender is refused, it does stop the running of interest. In addition, if the creditor should bring suit, the person who has tendered the correct amount is not liable for court costs. The debtor must, however, hold himself in readiness to pay at any time. In other words, the debtor must keep his defense good.

(4) Time of Performance. If a contract does not specify the time when the contract is to be performed, it must be performed within a reasonable time. If a definite time is specified, then the question arises as to whether or not time is of the essence of the contract.

● If Watkins pays two weeks' rent on a boat to be delivered on August 15, the day his vacation begins, time is of the essence of the contract. He does not want the boat on August 20. If it is not delivered on or before August 15, he may reject delivery at a later date and recover his payment.

On the other hand, Atkins may contract to build and complete a house for Hurley by September 1. He does not complete it until October 1. Time here is not of the essence of the contract, and Hurley must accept and pay for the house. He may, however, deduct whatever amount he may have been damaged by the delay.

Voluntary Agreement of the Parties. A contract is a mutual agreement. The parties are as free to change their minds by mutual agreement as they are to agree in the first place. Consequently, whenever the parties to a contract agree not to carry out its terms, the contract is discharged. The contract itself may recite the events or circumstances which will automatically terminate the agreement. The release of one party to the contract constitutes the consideration for the release of the other. If Walker agrees to build a house for Troelson, and Troelson agrees to pay Walker $20,000 upon completion of the house, they may at any time mutually agree to terminate the contract.

Breach of the Contract by One of the Parties. When one of the parties fails or refuses to perform the obligations assumed under the contract, there is a breach of the contract.

If one party, prior to the time the other party is entitled to performance, announces his intention not to perform, there is an anticipatory breach of the contract. In either case the nonbreaching party is, if he so elects, discharged from his obligations. He then has three possible courses of action open to him:

1. Sue for damages
2. Rescind the contract
3. Sue for specific performance

(1) SUE FOR DAMAGES. Whenever there is a breach of contract, or an anticipatory breach, the innocent party may immediately bring suit for damages. The amount of damages sustained is a matter of proof.

If he fails to prove that any damages have been sustained, he can recover only *nominal damages*, such as one dollar. This throws the court cost, however, on the one who breached the contract. The contract itself may have fixed the amount of damages in the event of default, such damages being known as *liquidated damages.* The amount fixed must be reasonable.

The purpose of damages is to compensate the aggrieved party, not to be a source of profit except when lost profits are the measure of damages. Furthermore, one must use all due diligence in mitigating damages.

- Mary Lande rented two rooms to four adults for nine months. The rent amounted to $540, payable $60 each month. At the end of two months the tenants moved out without cause. The maximum damages amounted to $420, but Lande had to attempt to rent the rooms for the remaining seven months. Any rent received before judgment was obtained would be a credit against the $420.

- Grant was employed for twelve months by the Blank School of Commerce. He was discharged without cause at the end of three months. Grant should seek suitable employment elsewhere. If he failed to find such employment, his damages would be nine months' salary. If he did find work, his salary at the new job would reduce the maximum damage.

(2) RESCIND THE CONTRACT. The aggrieved party, when a contract is breached, may elect to rescind the contract. He then is released from all obligations not performed by him. If he has executed his part of the contract, his remedy is to sue for recovery of what he parted with. He does not ask for damages when he elects to rescind.

(3) SUE FOR SPECIFIC PERFORMANCE. Sometimes neither a suit for damages nor rescission will constitute an adequate remedy. The injured party's remedy under these circumstances is a suit in equity to compel specific performance, that is, the carrying out of the specific terms of the contract.

This remedy is available in most contracts for the sale of real estate or any interest in real estate, and for the sale of rare articles of personal property, such as a painting or an heirloom, the value of which cannot readily be determined. There is no way to measure sentimental value attached to a relic. Under such circumstances mere money damages may be inadequate to compensate the injured party. The court may compel specific performance under such circumstances.

- Hurley contracted to buy from Lester an old coffee urn which had formerly been in the Hurley family before the Revolutionary War. The contract price was $25. Later Lester was offered $40 by an antique dealer and refused to sell to Hurley. The court would compel specific performance in this instance because a similar one could not be bought elsewhere, and the sentimental value attached to it would not be attached to another even though it were the same kind.

Impossibility of Performance. If the act called for in a contract is impossible of performance at the time the contract is made, no contract ever comes into existence. Frequently, impossibility of performance arises after a valid contract is formed. This type of impossibility discharges the contract under certain circumstances. If the impossibility can reasonably be anticipated, such as one due to a strike, a tornado, or any other common catastrophe, the promisor is not discharged unless the contract itself provides for its discharge upon the occurrence of such events. The most common causes of discharge by impossibility of performance occurring after the contract is made are:

1. Destruction of the subject matter
2. New laws making the contract illegal
3. Death or physical incapacity in personal service contracts

(1) Destruction of the Subject Matter. When there is a contract involving specific subject matter, which is subsequently destroyed, the contract is discharged. If the Georgia Bulldog Band contracts to play for a dance in a particular hall, and before the date of performance the hall is destroyed by fire, the contract is

discharged because of impossibility. Also, contracts for the sale of specific personal property are discharged when the property is destroyed through no fault of either party prior to the sale. If the sale, however, is not for specific goods, but merely a quantity of goods of a designated grade, destruction will not discharge the contract. For example, a contract to sell and deliver 1,000 bushels of No. 1 wheat is not discharged by the destruction of all the seller's wheat if no specific 1,000 bushels were specified in the sale.

(2) NEW LAWS MAKING THE CONTRACT ILLEGAL. If an act is legal at the time of the contract but is subsequently made illegal, the contract is discharged. Under local option laws alcoholic beverages may be banned if a referendum approves such action. All executory contracts for the sale of alcoholic beverages in that locality are discharged when the ban becomes effective.

• The Gates Construction Company contracted with Segrest to build a filling station on Segrest's property. After the contract was entered into, but before work began, the City Council passed a zoning ordinance restricting the site of the proposed filling station to residential purposes. The contract was fully discharged by this ordinance.

(3) DEATH OR PHYSICAL INCAPACITY. If the contract calls for personal services, death or physical incapacity of the promisor discharges the contract. The personal services must be such that they cannot readily be performed by another or the personal representative of the promisor.

Such acts as the painting of a portrait, representing a client in a legal proceeding, and other services of a highly personal nature are discharged by death or incapacity. A contract, however, to build a dwelling would not be discharged because any competent construction man can build it according to the specifications.

Discharge by Operation of Law. Under certain circumstances the law will effect a discharge of the contract or at least the law will bar all right of action. The most common ways by which the law operates to discharge contracts are:

1. Bankruptcy
2. Statute of Limitations
3. Alteration of written contract

(1) BANKRUPTCY. It is not uncommon for individuals and business firms to be overwhelmed with financial obligations. The law permits these individuals and firms to petition the court for a decree of voluntary bankruptcy. Creditors may, under certain circumstances, force one into involuntary bankruptcy. (Bankruptcy is treated fully in Chapter 46.) In either event, all rights of action to enforce the contracts of the bankrupt are barred except for certain classes of debts, such as wages for the preceding three months, taxes, alimony, and court costs. However, a creditor's right of action is revived by the debtor's promise to pay made after his discharge in bankruptcy.

(2) STATUTE OF LIMITATIONS. When one party to a contract breaches it, the other party has the right to sue for breach of contract, but he must exercise this right within the time fixed by law. This time varies from state to state and for different types of debts. For open accounts, called accounts receivable, the time varies from two to seven years, while for notes it varies from four to fifteen years.

After a person has brought suit and obtained judgment, the judgment must be enforced by having the property of the debtor levied upon and sold. If this is not done, the statute of limitations operates even against judgments. The time varies from five to twenty-one years.

In some cases the time is calculated from the date of the account, in others from the due date, and in still others from the date of the last payment if the debt has been partially paid. In the case of accounts receivable involving several purchases, the time starts from the date of the last purchase. If the promisor leaves the state, the statute of limitations ceases to run during the time he is beyond the jurisdiction of the court.

• In a state where the Statute of Limitations is three years for open accounts, Parrish owed the Elite Department Store $400, the last purchase being made June 1, 1951. He made a payment on July 1, 1951, and then left the state and was gone two years. In April, 1955, the Elite Department Store sued for the account and Parrish pleaded the Statute of Limitations. His plea was rejected. Since he was absent from the state for two years, the three years would expire June 30, 1956.

A debt that has been outlawed by a statute of limitations may be revived. This is done in some states by a written acknowledgment of or a promise to pay the debt, in others by part payment after it has been outlawed, and in still others by the mere payment of the interest. After the debt is revived, it is a new obligation and runs the full period of the statute of limitations again.

(3) Alteration of Written Contract. Written contracts contain the provisions upon which the minds of the parties have met. If one of the parties alters one of these provisions, the old contract is discharged and the minds have not met on the altered form of the contract. To discharge the contract, the alteration must be done intentionally and without the consent of the other party. In most states the alteration must also be material, although it need not injure the other party. If a note is noninterest-bearing and the holder adds the term "with 6% interest from date," the maker is discharged. (If the holder is an innocent purchaser, the maker is still liable for the principal of the note. This is set out more fully in Chapter 24.)

Questions

1. State the ways in which a contract may be terminated.

2. If one party does not perform every detail of a contract, is the other party released from his obligations under the contract?

3. If one party contracts to perform a contract "to your absolute satisfaction," may the other party avoid the contract merely by claiming that he is not completely satisfied?

4. If a debtor tenders payment of money but payment is refused, is the debt discharged?

5. If a check is accepted in payment, when is the contract performed?

6. When is time of the essence of a contract?

7. Under what conditions may one sue for specific performance of a contract rather than sue for damages?

8. A professional performer agreed to put on a program for a club for a $200 fee. Due to illness, he was unable to perform. Could he be sued for breach of contract?

9. What effect does bankruptcy have upon the bankrupt's obligations?

10. How may the right of a person to collect payment under the terms of a contract be affected by a statute of limitations?

Case Problems

1. The Hope Manufacturing Company entered into a contract with the Georgia Well and Supply Company to fabricate for the latter company certain sizes of well casings. A given quantity was to be deliverd on the first of each month. Due to a heavy flood which seriously damaged the Hope Manufacturing Company plant, it was unable to fill its order for several months. The Georgia Well and Supply Company sued it for damages, alleging breach of contract. Was it entitled to damages?

2. Mary Lou Collins was bookkeeper-secretary for the Dudley Wholesale Company. She received a check from a customer for $1,890 in the lower left hand corner of which were these words, "In full of account." She checked the accounts receivable ledger and found that the balance of

the account was $2,190. Consequently she marked out the words, "In full of account" and deposited the check. What was the effect of this act?

3. Daniel tendered a certified check in payment of his account. Cohen refused the check "because the amount is incorrect." Later Cohen sued Daniel on the account. Daniel proved that he had tendered a certified check for $500 as the full amount due, and he offered before the trial started to pay this amount. Cohen refused to accept it, claiming $700. The jury awarded Cohen a judgment for $500. Who must pay the court costs? Did Cohen use his knowledge of law wisely in this case?

4. The N & O Restaurant had a contract with the O'Kelley Dairy Farm to purchase ten gallons of raw milk a day for twelve months. About one month after this contract was signed, the city council passed an ordinance prohibiting the serving of raw milk in the city's public eating places. The N & O Restaurant stopped its purchases of milk from O'Kelley and O'Kelley sued for breach of contract. Was he entitled to collect?

5. Harmon employed Darwin to paint his house inside and out for $800. Darwin finished the job but, through an oversight, failed to paint the eaves boards on one end. Harmon offered Darwin $750, claiming he was withholding $50 for damages. Darwin offered to return and complete the job, which would require about two hours' work. Harmon refused to let him complete the job, and Darwin sued for $800. Who, in your opinion, was entitled to win the case?

6. Harbin contracted with Campbell to wire Campbell's house for $300. One week later, Harbin with his two helpers called at Campbell's residence and reported ready to begin the wiring. Campbell refused to let them enter the house. Being unable to get anyone else to wire it for less than $350, Campbell called Harbin and told him to go ahead and wire the house. Harbin refused and Campbell sued him for breach of contract. Was Harbin liable for damages?

7. Hobbs entered into a written contract with Raub to sell Raub his house for $17,500, deed to be delivered within two weeks, at which time payment was to be made. When the time came to complete the sale, Hobbs refused to execute and deliver the deed since another buyer was willing to pay $18,500. What were Raub's rights?

Cases for Review of Part II

1. Wilkisins and his wife were unable to read, write, or speak English. They entered into a contract with Sheehan and O'Keefe to exchange real estate and to execute a mortgage evidenced by a promissory note for the balance due. All the dealings were carried on through an interpreter. There was no evidence of fraud or other misconduct of any kind on the part of Sheehan and O'Keefe. Wilkisins and his wife brought action to nullify the contract because they never assented to its terms. (Wilkisins vs. Sheehan, 258 Mass. 240) Was this an enforceable contract?

2. The Texas and Pacific Railway Company entered into an oral contract with Warner whereby Warner agreed to grade the ground and place railroad ties, and the railroad agreed to build a switch for Warner for shipping purposes. The railroad company further agreed "to maintain the switch as long as he (Warner) needed it." The Railway Company failed to perform its part of the contract and Warner sued for damages. (Warner vs. Texas and Pacific Railway Company, 164 U. S. 418) Was this oral contract enforceable?

3. Poel and Arnold offered by letter to sell the Brunswick Company twelve tons of rubber at $2.42 a pound. The Brunswick Company accepted the offer on condition that the rubber should be delivered when requested, and further that the acceptance must be acknowledged. Poel contended that this conditional acceptance constituted a counteroffer which was never accepted. (Poel vs. Brunswick-Balke-Callender Co., 216 N. Y. 310) Do you agree?

4. Jack Scanlon executed a promissory note in favor of the Samuels Shoe Company for $550. The note was indorsed by Mrs. Louise Frensley, the mother of Jack Scanlon. Mrs. Frensley indorsed the note because an agent of the Samuels Shoe Company threatened to prosecute her son for an alleged felony. (Samuels Shoe Company vs. Frensley, 151 Oklahoma 196) Was she liable on the note?

5. Shaw by wire offered to let Braver have space on the Warren ships to transport cattle from Boston to Liverpool. This offer was sent at 11:30 A. M. This telegram containing the offer was received by Braver in New York at 12:16 P. M. He immediately accepted the offer by wire at 12:28 P. M. and this acceptance was received by the offeror at 1:20 P. M. of the same day. At 1:00 P. M., or twenty minutes before the

wire of acceptance was received by the offeror, he sent a revocation of the offer. This withdrawal did not reach Braver until 1:43 P. M. The defendant contended that the offer was withdrawn before acceptance, and hence, there was no contract. (Braver vs. Shaw, 46 N. E. 617) Do you agree?

6. T. Ford Leggett contracted with M. M. Vinson to have Vinson construct a building for a fixed price. Vinson worked on the building several weeks, but upon realizing that he was losing money on the contract, he induced Leggett to agree to pay an additional sum. There was no change in the original contract, the additional compensation being for the same specifications included in the original contract. When the building was completed, Leggett refused to pay the additional sum and Vinson sued for that amount. (Leggett vs. Vinson, 155 Miss. 411) Was he entitled to collect?

7. Edward Coody, an Indian citizen, owned certain lands in the Cherokee reservation. While intoxicated he entered into several contracts with one D. R. Coody whereby he leased and mortgaged his land. After recovering he attempted to disaffirm his contracts with D. R. Coody on the ground of incompetency due to intoxication. His intoxication was so extensive that he could not understand the nature of the contracts. (Coody vs. Coody, 39 Okla. 719) Was he bound on them?

8. Patrick was the manager of a mine in which Davis had an interest by reason of a debt owed to Davis by the mine owners. The mine operators were dilatory in paying Patrick for his services and he planned to quit his job. Davis, realizing Patrick's worth to the business, promised Patrick that he would see that his salary was promptly paid if he would not quit. This oral promise was made because Davis felt that his debt would be made more secure thereby. When Patrick demanded that Davis comply with his promise, Davis refused, contending that his oral promise was not binding. (Davis vs. Patrick, 141 U. S. 479) Do you agree?

9. Hirth entered into an oral agreement with Graham whereby Graham contracted to sell Hirth some standing timber growing on Graham's land. The contract was complete in every detail except that it was oral. Before the timber was cut, Graham changed his mind and refused to permit Hirth to cut and market the timber. Hirth sued for breach of contract. (Hirth vs. Graham, 50 Ohio St. 57) Was this oral contract enforceable?

Part III
SALES

Chapter 12

Sales of Personal Property

Importance of Sales Contracts. In terms of the number of contracts as well as in the dollar volume, contracts for the sale of goods—tangible personal property—constitute the largest class of contracts in our economic system. Every time one purchases a package of cigarettes, he enters into a sales contract. If the cigarettes contained some harmful substance, the sale could be the basis of a suit for thousands of dollars in damages.

For a long time the law of sales varied considerably from state to state. Few laws applied to every state in the union. To overcome this weakness, the Uniform Sales Act was drawn up. Up to this time almost three fourths of the states have adopted the Uniform Sales Act, and the other states have brought their laws dealing with sales more in line with the Uniform Sales Act. For this reason the laws set forth in these chapters on sales are based on the Uniform Sales Act.

Sales and Contracts to Sell. Under the Uniform Sales Act, a distinction is made between a sale and a contract to sell at a future date.

A *sale* of goods is an agreement whereby the seller transfers the title in goods to the buyer for a consideration called the price. It is a contract in which the ownership changes hands at the moment the bargain is made regardless of who has possession of the goods.

A contract to sell goods is a contract whereby the seller agrees to transfer the title in goods to the buyer for a consideration called the price. This is a contract in which one promises to buy or to sell in the future.

The important distinction between a sale and a contract to sell is that in the former the title, or the ownership of the subject matter, is transferred at once; in the latter it will be transferred at a later time. A contract to sell is not in the true sense of the word a sale; it is merely an agreement to sell.

Since in a sale title passes to the buyer immediately, and in a contract to sell, title passes at some future date, it is extremely important to distinguish between the two. Except in rare instances, title to personal property is held by someone at every moment of time. There can be no such thing as an intervening period during which time title rests neither with the seller nor the buyer. The risk of loss, with the exceptions set out later in this chapter, is borne by the owner. Also, any increment in the property belongs to the one who has the title. It is essential, therefore, to have certain definite rules to aid the courts in determining when title passes if the parties to the contract are silent as to when title passes. If the parties, themselves, agree as to when title passes, then the courts will enforce this agreement. When the parties are silent and the court must decide, the first task the court must perform is to determine whether or not it is a sale or a contract to sell.

● Lester sold Roger fifty dairy cows for $15,000 and agreed to have them vaccinated at his expense before delivering them to Roger. One month elapsed before he was able to get all of them vaccinated. During this time five calves were born. The court held that the calves belonged to Lester because title had not passed. Had five of the dairy cows been frozen to death in a blizzard, it would have been Lester's loss. Since something remained to be done by the seller, this was a contract to sell. Therefore, title remained with Lester and he received any increment and bore all losses. Had it been a sale, Roger would have received the increment and would have borne any loss.

Price. The consideration in a sales contract must be expressed in terms of money or money's worth. The actual payment may be made in property or services, but the value of these must be converted to a price in order for it to be a sale. This is significant for the reason that the law of sales does not apply to barter contracts and other exchanges of property. For example, if Wilson agrees to exchange his record player with Kaplan for his (Kaplan's) television set, the contract is one of barter, not of sale.

H. Armstrong Roberts

A Salesman Must Understand the Law of the Sale of Personal Property.

Frequently the sales contract is an express contract, but some of its terms are implied. In a contract of sale, the price may be implied, in which case the courts will consider the market price a reasonable price. In this event, however, the seller and the buyer must both clearly imply by their conduct that they are willing to contract for a reasonable price. Unless the price can definitely be fixed, no contract results since their minds have not met. This situation would occur when the contract, or apparent contract, simply stipulates that the price is to be fixed at a later date. If it stipulates that the price is to be fixed later by a third party or by market quotations, then the price would be determinable and an enforceable contract would result.

Goods Not Yet in Existence. Goods that are not in existence at the time the contract to sell them is made, may be classified as:

1. Future goods
2. Potential goods

(1) FUTURE GOODS. *Future goods* are goods which the seller does not now own. He expects to acquire them in the future by purchase or by manufacture. The Uniform Sales Act clearly stipulates that any contract purporting to sell future goods is a contract to sell and not a contract of sale. This law was not passed to hinder a man in making any type of contract he wishes, but it was necessary to enable the court to determine the rights of the parties under certain contingencies.

• Taylor, a shoe manufacturer, contracted to sell the Mitchell Shoe Store 2,000 pairs of shoes. At the time this contract was made, the shoes had not been manufactured. After they were manufactured but before they were shipped, Taylor's creditors levied upon the shoes. Taylor claimed they were not his shoes since he had sold them to the Mitchell Shoe Store. Since the shoes at the time of the contract were not in existence, they were future goods. Consequently, this was merely a contract to sell, not of sale. The title rested with Taylor until the shoes were shipped. Since the shoes belonged to Taylor, his creditors could levy on them and sell them for Taylor's debts.

(2) POTENTIAL GOODS. Closely akin to future goods are potential goods which the seller owns at the time of the contract. They consist primarily of agricultural products that are to be produced in the future. Fish that are to be caught from one's own fish pond are potential goods, but fish to be caught from the ocean, for example, are future goods. To be *potential goods*, the seller must own the source from which they are to be produced or caught. The Uniform Sales Act makes no distinction between future goods and potential goods. Neither class can constitute the subject matter of a contract of sale, only to sell. Many of the thirteen states which have not adopted the Uniform Sales Act permit a contract of sale of potential goods, but no state recognizes a contract of sale for future goods.

Bill of Sale. A *bill of sale* is written evidence of one's title to tangible personal property. It is not necessary to have evidence of title; but should one's title be questioned, such evidence is highly desirable. Most states specifically require all automobile owners to have a bill of sale. One should not purchase an automobile unless the seller can produce his bill of sale as proof that he has title to the car. If one buys a stock of merchandise in bulk, a house trailer, livestock, and many other relatively expensive items, such as jewelry and furs, he should demand that the seller give him a bill of sale. This serves two purposes: (1) If the buyer wishes to resell the goods and the prospective buyer demands proof of title, he can produce his bill of sale; (2) if any question arises as to whether or not he came into possession of the goods legally, he has his bill of sale as proof.

● Flanders purchased an expensive watch from Sanders, a man whom he had never seen before. The watch had been stolen from the Dawsoin Jewelry Company. Flanders was suspected of being the thief. To prove his innocence, he produced a bill of sale which Sanders had given him. This did not permit him to keep the watch, but it did exonerate him from the charge of theft.

Illegal Sales. Many difficulties arise over illegal sales, that is, the sale of goods prohibited by law, such as alcoholic beverages in a "dry" locality. If the sale is fully executed, the court will not intervene to aid either party. If an innocent party through fraud is induced to enter into an illegal sale, the court will compel a restoration of the goods he has transferred.

If the illegal sale is wholly executory, the transaction is a contract to sell and will not be enforced. If it is only partially executory, the courts will still leave the parties where it found them unless the one who has performed is an innocent victim of a fraud.

If the sale is divisible and a part is legal and a part illegal, the court will enforce the legal part. As a rule the nature of the contract, not the nature of the goods, determines its divisibility. If the sale involves several separate and independent items, but are a lump-sum sale, then the sale is indivisible. If any part is illegal, the entire sale is illegal. If the individual items are separately priced, the sale is divisible.

● The Athens Wholesale Company shipped a carload lot of merchandise to the Acme Company. The shipment contained $1,000 worth of colored oleomargarine, the sale of which was illegal in that state. All the merchandise was priced separately. The Acme Company refused to pay, claiming that it was not bound because of the illegality. This defense was not good, except for the $1,000, because the sale was divisible. The court would enforce the legal part.

Questions

1. Why is the Uniform Sales Act important?

2. Distinguish clearly between a sale and a contract to sell.

3. Why is it important to make a distinction between a sale and a contract to sell?

4. What is the one feature that distinguishes a sales contract from a contract to barter?

5. If the price in a sales contract is not stated, what may the court consider to be a reasonable price?

6. (a) What are future goods?
(b) Can future goods ever constitute the subject matter of a contract of sale?

7. How do potential goods differ from future goods?

8. (a) What is a bill of sale?
(b) Is a bill of sale necessary to pass title?

9. In an illegal contract of sale, will the courts restore the parties to their former position upon the petition of one party?

10. If a sale is divisible and part is legal and part is illegal, what determines its divisibility?

Case Problems

1. Lasher, the purchasing agent of the Hertz Company, purchased a used bookkeeping machine from the Adams Bookkeeping Service. The selling price of the machine was $3,200. About two weeks later, a representative of the manufacturer of the machine demanded possession of the machine claiming it was only rented to the Adams Bookkeeping Service. He showed Lasher the rental agreement as proof of his statement. What should Lasher have done to avoid this loss?

2. The Fox Fur Shop contracted to sell Adele a fur coat for $4,500. The contract stipulated that the title was to remain with the Fox Fur Shop but that when the contract became a contract of sale, a bill of sale would be issued to Adele. The next day Adele called at the office of Fox Fur Shop to demand a bill of sale. The manager was out but Mamie, his secretary, attempted to placate Adele. Mamie read the contract and saw that it said, "A bill of sale will be issued as soon as this becomes a contract of sale." Mamie, thinking it was already a contract of sale, issued to Adele a bill of sale. Adele then sold the coat for cash and disappeared. What error did Mamie make?

3. Paul, aged seventeen but married, purchased about $50 worth of groceries from the Burkhart Food Mart on credit. The $50 included $5 for cigarettes. There was a state law making it illegal for a merchant to sell cigarettes to one under 18 years of age. Paul learned of this and refused to pay any part of the $50 since the sales contract is illegal. Was he correct in his contention?

4. Smith entered into a written contract with Denfield to purchase 100 bales of cotton at the market price. Denfield was to pick, bale, and deliver the cotton to Smith's warehouse. Before the cotton was picked, a flood destroyed the entire crop. Who must bear the loss?

5. Before the pecan season opened in Albany, Georgia, Thompson Brothers entered into a contract with Davis, a pecan grower, to purchase all his pecans "at the market price." After Davis had delivered 20,000 pounds of pecans, he asked Thompson Brothers for a settlement. He produced a New York paper showing the market price for pecans in New York to be 19 cents. In Albany they were 17 cents a pound. Could Davis collect 19 cents a pound?

Chapter 13

Formalities of a Sale

section 17

Form of Contracts Pertaining to Sales. Unless a statute provides otherwise, a sale of property or a contract to sell property may be (1) oral, (2) written, (3) implied from the conduct of the parties, or (4) a combination of two or more of these. Generally the law does not prescribe any particular form for most sales contracts; but many executory contracts of sale and contracts to sell are required by the Statute of Frauds either to be in writing or to meet some other specific requirement. Unless the contracts meet these requirements, the courts will not enforce them.

Requirement of the Statute of Frauds. In addition to the five classes of contracts required by its fourth section to be in writing (pages 83 to 87), the Statute of Frauds requires, under its seventeenth section, that certain contracts to sell and sales of goods, wares, and merchandise, as well as other forms of personal property, must be in writing.

In the main, the seventeenth section of the Statute of Frauds provides that no contract for the sale of any goods, wares, or merchandise, or of other kinds of personal property, in which the price is more than a specified sum, is enforceable unless:

(1) Some of the goods have been accepted and received by the buyer with the intent to retain them; or

(2) Something of value has been given by the buyer to bind the contract or in part payment thereof; or

(3) A note or memorandum of the agreement has been made and signed by the parties to be charged by the contract, or by their authorized agents.

In most of the states, any contract pertaining to the sale of personal property for more than the amount fixed by statute must meet one, but only one, of the three provisions listed above. If it meets either the first or the second provision, the contract, regardless of the amount, may be oral without losing its enforceability. The exceptions to this general rule are (1) Florida and Iowa, in which all sales contracts, regardless of the amount, must be written in order to be enforceable unless they meet the first or second provision and (2) Kansas, Louisiana, North Carolina, Texas, Virginia, and West Virginia, in which no sales contract must be written, regardless of the amount, in order to be enforceable. The table on page 125 (which is, of course, subject to statutory change at any session of a state legislature) summarizes the maximum amounts for which sales may be made in the several states, Alaska, the District of Columbia, and Hawaii, without coming under the Statute of Frauds (that is, the maximum amounts which may be proved orally).

If a contract does not meet the requirements of the Statute of Frauds, it is not void, merely invalid. If both parties elect to abide by its terms even though they are not legally bound to do so, neither one can later change his mind.

Sales Within the Statute of Frauds. If a sale is for an amount less than the sum specified in the particular state statute, it is enforceable without reference to the Statute of Frauds. Millions of sales occur daily for amounts less than the statutory sums. If all these had to meet the rigid tests of the Statute of Frauds, the wheels of commerce would be unduly impeded. The purpose of the act is to discourage perjury. The temptation to commit perjury is weak when the amount involved is small. Then, too, one does not engage in litigation simply because he has a right to do so. If the expense of litigation is greater than the loss sustained for a breach of contract, it is cheaper and better to forego enforcing one's rights.

Frequently one makes several purchases the same day from the same seller. The question may then arise as to whether or not this is one sale or several sales. In Alabama, for example, all sales of less than $500 may be made by oral contract. If one purchases five items from the same seller in one day, each one having a sale price of less than $500, but in the aggregate they are in excess of $500, must this contract meet the requirement of the Statute of Frauds? If the several items are part of the same sales transaction, it is one sale and must meet the requirement of the Statute. If all purchases are made during the same shopping tour and all are to be delivered at the same time and place, the several items are part of the same transaction.

Acceptance and Receipt. An oral contract of sale for any amount is enforceable if there are both an acceptance and a receipt of the goods. If the goods are divisible, acceptance and receipt of any part of them will meet the requirements of the statute. In some sales, such as that of a fur coat, the goods are not subject to a division; in other sales, such as a thousand bushels of wheat, they are.

Acceptance is the assent of the buyer to become the owner of specific goods; *receipt* is taking possession of all or any part of the goods. The receipt may be actual or constructive. If Admire buys from Taylor a thousand railroad ties stacked along the side of the highway, and Taylor says, "They are yours; haul them away when you are ready," there is a constructive delivery, and the contract does not come under the Statute of Frauds because there was both an acceptance and a receipt.

Sometimes goods are received for the purpose of making an examination. Here the receipt precedes the acceptance. If the goods are afterwards rejected, no contract is consummated. If, however, the buyer asserts ownership by act or word, he indicates an acceptance, and the sale is completed.

None (all sales may be oral): Kansas, Louisiana, North Carolina, Texas, Virginia, West Virginia.

No amount (all sales must be written): Florida, Iowa.

Minimum amount, $30 (all sales for $30 or more must be written): Arkansas, Missouri.

Minimum amount, $50 (all sales for $50 or more must be written): Alaska, Colorado, District of Columbia, Georgia, Maryland, Minnesota, Mississippi, Nevada, New Mexico, New York, Oklahoma, Oregon, South Carolina, Vermont, Washington, Wisconsin, Wyoming.

Minimum amount, $100 (all sales for $100 or more must be written): Connecticut, Michigan, Hawaii.

Minimum amount, $200 (all sales for $200 or more must be written): Montana.

Minimum amount, $500 (all sales for $500 or more must be written): Alabama, Arizona, California, Delaware, Idaho, Illinois, Indiana, Kentucky, Maine, Massachusetts, Nebraska, New Hampshire, New Jersey, North Dakota, Pennsylvania, Rhode Island, South Dakota, Tennessee, Utah.

Minimum amount, $2,500 (all sales for $2,500 or more must be written): Ohio.

Minimum Amounts of Sales to Which the Statute of Frauds Applies.

• Dawson offered to sell his automobile to Talmadge for $1,800. Talmadge asked for the privilege of driving the car before deciding. Dawson agreed to let him keep the car overnight and drive it as much as he wished. Talmadge drove to the Orange Bowl football game and was gone four days, driving 2,000 miles. The car was damaged to the extent of $100. Talmadge returned the car stating that he was not satisfied with it. He was liable since his acts clearly indicated an assent by keeping the car beyond the time agreed upon.

Part Payment. A sales contract need not be in writing if a part or all of the purchase price is paid at the time the contract is entered into or at a subsequent date. There need not be a receipt of the goods, only a payment or part payment or something of value to bind the bargain. The payment need not be in money, but whatever is given must have its value stated in money's worth; otherwise the transaction is a barter, not a sale.

A check, draft, note, or due bill is usually not a payment within the meaning of the Statute of Frauds. These are only conditional payments. But if a check is cashed before rescission is attempted, the sale is valid even though it is based on an oral contract. If the seller accepts a check, draft, note, or similar conditional payment as an "absolute" payment, however, the requirement of part payment of the Statute is met. There must be some concrete evidence that the seller is accepting the instrument as an absolute payment. This might be and usually is in the form of an indorsement on a check as follows: "Pay to the order of John Smith without recourse to me if the check is not paid. Adam Stoltz." In the absence of this or some similar proof that the check is being accepted as absolute payment, the courts will interpret the check to be a conditional payment.

- Jones sold Greiner a trailer for $650, and Greiner gave a check for $10 as evidence of good faith. One hour later Jones cashed the check at the bank on which it was drawn. The next day Greiner informed Jones that he had changed his mind and would not go through with the deal since it was oral. The contract was binding, however, because the check had been cashed. Had Greiner notified Jones before the check had been cashed, the contract would have been canceled, as the check was not a part payment. Had Greiner indorsed a check to Jones, and he (Jones) had agreed to accept it "good or bad," this check would have been a part payment.

Note or Memorandum. The third factor which may make it unnecessary to have a written contract for the sale of personal property is a written note or memorandum of the sale. This note is required to be almost as complete as a written contract. It must contain a description of the goods sold, the price, terms, time, and place of delivery, and be signed by the party to be charged, that is, the one to be sued for breach of contract or specific performance. The memorandum need not be formal. Letters, telegrams, invoices, and sales tickets are adequate if they contain the information set out above.

• Mrs. Fortson purchased a set of books for $150 from a door-to-door salesman. She paid nothing down, the full purchase price to be paid upon delivery. An invoice of the sale was made out and Mrs. Fortson signed it. When the books came Mrs. Fortson refused to accept them, claiming that the contract was unenforceable because it was oral. Her defense was invalid since the signed invoice was an adequate memorandum of the sale.

Contracts for Labor and Materials. A contract for labor and materials is not a sale and need not meet the requirements of the Seventeenth Section of the Statute of Frauds. The courts are in complete accord that service contracts need not be in writing, but are divided on the criteria used to distinguish a sale from a contract for labor and materials. There are two rules applied by the various courts in the United States: the Massachusetts Rule and the New York Rule. Some state courts use one rule, some the other.

(1) MASSACHUSETTS RULE. Under the Massachusetts rule, when the goods that are made up in accordance with the buyer's order are different from those produced for the general market, the contract is for labor and materials, and is not a contract of sale. On the other hand, if the goods are suitable for trade in the ordinary course of business, the agreement is a contract to sell and comes under the Statute of Frauds. This rule, often called the American rule, has been adopted by the Uniform Sales Act and most states follow it.

(2) NEW YORK RULE. A few states follow the so-called New York rule, which differs from the Massachusetts rule in only one particular. If the goods are not in existence at the time of the contract, but are to be manufactured on the order of the buyer, the agreement is a contract for labor and materials regardless of whether or not the goods are suitable for trade in the ordinary course of business.

• Tucker ordered a suit tailor-made, the price being $135. The tailor made the suit according to the special measurements required. Tucker was slightly deformed so that an odd cut suit was required. He made no down payment at the time the suit was ordered, and no memorandum of the order was signed by Tucker. When the suit was finished, Tucker refused to accept it claiming he was not bound by the contract since it was oral. This defense was invalid because the suit was not suitable for the usual trade. It was, therefore, a contract for labor and materials, and did not need to be in writing.

Auction Sales. A sale by auction need not be in writing, nor need it meet the other conditions set out in this chapter. The clerk or the auctioneer need only record the sale in his books. Since he is the agent for both parties, he has the power to sign a memorandum for either party. The sales book is a sufficient memorandum.

Questions

1. What contracts are covered by the seventeenth section of the Statute of Frauds?

2. (a) If all of the goods, or part of them, are delivered at the time of the contract, must the contract be in writing? (b) Can there be a delivery of the goods without an acceptance?

3. In your state, to what sales does the Statute of Frauds apply?

4. What is a constructive delivery of goods?

5. What constitutes part payment?

6. How does a written memorandum differ from a written contract?

7. (a) Can an exchange of letters constitute a memorandum?

(b) Is a sales ticket that is signed by the buyer a sufficient memorandum?

8. Wherein does a contract for labor and materials differ from a contract of sale?

9. In what particular does the Massachusetts Rule differ from the New York Rule?

10. What kind of writing meets the requirements of a note or memorandum for an auction sale?

Case Problems

1. Hammond, manager for a supermarket, ordered by telephone 400 bushels of peaches from Hardigree. He stipulated, "The peaches must be first grade and free from defects." When the peaches were delivered, Hammond opened one bushel before the truck was unloaded and the peaches seemed to be as ordered. He made no further comment. After the peaches were all unloaded and opened, he found they were badly bruised by hail and every bushel contained some rotten ones. He called Hardigree and asked him to come and get the peaches. Hardigree refused. The peaches remained in the warehouse for ten days while the argument between Hammond and Hardigree as to their rights persisted. During that time the peaches became a total loss. What fundamental error did Hammond make?

2. Mrs. Jane Langley inspected some carpet material on display at the Sinkwich Furniture Mart. The salesman quoted her a certain price per square foot, the carpet material to be cut individually to fit her living room, a wall-to-wall type of carpet. She orally agreed to purchase it. Her living room had a very odd and unusual shape. After the carpet was cut and laid, Mrs. Langley was keenly disappointed in its appearance. She had faintly remembered from her business law course that an oral sales contract under certain conditions is invalid. She refused to pay for it and demanded that the seller take it up. What were the rights of the parties here?

3. The Glo-Coat Paint Company offered to sell the Lull Paint Store a quantity of paint of various grades and colors. The value of the bulk lot was $5,575. The owner of the Lull Paint Store orally agreed to buy it, but the seller insisted on a written memorandum of the sale to make it comply with the Statute of Frauds. Lull was in a quandary. He really wanted the paint as it was a very good price, but there was a possibility he would sell his paint store in a few days, in which case he would not want it. He drew up a memo as follows: "It is hereby agreed that were I to buy the paint herein described, I will pay cash on the day of delivery, which is to be not later than one week from today." Both parties signed the memo. Lull sold his paint store the next day and notified the Glo-Paint Company that he would not buy the paint. The Glo-Paint Company sued him for breach of contract, alleging that they were inveigled into signing a trick memo. Was the Lull Paint Store liable on this contract?

4. Lemly went into a men's clothing store and purchased a suit for $75. He was to pay for it when it was altered. Later in the morning he returned and selected a pair of shoes for $15 and three shirts for $15. He was to pay for all and take delivery when the suit was ready. In that state all sales for more than $100 came under the Statute of Frauds. Lemly changed his mind and decided not to take the items. Was Lemly bound on this oral contract?

5. Joel, sales manager for the Dobbs Building Materials Company, sold Wilson $6,000 worth of building materials. Joel wrote down the items on a purchase order as Wilson listed them. Joel agreed to take in part payment a due bill which was drawn by Downs Motor Company in favor of Wilson. This due bill was assigned in writing to the Dobbs Building Materials Company. Joel interpreted this to meet the requirements of a memo under the Statute of Frauds. Wilson signed nothing else and made no other payment at the time. He later canceled the order and demanded a return of the due bill. Was Wilson bound on this contract?

6. Haines orally contracted to buy Justus's trailer for $1,500. To bind the bargain he gave Justus a check for $50 and agreed to pay the balance the following day, at which time he would take possession of the trailer. The next day Justus returned the check and refused to consummate the sale. Haines brought suit for breach of contract. Was he entitled to judgment?

7. Hancock orally agreed to buy a piano from Campbell for $750. He gave a check for the purchase price. Later during the day Campbell found another purchaser who was willing to pay $800. He destroyed the check and notified Hancock the sale was off. Did he have the right to do this?

8. Sanders entered into an agreement with Milo, a cabinet maker, whereby the latter agreed to furnish the material and to make a mahogany desk for Sanders at a stipulated price. After the desk was finished, Sanders refused to accept it, contending that his oral promise did not bind him. Was this a contract for the sale of goods or a contract for labor and materials under the New York rule? Under the Massachusetts rule? What is the difference?

Chapter 14

Transfer of Ownership

Passing of Title. In a sale there is always a specific, definite time when title or ownership passes from the seller to the buyer. If the goods are lost, stolen, or damaged, the loss generally falls upon the owner. Also, if there should be a gain or an increase, or a loss or a decrease, the increase or gain inures to the owner and the decrease or loss is his also. It is important, then, to have definite rules to enable the court to determine when title passes. If the parties expressly state when title is to pass, no dispute need arise. Furthermore, in most cash sales where delivery is made immediately, there is little difficulty in determining when title passes. But if delivery is to be made at a future date, if the goods are not separated from a mass, or if something remains to be done, it frequently is difficult to determine the exact time when title passes.

Seller's Title. Only the owner of property can pass title to it. If one does not own property, he cannot vest others with good title to it. The seller can pass only such title as he has. A man may steal property and sell it; but no subsequent purchaser, even though there be a hundred of them, can ever acquire title to the property because the real owner has never parted with the title. The innocent purchasers can look only to their sellers for damages.

One fundamental exception to this rule is that when one of two innocent persons must suffer loss by reason of the wrongdoing of another, the loss should fall on the one whose conduct enabled the wrongdoer to cause the injury. This rule applies in each of the following four situations.

(1) Transfer of Possession to Agent or Dealer. If the owner of personal property transfers possession to an agent, dealer, commission merchant, or similar person so that he is clothed with the apparent authority to sell, this person has the power to transfer title to an innocent third party. If the courts adhered strictly to the law that only the owner may pass title, many lines of business could not operate. This is especially true of commission merchants, sometimes called *factors*, who take possession of other people's property under a contract to sell it and receive a commission for their services. They can transfer good title to the buyer even though they do not own the property. This same law applies to all firms or persons, whether it is their common business to sell on commission or not, who are intrusted with the possession of personal property in such a way as to indicate that they have the right to sell.

- Spratlin left his house trailer with the Green Trailer Corporation with instructions to sell "upon my prior approval of the terms of sale." The Green Trailer Corporation sold the trailer to Hartwell upon terms highly unsatisfactory to Spratlin and without his approval. In spite of this betrayal of trust, Hartwell got good title to the trailer because the Green Trailer Corporation had possession in a manner that clearly indicated its right to sell.

(2) Sale by One Having Only a Conditional Title. In sales on the installment plan whereby the seller retains title until the terms of the sale are complied with, the buyer may sell the goods and under certain conditions pass good title to them. To prevent this loss, the seller must have his conditional sales contract recorded.

- Rankin purchased a watch from the Pollock Jewelry Company on the installment plan. The manager of the Pollock Jewelry Company failed to have the contract recorded in the proper place. Rankin sold the watch to Norton while there was still an unpaid balance of $42.50 on the watch. Norton got title to the watch free of this lien because he had no notice of any limitation on Rankin's title.

(3) SALE BY ONE WHO HAS VOIDABLE TITLE. In Chapter 5 it was pointed out that all contracts evidenced by fraud, duress, or undue influence were voidable. If such a voidable contract is a sales contract and if the buyer is the one who committed the wrongdoing, he has only a voidable title. When the seller elects to avoid the sales contract, he has the right to regain both possession and title of the article sold. If, before he regains title, the buyer resells the article to an innocent purchaser, that purchaser obtains good title even though the seller did not have good title. This would not be true if the first sale was the result of forgery or mistake since then the buyer's title would rest upon a void contract.

● Malone by fraud induced Garard to sell some road machinery valued at $30,000. Malone immediately sold this machinery to the Davidson Construction Company. When Garard learned of the fraud, he rescinded the contract. Since the Davidson Construction Company was an innocent purchaser, it got good title to the machinery.

(4) NEGOTIABLE INSTRUMENTS. The most important exception pertains to negotiable instruments. This will be discussed fully in Chapters 22 and 23.

Types of Goods. Under the Uniform Sales Act there are three classes of goods:

1. Ascertained or specific goods
2. Fungible goods
3. Unascertained goods

(1) ASCERTAINED OR SPECIFIC GOODS. Goods that are in existence and are specifically selected and set aside by the seller with the assent of the buyer are *ascertained or specific goods.*

(2) FUNGIBLE GOODS. Goods that are in mass, but of the same grade or quality, such as wheat, lumber, and coal, are *fungible goods.* If a man buys 500 bushels of

No. 1 wheat out of a bin containing 10,000 bushels of No. 1 wheat, he owns one-twentieth of the mass. This would not be true if the bin contained 10,000 bushels of several grades and the buyer bought only No. 1 wheat. In most states the law considers fungible goods as ascertained goods.

(3) UNASCERTAINED GOODS. Goods that are part of a mass of goods of varying quality and value are *unascertained goods.* Title does not pass until they have been separated from the mass.

Intention of the Parties. It is a well-established rule of law that title to goods passes when the parties intend for it to pass. If their intentions are clearly expressed at the time the contract is made, disputes seldom arise. When the parties are silent as to when title is to pass, then the time of passage of title must be inferred from their conduct or the nature of the transaction. Over the years the courts have achieved a high degree of uniformity throughout all the states by adopting seven rules which help in determining the true intention of the parties.

(1) IF SPECIFIC GOODS ARE IN A DELIVERABLE STATE AT THE TIME OF THE CONTRACT, THE TITLE PASSES IMMEDIATELY. The average sales contract consists of a brief, definite offer and an equally brief acceptance. The following is a typical illustration taken from an actual court case:

- *A* says to *B*, "I will sell you this horse for $50." *B* replied, "I will take him." Neither said anything as to when the $50 was to be paid or when delivery was to be made. Nevertheless, title to the horse passed to *B* as soon as he uttered the words, "I will take him." This is true even though goods are sold on credit or where delivery is expressly stated to be at a future date. The court fixes the time when title is to pass if the parties fail to do so.

(2) If Something Remains to Be Done Before Specific Goods Are Put in a Deliverable State, Title Does Not Pass Until Such Thing Is Done. It is not unusual for the contract to sell to contain a provision that the selling price is not for the goods in their present state but in a state described in the offer and the acceptance. An example would be an agreement whereby the seller promises to repair and revarnish a sewing machine as a part of the selling price. Title would not pass until the machine is repaired and revarnished.

If the thing that remains to be done is merely weighing, sorting, counting, or measuring to determine the quantity, passing of title in most states does not depend on the performance of this act. If one buys 500 bushels of wheat from a bin of 10,000 bushels of the same grade, for example, the 500 bushels would have to be measured, but title would pass even before this is done unless otherwise agreed upon.

● Atlee sold Carlson a piano for $800. It was agreed that Atlee was to have the piano tuned before he delivered it. Before this was done, a fire completely destroyed the piano. The loss fell upon Atlee because title remained with him.

(3) If Goods Are Delivered to the Buyer on a "Sale or Return" Basis, Title Passes Immediately to the Buyer, but the Buyer May Revest Title in the Seller. The contract may fix the time limit upon the buyer's option to retain or return the goods. If he keeps them beyond this time, such an act constitutes a waiver of his right to return the goods. If no time is fixed by agreement, then a reasonable time will be allowed. What constitutes a reasonable time is a question of fact.

The buyer may expressly waive his right to return the goods before the expiration of either the agreed time or a reasonable time. In that event, the title of the buyer becomes absolute.

● Rochester purchased a second-hand tractor from Fleeman. The agreement stipulated that Rochester was to have the tractor with the right to return it in thirty days if he was not satisfied with it. Ten days after the sale, the creditors of Rochester levied upon the tractor. Since Rochester had not exercised his right to return the tractor before the levy, he could not do so afterwards; the creditors could sell it to satisfy their debts. Had the tractor been stolen or destroyed before Rochester had indicated an intention to return the tractor, the loss would have fallen on him.

(4) IF GOODS ARE DELIVERED TO THE BUYER "ON APPROVAL," THE TITLE REMAINS WITH THE SELLER UNTIL THE BUYER INDICATES HIS APPROVAL BY WORD OR ACT. In a sale "on approval," the title remains with the seller and thus the risk of loss must be borne by him. If there is an increase, as is often the case with animals and livestock, the increase belongs to the seller. The title vests in the buyer as soon as he expressly indicates his approval or commits some act which indicates approval.

● Mary Jones purchased an evening gown "on approval," and promised to return it in two days if her mother did not like it. Mary decided to wear the gown to a formal dance so that she would be better able to determine if the gown was becoming to her. The next day the gown was stolen through no fault of her own. The loss was Mary's because her wearing the gown to a formal dance was an act of approval.

(5) IN A CONTRACT TO SELL UNASCERTAINED OR FUTURE GOODS BY DESCRIPTION, TITLE DOES NOT PASS TO THE BUYER UNTIL THE GOODS HAVE BEEN APPROPRIATED TO THE CONTRACT. If the goods to be delivered have not been ascertained or are not in existence, title cannot, in most states, pass to the buyer at the time of the sale. They must first be ascertained or acquired, but this alone does not pass title. They must be "appropriated to the contract," which means either delivered to the buyer directly or delivered to a transportation company for hauling. Title passes as soon as the goods are placed with the transportation company. The parties may, of

course, expressly agree otherwise, in which case, the goods are appropriated to the contract when the terms of the contract regarding the passing of title have been carried out.

● Range bought all the potatoes which Bramlett expected to harvest from his potato crop. The potatoes had been planted at the time of the contract but were not mature. Bramlett was to dig the potatoes, sack them, and then notify Range. The potatoes were "appropriated to the contract" as soon as these three conditions were met. Title passed as soon as Bramlett notified Range that the potatoes were sacked.

(6) IF THE CONTRACT TO SELL SPECIFIC GOODS REQUIRES THE SELLER TO DELIVER THE GOODS TO THE BUYER OR TO A PARTICULAR PLACE, THE TITLE DOES NOT PASS UNTIL THE GOODS REACH THEIR DESTINATION. The goods are appropriated to the contract as soon as they are delivered to the buyer or to the place designated in the contract. In many instances, the goods are shipped C.O.D. The terms C.O.D. have no effect upon the passing of title. Possession cannot pass to the buyer until the purchase price is paid, but the passing of title can precede the passing of possession.

If the terms are f.o.b. destination, title does not pass until the goods reach the buyer.

● Biscoe ordered thirty bales of cotton from the Hobson Cotton Exchange, the cotton to be delivered by the seller's truck to the Biscoe Textile Company's warehouse. The truck was wrecked and the cotton was destroyed. The loss had to be borne by the seller because title did not pass until the cotton was delivered to the place designated in the contract.

(7) IF THE GOODS ARE TO BE DELIVERED AT THE BUYER'S EXPENSE, AS, FOR EXAMPLE, WHEN THE TERMS ARE F.O.B. SHIPPING POINT, TITLE PASSES AS SOON AS THE GOODS ARE DELIVERED TO THE TRANSPORTATION COMPANY. When the terms, however, are f.o.b. shipping point, or in other cases where the goods are to be deliv-

ered at the buyer's expense, title passes as soon as the goods have been delivered to the common carrier for transportation, unless there is an express agreement to the contrary.

Conditional Sales. The seller of goods may deliver the possession of the goods to the buyer but retain title to them. Such a sale is known as a *conditional sale.* In a conditional sale the price is usually payable in installments. Common examples of conditional sales are installment sales of automobiles, television sets, refrigerators, and furniture.

The chief purposes of a conditional sale are:

1. To protect the seller against third parties who may purchase the article.
2. To obtain a preferred lien against the article for the unpaid purchase price
3. To facilitate a collection if the account is in default

(1) TO PROTECT THE SELLER AGAINST THIRD PARTIES WHO MAY PURCHASE THE ARTICLE. Possession is presumptive evidence of ownership. If the buyer under a conditional sales contract is inclined to do so, he can sell the article to an innocent third party. If the article was merely sold on credit, but title was permitted to pass, the third party would obtain a title superior to the original seller. Under a conditional sale the seller can assert title to the article even against an innocent third party. Under the common law the seller is not required to record the conditional sales contract in order to protect his interest. A majority of the states have amended the common law to require the seller to record his conditional sales agreements. This record is constructive notice to everyone that the seller retains title. It is not necessary that the innocent third party actually see the record. Usually there is a conditional sales book in the county or city clerk's office for the recording of conditional sales contracts.

Conditional Sales Agreement, made this eighth day of March, 19__, between the JOHN REGIS CO., Dayton, Ohio, hereinafter called the "Seller," and John Burroughs, residing at 362 Forest Avenue, in the city of Dayton, State of Ohio, hereinafter called the "Buyer."

WITNESSETH: That the buyer has this day conditionally purchased from the seller, subject to the terms and conditions hereof, certain personal property, as listed below:

DESCRIPTION	SERIAL NO.	PURCHASE PRICE
one RCA Television Receiver, Model TC167	A-1575273	$ 412.00
Salesman	Total	$ 412.00

The buyer agrees to pay the seller for said property and the use thereof the sum of $52.00 Dollars on the signing of the contract, and $20.00 Dollars on the first day of every month hereafter.

The title in the property above described shall remain in the seller until the terms of this contract have been fully complied with. In case of any default in the performance of the terms and condition hereof, or in the event the seller deems itself insecure, the seller shall have the right to declare the full unpaid amount immediately due and payable and/or retake all the property. Buyer agrees not to move, sell, mortgage, encumber, pledge, or otherwise dispose of the property until paid for in full. Upon the performance by the buyer of all the conditions of this contract, title to the property is to vest in the buyer. It is mutually agreed that this instrument sets forth the entire contract.

In Witness Whereof, the parties to this instrument have hereunto set their hands and seals at Dayton, Ohio, on the date hereinabove stated.

READ THIS BEFORE SIGNING.

JOHN REGIS COMPANY

By Charles H. McConnell Signature John Burroughs

A Conditional Sales Contract.

(2) To Obtain a Preferred Lien Against the Article for the Unpaid Purchase Price. The creditors of the buyer, after having obtained judgment against the debtor, may proceed to levy on all the assets of the buyer to collect their unpaid claims. In such an event, the seller has a prior lien on the article he sold. The creditors may sell it, but the seller must have his claim paid in full before the other creditors get anything from the proceeds. This is true under the common law, but in those states requiring the agreement to be recorded, no preference exists unless it is recorded, or the seller notifies the bidders at the sale of his interest.

(3) To Facilitate a Collection if the Account Is in Default. If the seller retains title to personal property under a conditional sales agreement, he has the right in most states to repossess it since it belongs to him. He may use any peaceable means which he deems necessary. If the buyer refuses to return the goods, the seller may resort to court action to compel a return. After the goods are repossessed, some states require the seller to resell the goods and apply the proceeds on the unpaid purchase price. If the proceeds are less than the unpaid balance, the seller may sue for the deficit. If there is an excess, this goes to the buyer after all costs and expenses are paid. Other states permit a repossession but do not require a resale. The title revests in the seller and he is free to do as he chooses.

Risks. Although title remains with the seller in a conditional sales contract, the risks of ownership fall on the buyer. If the property is destroyed, stolen, lost, or damaged, the buyer still must pay the balance due. This is not true, of course, if the contract provides otherwise.

Bulk Sales Laws. The purpose of state bulk sales laws is to prevent a merchant from defrauding his creditors by purchasing stock on credit and then selling the entire stock to another merchant. The goods can be sold item by item, but not in bulk.

The first requirement under the bulk sales laws is that the seller under oath must deliver to the buyer a written list of all his creditors with their addresses and the amounts owed to each. The second requirement is that the buyer, within a specified time and before taking possession of the goods or paying the purchase price, must notify these creditors of the proposed sale, the price, and conditions. The buyer, having given such notice, has no further liability, and it is the responsibility of the creditors to protect themselves. If they do nothing, the purchaser takes the goods free of the creditors' claims.

Questions

1. In a sale for cash with delivery made at the time of the sale, when does the title pass?

2. What are the exceptions to the general rule that only the owner can pass title?

3. (a) Define ascertained or specific goods.
(b) Define fungible goods.

4. If specific goods are in a deliverable state at the time of the contract and the parties are silent as to when the title is to pass, when does title pass?

5. In a contract to sell specific goods in which the seller must do something to the goods before they are ready to deliver, when does title pass?

6. If a television set is sold on approval, when does title pass?

7. If the Climax Hosiery Mills buys all of John's Cotton and John is to pick, bale, and deliver the cotton, when does title pass?

8. (a) If Jones purchases a piano and the seller is to deliver it to 237 Hope Street, when does title pass?
(b) If the Davis Furniture Exchange buys $10,000 worth of furniture f.o.b. Chicago, when does title pass?

9. In a conditional sales contract, who has the risks of ownership before the conditions are met?

10. What is the purpose of the bulk sales law?

Case Problems

1. Lowe of New York, who owned and operated a supermarket, purchased a carload of lettuce from the Produce Exchange in California. The seller described the lettuce as "first class." The terms were "f.o.b. Los Angeles." When the lettuce arrived in New York, Lowe examined it and found it to be second class. He refused to pay the freight and accept it. A week went by while Lowe, the railroad, and the Produce Exchange argued as to what disposition should be made of the lettuce. During that week the lettuce deteriorated and became worthless. The purchase price was $3,500; the value of a similar quantity of second-class lettuce was $2,700; and the freight was $400. Discuss the rights of all the parties.

2. Martha Doan bought a fur coat from the Elite Department Store. She paid cash for it but asked the store to hold it for her a few days. The next day the store sold the coat again to Peggy Matney. Miss Doan brought suit against Miss Matney to obtain possession of the coat. Discuss the rights of these two parties.

3. Smith sold Ling a radio for $75, cash to be paid within two weeks. Smith agreed to supply two new tubes before delivering the radio to Ling. It was further expressly agreed that the radio should belong to Ling as of the time of the sale even though delivery was not made then. Before delivery was made the radio was destroyed by fire due to no fault of Smith's. Who had to bear the loss?

4. The Davis Insurance Agency agreed in February to purchase from the Ajax Calendar Company 5,000 calendars of a particular description. The name Davis Insurance Agency was to be printed in bold letters on the calendars. It was specifically agreed that title was to pass "when the calendars were in a deliverable condition." In August, after the calendars had been printed and made ready for delivery but before they were packed, a fire destroyed all the calendars. Who must bear the loss?

5. Mrs. Jones took her three children to the Baxter Tot Shop to purchase each of them a coat preparatory to their starting back to school. She selected a coat for each one, the total purchase price amounting to $110. She paid $50 and agreed to pay the balance when the coats were delivered. The seller was to alter each of the coats to meet each child's measurements. There was no charge for these alterations. He said "They will be ready on or before Friday." Thursday night the store was burglarized, and the three coats were among those things taken. The coats had been altered, but Mrs. Jones had not been notified. Who must bear this loss?

6. The Troutman Boat Company had for some time been attempting to sell McCracken of Cedar Rapids a boat at a price of $2,700. Mr. Troutman promised McCracken to wire him later in the day and tell him his very best terms. He wired McCracken the offer. The offer contained this clause: "Title is to pass at the site of the boat." The telegraph company's secretary typed it up "at the sight of the boat" although Mr. Troutman had spelled the word for her. McCracken accepted the offer and wired $100 as a binder as agreed. In shipment the boat was damaged to the extent of $700 due to a hurricane. Who must bear the loss, McCracken or The Troutman Boat Company?

7. Mary, a widow, took her insurance money which she received upon her late husband's death and purchased The Thrift Dress Shop, hoping thereby to earn a living for her three minor children. The purchase price was $4,500. Soon after she took over the business, she found there were $3,000 in unpaid bills. The seller had assured her all bills were paid. Must Mary pay this $3,000?

8. Coleman was the bookkeeper for the Anawalt Auto Stores. The store sold Brandt four truck tires on a conditional sales agreement. The manager said to Coleman, "After you record the sale, be sure to file the conditional sales contract." He filed it under "Ti" for Tires. They discovered later that the buyer had sold the tires and the seller planned to take legal action to regain them. In checking at the county clerk's office, it was found that the contract was never filed with the clerk for recording, nor could they find the contract. Could the seller compel the second buyer to pay for them or give up possession?

Chapter 15

Warranties of the Seller

Nature of Warranties. In making a sale, a seller often "warrants" or "guarantees" that the article will measure up to a certain standard or will operate in a certain manner. The statement of the seller in which he "warrants" or "guarantees" the article is known as an *express warranty.* It is a warranty because it is a representation about the goods; it is express because the seller actually and definitely expresses it. By his warranty the seller agrees in effect to make good any loss or damages that the purchaser may suffer if the goods are not as they are represented.

If a warranty is made at the time of the sale, it is considered to be a part of the contract and is therefore binding. If a warranty is made after a sale has been completed, it must be supported by a separate or additional consideration because it is a promise made by the seller that is not a part of the sales contract.

Certain warranties, such as the seller's right to sell the goods, are imposed on all sellers by law. Since they are not expressed by the seller but are nevertheless an essential part of sales contracts, they are called *implied warranties.*

Express Warranties. An express warranty need not consist of any particular words to be binding on the seller. The words "warrant" or "guarantee" need not be used. If a statement or a promise is such that a reasonable interpretation of the language leads the buyer to believe there is a warranty, the courts will construe it as such. A seller is bound by the ordinary meaning of his words, not by his intentions.

The seller can use the word "warrant" or "guarantee" and still not be bound by it if an ordinary, prudent man would not interpret it to constitute a warranty. If the seller of a car says, "I'll guarantee that you will not be sorry if you buy the car at this price," no warranty exists as this is mere conjecture, even though the word "guarantee" was used.

Representations. A *representation* is a statement made prior to the sale for the purpose of inducing the sale. A representation differs from a warranty. To be a warranty there must be two elements in the statement: First, there must be an affirmation about the quality or condition of the article sold; and second, the seller must intend to make this a warranty. Thus every warranty is a representation, but a representation may not be a warranty. There are two reasons why it is necessary to make this a distinction. First, a warranty must be true, even though it is immaterial. Representations need not be true if they are immaterial. Also representations may be both untrue and material and still be irrelevant if the buyer does not rely on them.

Most so-called representations are mere "sales talk" or "puffing." The law holds that a seller may praise his wares, even extravagantly, without obligating himself on his statements or representations. If the representations can be classed as "opinions," "sales talk," "puffing," or similar expressions, they do not give cause for legal redress. Some "shady" merchants have made an art of making opinions sound like warranties. A person should not be misled by such borderline expressions as "best on the market for the money," "these goods are worth $10 if they are worth a dime," "experts have estimated that one ought to be able to sell a thousand a month of these," and many others which sound very convincing, but which have been held to be mere expressions of opinion.

The second reason why one must distinguish between a representation and a warranty is in the remedy. If there is a breach of warranty, the result is a breach of contract. The innocent party has only one of the remedies described later in this chapter. If it is a false representation, it is a tort or legal wrong and gives the injured party the right to sue for damages over and beyond the contract itself. A false representation then may give the buyer wider legal remedies than a breach of warranty.

The rule that a statement of opinion or belief does not constitute a warranty must be qualified in one respect. If the seller does not warrant but expresses an opinion that the article is first-class merchandise when he knows that it is not first-class, the statement becomes a warranty. He in substance warrants that his opinion is sincere.

- Makurath sells Sooter a house. He refuses to warrant that all water pipes and plumbing are in first-class condition, but he expresses the opinion that they are. As a matter of fact, he knows that some of the concealed pipes are broken. He thus warrants that his opinion is sincere and can be held for breach of warranty.

Warranties in Written Contracts. In oral contracts it is often impossible to distinguish between a warranty and a representation. Written contracts create no such difficulties. If the statement is not incorporated into the written contract, it is not a warranty. The unscrupulous seller who knows this law is inclined to be very generous in his warranties during the bargaining stage of the sale. When the sales contract is reduced to writing, he is careful to omit the warranties that he made orally. The buyer must be equally versed in the law of sales.

Defects. Even when the words used constitute an express warranty, no effect will be given to them unless the buyer relied on them, or was materially influenced by them in agreeing to the contract. If there are defects that are actually known to the buyer, or defects that are so apparent that no special skill or ability is required to detect them, an express warranty cannot be invoked to cover them. If Ross says, "I guarantee this car to be in first-class condition in every respect," there is no breach of warranty if the car clearly has four threadbare tires. The courts assume that the clear implication of his words is, "except for the defects which you can clearly see." This would not be true if the seller used any scheme or artifice to conceal the defect. The seller must not do anything that is for the purpose of diverting the attention of the buyer from the defects.

Implied Warranties. An implied warranty differs from an express warranty in that it is created by the operation of law rather than by statements made by the seller. It is implied from the very nature of the transaction and the surrounding facts and circumstances as well as custom and usage. The seller cannot avoid liability by insisting that he made no such warranties, unless he expressly stated that he did not warrant it.

The two most common types of implied warranties are:

1. Warranty of title
2. Warranty of quality

(1) WARRANTY OF TITLE. If the seller has goods in his possession at the time of the sale, there is an implied warranty that he either has title to them or has the right to transfer title. In some states the warranty of title applies even though the goods are not in the seller's possession at the immediate time of the sale. If the contract is one to sell, the seller warrants that he will have title to the goods at the time when the title is to pass. Neither of these implications will apply if the buyer personally knows that the seller does not have title or that he is merely selling whatever interest he may have in the goods.

• Smith stole a watch from the Crown Jewelry Company and sold it to Cooper for $75. Cooper did not know it was stolen. He later sold it to Wilson, who took it to the Crown Jewelry Company to be repaired. They recognized the watch as theirs and refused to return it to Wilson. Wilson then sued Cooper for the price of the watch. He was able to collect because Cooper impliedly warranted that he had good title. It mattered not that he was innocent. He obtained possession from a thief and got no better title than the thief had.

This rule of implied warranty of title does not hold true when one sells goods in a representative capacity, such as when an executor, trustee, or sheriff sells property under an order of the court or in an official capacity. In such a case the buyer assumes the risk that someone having a superior title will claim the article.

If the seller expressly states that he does not warrant the title, the buyer assumes all the risks since the seller did not leave his intentions to be ascertained by implication. Implication is invoked by the courts only when the true intentions of the parties cannot be ascertained.

(2) WARRANTY OF QUALITY. At one time there was no implied warranty of quality. The rule of *caveat emptor*, "Let the buyer beware," was the law of the market place. This is still the primary law that applies to ordinary sales. It applies particularly to what are called "over-the-counter" sales where the buyer can see and inspect the goods. In sales of this kind the law presumes that the buyer can demand an express warranty of quality if he does not trust his own judgment. If he does not avail himself of this bargaining right, he buys without recourse to an implied warranty of quality. There are four exceptions to this rule.

(*a*) *When goods are bought for a particular purpose, there is an implied warranty that they are fit for that purpose.* To avail oneself of this law, the article must be bought for a particular purpose, the purpose must be made known to the seller, and the buyer must rely on the seller's skill and judgment. If these three conditions are met, the merchandise must be fit for the purpose for which it was bought. If any one of these conditions is absent, there is no breach of warranty. This situation frequently arises when one purchases an article by trade name or brand name. If the buyer accepts whatever brand is offered, it must be fit for the purpose for which it was bought. But if the buyer orders by trade name or selects the brand that he thinks most likely will serve his purpose, he does not rely on the seller's skill and judgment.

● Westfall, a crippled soldier, ordered an automobile that could be steered while standing, since a spinal injury made it impossible for him to drive while sitting. The car was satisfactory in every particular, but the steering device was so constructed that it was impossible for him to stand while driving. He was not liable for the purchase price because there was an implied warranty that the car was fit for the particular purpose. Westfall had made known to the seller the use to which the article was to be put.

(*b*) *When goods are sold by sample, there is an implied warranty that the bulk of the goods will correspond with the sample in kind and quality. When goods are sold by description, there is an implied warranty that they will answer the description.* If the goods fail to conform to the sample or the description, the buyer may reject them.

● The Collins School of Business purchased 1,000 reams of typing paper "just like the sample enclosed which was left by your salesman." The paper when received was a slightly different quality than the sample. It was not so heavy and was a shade darker in color, though of good quality. Since the paper received was not "just like the sample," there was no obligation to keep it and pay for it because of the breach of warranty.

(*c*) *When goods are sold for human consumption, there is an implied warranty that they are wholesome*

In the Sale of Food Products There Is an Implied Warranty That the Food Is Fit for Human Consumption.

and fit for consumption. It matters not that the buyer inspected the food or failed to indicate that he relied on the seller's skill and judgment.

- The Wholesale Baking Company sold some pastries to Harriett Gates. The pastries contained contaminated materials causing severe illness on the part of the purchaser and her children. She was entitled to recover damages for a breach of warranty that the goods were fit for human consumption.

(*d*) *In the sale of goods for resale, there is an implied warranty that the goods are of merchantable quality unless the buyer assumes this risk by inspecting the goods or otherwise showing his approval.* If a dealer orders a carload of lettuce which ordinarily sells for twenty cents a head and he is unable to inspect the lettuce, there is an implied warranty that the lettuce is merchantable at approximately that price. It is not sufficient that the lettuce can be sold at some price.

Remote Purchaser. A suit for breach of warranty is based on a contractual relationship existing between the buyer and the seller. If a manufacturer sells a retailer defective merchandise, and the retailer in turn sells it to the consumer, there is no contractual relationship existing between the manufacturer and the remote purchaser. For this reason, until recently no suit for breach of warranty could be maintained against the manufacturer. The modern trend of court decisions is to give the remote purchaser one of two courses for redress. The first is a suit for damages, not for breach of warranty, but for tort. To do this, the purchaser must prove fraud or negligence on the part of the manufacturer. The other remedy is to treat the retailer as the agent of the manufacturer, thus creating a contractual relationship with the remote purchaser. These remedies are not yet permitted in all states, but the trend is in this direction.

Remedies for Breach of Warranty. If the seller is guilty of a breach of warranty in the sale of any article, the law allows the buyer to choose one of four remedies. He must weigh all the facts carefully to determine which of these remedies is most advantageous to him. He can have one and only one. These remedies are:

(1) Keep the merchandise and bring suit against the seller for any damages he has sustained. Frequently there has been a breach of warranty, but no damage was sustained. In such case this remedy is of little value.

(2) If the goods were bought on credit, the purchaser may deduct from the purchase price the damages he has sustained. In this event he keeps the goods. If he overestimates the damages, the seller would have to sue the buyer so that the actual damages could be judicially determined.

(3) If title has not passed to the buyer at the time the breach of warranty is discovered, the buyer can refuse to accept the goods and then can sue the seller for any damages he has sustained. He must make sure title has not passed before he attempts to exercise this remedy. Again, if he has not been damaged materially, there is no merit in bringing a suit for damages.

(4) If title has passed to the buyer, he should return the goods or offer to return them, assuming he does not wish to keep them. If the seller refuses to take them back, the buyer should hold them, unless they are perishable, until the respective rights have been judicially determined. While awaiting the outcome, the buyer must not permit the goods to deteriorate. Even if he returns the goods, he may still sue for damages.

Questions

1. Define express warranty.

2. What are implied warranties?

3. May one warrant an article sold and still actually not make an express warranty? Explain.

4. Distinguish between a representation and a warranty.

5. Is the statement, "This fish bait is so good you will have to hide behind a tree to put it on a hook," a warranty or sales talk?

6. Is an expression of an opinion ever a warranty?

7. Name the two most common types of implied warranties.

8. What warranty does the seller make when he sells by sample?

9. If the buyer of food for human consumption inspects the food, what liability, if any, does the seller have?

10. What are the remedies for a breach of warranty?

Case Problems

1. Branch, a cattleman, purchased from the Hay Seed Company, 2,000 pounds of reseeding crimson clover seed. The seller said, "This is the Dixie strain of reseeding clover, and I guarantee you won't have to worry about its reseeding." There are several strains of crimson clover, some reseeding, some not. The Dixie strain is the most reliable. Branch later learned his seed was not the Dixie strain. It did reseed satisfactorily, but Branch could not market his seed as Dixie seed. He sued the Hay Seed Company for breach of warranty. Was he entitled to collect damages?

2. The Vulcan Metals Company purchased in bulk the Simmons Manufacturing Company, a manufacturer of vacuum cleaners. The seller made these statements about its cleaner: (1) It is clean, economical, efficient, and perfect in the smallest detail; (2) a child of six can operate it; (3) it works completely and thoroughly; (4) and it has never been placed on the market." All of these statements were absolutely false. The vacuum cleaner was almost worthless. Which statement, if any, was a warranty and which ones were mere sales talk?

3. The Virginia Supply Company sold Lewis, a groceryman, 500 bushels of No. 1 Idaho potatoes. The sale was by correspondence. The potatoes were shipped by truck and accepted by Lewis. Four days later, after several customers had complained about the poor quality of the potatoes, Lewis notified the seller that he would not pay for the potatoes and offered to return them, claiming a breach of warranty. Was there a breach of warranty in this case?

4. Westbrook, purchasing agent for a chain grocery store, called at the office of the Hayden Preserve Company preparatory to ordering some preserves. On the desk of the president of the preserve company were four jars of preserves, each having a brand name. They were of the consistency and quality of preserves that Westbrook wished to buy. He asked to be allowed to enter the canning room and warehouse to inspect the product further. He was told that was inconvenient since the preserves were in sealed boxes, but if he insisted, they would do so. He ordered a carload of the preserves without further inspection, but they were not at all like the four jars which he examined. The buyer refused to pay for the preserves claiming a breach of warranty in a sale by sample. The seller contended that they did not represent these four jars to be samples but sold only by brand names. Was there a breach of warranty?

5. A manufacturer of combs to be used by professional hairdressers sold some combs to a dealer who in turn sold them to a hairdresser. When the combs came in contact with the hairdressing machines, they ignited and caused serious injury to Mrs. Dale. She sued the manufacturer for breach of warranty. Was this the proper remedy?

6. Young was branch manager for the Free-Fit Shoe stores. He purchased 1,000 pairs of overshoes that were expressly guaranteed to be waterproof and seamless. The shoes delivered had two seams and were not 100 per cent waterproof. The purchase price was $5,000, and Young estimated that the shoes were not worth more than $4,000. The shoes had been purchased on credit. Young kept the shoes and withheld $3,000 from the purchase price as damages. The seller sued for $1,000, admitting the $1,000 damages, and obtained judgment for this amount. What error did Young commit in selecting his remedy?

7. A salesman in an effort to sell a college student an encyclopedia set for $70 showed him proofs of advertisements that were to be run soon fixing the price for the same books at $210. "This is the last chance to buy at this price" was repeated over and over. The salesman also said, "I guarantee that you can pass any business law exam if you learn all the answers in this encyclopedia." The college student bought the books but failed his examination. Also, the price did not go up. The purchaser wished to rescind the contract. Could he do so?

8. The defendant wrote to the plaintiff for information and prices on a road-finishing machine. In his letter he stated that the machine must be for 16″ x 18″ finishing work on a concrete pavement and "must pass the specifications of the Michigan State Highway Department." The machine that was delivered failed to do the work. The defendant refused to pay the notes that he had given in payment of the purchase price.

(a) Did the purchaser expressly or impliedly make known the purpose for which the machine was to be used?

(b) Did the buyer rely on the seller's skill or judgment?

9. The Heller Typewriter Exchange sold McBroom a secondhand typewriter. McBroom wanted the typewriter just for personal use. He used the "hunt-and-peck" system. The seller assured McBroom that a good typist could attain a speed of 150 words a minute on this machine although he knew it was impossible to make over 80 words a minute. He also guaranteed that it was in perfect condition, that it was "the best buy in town," and that McBroom could no doubt sell it for $15 more than he was paying for it. McBroom later learned that he could buy a similar machine for $5 less and that it was impossible to attain a speed of more than 80 words a minute; otherwise, the machine was just as represented. He offered to return the machine and demanded the return of his money. The seller refused so McBroom brought suit. Who was entitled to win the case?

Cases for Review of Part III

1. J. Maiman and Sons, through their agent, Jacob Maiman, purchased by an oral contract from Harry Brussell some machines valued in excess of $500. Because of a strike in the J. Maiman & Sons plant in Philadelphia the agent requested that the machines be sent to the buyer's factory at Skippack. The seller complied and the machines were installed by the employees of the Skippack Company under the supervision and direction of the seller. The purchaser later attempted to avoid the contract, and contended that the Statute of Frauds required such a contract to be in writing. (Brussell vs. Maiman, 11 Pa. Supp. 54, 1933) Do you agree?

2. The Cudahy Packing Company purchased a carload of eggs from Jacob Narzisenfeld. The agent who did the buying for the packing company inspected the eggs before the purchase, and the seller made no warranty as to quality. There was no evidence that the seller knew the eggs were too old. The buyer refused to pay for the eggs and claimed damages from the seller alleging a breach of warranty of both quality and merchantability. The eggs had to be sold at a greatly reduced price because of the deterioration in quality. (Cudahy Packing Company vs. Narzisenfeld. Circuit Court of Appeals, Second Circuit, 1924, 3 F. [2nd] 657) Was there a breach of warranty?

3. The Technical Economist Corporation purchased from Moores some secondhand refrigerating machinery. A check for $500 was given as a deposit with the understanding that it was to be applied on the purchase price of $14,000. Other than this check everything relating to the contract was oral. Later the check was returned to the Technical Economist Corporation and Moores refused to carry out any part of the contract. Moores contends that since the contract was oral he was not bound to carry out its terms. (The Technical Economist Corporation v. Moores, 255 Mass. 591) Was this contract enforceable?

4. The Slayden-Kirksey Woolen Mills sold its merchandise by supplying its salesmen with samples of its merchandise and taking orders from the samples. Spring purchased several dozen trousers of several different grades. When the trousers were delivered, only a few corresponded to the samples. The others were returned and payment refused. The Slayden-Kirksey Woolen Mills Company sued for the contract price. (Spring vs. Slayden-Kirksey Woolen Mills, 106 Ill. Appeals, 579) Was Spring liable?

5. The J. C. Weeter Lumber Company purchased some stoves and heaters from the Detroit Vapor Stove Company. At the time of the sale the seller stated "these stoves are the best and finest on the market. They will sell like hot cakes, and you will have to buy another carload before the season is over." None of these statements proved true, and the buyer attempted to recover the purchase price on the grounds of a breach of warranty. (Detroit Vapor Stove Company vs. J. C. Weeter Lumber Company, 61 Utah 503) Could the buyer recover?

6. The Max Furniture Store ordered a quantity of furniture from the Morris Furniture Company, manufacturers. The order consisted of an unsigned letter in which the furniture ordered was itemized, described, and price indicated. About two weeks later, but before any goods were shipped, the buyer wrote a letter to the manufacturer in which this statement was made: "Hold our order of September 17 until we give you further notice." This letter was signed and referred to the unsigned order described above. The buyer refused to accept the goods when they were shipped, and the seller sued for the invoice price. (Morris Furniture Company vs. Brauerman, 210 Iowa 946) Was the Morris Furniture Company entitled to collect?

7. Bernadette, Joseph and Company sold watches to Van Buren of New York. The contract provided that the sale to Van Buren was on a "sale or return" basis, the option resting with Van Buren. Shortly after their receipt, the watches were stolen due to no fault of Van Buren's. Because of this Van Buren refused to pay for the watches. (Bernadette, Joseph & Co. vs. Van Buren, 209 N. Y. S. 559) Did he have to pay for them?

8. The James Butler Grocery Company sold a can of peaches to Mrs. Martha Griffin. Because of the unfit condition of the peaches, Mrs. Griffin became gravely ill. She sued the James Butler Grocery Company for damages, alleging a breach of an implied warranty that the peaches were fit for human consumption. The seller sought to evade liability on the grounds that it bought the peaches from a cannery in California and knew no more about the contents of the can than the purchaser. (Griffin vs. James Butler Grocery Company, 108 N. J. L. 92, 156 A. 636) Could Griffin collect damages?

Part IV
BAILMENTS

Chapter 16

Bailments in General

Characteristics of a Bailment. A *bailment* is the transfer of possession, but not the title, of personal property (never real property) by one party, usually the owner, to another party on condition that the identical property will be returned to him or his agent at a future date. The one who retains title but gives up possession is called the *bailor*. The one who acquires possession but not the title is called the *bailee*.

In a bailment two conditions are always present:

(1) There must be both a delivery and an acceptance of personal property.

(2) The bailor must expect to get back the same property, though it may be considerably altered in form.

If either one of the preceding conditions is absent, the transfer may be a sale, a barter, or a gift; but it is not a bailment.

Some typical business transactions resulting in a bailment are:

(a) A motorist leaves his car with the garage for the purpose of having it repaired.

(b) A family stores its furniture in a warehouse.

(c) A student borrows a friend's dinner jacket to wear to a formal dance.

(d) A hunter leaves his jewelry with a friend for safekeeping while he goes on an extended hunting trip.

The Bailment Agreement. A bailment is based upon an agreement, express or implied, between the bailor and the bailee. If the agreement is the result of written or spoken words, the bailment is express. If the agreement is indicated by the conduct of the parties, the bailment is implied. When a man checks his hat and coat as he enters a restaurant, nothing may be said, but the bailment is implied by the acts of the two parties. When one finds lost property, the bailment is implied by law.

Delivery and Acceptance. A bailment can be established only if there are both a delivery and an acceptance of personal property. The delivery and acceptance may be actual or constructive. They are actual when the goods themselves are delivered and accepted. They are constructive when there is no physical delivery of the goods, but when control over the goods is delivered and accepted.

- Garber hired Hoyt's car. Hoyt gave Garber a parking lot check and said, "The car is in the parking lot at Third and Court Streets." Garber did not call for the car immediately. Nevertheless Garber became a bailee because there was a constructive delivery and acceptance.

Return of the Bailed Property. In a bailment the bailee must return to the bailor the identical goods bailed. If a farmer delivers wheat to a miller, a bailment is established if he expects to get back flour made from this same wheat. If he expects to get back flour made from any wheat of like grade, there is an exchange of personal property, but not a bailment.

Loss of the Bailed Property. As a general rule, any loss due to the theft or damage of personal property falls upon the owner. This may not be true if a bailment exists. Thus it is often very important to ascertain if there is in fact a bailment. If a bailment exists, the owner may in some instances, in case of loss or damage, shift the burden to the bailee. To do this, he must prove negligence on the part of the bailee. The degree of negligence required to hold the bailee liable in the event of damage to the bailed property varies according to the class of bailment.

Classification of Bailments. For convenience, bailments are usually divided into the following three groups:

1. Bailments for the sole benefit of the bailor
2. Bailments for the sole benefit of the bailee
3. Bailments for the mutual benefit of both parties

The following chart illustrates the difference in the degree of care required in the classes of bailments:

Type of Bailment	Degree of Care Required	Degree of Negligence Necessary to Hold the Bailee Liable
Bailment for the sole benefit of the bailor	Slight care	Gross negligence
Bailment for the sole benefit of the bailee	Great care	Slight negligence
Mutual-benefit bailment	Ordinary care	Ordinary negligence

Negligence is a failure to take that degree of care required by the circumstances.

(1) BAILMENTS FOR THE SOLE BENEFIT OF THE BAILOR. If one is in possession of another's personal property for the sole benefit of the owner, a bailment for the sole benefit of the bailor exists. The bailee receives no benefits in the way of compensation or else it would not be a bailment for the sole benefit of the bailor. Any benefit that the bailee receives must be from the nature of the property, and not a part of the contract. For example, a man asks a friend to keep his piano in his home until he, the owner, is able to rent larger quarters. The friend may play the piano and otherwise receive all the benefits of ownership while it is in his possession without this constituting a consideration. If the pleasure which the bailee received from possessing the piano in no way induced him to take care of the piano, there was no

benefit, in the eyes of the law, derived from the act. Not all gratuitous services have the possibility of benefit to the bailee. If a farmer agrees, gratuitously, to haul a load of hay to town for a neighbor, this is clearly a bailment for the sole benefit of the bailor.

- Askew planned a trip through Atlanta. Bolton asked him to deliver, as a favor, a watch to his son in that city. Askew placed the watch in his coat pocket. He parked his car in Atlanta in the downtown section, left the doors unlocked, the windows lowered, and his coat on the front seat while he ate lunch. The coat and the watch were stolen. A jury would have to decide whether or not Askew exercised reasonable care of the watch.

Another example of a bailment for the sole benefit of the bailor occurs when one person loses an article and another person finds it. In this case the loser is the bailor, and the finder is the bailee. The finder is under no obligation to take possession of the lost property. During the time that he has possession of the goods as a bailee, even though the bailment is for the sole benefit of the bailor, he nevertheless assumes certain responsibilities. He is liable for lack of reasonable care which, as in the case of other gratuitous bailments, requires only slight attention and diligence in the protection of the property. After a reasonable time has elapsed and reasonable diligence has been exercised to find the owner, or after statutory requirements have been met, the bailment comes to an end and the finder becomes the owner of the found property.

(2) Bailments for the Sole Benefit of the Bailee. If the bailee has possession and use of another's personal property, and the owner of the property receives no benefit or compensation for its use, a bailment for the sole benefit of the bailee exists. This type of bailment arises as a rule through borrowing someone else's property. The bailee must exercise extraordinary care over the prop-

erty and is liable for negligence if he fails to do so. The bailee is not an insurer of the bailed property since any loss or damage due to no fault whatever of the bailee falls upon the owner. If Petras borrows Walker's diamond ring to wear to a dance and is robbed on the way to the dance, the loss falls upon Walker, the owner. Petras was not negligent.

Even though the bailor receives no benefit from a bailment for the sole benefit of the bailee, he must inform the bailee of any known defects. If the bailee is injured by reason of a defect, the bailor is liable for damages, provided he knew of the defect and failed to inform the bailee.

- Bolen borrowed a truck from Jernigan to move his household goods. Bolen paid nothing for the use of the truck. Jernigan failed to notify Bolen that the brakes on the truck would not hold. As a result, Bolen was injured. Jernigan was liable for damages since he failed to notify Bolen of the defect. The bailor, Jernigan, was under no obligation to furnish safe property, but he was liable for failure to notify the bailee of known defects.

(3) Bailments for the Mutual Benefit of Both Parties. The largest volume of bailments are those for the mutual benefit of both the bailor and the bailee. Some common bailments of this type are: machinery left with

A Mutual Benefit Bailment Is Created When a Fee Is Paid for the Use of Library Books.

American Telephone & Telegraph Company

a mechanic to be repaired, laundry and dry cleaning contracts, the rental of personal property, such as an automobile or a typewriter, and material left with a fabricator to be converted into a finished product for a price. The bailee must take ordinary care of the bailed property.

• Green rented a You-Drive-It automobile from Trestle Motors Company. While driving to Denver, he collided with a car driven by White, and both cars were wrecked. The roads were coated with ice, and Green was driving at the time of the collision down a fairly steep grade at about forty miles an hour. Visibility because of snow was about 200 feet. Green was liable to the Trestle Motors Company for damages to the car. Forty miles an hour, under the conditions described, was faster than an ordinary prudent man would have driven his own car.

Had the Trestle Motors Company furnished Green with a car which had a defect that caused the accident, not only would Green not have been liable, but the Trestle Motors Company would have been liable to Green for any damages sustained by him. In a mutual-benefit bailment of this type, the bailor must furnish safe property, not just inform the bailee of any known defects.

In most cases of mutual-benefit bailment the bailee makes a charge for services rendered. This is true in all repair jobs, laundry, dry cleaning, shoe mending, and storage bailments. The bailee has a lien, and usually a first lien, against the bailed property for his charges. If these charges are not paid, the bailee is under no obligation to return the bailed goods. After a reasonable time the bailee may advertise and sell the property for his charges. If any money remains from the proceeds of the sale after expenses and his charges are paid, he must turn it over to the bailor.

If the bailee parts with possession of the property before he has been paid, in most states he loses his lien. If he later regains possession of the same property, his lien is not re-established for the old charges, except in a few states where, by special statute, this right is given to the bailee.

Use of the Bailed Goods. When a bailment is for the sole benefit of the bailor, the bailee has no right to use the property for his own purpose. This rule may be altered if use of the goods is for their benefit or is necessary to preserve them.

If the bailment is for the sole benefit of the bailee, the use is strictly limited to the use agreed upon by the parties at the time the contract was formed. If the bailee uses the property in any other way, he is liable for any resulting damage regardless of his negligence.

- McDougall borrowed Brandt's car to drive to Momence; but, instead of driving to Momence, he drove to Sheldon. While he was driving to Sheldon, the car was badly damaged in an accident although McDougall was in no way negligent. McDougall was liable, however, even in the absence of negligence because the accident would not have happened had he not gone to Sheldon. He had borrowed the car to drive to Momence and therefore had no right to drive it to Sheldon.

If a bailment is for the mutual benefit of both parties, the wrongful use of the property makes the bailee liable for any damages caused by that use. In the case of wrongful use, the amount of care that was exercised by the bailee is immaterial.

Duties and Obligations of the Bailor. In all types of bailments the bailee has the right to receive bailed property that is safe to keep or use, or to be apprised of the dangerous nature of the article bailed. For example, when *A* borrows or rents *B*'s truck, *B* must inform *A* if the brakes are deficient. If *B* fails to do so and *A* is injured, *B* is liable for damages. When the bailment is for the sole benefit of the bailee, the bailor is liable for any injury due to a failure to inform the bailee of any known defects. The bailor is not liable if the injury is due to an unknown defect. When it is a mutual benefit bailment, the bailor is liable for any injury caused not only by any known defects if he fails to inform the bailee, but also by any unknown defects. When one rents or leases to another a car, boat, airplane, or other goods, he warrants that the devices are suitable and trustworthy.

Bailee's Duty to Protect Property. Often bailed property is damaged or destroyed not by any negligence by the bailee in the use of it, but by some act having nothing to do with its use. One of the most common causes of loss is the failure to insure the property. In the absence of a promise supported by a consideration to insure the property, the bailee is under no obligation to insure it. But the bailor may as a part of the contract of bailment bind the bailee to insure the bailed property. A failure of the bailee to do so subjects him to full liability for all losses due to a failure to insure.

- The Ellison Furniture Mart sold Haley some furniture valued at $1,500. Since Haley was not yet in a position to accept delivery of the furniture, he asked the seller to store it for him and to insure it while in storage. The property was destroyed by fire caused by lightning before any insurance had been placed on it. The Ellison Furniture Mart was liable for this loss because its promise to insure was a part of the whole transaction and this was supported by a consideration.

Another cause of loss not due to the use of property is a failure to return it on time or returning it to the wrong party in good faith. In both cases the bailee is liable if the loss is due primarily to this breach of duty to return the property on time to the owner. The bailee is liable for all loss due to the wrongful conversion of the property regardless of any degree of negligence.

Sale of Bailed Property by the Bailee. Possession of property is not proof of ownership. One who purchases property from a bailee ordinarily does not get good title to it. There are situations, however, where the bailor may not deny that the bailee had the right to sell the property. This is particularly true in goods put out on consignment with a commission merchant or factor. In these cases a mutual benefit bailment exists even though the bailor does not expect to get the bailed property back. The purpose of the bailment is to have the property sold and the proceeds remitted to the bailor. The bailee has the power to sell all goods under these types of contracts regardless of any restriction upon his right to sell, unless the buyer knows of the restriction.

The bailor may by his act mislead an innocent third person into believing that the bailee owns the property. An instance of this type is shown in the following illustration:

- Jessie borrowed Logan's wagon. With Logan's knowledge and consent Jessie had painted in bold red letters on the side of the wagon these words: "Jessie's Transfer." Jessie sold the wagon later to Donovan. Donovan obtained good title to the wagon because Logan was estopped to deny that it was Jessie's Wagon. Logan's act enabled Jessie to mislead Donovan into believing that Jessie owned the wagon.

Pledge or Pawn. One type of bailment is the deposit of personal property as security for some debt or obligation. If the security is tangible property, such as livestock, a radio, or an automobile, it is a *pawn.* If the security is intangible property, such as notes, bonds, or stock certificates, it is a *pledge.* In each case the transaction is a mutual-benefit bailment.

Questions

1. In a contract of bailment, is the owner the bailor or the bailee?

2. (a) If one sends a suit to be cleaned, is this a bailment? (b) If one enters a restaurant and hangs his coat on a hook provided for the convenience of the customers, is this a bailment?

3. Give an example of a contract of bailment without an actual delivery of the goods to the bailee?

4. If one delivers logs to a sawmill to be cut into lumber and the lumber from these logs is delivered back to the owner, is this a bailment?

5. (a) If Davis asks Hall to keep his car for him while he is away and Hall receives no benefit from the transaction, what kind of bailment is this?

(b) If Davis pays Hall $24 for his services, what kind of bailment would it be?

6. What is the difference in the degree of care required of Hall in the situations in Question 5?

7. If Jones loans his car to Smith as a favor and Smith is injured because the car had very defective brakes, what remedy does Smith have against Jones?

8. In a bailment for the sole benefit of the bailor, how may the bailee use the goods?

9. In a bailment for the mutual benefit of both parties, the bailee used the property contrary to the agreement. Is the bailee liable for damages if the property is damaged due to no negligence on the part of the bailee?

10. (a) Define a pawn.

(b) Define a pledge.

Case Problems

1. The Bronson Typewriter Exchange sold an electric typewriter to Holmes, who was to pick up the machine the following day. The next day Holmes telephoned the Bronson Typewriter Exchange and asked that the machine be delivered to 237 Hull Street. Miss Hayes, the secretary, attached a memo to the machine that it was to be delivered to 237 Hull Street. Because of her poor penmanship, the truck driver read it 237 Hall Street. He delivered it at that address. The machine was stolen before the error was detected. Who must bear the loss, Holmes or the Bronson Typewriter Exchange?

2. The Bailey Transfer and Storage Company received from Hill some household furniture to be stored in their brick warehouse. About one month later the storage company, without Hill's knowledge or consent, moved the furniture to a new location in a less fireproof building. Hill's fire insurance policy showed the location of his furniture as 1416 Main street, the location of the brick warehouse. The policy also contained a clause which limited the company's liability if the property was moved to a new location without the insurance company's consent. The property was destroyed by fire through no negligence on the part of the storage company. The fire insurance company refused to pay. Could Hill collect for the loss from the Bailey Transfer and Storage Company?

3. The McDougal Fur Storage Company received for storage a mink coat, valued at $4,000, from Sheldon. Mrs. McDougal, wife of the owner of the storage company, wore the coat to an exclusive club. While there, a robbery occurred in which the mink coat was taken. Must the McDougal Fur Storage Company compensate Sheldon for the loss?

4. The Bargain Corner had a stock of merchandise valued at $20,000. Of this amount $15,000 belonged to the proprietor and $5,000 was stocked on consignment. There was a fire insurance policy of $10,000 on the stock owned by the Bargain Corner proprietor, but none on the consigned merchandise. A fire loss results in a damage of $8,000 on the stock, $2,000 of which was on the consigned goods. The proprietor of the Bargain Corner was in no way negligent in causing the loss. Must he use $2,000 of the insurance proceeds to apply on the loss of the consigned goods?

5. Hicks orally sold Smith all his spring lambs and gave Smith one week to take them away. Hicks agreed to care for the lambs without charge until Smith came for them, at which time Smith was to make payment. Two days later the lambs were frozen to death in a blizzard. Hicks made no effort to get them to shelter, and there was some evidence to indicate that he might have saved some of them had he put them in shelter. Smith refused to pay for the lambs. Must he pay for them?

6. Henry asked to borrow his employer's car to drive to Booneville on personal business. There were two roads to Booneville. By the usual route, the distance was ten miles; by the other route, it was twenty miles. Henry went the long way so that he could pick up his girl friend and take her with him. While driving at forty miles an hour around a bad curve, he ran into another car parked on the wrong side of the road. There was conflicting evidence as to whether or not he was driving with both hands. His employer demanded that Henry pay the $75 repair bill. Was he legally bound to pay it?

7. Oliver was a cabinet maker, specializing in solid walnut cabinets. The customers supplied the walnut lumber and the patterns and Oliver did the work. Under this plan Westfall delivered some walnut lumber valued at $75 to Oliver to be converted into a table and a cabinet. Oliver left this lumber lying out in the weather for two weeks, during which time it became unusable and virtually valueless. Westfall sued Oliver for the value of the lumber. Was he entitled to collect?

8. Froemke left his radio at the Classic City Radio Shop to be repaired. At the same time Froemke had the radio shop install a television set with the understanding that if he approved the set, the radio would be taken as a part payment, the value of the radio to be fixed at the time of purchasing the television set. Before Froemke decided to buy the set, the radio was destroyed by fire due to no fault of the radio shop. The radio shop refused to allow Froemke anything for the radio even though Froemke exercised his option to buy the television set. Who had to bear the loss of the radio?

9. Darlene rented a horse from the Oakhill Stables to ride in a horse show. Instead of participating in the horse show, Darlene changed her mind and rode to a friend's home in the country. While returning to town the horse became frightened, ran away, and was seriously injured. Darlene was in no way negligent. Was she liable for the loss?

Chapter 17

Common Carriers

Definition. A *carrier* is engaged in the business of transporting either goods or persons, or both. A carrier of goods is a bailee. Since a fee is charged for such service, the bailment is one for the mutual benefit of both parties. The general law of bailments, however, does not apply to all carriers of goods. For this reason it is necessary to classify carriers so that the laws governing each class may be set out.

Classification of Carriers. Carriers are usually classified into two groups:

1. Private carriers
2. Common carriers

(1) PRIVATE CARRIERS. A *private carrier* is one who, for a fee, undertakes to transport goods or persons. He does not hold himself out to the public as being able and willing to serve all who apply. He transports only under special instances and special arrangements. Since he conducts his business for profit, he is anxious to serve all as far as it is profitable for him to do so. He is free to refuse service if it is unprofitable, a freedom denied to common carriers. The most usual types of private carriers are taxis, trucks, moving vans, railroads, and ships owned by mining and other companies for transporting their goods only, and private delivery services.

Private carriers' contracts for transporting goods are mutual-benefit bailments, and the general law of bailments as well as of contracts governs them. Under the law of contracts one may limit his liability for his own negligence. In the absence of such a limitation the law of mutual-benefit bailments applies. Any state or city may impose certain limitations upon these private carriers, but such limitations are seldom extensive.

(2) COMMON CARRIERS. A *common carrier* is one who undertakes to transport goods or persons for all who apply for that service. The nature of the services rendered determines whether or not one is a common carrier. If one's business of transporting goods is so extensive as to be affected with a public interest, he will be deemed a common carrier.

A common carrier must serve all who apply without discrimination. If he fails to do so, he is liable for any damages resulting from such a refusal. He may refuse service because it is not one for which he is equipped. For example, an express company does not have to accept lumber for transportation. Also, a common carrier may refuse service if its equipment is inadequate to accommodate additional customers in excess of the normal demands.

Provided he has room, a common carrier of persons must carry without discrimination all fit persons who may apply for passage. He is not, however, required to transport (a) any person who requires unusual attention, unless that person is accompanied by an attendant, (b) any person who intends to cause an injury to the carrier or the passengers, (c) any person who is likely to harm passengers, such as a person with a contagious disease, or (d) any person who is likely to be offensive to passengers, such as an intoxicated person.

The usual types of common carriers of persons are railroads, bus lines, airplanes, ships (both ocean and river), and street railways. Common carriers that are public monopolies are subject to regulations as to prices, services, equipment, and other operational policies. This public regulation is in lieu of competition as a determinant of their prices and services.

A Common Carrier May Be Liable for Loss or Damages to Goods that It Transports.

Harold M. Lambert

Liability of Common Carrier of Goods for Loss. With but five exceptions noted below, a common carrier of goods is liable for loss or damage without reference to negligence. He thus approaches the status of an insurer since he assumes the risks inherent in transporting goods.

The common carrier is not liable as an insurer for losses arising from:

1. Acts of God
2. Acts of a public authority
3. Inherent nature of goods
4. Acts of the shipper
5. Acts of public enemy

(1) ACTS OF GOD. If the loss to goods being transported is due to floods, snowstorms, tornadoes, lightning, or fire caused by lightning, the carrier is not liable since these are considered acts of God. These acts, however, must be the immediate, not the remote, cause of the damage.

● A freight train was delayed two hours while the tracks were being repaired. The repairs could have been made at any time since the needed repairs did not render the tracks unusable. While the train was waiting for the repairs to be completed, a tornado swept across the track and several thousand dollars' worth of livestock were killed. The evidence showed that had the train been traveling all the time it was being delayed, it would have been beyond the path of the tornado. The delay was the direct cause and the tornado the remote cause of the damage, so the carrier was liable.

(2) Acts of Public Authority. Any loss to goods being transported due to public authority is borne by the shipper, not the carrier. Illicit goods may be seized by public officials, or health officials may seize goods that are a menace to health. The carrier is not liable for any loss due to these and similar acts.

(3) Inherent Nature of the Goods. Some goods, such as vegetables, are highly perishable. If the carrier uses the most modern methods of refrigeration or other means of minimizing loss, he is not liable for damage due to the inherent nature of the goods. The most common types of loss due to the inherent nature of the goods are: decay of vegetables, fermentation or evaporation of liquids, and the death of livestock as a result of natural causes or the fault of other animals. The loss must have been in no way due to the negligence of the carrier.

(4) Acts of the Shipper. If the loss is due directly to the act of the shipper, the carrier is not liable. The most common cause of this type of loss is improper packing. If the packing is clearly improper, the carrier should refuse to accept the goods. If the improper packing cannot be detected by inspection, and a loss results, the carrier is relieved from liability. Other instances are misdirection of the merchandise and failure to indicate fragile contents.

- Smith placed some valuable pieces of cut glass in his trunk and shipped the trunk without indicating its contents. The glass was completely destroyed. The carrier was excused from liability because the shipper failed to indicate the fragile nature of the contents.

(5) Acts of Public Enemy. If the loss or damage to goods is the result of organized warfare or border excursions of foreign bandits, the carrier is not liable. This cause of loss has all but vanished in America. Mobs, strikers, and rioters are not listed as public enemies in interpreting this exclusion.

Liability of Carrier Before and After Transportation. Frequently, goods are delivered to the carrier before they are ready for transportation. The carrier may be instructed to hold the goods until shipping instructions are received, or the carrier may delay shipment until the freight charges are paid. In either event, the carrier is liable only as a warehouseman, that is, a mutual-benefit bailee. The carrier's role as an insurer does not arise until the goods are ready to be transported.

Limitations upon the Carrier's Liability. A carrier may attempt to limit or escape the extraordinary liability imposed upon him by law. This is most often done by a contract between the shipper and the carrier. Since the bill of lading is the written evidence of the contract, the limitations on the carrier's liability are set out in this document. Since the shipper does not have any direct voice in the preparation of the bill of lading, the law requires all carriers to have the printed bill-of-lading form approved before it is adopted. For interstate commerce this approval is given by the Interstate Commerce Commission. The states have similar bodies to regulate purely intrastate commerce. These bodies have approved a few provisions whereby the carriers limit their liability. But in addition to the uniform limitations set out in the printed form of bill of lading, space is left for any additional limitations which the shipper and the carrier may agree upon. All of these acts are governed by the Uniform Bills of Lading Act, adopted in 31 states, and the Federal Bills of Lading Act. In general the limitations upon the carrier's liability permitted by these acts fall into the following classes:

(1) A carrier is permitted to limit by agreement his loss to a specified sum or to a specified per cent of the value of the goods. The freight rates must be uniform for all shippers. Carriers are prohibited from either reducing or raising the rates without prior approval.

They may, however, as a consideration for the shipper's agreement to permit the carrier to limit his liability, reduce the rate a reasonable amount. The shipper must be given the right to ship his wares under either rate.

(2) Most states permit the carriers to exempt themselves from liability due to certain named hazards. The most common named hazards are: fire, leakage, breakage, spoilage, and losses due to riots, strikes, mobs, and robbers. Some states specifically prohibit an exemption for loss by fire. Before these exemptions are valid, they must be specifically enumerated in the bill of lading or shipper's receipt. In all cases the exemptions are not effective if the loss is due to the negligence of the carrier. No consideration in the form of a reduced rate need be given to justify these limitations.

(3) Livestock shipments create many problems for carriers, and delay in transportation for any cause may result in serious losses or extra expense for feed. Most states allow some form of limitation upon the carrier's liability if the loss is due to a delay over which the carrier has no control.

Duration of Carrier's Liability. During most shipments the carrier at one stage of the shipment is an extraordinary bailee and liable as an insurer with the exceptions set out above. At another stage of the shipment the carrier is an ordinary bailee, and thus subject to far less risk. For example, if goods are delivered to a carrier with instructions not to ship until notified to do so, the carrier is an ordinary bailee during this waiting period. If the goods are damaged or destroyed, the carrier is not liable if ordinary care is taken of the goods. This is also true after the goods arrive at their destination if the consignee does not call for them within the time fixed by law. At all other times the carrier is liable for all loss or damage with the exceptions named, regardless of negligence. It is then often of the utmost importance to both the carrier and the shipper or the consignee to know at the time of the loss what class of bailment existed. The problem is to determine the exact moment the carrier's liability as a carrier begins and ends.

(1) COMMENCEMENT OF THE CARRIER'S LIABILITY. The carrier often comes into possession of the goods prior to the time they are to be shipped. This is particularly true when the goods are delivered in parts but shipment is not to take place until all goods have been delivered. During this interval the carrier is an ordinary bailee of those goods in its possession. As soon as everything has been done to make the goods ready for shipment, the carrier becomes liable as an extraordinary bailee.

At other times the goods are delivered but the shipper asks that shipment be delayed a specified time or until further instructions. During this time the carrier is an ordinary bailee and is liable only for loss due to ordinary negligence.

(2) TERMINATION OF THE CARRIER'S LIABILITY AS A CARRIER. After the goods arrive at their destination, three separate rules prevail. The Massachusetts Rule holds that the carrier's role of insurer ceases as soon as the goods are unloaded and placed in the freight warehouse. The New Hampshire Rule, which is followed in most states, holds that the carrier's role of insurer continues until the shipper or the consignee has had a reasonable time to remove the goods. For interstate commerce the Federal Rule holds that the consignee has a reasonable time after notice of arrival has been received. The Federal Rule, therefore, holds the carrier liable as an insurer for a slightly longer time than the New Hampshire Rule, and the latter rule in turn holds the carrier liable as an insurer slightly longer than the Massachusetts Rule.

Initial and Connecting Carriers. Under the federal laws the initial carrier is charged with liability for the loss or damage even though it occurs on a connecting line.

The initial carrier may then compel the connecting carrier to reimburse it. Most of the states follow this same rule for intrastate commerce, although in a few states the liability of the initial carrier ends as soon as the goods are delivered to the connecting carrier.

Bill of Lading. A *bill of lading* is a document of title and is evidence of the contract between the shipper and the carrier. Title to the goods described in the bill of lading may be passed by transferring the bill of lading to the purchaser. Since the bill of lading names the consignee, the carrier should deliver the goods to him only, or to one whom he has designated as the proper person to receive the goods.

There are two types of bills of lading:

1. Straight bills of lading
2. Order bills of lading

(1) STRAIGHT BILLS OF LADING. Under this type of bill of lading the consignee alone is designated as the one to whom the goods are to be delivered. The consignee may transfer his rights to another, but as a rule the third party obtains no better title than the shipper or the consignee had. He may under certain circumstances get larger rights than the consignee. If the bill of lading contains a recital as to the contents, quantity, or weight of the goods, the carrier is bound to a bona fide transferee as to the accuracy of these descriptions unless the bill of lading itself indicates that the contents of packages are unknown to the carrier.

- Davis crated 100 dozen candy bars and shipped them to Looney. The bill of lading stated the contents to be 100 dozen candy bars, but stated that this was based on the statement of the shipper. Looney transferred the bill of lading to Lester who discovered that the crate contained only 80 dozen. The railroad was not liable to Lester, the transferee, however, because he had notice from the bill of lading that the actual count was unknown to the carrier.

(2) ORDER BILLS OF LADING. Under the common law a bill of lading is not negotiable. Under the Uniform Bills of Lading Act and the Federal Bills of Lading Act, goods may be shipped to a designated consignee or his order, or merely "to the bearer" of the bill of lading. The bill of lading must be presented before the carrier can safely deliver the goods. If the goods are delivered to the named consignee and later a bona fide innocent purchaser of the bill of lading demands the goods, the carrier is liable to the holder of the bill of lading.

• The Clark Milling Company shipped a carload of flour to Rose and Rogers in South Carolina. The order bill of lading was attached to a draft and sent to a bank at the point of destination. The consignee, without paying the draft or obtaining the bill of lading, was permitted to receive the flour. The carrier was held liable for delivery of the flour without demanding that the consignee present the bill of lading. (N. & W. Ry. Co. vs. Aylor, 153 Va. 575)

Liability of Common Carrier of Persons. The carriers of passengers are not insurers of the passengers' safety, but they are required to exercise the highest degree of care possible, consistent with practical operation. The liability of the carrier begins as soon as the passenger enters the station or waiting platform and does not end until he has left the station at the end of the journey. The degree of care required is only ordinary care while the passenger is in the station. After the passenger boards the bus, train, plane, or other vehicle, the utmost care is required.

Rights of Common Carriers of Persons. Common carriers of persons have the right to prescribe the place and time of the payment of fares, usually before boarding the train, bus, or other vehicle. They also have the right to prescribe certain rules of conduct while transporting passengers so long as these are reasonable and for the convenience of the other passengers. They may stop the vehicle and remove any passenger who refuses to pay his fare or whose conduct is offensive to the other passengers. They also have the right to reserve certain coaches or seats for special classes of passengers, usually those who have paid extra charges for reserved seats.

• Riley boarded a train in Buffalo to go to Chicago. When the conductor demanded a ticket, Riley claimed that he had lost his. The conductor demanded that Riley pay his fare again and he refused. Riley was forcibly removed from the train at the next station. He later found his ticket. He sued the railroad for forcibly removing him and for damages due to delay in reaching his destination. The court held that since no more force than necessary was used, the railroad was not liable for damages. It further held that Riley's proper remedy was to have paid his fare a second time and then later he could have demanded a refund.

Duties of Common Carriers of Persons. A carrier's duty to its passengers consists of two broad groups:

1. Duty to provide reasonable accommodations and services

2. Duty to provide reasonable protection to its passengers

(1) Duty to Provide Reasonable Accommodations and Services. When a traveler purchases a ticket from a common carrier, a contract is formed between the carrier and the passenger. This contract entitles the passenger to a seat. If there is no seat available, he may get off at the next station and demand a refund of his fare. He may also sue for damages for breach of contract. The carrier must also notify the passenger of the arrival of the train, bus, or airplane at his destination and stop long enough to permit the passenger to disembark. A personal notice is not necessary, only a general announcement. If this is not done and a passenger is carried beyond his destination, he may sue for any damages suffered.

(2) DUTY TO PROVIDE REASONABLE PROTECTION TO ITS PASSENGERS. Common carriers of passengers are not insurers of the absolute safety of passengers, but must exercise extraordinary care to protect them. Any injury to the passenger by an employee or fellow passenger subjects the carrier to liability for damages, provided the passenger is without blame. The vehicle must stop at a safe place for alighting and passengers must be assisted when necessary for alighting. Transportation may be denied to invalids unless someone accompanies them; but if they are accepted, reasonable assistance must be rendered to them.

• Belcher was traveling by train to Sedalia, Missouri. The conductor called out the station, but because Belcher was deaf, he did not hear the station announcement. As a result, he was carried on to Kansas City. The carrier was not liable for damages because it did all that the law requires. The carrier cannot guarantee that every passenger will hear the announcement.

Definition of Baggage. *Baggage* consists of those articles necessary for personal convenience while traveling. Articles carried by travelers on similar missions and destinations constitute the test rather than what passengers in general carry. For example, fishing paraphernalia is baggage for a man on a fishing trip, but not for the ordinary traveler. Also, a lady's watch is not baggage when carried in a traveling bag by a man. Any article carried for the accommodation of one who is not a passenger is not baggage. Samples carried by salesmen are not baggage. The carrier is, of course, liable for the loss of these articles the same as for baggage, but the passenger is not entitled to have them transported without extra charge. They are freight, not baggage.

Liability for Baggage. The liability of a common carrier for baggage is the same as that of a common carrier of goods. The common carrier is an insurer of the baggage with the five exceptions noted in the section on common carriers of goods. It is necessary to distinguish between baggage retained in the possession of the traveler and that carried in the baggage car or other space. In the first type, the carrier must exercise reasonable care.

A reasonable amount of baggage may be carried as a part of the cost of the passenger's fare. The carrier may charge extra for an amount in excess of a reasonable value, usually $100.

Questions

1. What law governs private carriers?

2. Is a common carrier liable for the loss or damage to goods being transported regardless of negligence?

3. Must a common carrier serve all who apply?

4. (a) Name some acts which the law tends to call acts of God.

(b) Is there a difference between a loss caused by an act of God when the act is remote rather than the direct cause?

5. What acts of the shipper will relieve a common carrier for liability for loss?

6. When does the common carrier's liability begin?

7. When goods must be transported by two or more carriers before reaching their destination, which carrier is liable?

8. (a) What is a bill of lading?

(b) What is the difference between a straight bill of lading and an order bill of lading?

9. To what extent are common carriers responsible for the safety of passengers?

10. What is the liability of a common carrier for baggage carried by a passenger?

Case Problems

1. The Baxter Machine Company shipped an expensive machine to the Buford Mining Company in Denver by a straight bill of lading. An agent of the Buford Mining Company called at the office of the Stern Engineering Corporation and offered to sell them the machinery, stating that their plans had been altered and they would have to return it. The Stern Corporation purchased the machinery and received the bill of lading by indorsement. Three days later they inquired of the railroad if the machinery had arrived and were told that it had already been delivered to the consignee, the Buford Mining Company. It developed that this latter company, after it got possession of the machinery, had sold and delivered it to the Rocky Mountain Mining Company. The Stern Engineering Corporation sued the railroad for the value of the machinery, alleging it had delivered the machinery to the wrong party. Was the railroad liable?

2. Hardin delivered 42 bales of cotton to the Georgia Railroad with instructions to hold them until the following day when an additional 58 bales would be delivered, making a total shipment of 100 bales. The 42 bales were stacked on the loading platform. That night a fire destroyed the 42 bales. There was no negligence on the part of the railroad in starting the fire or in preventing its spread. Hardin sued the railroad for the value of the cotton, alleging that it was liable as a common carrier. Was Hardin entitled to collect?

3. Thomas owned a large truck in which he hauled fresh vegetables for a produce exchange from Florida to Atlanta. On the return trip he often carried freight at rates considerably below that charged by the railroad. On one of these return trips, the Glenn Jewelry Company shipped two cases of jewelry valued at $2,500 to its branch store in Orlando. The jewelry was stolen through no fault of Thomas. The Glenn Jewelry Company sued Thomas as a common carrier for the value of the jewelry. Was he liable?

4. A jewelry salesman was traveling on a train to a college town to sell class rings, fraternity and sorority pins, and other types of jewelry to college students. His bag containing $1,000 worth of samples was stolen. The baggage was given to the porter and he stacked it with the baggage belonging to the other passengers. Was the carrier liable for its loss assuming no extra charge was paid for the baggage?

5. The Devon Seed Company ordered a carload of seed from the Newberry Seed Corporation. When the seed arrived, the car was placed on a siding where the consignee by agreement was to unload it in his truck and at his expense. This car was placed on the siding at 10 a.m., but the Devon Seed Company was not notified that day. During the night a riot occurred, and the seed was thrown out of the car and destroyed by a heavy rain. Loss by riot had not been excluded in the bill of lading. Was the carrier liable for this loss under the New Hampshire rule, the Massachusetts rule, the Federal rule?

6. Roberts purchased a ticket for a trip to Denver. He boarded the train and took a seat. When the conductor called for his ticket he could not locate it. The conductor required him to pay his fare in cash and Roberts refused. At the next station Roberts was ordered to leave the train but he refused to do so. The train policeman was called and Roberts was forceably removed. As a result he was twenty-four hours late in keeping an appointment, resulting in a loss of $20,000. He sued the railroad for the loss plus additional damages for his injured pride in being forceably removed from the train. Was the carrier liable?

7. The Holland Brothers were large producers of fruits and vegetables. Their farm adjoined the railroad tracks. They built a loading platform beside the tracks and would place their packaged fruits and vegetables on this platform. The railroad had permitted them to do this for several years. The train would stop and the railroad's employees would load the freight. When the train got into town about twenty miles away, the freight would be weighed and a bill of lading made out. The Holland Brothers loaded the platform with freight and left it for the railroad to pick up. Because of a strike, the train did not run that day and a hard freeze destroyed all the fruit and vegetables. The railroad refused to compensate the Holland Brothers for the loss, claiming there had been no delivery and receipt of the freight. Was this contention correct?

8. The Associated Farmers Warehouse Corporation shipped a load of wheat by river boat to St. Louis. The boat struck a tree trunk that had been washed into the river channel by a recent flood. The boat sank, and all the wheat was destroyed. Was the carrier liable for this loss?

Chapter 18

Hotelkeepers as Bailees

Exceptional Bailments. When a guest registers at a hotel, the hotelkeeper enters into a contract of bailment with him with respect to the guest's luggage and other personal property. From early times, however, the innkeeper has been held to an extraordinary degree of liability for the safety of the personal property of his guest, the traveler, or the transient. Since the hotelkeeper's occupation is that of a public calling, the law exacts from him a higher degree of care than it does from a bailee in an ordinary mutual-benefit bailment. Like those of carriers described in the preceding chapter, the contracts of hotelkeepers are specially designated exceptional bailments. For this reason a hotelkeeper's liability for the safety of a guest's property cannot be determined from the law of bailments in general.

Who Is a Hotelkeeper? Under the old common law an innkeeper was one who provided a traveler with lodging, food, drink, and a stable for the traveler's horses. If any one of these services was not supplied, one was not an innkeeper, and thus not held to strict accountability for the care and safety of the guest. This narrow common law rule has been so modified that today "innkeeper" is synonymous with "hotelkeeper." Today a *hotelkeeper* is one who supplies lodging to transients. He may supply food or entertainment, but lodging to the transients is the cardinal test.

Those Who Are Not Hotelkeepers. Because of the narrow dividing line between a hotelkeeper and one who keeps a boardinghouse, tourist home, or hotel apartment, it is important to know who is not a hotelkeeper. If one provides rooms only or room and board to permanent guests, but does not hold himself out as able and willing to accommodate transients, he is not a hotelkeeper, and thus is not held to the strict accountability of the common law. A tourist home is not an inn if the owner does not hold himself out as willing to accommodate all who apply so long as he has room. Some states have held that when a tourist home, by roadside advertising, attempts to attract transients, it is an inn. If the service is provided only seasonally or at infrequent intervals, a tourist home is not an inn. Modern motels, auto courts, and tourist cabin establishments are usually classed as inns. Apartment hotels that cater only to permanent residents are not inns, although a hotel may cater to both permanent guests and transients. In that event, it is an inn.

Duties and Liabilities of a Hotelkeeper. The duties and liabilities of a hotelkeeper are:

1. Duty to serve all who apply
2. Duty to protect a guest's person
3. Duty to care for the guest's property

(1) DUTY TO SERVE ALL WHO APPLY. The basic test of a hotelkeeper is that he holds himself out as willing to serve all who apply without discrimination. He is liable for damages to the person rejected. He may turn people away such as a drunken person who would be highly offensive to his other guests. If his rooms are all filled, he may turn all other applicants away without liability for damages.

(2) DUTY TO PROTECT A GUEST'S PERSON. A hotelkeeper is not liable as an insurer of a guest's safety. He must use ordinary care for the safety of those who are on his premises as guests, but not for a mere visitor or a patron of the newsstand or lunch room. He must provide fire escapes and also have conspicuous notices indi-

cating the direction of the fire escapes. He is not liable for an injury due to a fire if he was in no way negligent in starting the fire. If he is negligent in preventing the spread of the fire or in directing the guests to fire escapes, he is liable.

(3) Duty to Care for the Guest's Property. The hotelkeeper is an insurer of the guest's property except for losses occurring from:

(a) An act of God
(b) Act of public enemy
(c) Negligence or fault of the guest
(d) The inherent nature of the property itself
(e) Accidental fire, provided neither the hotelkeeper nor his servants were negligent

Under the common law the innkeeper was an insurer of the guest's property unless the loss or damage was due to one of the five acts listed above. By statute in every state this liability has been modified to some extent.

The hotelkeeper may provide a safe where a guest may deposit his valuable articles. If the guest fails to do this, the hotelkeeper is released from liability as an insurer. Notice to this effect must be posted either in the room or at the registration desk. Also, most statutes limit a hotel's liability to a designated sum varying from $500 in New York to $250 in Illinois. Other states permit the hotelkeeper to limit his liability by contract with the guest. This is usually done by posting a notice.

Who Are Guests? Before a hotelkeeper can be held liable for either injury to the person or for loss of property, the injured party must be a guest. To be a *guest* one must be a transient, not a permanent resident. Also, he must have been received as a guest. If one enters the hotel to attend a ball or other social function or to visit a guest, he himself is not a guest. If one enters a hotel with the intention of becoming a guest, but before registering he changes his mind, he is not a guest.

• Holoban entered a hotel and gave his baggage to the porter. He intended to register, but before he did so, he changed his mind. In the meantime, his baggage was lost. The hotel was in no way negligent. The hotel was not liable since Holoban had not become a guest.

• Day, while walking up the marble steps to register at a hotel, slipped and was seriously injured. The steps were slippery due to the gross negligence of the hotel. It was held that Day became a guest as soon as he entered the premises of the hotel for that purpose. The hotel was liable for ordinary care. Since the hotel was grossly negligent, it was liable to Day.

Lien of the Hotelkeeper. A hotelkeeper has a lien on the baggage of his guests for the value of the services rendered. This lien extends also to all wearing apparel not actually being worn, such as an overcoat, a fur coat, or an extra suit. Since the hotelkeeper is an insurer of all goods brought to the hotel by the guest, the lien extends to all these goods even if they do not belong to the guest. The only exception to this rule is that the lien does not attach to the property of another, if the proprietor or manager of the hotel knows of the true ownership. Some states have slightly modified by statute these strict common law rules; but for the most part, they are still in effect.

The lien of the hotelkeeper attaches only to baggage. It does not apply to an automobile, for example. If the hotel provides storage facilities for the guest's car, the car cannot be held if the guest fails to pay his hotel bill. If there is a separate charge for car storage, this charge (but not the room charge) must be paid before the car can be removed.

If the charges are not paid within a reasonable time, the hotelkeeper may sell the baggage or other goods and pay the charges. Any residue must be returned to the guest.

Boardinghouse Keepers. The laws of a hotelkeeper do not apply to boardinghouse keepers. The boardinghouse keeper has no lien under the common law, but most states have given this right to boardinghouses by statute. The chief difference in the common law relating to a hotelkeeper and a boardinghouse keeper is that the latter need take only ordinary care of the property of the boarder or lodger. He is in no way an insurer. Also, he does not have to accept all who apply. He may choose his clients using whatever test of discrimination he wishes.

At common law the boardinghouse keeper is not given a lien on the goods of a boarder as security for an unpaid account; in some states, however, he is given such a lien by statute. Some of these state laws make it a criminal offense for a boarder owing a board bill to leave his boardinghouse secretly. Under the federal Constitution no one can be imprisoned for a debt. These state laws comply with this constitutional restriction by making the crime consist of "leaving without paying the board bill," not just a failure to pay it.

● River, a college student, owed a boarding bill in a state where it was a criminal offense to leave without paying the bill. At night his fellow students lowered him and his baggage from a second-story window. He departed to another state. The boardinghouse keeper had him extradited and tried for running away without paying a board bill.

Questions

1. How does the law of mutual-benefit bailment apply to a hotelkeeper for the guest's baggage and personal property?

2. Who is a hotelkeeper?

3. (a) Are apartment hotels that cater only to permanent tenants hotelkeepers?

(b) May a hotelkeeper refuse to accept anyone who applies?

4. Is the hotelkeeper liable for the safety of a patron of a newsstand in the hotel lobby?

5. Who is liable for the injury to a guest by fire if the hotel was in no way negligent?

6. If a guest has $4,000 worth of jewelry and expensive clothes while staying at a hotel and the property is stolen due to no fault of the hotel, who is liable for the loss?

7. When does one become a guest of the hotel?

8. If a guest's baggage is held by the hotel as a lien for the payment of the hotel charges, what disposition may be made of the property?

9. What is the chief difference in the law relating to a hotelkeeper and a boardinghouse keeper?

10. (a) Under the common law can a boardinghouse keeper hold a roomer's baggage and clothes for his unpaid room rent? (b) May one be imprisoned for leaving without paying his board bill at a boardinghouse?

Case Problems

1. Miss Seagraves, an actress, spent some time at an exclusive hotel in Florida. When she got ready to leave, she had an unpaid hotel bill of several hundred dollars. She was unable to pay the bill, and the hotel notified her that she could not remove her baggage from the room. Although the temperature outside was 96, she put on her expensive mink coat, adorned herself with all her expensive jewelry, and then attempted to leave without her baggage. The hotel contended it was entitled to a lien on her coat and her excess jewelry. Was its contention correct?

2. Arnold registered as a guest at the Colonial Hotel. After his baggage was placed in his room, he left the hotel but failed to lock the door to his room. During his absence, his baggage was stolen. Must the hotel pay for the baggage?

3. Martin was a guest in the Savoy Hotel. He deposited his overcoat, baggage, and a few other items with a check girl and received a check stating in bold letters that the hotel would not be liable for any loss of the items checked. The items were delivered by the check girl to the wrong guest, and Martin was never able to locate them. The hotel contended its liability had been limited by contract when the items were checked. Was this contention correct?

4. The Greenway Auto Court had signs along the highway soliciting all travelers to become guests. John L. Hewess, a labor leader, applied for accommodations. Because the owner of the auto court was violently opposed to unions, he refused Hewess accommodations although he had vacant rooms. Hewess sued for damages. Was the Greenway Auto Court liable?

5. The law in Georgia requires all hotels to provide devices to prevent a fire from spreading from one floor to another. A fire of undetermined origin started on the fifth floor of the Fenwick Hotel. Because of open stairways the fire spread quickly to the upper floors, and many guests lost their lives on the fifth, sixth, and seventh floors.

(a) If the hotel was not negligent in starting the fire, was it liable for the loss of life on the fifth floor?

(b) Was it liable for the loss of life on the sixth and the seventh floors?

6. Hawkins registered at a hotel and was assigned a room. During the night the hotel caught fire; neither the hotel nor its employees were negligent. When Hawkins was awakened, he could not leave by the stairway, so he sought the fire escape. Since there were no signs directing him to the fire escape, he could not find it. Seeing no other way out, he jumped from a second-floor window and was injured. All his baggage was destroyed. Hawkins brought suit against the hotel to collect for the value of his baggage and compensation for his injuries. Discuss the rights and obligations of the parties.

7. Rice, a traveling salesman, registered at the Unique Tavern and was assigned a room. Desiring to keep an appointment with a customer before going to his room, Rice had the clerk send his suitcase to his room, where it was stolen through no fault of Rice. What was the liability of the Unique Tavern for the loss of the suitcase?

8. Porter was a guest at the City Hotel. The hotel provided a safe for the deposit of jewels and other valuable articles. Proper notice of this service was posted on the door, according to the provisions of the law. Porter ignored this notice and retained possession of his valuables. They were stolen while he was a guest. He brought a suit for damages.

(a) Was the posting of the notice on the door sufficient, or must the hotelkeeper inform the guest of the protection provided?

(b) In your judgment was the hotelkeeper liable in this case?

Cases for Review of Part IV

1. Edgar Perera delivered about $15,000 worth of jewelry to the Panama-Pacific International Exposition Company. The delivery was made on consignment with the understanding the Exposition Company would display the jewelry and also sell it if possible. Ownership remained with Perera; the Exposition Company had possession only for the purpose of sale on commission. The jewelry was displayed at the Panama-Pacific Exposition along with other types of products. The jewelry was stolen by unknown parties. The Exposition Company exercised the usual type of care for similar exhibits. Perera brought suit to collect the value of the jewelry. (Perera vs. Panama-Pacific International Exposition Company, 179 Calif. 63) Was the company liable?

2. The Wallblom Furniture and Carpet Company operated a retail furniture store and furniture storage facilities. The receipts for storage showed the street address of the storage business. They later moved their storage business to a new location and transferred all the contents of the old building to the new building. No notice of this transfer was given to the customers. The new building with all its contents was destroyed by fire. There was no insurance to cover the furniture stored, and it was not customary for storage firms to carry such insurance. W. S. McCurdy, one of the customers who had delivered furniture for storage to the old address, brought suit to recover the value of his furniture. (McCurdy vs. Wallblom Furniture and Carpet Company, 94 Minn. 326) Was he entitled to collect?

3. Stella Gottlieb was a designer of wallpaper. She designed patterns and submitted these original creations to prospective manufacturers of wallpaper. Her designs were her only stock in trade. She submitted a number of designs to the agents of the Wallace Wall Paper Company with the express understanding that they were to examine the designs and return them to her. The designs were delivered in person to the president and the vice-president of the corporation at their room in the Breslin Hotel. During the day the designs disappeared and could not be found. No copies of the designs were kept, so Gottlieb sued the Wallace Wall Paper Company for their value. (Gottlieb vs. Wallace Wall Paper Company, 140 N. Y. S. 1032) Was she entitled to damages?

4. Nixon owned a warehouse used for storing wheat for his customers. Wheat of like grade was deposited in bins, and the owner was given a warehouse receipt showing the number of bushels and grade of wheat left with Nixon. It was the custom to return to the wheat owner the correct number of bushels of wheat of like grade that was left in the warehouse, but no promise was made to return exactly the same wheat. Rice deposited wheat with Nixon, and soon thereafter the warehouse and all the wheat was destroyed. Rice demanded payment from Nixon for the value of the wheat contending there was a sale, not a bailment. (Rice vs. Nixon, 97 Ind. 97) Do you agree?

5. The Standish Hotel served both transient and permanent roomers. McIntosh rented a room at a fixed rent by the month and occupied the room as a lodger rather than a transient. He was a resident of Portland where the hotel was located. While McIntosh was away for a few days, but still retaining possession of his room, a burglar entered the room and stole clothes and other articles valued in excess of $100. There was no evidence that the hotel was negligent in any way. McIntosh brought suit against the hotel for the value of the stolen property. (McIntosh vs. Schops, 92 Oregon 307) Was he entitled to recover?

6. Holohan, a traveling salesman, turned his valises over to the porter of the Tulane Hotel with the intention of going there, but he changed his mind and did not become a guest of the hotel. When Holohan went to the Tulane Hotel to claim his valises, only one of them could be found. Holohan brought a suit to recover the value of the lost baggage. (112 Tenn. 214) Could Holohan recover as a guest?

7. Burrowes desired to ship his tent show from Loup City, Nebraska, to Ashton, Nebraska. He had the Chicago, Burlington, and Quincy Railroad place an empty car on the railroad siding where he could load the tents. On Sunday afternoon the car was placed on the siding and some of the goods were placed in it that afternoon. During the night the car and its contents were totally destroyed by fire. No bill of lading had been made out, nor were the railroad officials in any way negligent in causing the fire or preventing its spread. Burrowes brought suit against the Chicago, Burlington, and Quincy Railroad to recover the value of the lost merchandise. (Borrowes vs. Chicago, Burlington, and Quincy Railroad, 85 Nebr. 497) Was he entitled to recover?

8. The Atlantic Coast Line Railroad agreed to supply space on its platform to Singleton for the purpose of storing cotton pending instructions to ship. The contract was in the form of a lease since the cotton was to remain on the platform more for storage than for transportation. The lease provided that the Atlantic Coast Line Railroad was not to be liable as a shipper while the cotton was stored on the platform, and exempted the railroad for all loss even though caused by the negligence of the railroad. In accordance with this lease Singleton placed a quantity of cotton and hay on the platform and it was destroyed by fire due to the negligence of the employees of the railroad. Singleton brought suit to recover under the railroad's liability as a common carrier. (Singleton vs. Atlantic Coast Line Railroad Company, 203 N. C. 462) Was he entitled to recover?

9. Mrs. Julia Hasbrouck obtained passage on the New York Central and Hudson Railroad to make a trip to Natick, Massachusetts, to visit her daughter, a college student in that city. In her baggage were four rings valued at about $1,500. Mrs. Hasbrouck was socially prominent and was in the habit of wearing expensive jewelry at all social functions. The baggage was checked with the railroad and the usual excess value was declared and the charges paid. When she arrived at her destination her baggage was returned to her, but the jewelry was missing. The railroad refused to pay her claim contending that so much jewelry, four diamond rings, was not properly baggage, and therefore the railroad was not liable for its loss. (Hasbrouck vs. New York Central and Hudson Railroad Company, 202 N. Y. 363) Was the railroad liable for the loss?

10. Swain, a traveling salesman, entered the Connor Hotel intending to stay all night. He placed his suitcase on a bench provided for that purpose. Because there were no vacant rooms, Swain did not register at that time. Later in the day, however, he registered and was assigned a room. In the meantime his suitcase had been lost. (224 S. W. 123) Was the hotel liable for the loss of the suitcase?

Part V
NEGOTIABLE INSTRUMENTS

Chapter 19

Nature of Negotiable Instruments

Definition of a Negotiable Instrument. A *negotiable instrument* is a written instrument drawn in a special form, which can be transferred from person to person as a substitute for money or as an instrument of credit. Such an instrument must meet certain definite requirements in regard to form and the manner in which it is transferred. Since a negotiable instrument is not money, a person is not required by law to accept one in payment of a debt due him unless he wishes to do so.

History and Development. In the days of sea pirates and land robbers the shipment of money in settlement of debts between traders was a risky business. The need for instruments of credit that would permit the settlement of claims between distant cities without the transfer of money has existed as long as trade has existed.

There were references to bills of exchange or instruments of credit as early as 50 B.C. Their widespread usage, however, began about 1200 A.D. At first these credit instruments were used only in international trade, but they gradually became common in domestic trade.

Prior to about 1400 A.D. all disputes between merchants were settled on the spot by special courts set up by the merchants. The decisions of these courts became known as the *law merchant*. Later the common law courts of England took over the adjudication of all disputes including those between merchants, but these common law courts retained most of the customs developed by the merchants and incorporated the law merchant into the common law. Most, but by no means all, of the law merchant dealt with bills of exchange or credit instruments. The colonists brought these laws to America. After the Revolution each state developed the common law dealing with credit instruments in its own way so that by 1890 much confusion existed. In 1895 a commission was appointed by the American Bar Association and the American Bankers Association to draw up a Uniform Negotiable Instrument Law. The commission in 1896 proposed a Uniform Act. This act has since been adopted in all the states.

Transfer of Negotiable Instruments. *Negotiation* is the act of transferring a negotiable instrument, such as a draft, a check, or a promissory note, to another party in such a manner that the instrument is payable to that party. The simplest way for a person who owns a negotiable instrument to negotiate it is to write his name on the back of the instrument and deliver it to the other party. When a person writes his name on the back of a negotiable instrument before he delivers it to someone else, he is said to *indorse* the instrument.

If a negotiable instrument is payable to the "order" of some specified party, that person must indorse the instrument when he transfers it to someone else. If a negotiable instrument is payable to "bearer" (the person who holds the instrument) rather than to the order of a specified person, the holder may transfer it merely by delivery to another person.

When a negotiable instrument is transferred to one or more parties, these parties may acquire rights that are superior to those of the original owner. Parties who acquire rights superior to those of the original owner are known as holders in due course. It is mainly this feature of the transfer of superior rights that gives negotiable contracts a special classification all their own.

The law has clothed negotiable instruments with special advantages as a means to promote and to encourage commerce. How this is done will be more evident as the subject is developed.

Classification of Negotiable Instruments. The basic negotiable instruments may be classified as follows:

1. Bills of exchange
2. Promissory notes

Inasmuch as these negotiable instruments are discussed in detail in succeeding chapters, a definition of each type will suffice at this time.

(1) BILLS OF EXCHANGE. A *bill of exchange* is "an unconditional order in writing addressed by one person to another, signed by the person giving it, requiring the person to whom it is addressed to pay on demand, or at a fixed or determinable future time, a sum certain in money to order or to bearer." The three main divisions of bills of exchange are drafts, trade acceptances, and checks.

(2) PROMISSORY NOTES. A *promissory note* is "an unconditional promise in writing made by one person to another, signed by the maker, engaging to pay on demand, or at a fixed or determinable future time, a sum certain in money to order or to bearer."

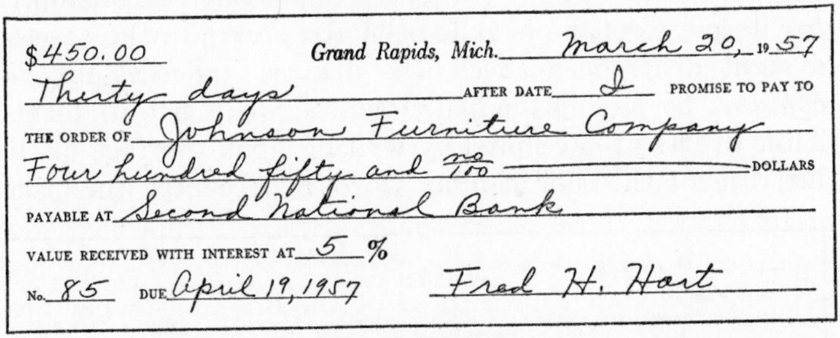
$450.00 Grand Rapids, Mich. March 20, 1957
Thirty days AFTER DATE I PROMISE TO PAY TO
THE ORDER OF Johnson Furniture Company
Four hundred fifty and no/100 DOLLARS
PAYABLE AT Second National Bank
VALUE RECEIVED WITH INTEREST AT 5 %
No. 85 DUE April 19, 1957 Fred H. Hart

Promissory Note

There are commercial instruments other than bills of exchange and promissory notes which are usually negotiable. Bonds and certificates of deposit, for example, are negotiable in form under certain circumstances. Whether or not they are negotiable depends upon their wording.

Parties to Negotiable Contracts. Each party to a negotiable instrument is designated by a certain term depending upon the type of instrument. Some of these terms are common to all types of negotiable instruments, while others are restricted to one type only. The same individual may be known by one term at one stage and may be designated by another term at a later stage through which the instrument passes before it is collected. These terms are payee, drawer, drawee, acceptor, maker, bearer, holder, indorser, and indorsee.

PAYEE. The party to whom any negotiable instrument is made payable is called the *payee.*

DRAWER. The person who executes any bill of exchange, such as a draft, a trade acceptance, or a check, is called the *drawer.*

DRAWEE. The person who is ordered to pay a bill of exchange is called the *drawee.*

ACCEPTOR. When the drawee accepts a bill of exchange, that is, indicates his willingness to assume responsibility for its payment, he is called the *acceptor.* In the case of a sight draft or a check, the drawee indicates his *acceptance* by paying the instrument according to its terms. Time drafts are accepted by writing upon the face of the instrument these or similar words: "Accepted this 10th

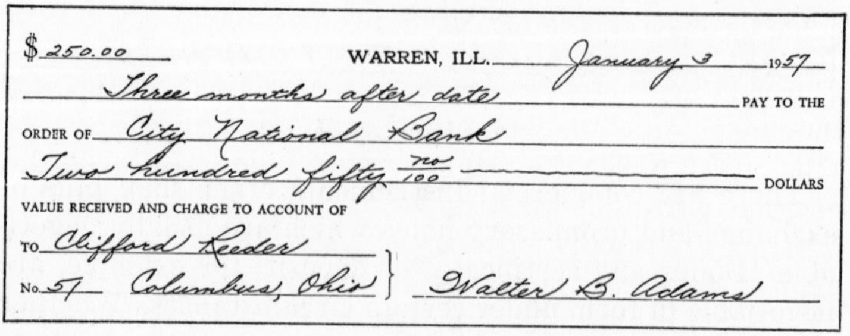
$250.00 WARREN, ILL. January 3 1957
Three months after date PAY TO THE
ORDER OF City National Bank
Two hundred fifty no/100 DOLLARS
VALUE RECEIVED AND CHARGE TO ACCOUNT OF
TO Clifford Reeder
No. 57 Columbus, Ohio } Walter B. Adams

Draft

day of June, 1956. John Daws." This indicates that John Daws is willing to perform the contract according to its terms.

MAKER. The person who executes a promissory note is called the *maker*. He is the one who contracts to pay the amount due on the note. His obligation is similar to that of the acceptor of a time draft.

BEARER. Any negotiable contract may be made payable to "bearer." The payee of such an instrument is the *bearer*. If the payee is "Myself," "Cash," or another similar name, these terms are equivalent to bearer.

HOLDER. Any person who has possession of a delivered negotiable instrument is called the *holder*. The payee is the original holder.

INDORSER. When the payee of a draft, a check, or a note wishes to transfer the instrument to another party, he must indorse it. He is then called the *indorser*.

INDORSEE. A person who becomes the holder of a negotiable instrument by indorsement is called the *indorsee*. If he obtains possession of a "bearer" instrument, he is merely another holder unless he required the preceding holder to indorse it. This he can do even though the indorsement is not necessary to transfer title.

Negotiation and Assignment. In some respects negotiation and assignment are the same; in others they are different. In each case there are original parties. In a promissory note, for example, the original parties are the maker (the one who promises to pay) and the payee (the one to whom the money is to be paid). Between the original parties, both a nonnegotiable and a negotiable contract are equally enforceable. Also, the same defenses against fulfilling the terms of the contract may be set up. For example, in either case, if one party to the contract is a minor, he may set up his incapacity to contract as a defense against carrying out the agreement.

Although nonnegotiable and negotiable instruments are alike in the rights given to the original parties, they are different in the rights given to subsequent parties. When a nonnegotiable contract is transferred by assignment, the assignee receives only the rights of the assignor and no more. (See Chapter 9.) If one of the original parties to the contract has a defense that is valid against the assignor, it is also valid against the assignee. When an instrument is transferred by negotiation, however, the party who receives the instrument in good faith and for value will ordinarily have rights that are superior to the rights of the original holder. The nature of these rights and the conditions under which they are received are discussed in later chapters.

- Tate owed Danner $500 due in ninety days. Soon after this debt was incurred by Tate, he sold Danner a television set for $300 with the general understanding that a settlement of both claims would be made at the same time. Danner, before the due date, assigned his right to receive $500 from Tate to Bolton. When Bolton demanded payment from Tate, he claimed the right of offset to the amount of $300. He was allowed to do this because Bolton received by assignment no better rights than Danner had.

- Under the same facts set out above, Tate gave Danner a negotiable note for $500 due in ninety days. Danner then sold this note to Bolton, an innocent purchaser. In that event, Tate could not offset his contract to receive $300 against his contract to pay $500. Since the contract was a negotiable one and Bolton was an innocent purchaser, he, Bolton, obtained rights greater than Danner. This was not possible under assignment.

Questions

1. What is a negotiable instrument?

2. Explain what is meant by the statement that a negotiable instrument can be used as a substitute for money.

3. How is a negotiable instrument negotiated?

4. How does one indorse a negotiable instrument?

5. Who is the payee of a negotiable instrument?

6. What is the difference between the drawer and the drawee of a bill of exchange?

7. When the drawee accepts the bill of exchange, what is he called?

8. What does the maker of a promissory note contract to do?

9. Who is the indorser of a negotiable instrument? The indorsee?

10. How do assignment and negotiation differ?

Case Problems

1. (a) Name the parties to this promissory note?

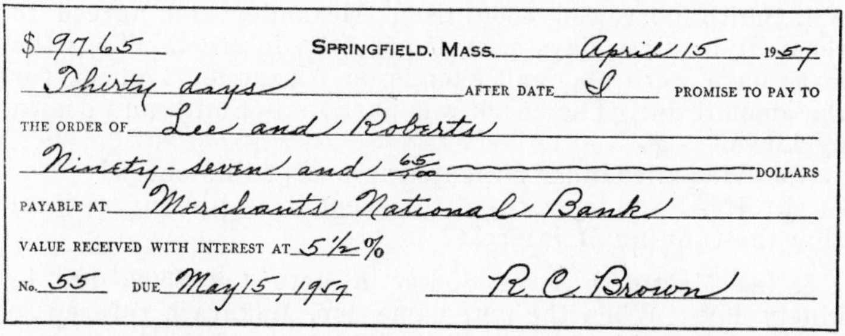

$97.65 SPRINGFIELD, MASS. April 15 1957

Thirty days AFTER DATE I PROMISE TO PAY TO

THE ORDER OF Lee and Roberts

Ninety-seven and 65/100 DOLLARS

PAYABLE AT Merchants National Bank

VALUE RECEIVED WITH INTEREST AT 5½%

No. 55 DUE May 15, 1957 R. C. Brown

(b) Assume that when this note was due, Brown refused to pay it, claiming that when he executed this note in payment of merchandise, Lee and Roberts guaranteed the merchandise to be like the sample exhibited when the order was taken. The merchandise was in no way like the sample. If Brown could prove this point, would he have to pay the note?

(c) Would your answer be different if Lee and Roberts sold the note before maturity to an innocent purchaser and this innocent purchaser demanded payment on the due date?

2. (a) Who is the payee in this trade acceptance?

(b) Identify the drawer and the drawee in this instrument?

TRADE ACCEPTANCE

No. 101 Peoria, Illinois, March 4, 19

To Brown Store Company Cleveland, Ohio

On June 2, 19 (DATE OF MATURITY) Pay to the order of Ourselves

Five hundred and no/100 Dollars, ($ 500.00)

The obligation of the acceptor hereof arises out of the purchase of goods from the drawer. The drawee may accept this bill payable at any bank, banker or trust company in the United States which he may designate.

Accepted at Cleveland *on* March 7 *19*

Payable at Pioneer Trust Company *Bank*

Brown Store Company (SIGNATURE OF ACCEPTOR)

By D. C. Brown, Prest.

By Smith, McCord & Company

By A. M. Smith, Treasurer

3. Strong of San Diego owed Lawson of Richmond, Virginia, $5,000. Bell of Richmond owed Strong $5,000. Show how by means of a draft, check, or other negotiable instrument that Strong could pay Lawson the $5,000 he owes him and collect the $5,000 Bell owes him without sending any money across the country.

4. Smith borrowed $500 from Alexander and agreed to repay it in sixty days with 6 per cent interest. When the sixty days were up, Smith tendered Alexander a check for the amount due. The check was payable to Smith and drawn by Lowe.

(a) Was Alexander obligated to accept this check?

(b) If Alexander refused to accept it, would this refusal stop the running of interest?

5. (a) Makurath gave Sooter a note for $500 due in ninety days. When the note came due, Makurath refused to pay it, claiming Sooter owed him $500 for work done. Assuming that Makurath was able to prove that Sooter owed him $500, did Makurath have to pay the note?

(b) Would your answer be different if Sooter had sold the note before maturity to an innocent purchaser and this innocent purchaser had demanded payment of Makurath?

Chapter 20

Bills of Exchange

Nature of a Bill of Exchange. A bill of exchange is commonly called a draft. It is drawn or executed by the drawer in favor of the payee, who has the drawer's authority to collect the amount indicated on the instrument. It is addressed to the drawee, who is ordered by the drawer to pay the amount of the instrument when the amount is demanded by the payee or some other party to whom the payee has transferred the instrument by indorsement. The drawee, after he has accepted the instrument, that is, after he has agreed to pay it, becomes the acceptor.

If a bill of exchange is payable in the same state in which it is drawn, it is called a *domestic bill of exchange.* If it is drawn in one state and payable either in another state or a foreign country, it is called a *foreign bill of exchange.* This distinction is important if the instrument is dishonored, as will be pointed out in Chapter 24 (page 253).

Forms of Bills of Exchange. There are two principal classes of negotiable instruments—bills of exchange and notes. This chapter deals with bills of exchange. There are several forms of bills of exchange, and employees who handle them must be able to recognize each one. The first step is to learn to recognize each of the three forms of bill of exchange:

1. Drafts
2. Trade acceptances
3. Checks

DRAFTS

Sight and Time Drafts. Any type of *draft* is a written order drawn and signed by one party (drawer), ordering another party (drawee) to pay either to the payee (who commonly is also the drawer) or to his order a definite sum of money. There are two kinds of drafts to meet the different needs of business:

1. Sight drafts
2. Time drafts

(1) SIGHT DRAFTS. A *sight draft* is a draft payable at sight or upon presentation by the payee or holder. It indicates that the amount is either due or past due and that the drawer is demanding payment at once.

$950.50 CLEVELAND, OHIO February 11, 19 57

At sight PAY TO THE

ORDER OF City National Bank, Gary, Indiana

Nine hundred fifty and 50/100 DOLLARS

VALUE RECEIVED AND CHARGE TO ACCOUNT OF

TO L. A. Britton GORDON ELECTRIC APPLIANCES

No. 167 Gary, Indiana BY B. J. Carter

Sight Draft

(2) TIME DRAFTS. A *time draft* has exactly the same form as a sight draft except that the drawee is ordered to pay the money a certain number of days after date or after sight rather than at sight. In other words, the drawer by drawing a time draft is indicating his willingness to give the drawee an additional credit period.

The payee should present the draft to the drawee for acceptance. Then when the credit period expires, that is, when the draft matures, it must be presented for payment. If the draft reads, "Sixty days after date," it matures or becomes due sixty days after the date of the draft regardless of the date it was accepted.

If the drawee is ordered to pay the draft a specified number of days after sight, it must be presented for acceptance because the due date is calculated from the date of the acceptance, not from the date of the draft. A failure to present such a time draft for acceptance may release the drawer from his liability to the payee. This is the primary reason the two forms must be identified.

Uses of Drafts. Prior to the rise of banks, drafts were used as a substitute for money when making foreign remittances. Now checks are used primarily for this purpose, sight drafts are used as instruments of collection, and time drafts are used to convert accounts receivable past due into notes receivable. At maturity the time draft in turn becomes an instrument of collection.

When drafts are used as instruments of collection, a bank is usually made the payee. When the drawee pays the draft to the bank, the bank in return remits to the drawer or holder, or else deposits the face of the draft less a collection charge to the credit of the drawer or holder.

Presentment for Acceptance. Not all presentments for acceptance are proper presentments. To be a proper presentment, these conditions must be met:

(1) TIME. The instrument must be presented for acceptance within a reasonable time. The court decides what is a reasonable time.

(2) PLACE. The instrument should be presented at the drawee's place of business. If he has no place of business, it may be presented at his home or wherever he may be found.

(3) HOUR. It must be presented for acceptance at a reasonable hour on a business day.

(4) PARTY. It must be presented to the drawee or to someone authorized either by law or by contract to accept for him.

Form of Acceptance. The usual method of accepting a bill of exchange is to write on the face of it these words:

"Accepted July 12, 1956

John Doe."

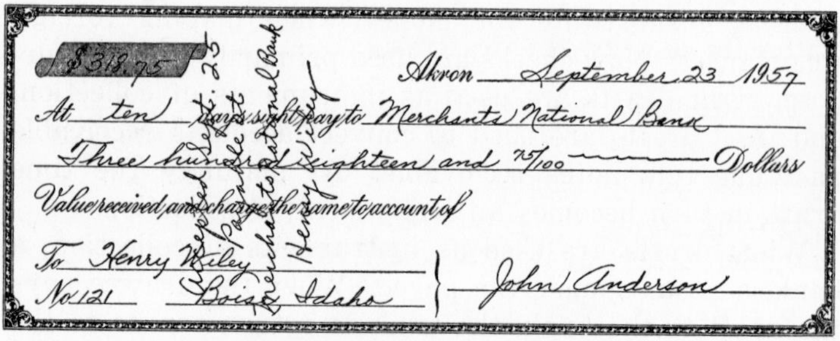
$318.75

Akron September 23 1957

At ten days sight pay to Merchants National Bank

Three hundred eighteen and 75/100 Dollars

Value received and charge the same to account of

To Henry Wiley

No. 121 Boise, Idaho

John Anderson

Accepted Sept. 23
Payable at
Merchants National Bank
Henry Wiley

An Accepted Time Draft

The drawee may use other words of acceptance, but the words used must indicate an intention to be bound by the terms of the contract. An oral acceptance is not permissible. The written acceptance may be on separate paper, but the payee has a right to treat this as dishonoring the draft if he chooses to do so. A telegram of acceptance has been held to be a valid acceptance if the payee is willing to treat it as accepted.

Presentment for Payment. All sight drafts and all accepted time drafts must be presented for payment. The law governing this type of presentment is developed more fully in Chapter 24.

Obligation of the Acceptor. When a draft is presented to a drawee for acceptance, he must either accept or return it. If it is not returned within a reasonable time, it is presumed to have been accepted. After the instrument has been accepted, the drawee is unconditionally and absolutely required to pay the amount of the instrument; he is therefore primarily liable for the obligation.

When the drawee accepts a time draft, he makes the following three admissions concerning the drawer:

(1) That the signature of the drawer is genuine.

(2) That he owes the drawer the amount shown on the draft.

(3) That the drawer has both the capacity and the authority to draw the draft.

The drawee, by accepting a draft, also admits the payee's capacity to indorse, but not the genuineness of the payee's indorsement.

Having made these admissions, the acceptor cannot later deny them against a holder in due course.

● O'Kelly forged Cohen's name as drawer to a draft for $3,000 payable to O'Kelly. He presented it to Smith for acceptance. O'Kelly then transferred the draft by indorsement to Berger. Later Smith learned that Cohen's signature was forged and refused to pay the draft when it became due. He could not avoid payment because he admitted the genuineness of Cohen's signature when he accepted the draft. It was then too late to raise the defense of forgery against Berger. He could proceed, of course, against O'Kelly.

TRADE ACCEPTANCES

Trade Acceptance. The *trade acceptance* is a time draft. Its use is confined to the sale of goods. It is a bill of exchange drawn by the seller on the purchaser of goods sold, and accepted by such purchaser. It is drawn at the time the goods are sold. The seller is the drawer, and the purchaser is the drawee. Both the trade acceptance and the time draft in accounting are notes receivable when accepted. The chief difference is that the trade acceptance is always given at the time the goods are sold, and the time draft may be given at the end of a credit period.

CHECKS

Checks. A *check* is a bill of exchange drawn on a bank and payable on demand. The chief legal differences between a check and a sight draft are:

(1) The death of the drawer of a check automatically revokes the authority of the bank, the drawee, to pay it.

(2) The drawer who draws a sight draft on a drawee with whom he has no funds commits no crime. It is a fraud, and in most states a crime also, to draw a check on a bank in which the drawer has no funds.

(3) If the holder of a check delays presentment for payment beyond a reasonable time, the drawer is released, provided he can prove an injury due to the delay. If the delay causes no injury, he remains liable until the Statute of Limitations has run on the check. Hence, he must keep funds in the bank for an indefinite period of time. Delay in presenting a sight draft can discharge the drawer regardless of injury.

(4) Presentment by the holder of a check for certification, that is, acceptance, discharges the drawer and all indorsers. This is not true of other bills of exchange.

(5) Acceptance (certification) of a check by the bank constitutes a warranty that the drawer has sufficient funds to pay it and that these funds are being earmarked for payment. No such warranty is given by the acceptor of a draft.

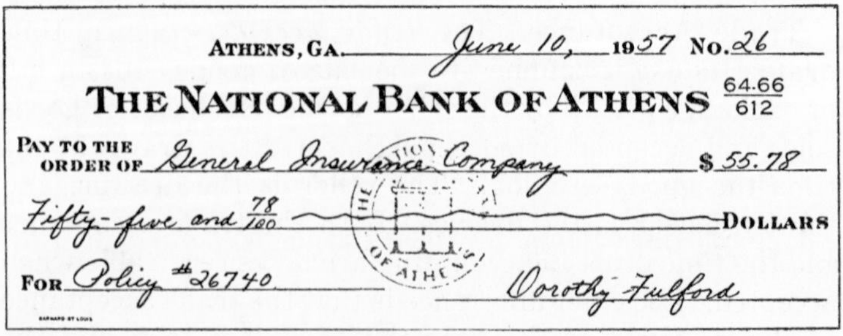

ATHENS, GA. June 10, 1957 No. 26

THE NATIONAL BANK OF ATHENS 64-66/612

PAY TO THE ORDER OF General Insurance Company $ 55.78

Fifty-five and 78/100 DOLLARS

FOR Policy #26740 Dorothy Fulford

Check

Special Kinds of Checks. There are three special types of checks, each one having a distinguishing characteristic:

1. Certified checks
2. Cashier's checks
3. Bank drafts

(1) CERTIFIED CHECKS. A *certified check* is an ordinary check which an official of the bank, the drawee, has accepted by writing across the face of the check the word "certified," or some similar word, and signed. Either the drawer or the holder may have a check certified. The effect of having it certified is to establish a primary liability on the part of the bank. The bank not only thereby guarantees the genuineness of the drawer's signature, but warrants that the drawer has sufficient funds to cover the check and that these funds have been earmarked in an amount equal to the check.

If the drawer has the check certified before delivering the check to the payee or holder, he merely adds, but does not substitute, the bank as a copromisor of payment. The drawer remains fully liable if the bank refuses or is unable to pay it. If the holder, however, has it certified, he substitutes the bank for the drawer as the one liable for its payment. The drawer is released from liability.

• Sherman Matney gave Garner a $10,000 check on a Grundy bank. Garner, not wishing to cash the check and carry the cash while traveling, had it certified. Before Garner arrived at his destination, the bank failed and its assets were insufficient to pay all its depositors. Garner was the loser since he could have received the cash at the time he had the check certified.

Had Matney been the one who had the check certified and mailed it to Garner, the drawer, Matney, would have remained liable, provided Garner was diligent in presenting it for payment.

(2) CASHIER'S CHECKS. A check that a bank draws on its own funds and that is signed by the cashier or

some other responsible official of the bank is called a *cashier's check.* Such a check may be used by a bank in paying its own obligations, or it may be used by anyone else who wishes to send a remittance in some form other than his own check.

(3) BANK DRAFTS. A *bank draft* is a check drawn by one bank on another bank. It is customary for banks to keep a portion of their funds on deposit with other banks. A bank, then, may draw a check on these funds as freely as any corporation may draw checks.

Postdated Checks. A check dated July 1, but drawn on June 21, is a *postdated check.* It is in effect a ten-day sight draft when so drawn. If the payee is willing to accept such a check, and funds are in the bank on July 1 to cover it, the transaction is a legitimate one. If a check is postdated for the purpose of defrauding someone, the drawer is guilty under the bad check laws.

Bad Checks. A check drawn on a bank in which the drawer has no funds is a *bad check.* Such act is a crime under the bad check laws in all states. If one gives a bad check in payment of an existing debt, as a rule no serious harm has been done. The debt merely remains unpaid just as if no check had been given. Some states do not make this a crime. If one induces another to part with money or other property, however, the drawer commits a fraud. Some states make the act equivalent to larceny. If the drawer can prove that there was no intent to defraud, no crime has been committed. The burden of proving this is on the drawer.

Presentment of a Check for Payment. Checks, unlike other bills of exchange, are given as immediate payment of accounts, not as an instrument of credit. For this reason, they should be presented for payment within a reasonable time after receipt. As a rule a "reasonable time" is interpreted to mean during banking hours of the next business day after it is drawn. If the payee and the bank are in different towns, then the payee should forward it for presentment not later than the next business day after it is drawn. In rural communities these times may be somewhat longer.

When the drawer gives a check, he should have funds in the bank to cover it. As far as the drawer is concerned, the payee could hold the check for months and still present it for payment. If the delay has not injured the drawer in any way, he cannot complain. If the bank should become insolvent, however, the payee's recovery would be limited to the drawer's pro rata share in the assets of the insolvent bank. This might mean that the payee could recover nothing on the check. The effect of delay is quite different with indorsers. If the holder through indorsement waits an unreasonable length of time to present the check for payment, all indorsers are discharged whether they have suffered a loss or not.

Questions

1. What is the difference between a domestic bill of exchange and a foreign bill of exchange?

2. Name three forms of bills of exchange.

3. State two types of drafts and tell the difference between them.

4. Why is a bank usually made the payee of a sight draft?

5. If an instrument is properly presented for acceptance, what conditions must be met?

6. When the drawee accepts a time draft, what admissions does he make concerning the drawer?

7. What is a trade acceptance?

8. What is the difference between a check and a sight draft?

9. (a) If the holder of a check has it certified, who is liable?

(b) If one bank has some of its funds deposited in another bank and draws a check on these funds, what is this type of check called?

10. What may be the effect of a delay in presentment for payment of a check?

Case Problems

1. Benson Brothers had an order from Holman of Cincinnati for $2,500. He wanted to purchase merchandise on sixty days' credit. Holman's credit was good, but he had the reputation of always denying that he received all the merchandise or claiming an error of some kind. Benson Brothers were willing to sell him the merchandise on credit but wanted to forestall any contention about the amount owed. Explain how they might accomplish this.

2. Dalton owed Harper and Son $3,200. When the account came due, he was unable to pay it. He drew a time draft on Turner for $3,200 and sent it to Harper and Son. Hand, the bookkeeper for Harper and Son, presented the draft to Turner for acceptance, and Turner wrote this on the draft: "The face of this draft is the correct amount I owe Harper and Son. A. Turner." Was this a proper acceptance?

3. Thomas J. Granger executed the following instrument:

> Chicago, Ill., April 10, 19—
>
> At sixty days' sight pay to the order of Charles Hudson five hundred dollars ($500) and charge the same to the account of
>
> To Albert W. Morris
> St. Louis, Mo. Thomas J. Granger

(a) Must this draft be presented for acceptance?

(b) To whom would it be presented?

(c) When should it be presented?

(d) If the drawee was out when it was presented and his secretary accepted it, would this be a proper acceptance?

(e) If the draft was presented on Sunday at the drawee's home, would this be a proper presentment?

(f) The drawee took the draft, and the next day returned it by mail with this memo attached: "I will pay this draft when it comes due. A. W. Morris." Was this a valid acceptance?

(g) If Hudson was not satisfied unless Morris wrote an acceptance on the face of the draft, what should he do?

(h) When Hudson received the draft with the acceptance written on a separate paper, he notified Granger that this was unsatisfactory and demanded that Granger pay him. Granger did this. Two months later Morris paid Hudson and Hudson accepted the money but never remitted it to Granger. Must Morris pay Granger?

4. Hartsfield owed Huff and Company $1,900. He wrote on a post card these words:

The First National Bank

Pay to the order of Huff and Company $1,900

Cordially yours,

A. W. Hartsfield.

He put a stamp on this post card and mailed it to Huff and Company. Since the owner of this company was on vacation, the bookkeeper held the post card until his employer returned about two weeks later. In the meantime The First National Bank went into receivership, and the assets of the bank were sufficient to pay only $900 on the post card. Who must bear the $1,000 loss, Hartsfield or Huff and Company?

5. Davison drew a check on June 7 payable to Lester Hardware Company. He dated the check June 12 and asked the Lester Hardware Company to hold the check until June 12 before cashing it, and he would have the money in the bank at that time to pay it. The Lester Hardware Company deposited the check on June 8, and it was returned marked "Insufficient Funds." Davison was indicted for giving a bad check. Was he guilty?

6. Holston Tobacco Company received a check by indorsement from Davis, a customer. The check was misplaced by the auditor, and it was two weeks before it was located. The check was immediately deposited but was returned since the drawer had no money in the bank. Must Davis make this check good?

7. Donaldson had a check for $800 drawn by Harvey on the Acton Bank. Since Donaldson was leaving on an extended trip and did not care to carry $700 in cash with him, he had the check certified. The bookkeeper at the bank

by error showed that Harvey's balance was $875, when in reality it was $185. Before the check was cashed, the bank auditor discovered the error and the bank refused to pay the check. Must the bank pay the full $800?

8. The following draft was sent to Milton V. Gray:

> Denver, Colo., June 20, 19—
>
> At sight pay to the order of Rocky Mountain National Bank for collection one thousand dollars ($1,000), and charge to the account of
>
> To Milton V. Gray
> Billings, Mont.
>
> R. W. Tate & Co.

(a) Who is the drawer of this draft?
(b) Who is to pay the draft?
(c) Must this draft be presented for acceptance?

9. (a) If the draft in the foregoing case read "At ten days' sight," would it require presentment for acceptance? If it were accepted on June 25, when would it be due?

(b) If this draft read "Ten days after date pay . . .," would an acceptance be necessary? If it were accepted on June 25, when would it be due?

10. Dotson drew a check on the First National Bank for $375, payable to Adkins. At the time the check was drawn, Dotson had sufficient funds in the bank to cover the check.

(a) If Adkins held the check without presenting it for payment, would this delay justify Dotson's drawing the money out of the bank at the end of four months?

(b) If the bank during the four months became insolvent and a receiver was appointed, was Dotson released from liability?

Chapter 21

Promissory Notes

Nature of a Promissory Note. Any written promise to pay money is a promissory note, but it may not be a negotiable instrument. To be negotiable, a note must contain the essential elements discussed in Chapter 22.

It is not necessary to use the word "promise," in a note but the substitute word or words must literally mean "promise." Such expressions as "I will pay" and "I guarantee to pay" have been held to constitute a "promise to pay."

The two original parties to a promissory note are the maker, the one who signs the note and promises to pay, and the payee, the one to whom the promise is made. If the payee transfers the note, he becomes an indorser and the new holder becomes the indorsee.

Liability of the Maker. The maker of a promissory note (1) expressly agrees that he will pay the note when it is due, (2) admits the existence of the payee, and (3) warrants that the payee is competent to transfer the instrument by indorsement.

- Massey made a note payable to Hess or order, and Hess indorsed the instrument to Frazier. Hess was an infant. When Massey refused to pay the note upon its due date, Frazier brought an action against him. Massey set up the defense that the infant was not competent to indorse the note to Frazier and therefore Frazier could not sue and recover on the note. The court held that Frazier could recover. Massey, by making the note payable to Hess, a minor, warranted the competency of Hess to negotiate the paper.

Types of Negotiable Notes. Any contract, the wording of which corresponds to the definition of a note set out in the early part of this chapter, is a negotiable note.

Many types of notes are known by special names that one who deals with them must know. These classes are:

1. Bonds
2. Interest coupons
3. Chattel mortgage notes
4. Collateral notes
5. Real estate mortgage notes
6. Judgment notes

(1) BONDS. A *bond* is a written contract obligation, generally issued by a corporation, a municipality, or a government, which contains a promise to pay a sum certain in money at a fixed or determinable future time to order or to bearer. It may contain, in addition to the promise to pay, certain other conditions and stipulations. If it is issued by a corporation, it is generally secured by a deed of trust on the property of the corporation.

Bonds, which are more formal than ordinary promissory notes, may be classified as (a) registered bonds, and (b) coupon bonds.

A *registered bond* is recorded under the name of the purchaser by the organization issuing it to guard against its loss or destruction. When a registered bond is sold, a record of the transfer to the new holder must be made under the name of that holder.

A *coupon bond* is so called because the interest payments are made by means of small notes or coupons attached to the bond itself. Coupon bonds are usually payable to the bearer; as a result, they can be negotiated by delivery.

(2) INTEREST COUPONS. A ten-year coupon bond with interest payable semi-annually has twenty interest coupons attached. At the end of each six months, the holder detaches one interest coupon. This coupon may be negotiated like a check or a negotiable promissory note. The coupon contains a promise to pay to the bearer a definite sum of money on demand, and thus may be classed as a special type of promissory note.

(3) Chattel Mortgage Notes. A *chattel* is personal property, as distinguished from real estate. A *chattel mortgage note* is a promissory note secured by a chattel mortgage on personal property, usually tangible personal property. The debtor keeps possession of the property. In some states he also retains title to the property; in others he keeps possession but gives title to the creditor, that is, the payee of the note. The mortgage provides that, in the event the note is paid, title to the chattel reverts to the debtor. In those states where title never rests in the creditor, in the event of default in the payment of the note, the creditor must sell the chattels and apply the proceeds to the note. If there is any residue, it goes to the debtor. If the mortgagee transfers title to the chattels to the creditor, in the event of default, he may sue to get possession of the chattels. In most states chattel mortgage notes are fully negotiable.

(4) Collateral Notes. A *collateral note* is a note secured by personal property; but unlike a chattel mortgage note, the debtor must deposit with the creditor the personal property, that is, the collateral. The collateral usually consists of stocks, bonds, or other written evidences of debt, but it may be any type of personal property. In the event of default, the creditor must comply strictly with the state law relative to selling the collateral. Any surplus remaining after all costs and the note are paid is payabe to the debtor, the maker of the note.

(5) Real Estate Mortgage Notes. A *real estate mortgage note* is in all respects the same as a chattel mortgage note except that the property given to secure the note is specific real estate rather than personal property. The owner of the real estate retains possession of it; but in the event of default, the holder of the note may sell the real estate. This subject is treated more fully in Chapter 43.

(6) JUDGMENT NOTES. In several states the law permits the use of *judgment notes,* which include a confession of judgment clause. This clause empowers the holder of the note to go into court and obtain judgment in the event the note is in default. The maker need neither be summoned into court nor receive any notice whatever. Except for this confession of judgment clause, these notes are ordinary promissory notes.

Questions

1. Must a promissory note contain the word "promise" to be enforceable?

2. Who is the payee of a note?

3. What are the obligations of the maker of a promissory note?

4. What is a bond and by whom are bonds usually issued?

5. What is the difference between a registered bond and a coupon bond?

6. How many coupons are there on a fifteen-year coupon bond if the interest is payable quarterly?

7. (a) Define a chattel.
(b) What is a chattel mortgage note?

8. (a) What is a collateral note?
(b) Of what does the collateral usually consist?

9. How does a real estate mortgage differ from a chattel mortgage note?

10. What is a judgment note?

Case Problems

1. Cook executed a judgment note for $2,000 payable to the Chicago Forge Company. Before the note was due, Cook discovered that the merchandise for which the note had been given in payment was defective. He planned to claim damages of $1,000 when payment of the note was demanded. When the note fell due, no demand was made for payment and Cook took no action. About two months later the holder, an innocent purchaser before the due date, confessed judg-

ment against Cook for the $2,000. Must Cook pay the full amount?

2. Green signed a note for $2,200, payable to the Bank of Dover. He simultaneously executed a chattel mortgage on 25 head of cattle as security for the note. When the note was due, Green was unable to pay it. The bank sold the cattle at a public sale, and the proceeds amounted to $3,800. The cost of the sale was $210, the accrued interest on the note was $120, and other necessary costs and expenses were $75. How would the $3,800 be distributed?

3. Darter owned fifty $1,000 coupon bonds, the interest payable semiannually. On one of the due dates of the interest coupons, Darter detached them intending to cash them at the bank. Before he did so, they were stolen and the thief cashed them at the Bank of Fargo. Darter sued the bank for reimbursement, claiming it should not have paid the coupons to the thief. Was Darter correct in his contention?

4. Ellett, the payee of a promissory note, was a minor. He transferred this note to Jackson, who took it for value and without knowledge of Ellett's infancy. Clancy, the maker of the note, refused to pay the holder on the ground that Ellett had no legal right to transfer it.

(a) What warranty of the maker of a note applies in this instance?

(b) Was the holder of the note legally entitled to collect? yes

5. Does the following instrument include a promise to pay?

> Thirty days after date it is agreed that either John Allen or any other holder may demand $575 from me and I assure you the demand will be granted.
>
> yes Signed: *B. A. Lert*

6. Combs was the holder of a $5,000 registered bond issued by the Realty Corporation. He failed to notify the Realty Corporation when he bought it from Alvey. Alvey received a semiannual interest check for $150, all of which had been earned after Combs bought the bond. Alvey cashed the check and kept the money. Combs sued both Alvey and the Realty Corporation jointly for the $150. Discuss the rights of all parties and give the correct verdict.

Chapter 22

Essentials of Negotiability

Requirements. The Negotiable Instruments Law sets forth seven definite requirements as to form with which an instrument must comply in order to be negotiable. If any one of these requirements is lacking, the contract is not negotiable even though it may be valid and enforceable as between the original parties to the instrument. These seven requirements are:

1. The instrument must be in writing and signed by the party executing it.
2. The instrument must contain either an order to pay or a promise to pay.
3. The order or the promise must be unconditional.
4. The instrument must provide for the payment of a sum certain in money.
5. The instrument must be payable either on demand or at a fixed or determinable future time.
6. The instrument must be payable to the order of a payee or to the bearer of the instrument.
7. The payee (unless the instrument is payable to bearer) and the drawee must be designated with reasonable certainty.

(1) A SIGNED WRITING. A negotiable instrument must be written. The law does not, however, require that the writing be in any particular form. The instrument may be written with pen and ink or with pencil; it may be typed or printed; or it may be partly printed and partly typed. If an instrument is executed with a lead pencil, it meets the legal requirements of negotiability; but a person might hesitate to accept it because of the ease with which it could be altered without detection.

There is little value to an unsigned form of any kind. On a negotiable instrument, as on other forms, a signature must be placed in order to show the intent of the promisor to be bound. The natural place for a signature is in the lower right-hand corner, but the location of the signature and its form are wholly immaterial if it is clear that a signature was intended. The signature may be written, typed, printed, or stamped. It may be a name, a symbol, a mark, or a trade name. The signature, however, must be on the instrument. It cannot be on a separate paper which is attached to the instrument.

From a legal standpoint, an odd or fictitious signature will bind the maker of a negotiable note as effectively as his real name. Here again, however, the question may later be raised as to whether or not the instrument is "complete and regular on its face" if the signature is of an odd nature. If any feature of the instrument is out of the ordinary, its legal negotiability may be nullified by prudent business customs.

The signature may be signed by another person who has been given authority to perform this act. When an agent signs for his principal or when an officer signs for his corporation, care must be taken not to make himself wholly liable or jointly liable with his principal or corporation. The two signatures below are the correct ones to use:

(a) The Acme Corporation
By *A. B. Jones*

(b) *A. B. Jones*
for The Acme
Corporation

Below are some odd or irregular signatures that are valid:

His
(a) Richard × Cooper
Mark

(b) "I, Thomas Morley," written by Morley in the body of the note, but signed on the typewriter in the usual place for the signature.

(c) "Snowwhite Cleaner," the trade name under which Glendon Sutton operated his business.

(2) An Order or a Promise to Pay. A bill of exchange, such as a draft, a trade acceptance, or a check, must contain an order to pay. A polite request or a suggestion to another to pay does not constitute an order. If the request is imperative and unequivocal, it is an order even though the word "order" is not used.

A promissory note must contain a promise to pay. The word "promise" need not be used—any equivalent words will answer the purpose—but the language used must show that a promise is intended. Thus the words "This is to certify that we are bound to pay" were held to be sufficient to constitute a promise.

(3) Unconditional. The order or the promise must be absolute and unconditional. Neither must be contingent upon any other act or event. If Baron promises to pay Noffke $500 "in sixty days, or sooner if I sell my farm," the contract is negotiable because the promise itself is unconditional. In any event he promises to pay the $500 in sixty days. The contingency pertains only to the time of payment, and that time cannot exceed sixty days. If the words "or sooner" were omitted, the promise would be conditional and the note would be nonnegotiable. It is well to emphasize here again, however, that the contract is valid even though it is nonnegotiable.

(4) A Sum Certain in Money. The instrument must call for the payment of money and money alone. It need not be American money, but it must be some national medium of exchange. It cannot be in scrip, gold bullion, bonds, or similar assets. Frequently, the instrument provides for the payment of either money or goods. If the choice lies with the holder, such a provision does not destroy its negotiability. If the option to pay in goods lies with the drawer or the maker, the contract is not

negotiable, but it may be enforced unless there is some valid defense to it.

> • Sixty days after date I promise to pay to the order of Ira Rasmussen $500 or 250 bushels of wheat at his option.
>
> Signed—*Frank Birchmore*
>
> This note is negotiable because it is at the option of the payee, Rasmussen. If the words "his option" were changed to read, "my option," the note would not be negotiable.

The sum payable must be a certain amount that is not dependent upon other funds or upon future profits.

> • In consideration for recommending Varney for a certain job, Fulton received the following instrument: ". . . we hereby agree to pay you the sum of $1,059 ninety days from date; the amount to be paid out of our profits on the 3 East 40th Street job." The court held that the statement on the note that the money was to be paid out of a particular fund destroyed its negotiability.

Not only must the contract be payable in money to be negotiable, but the amount must be certain from the wording of the instrument itself. A note for $5,000 provides that all taxes which may be levied upon a certain piece of real estate will be paid. This destroys its negotiability. The amount to be paid cannot be determined from the note itself. A provision providing for the payment of interest or exchange charges, however, does not destroy negotiability. Other terms which have been held not to destroy negotiability are provisions for cost of collection, a 10 per cent attorney's fee if placed in the hands of an attorney for collection, and installment payments.

Frequently, through error, a negotiable instrument calls for the payment of one sum in figures and a different amount in words. The amount expressed in words prevails because one is less likely to be in error in this amount. Also, if anyone should attempt to raise the amount, it would be much simpler to alter the figures than it would be the words.

(5) PAYABLE ON DEMAND OR AT A FIXED OR DETERMINABLE FUTURE TIME. An instrument meets the test of negotiability as to time if it is payable on demand—as in a demand note, or at sight—as in a sight draft, or when no time is specified—as in a check.

If the instrument provides for payment at some future time, the due date must either be fixed or so definitely stated that the due date can be determined. The date must be sure to arrive.

- Vaughn gave Marx an instrument containing the following provision: "I promise to pay Marx the sum of $450 when my son reaches the age of twenty-one." Such a condition rendered the instrument nonnegotiable because the time of payment was dependent upon a condition that might not happen. In other words, Vaughn's son might never reach the age of twenty-one.

- If Riggs promises to pay Burton $500 "sixty days after my marriage," the instrument is not payable at a determinable future time because the event is not certain to occur. If the words "after my death" were used instead of "after my marriage," the time would be determinable because the event is bound to occur.

Regardless of the wording used, if a due date is absolutely certain to arrive, it meets the test of the law. If the event is bound to occur but is such that it may not occur within a reasonable time, it is legally but not practically negotiable because no prudent person would want to accept it under normal conditions.

(6) PAYABLE TO ORDER OR BEARER. The two most common words of negotiability are "order" and "bearer." The instrument is *payable to order* when some person is made the payee and the maker or drawer wishes to indicate that the instrument will be paid to the person designated or to anyone else to whom he may transfer the instrument by indorsement.

It is not necessary to use the word "order," but it is strongly recommended. A note payable to "Smith and assigns" was held to be nonnegotiable. If it had been payable to "Smith or assigns," it would have been negotiable. Also "pay to the order of the holder" would be negotiable, but some people might hesitate to accept a check or other bill of exchange containing such wording. The law looks to the intention of the maker or the acceptor. If the words used clearly show an intention to pay either the named payee or anyone else whom he designates, the contract is negotiable.

The other words of negotiability, payable to bearer, indicate that the maker or the acceptor of a bill of exchange is willing to pay the person who has possession of the instrument at maturity. The usual form in which this word appears is this: "Pay to bearer" or "Pay to Lydia Lester or bearer." There are other types of wording that render a contract a bearer instrument. For example, if the payee is a fictitious person, it is a bearer instrument even though it contains the word "order." For example, "pay to the order of Payroll," is a bearer instrument. The same is true if it is payable to "cash," "holder," or a name that is clearly fictitious and that fact is known to the drawer.

The reason a clear distinction must be made between "order" negotiable contracts and "bearer" contracts is that title to the latter may be obtained by delivery only, while title to "order" instruments can be obtained only by indorsement and delivery.

(7) PAYEE AND DRAWEE DESIGNATED WITH REASONABLE CERTAINTY. When a negotiable instrument is payable "to order," the payee must be so named that the specific party can be identified with reasonable certainty. For example, a check which reads, "Pay to the order of the Treasurer of the Virginia Education Association" is not payable to a specific party, but that party can be ascertained with reasonable certainty and the check is

negotiable. If, on the other hand, the check is payable "to the order of the Treasurer of the Y.M.C.A." and there are three such organizations in the city, it would not be possible to ascertain with reasonable certainty who the payee is and the check would not be negotiable.

The drawee of a bill of exchange must likewise be named or described with reasonable certainty so that the holder will know to whom he must go for an acceptance or payment.

Execution and Delivery. The Negotiable Instruments Law states: "Every contract on a negotiable instrument is incomplete and revocable until delivery of the instrument for the purpose of giving effect thereto." Without this delivery there can be no force or effect to the contract. To constitute delivery the maker or drawer must give over control of the instrument to the holder for the sole purpose of giving effect to it, that is, making a binding obligation according to its terms. There can be a delivery without its being absolute, that is, without the delivery giving effect to the contract. If the delivery is made with the understanding, oral or written, that the instrument is not to become effective until some condition is met, this condition must be met before any liability arises under the contract. This is true only between the primary parties.

Delivery of an Incomplete Instrument. If a negotiable instrument is only partially filled out and signed before delivery, the maker or drawer is liable if the blanks are filled in according to instructions. If the holder fills in the blanks contrary to the authority given him, the maker or drawer is liable to the original payee only for the amount authorized.

Consideration. Negotiable instruments, like other contracts, must be supported by a valid consideration. In the hands of an innocent purchaser, consideration is conclusively presumed. It is not necessary to recite in the contract that there is a consideration to support it. Frequently, such a recital is made and this may destroy the negotiability of the contract.

A reference to the consideration in a note that does not condition the promise does not destroy negotiability. The clause, "This note is given in consideration of a typewriter purchased today," does not condition the maker's promise to pay. If the clause read, "This note is given in consideration for a typewriter guaranteed for ninety days, breach of warranty to constitute cancellation of the note," the instrument would not be negotiable. This promise to pay is not absolute, but conditional. Also, if the recital of the consideration is in such form as to make the instrument a part of another contract, the negotiability of the contract is destroyed.

● Mott inserted this statement in a note: "This note is a part of an agreement dated January 19, 1921." The court held that tying up the contract, which constituted the consideration for the note, with the note so that it all constituted one contract destroyed the negotiability of the note.

Nonessentials of Negotiability. Since the purpose of the Negotiable Instruments Law is to encourage the transfer of negotiable instruments freely from hand to hand, no minor detail is permitted to destroy an instrument's negotiability. Some of the details which have been held to be nonessential are:

The instrument need not be dated. The omission of a date may cause considerable inconvenience, but the date is not essential. The holder may fill in the correct date if the space for the date is left blank. If an instrument is due thirty days after date, and the date is omitted, the instrument is payable thirty days after it was issued or delivered. In case of dispute the date of issue may be proved.

The name of the place where the instrument was drawn or where it is payable is not specified. For contracts in general, one's rights are governed by the law where the contract is made or where it is to be performed. This rule makes it advisable for a negotiable instrument to stipulate the place where it is drawn and where it is payable, but neither is essential for its negotiability.

Questions

1. What are the requirements of a negotiable instrument?

2. In order for an instrument to be negotiable, where must the signature be placed?

3. How may an illiterate person sign a negotiable instrument?

4. If a promise reads, "I promise to pay $500 if the payee will give me a receipt," is this a conditional or unconditional promise to pay?

5. (a) Must a negotiable instrument call for payment in American money only?

(b) If a negotiable instrument calls for the payment of one sum in figures and a different amount in words, which one prevails?

6. When must a negotiable instrument be payable?

7. Explain the difference between "payable to order" and "payable to bearer."

8. Why is it important to designate the payee and drawee with reasonable certainty?

9. If an instrument is not supported by consideration, is it negotiable or nonnegotiable?

10. What is the effect on the negotiability of an instrument if it is not dated?

Case Problems

1. Lemly, the cashier-accountant for the Clemson Lumber Company, Inc., who was also the chief stockholder in the corporation, arranged a loan from the bank for $10,000 and signed it as follows:

Clemson Lumber Co., Inc.
John Lemly, Cashier.

Before maturity the note was sold to the Federal Reserve Bank of Atlanta, an innocent purchaser. The Clemson Lumber Company, Inc. became bankrupt and the holder of the note sued Lemly personally for it. Was he liable?

2. The Louisa National Bank signed the following instrument: "Received of Alice Mayo $7,500 in U. S. Bonds for which it promises to return to her or order said bonds within six months from date or to pay her at our option $7,500 in cash." Did this contract meet the requirement of the Negotiable Instrument Law that it must contain an unconditional promise to pay money?

3. Stanley was manager for the Anawalt Furniture Company. A customer selected furniture amounting to $700 and tendered in payment a check payable to the customer and drawn by A. W. Green. The check was for $750 in figures, but in words it stated: "Seven Hundred and No/100 dollars." The customer offered to indorse it and accept the $700 as the correct figure. Stanley interpreted this discrepancy to mean the instrument was not complete and regular on its face and therefore it was not negotiable. He refused to accept it and lost the sale. Was Stanley correct in his interpretation? NO, WORDS PREVAIL

4. Lamb executed a note for $7,000 payable to Sam Storey. The note was regular in every way except that it contained this clause, "payable within two years from date with 6% interest, but if paid within one year, no interest is to be charged." Storey sold the note before maturity to Hanson. Before Hanson could collect this note from Lamb, he had to prove it was negotiable. Was it negotiable?

5. The following instrument was delivered to Alexander Botts:

> Chicago, Ill., May 6, 19—
>
> One year after date, The Harpster Manufacturing Company will pay to Alexander Botts, on order, five hundred dollars, or, at his option, will issue to him five shares of the common stock of this corporation.
>
> The Harpster Manufacturing Company
> By G. E. Harpster, Mgr.

(a) Is this instrument negotiable? Why?

(b) Is the expression "will pay" equivalent to "promise to pay"?

(c) If this instrument contained the words "at its option" instead of "at his option," would the instrument be negotiable? Why?

6. Myrtle's Beauty Shop purchased some haidressing machines from the Welch Company for $800 and agreed to accept a trade acceptance when presented. The McDowell National Bank presented the bill of lading for the machines with a 90-day trade acceptance attached for acceptance. Myrtle, owner of Myrtle's Beauty Shop, accepted it and signed the acceptance: "Myrtle's Beauty Shop." Was this a proper signature?

7. Is the following instrument negotiable?

> Sixty days after my death I bind my heirs to pay to the Treasurer of the Y.M.C.A., or to anyone else whom he may designate, the sum of $5,000 with interest from the date of my death.
>
> Signed: Albert Sloan

8. Is the following instrument negotiable?

> To James Madison:
>
> Pay to the order of myself on January 3, 19—, $100, and also deliver to my order 100 bushels of wheat.
>
> Henry Clay
>
> Accepted December 1, 19—
> At Richmond, Virginia
> James Madison

Chapter 23

Negotiation and Discharge

Negotiation Defined. *Negotiation* is the transferring of a negotiable instrument in such a way as to constitute the transferee the holder of the instrument. The negotiation is usually, but not always, for the purpose of transferring title to the holder. Bearer instruments may be negotiated by delivery without any indorsement. This effectively invests ownership in the holder. In practice an indorsement is usually required even for bearer paper, although this adds nothing to the legality of the negotiation. It merely preserves a written chronological record of all negotiations. If the instrument is payable to "order," there can be a negotiation only by indorsement and delivery. The indorsement is the contract between the indorser and the indorsee or holder. The nature of the contract is fixed by the type of the indorsement.

Place of Indorsement. The usual place to indorse a negotiable instrument is on the back of the form. If the indorser's signature appears elsewhere and it cannot be determined in what capacity he signed, he will be considered an indorser. In any event, the indorsement must be physically attached to the contract. One may not wish to assume the liabilities of an indorser even though the instrument is negotiable. In that event he can assign it by writing out the assignment on a separate piece of paper.

If the maker or drawer misspells the name of the payee, the payee should first indorse exactly as the name appears on the instrument, and immediately following this, he should write his name correctly.

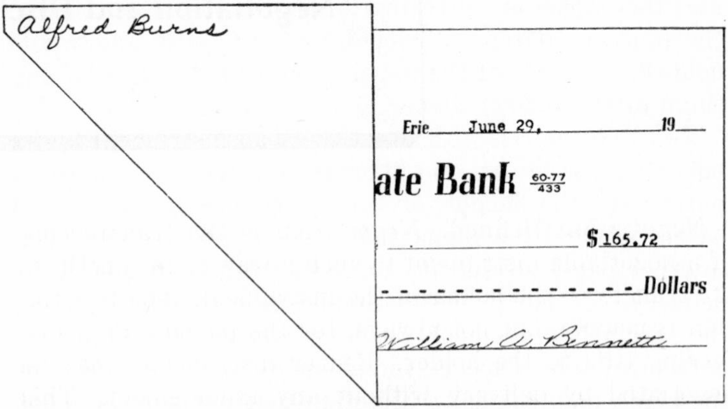

An Indorsed Check Folded to Show the Position of the Indorsement.

Kinds of Indorsements. The Negotiable Instruments Law lists five types of indorsements:

1. Blank indorsement
2. Special indorsement
3. Qualified indorsement
4. Restrictive indorsement
5. Conditional indorsement

Indorsement in Blank.

(1) BLANK INDORSEMENT. The most common type of indorsement is a *blank indorsement* which consists of the name only. If the instrument is payable "to order," a blank indorsement converts it into bearer paper. As has been indicated, title to bearer paper may be obtained by delivery only. Thus, the finder of a lost bearer instrument or a thief may collect from the maker if the maker is unaware of the defective title of the finder or thief, and the maker will be protected from any claims of the real owner. The real owner would have a claim against the finder or thief. If the finder or thief negoti-

ates the paper by delivering it to an innocent purchaser, the innocent purchaser would have full title and would hold the proceeds of the paper when collected free of any claim of the former owner.

To avoid the risk of losing title to an instrument by its being lost or stolen and thereafter sold to an innocent purchaser, the holder of an instrument converted to bearer paper by a blank indorsement may reconvert it to order paper so that it cannot be negotiated merely by delivery. He may do this by indorsing it to himself, using the special indorsement, or by converting the blank indorsement into a special indorsement by writing in over the blank indorsement a direction that payment be made to himself. If he negotiated it further, he would have to indorse it a second time.

(2) SPECIAL INDORSEMENT. A *special indorsement* designates the particular person to whom payment is to be made. The holder must indorse it before he can further negotiate it. He may, of course, indorse the instrument in blank, which makes it bearer paper. Each holder has the power to elect either a blank or a special indorsement. If the paper is bearer paper at the time of issuance either because it is stated to be payable to "bearer" or because the payee is fictitious, it stays bearer paper and can never be converted into an order instrument by means of a special indorsement.

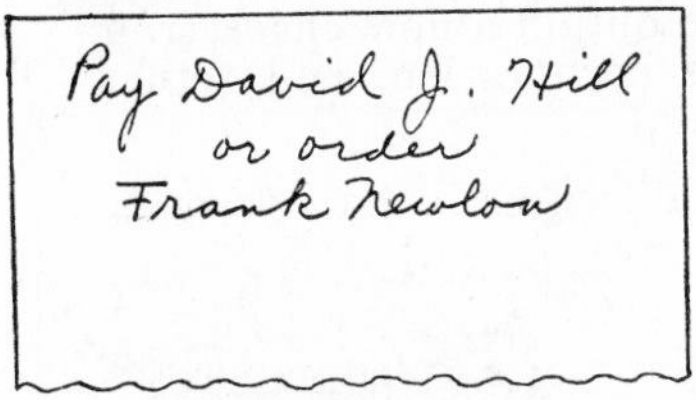
Pay David J. Hill
or order
Frank Newlon
Special Indorsement.

(3) QUALIFIED INDORSEMENT. A *qualified indorsement* has the effect of qualifying, that is, limiting the liability of the indorser. For example, if an agent receives checks in payment of his principal's claims which are made payable to the agent personally, the agent should and can elect to use a qualified indorsement. This is done

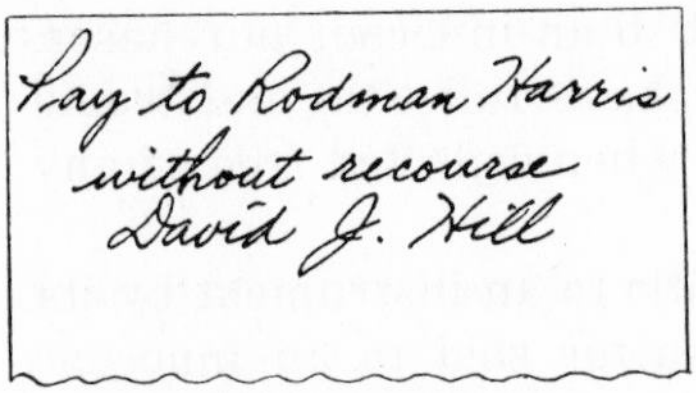

Qualified Indorsement.

merely by adding to either a blank or special type of indorsement the words "without recourse" immediately before the signature. This releases the indorser from liability for payment if the instrument is not paid because of insolvency or mere refusal to pay. The indorser still warrants that the instrument is genuine, that he has good title to it, that all prior parties had capacity to contract, and that the instrument to his knowledge is valid. If the agent wishes to avoid these liabilities, his recourse is to return the check to the drawer and have a new one made out to the principal.

- Fred Miller is a salesman for the Richmond Wholesale Grocery Corporation. In this capacity he receives a check from a customer of his principal made payable "to the order of Fred Miller." The Richmond Wholesale Grocery Corporation refuses to accept the check unless Fred Miller indorses it either in blank or by special indorsement. To avoid liability Miller should either indorse it "without recourse," regardless of the wishes of his employer, or else should obtain a new check from the customer, payable to the corporation, and return the old one.

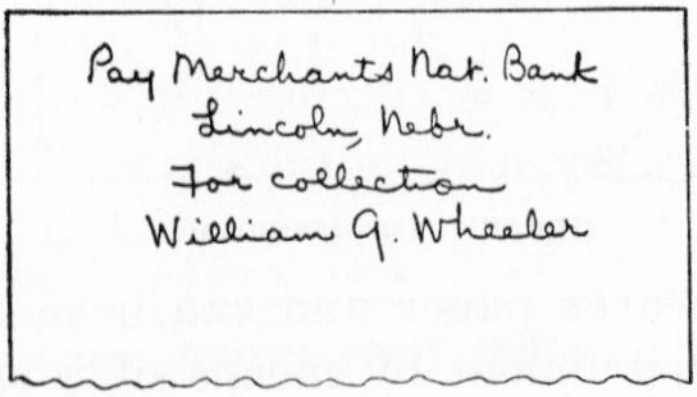

Restrictive Indorsement.

(4) Restrictive Indorsement. The Negotiable Instruments Law defines a *restrictive indorsement* as one that (a) prohibits the further negotiation of the instrument; (b) constitutes the indorsee the agent of the indorser; (c) vests the title in the indorsee in trust for, or to the use of, some other person. Several types of wordings are used in restrictive indorsements to achieve the results desired by this type of indorsement. If the only purpose of the restrictive indorsement is to pro-

hibit any further negotiation of the contract, the indorsement reads: "Pay to Vincent Dieball only." Dieball cannot negotiate this contract to any other person although he may assign it.

The most common use of the restrictive indorsement is to make the indorsee the agent of the indorser. In this case the indorsement reads: "Pay to the Cairo National Bank for collection." This indorsement transfers possession, but not title, to the indorsee, The Cairo National Bank is merely the agent of the indorser. When it collects the money, it holds the proceeds in trust for the indorser. If the Cairo bank finds it necessary to transfer the instrument to another bank for collection, it may do so but the second bank is merely the subagent of the indorser. It too must hold the money in trust for the indorser. This point becomes extremely important when the collecting bank goes into receivership before the proceeds are remitted to the indorser. In that event the receiver must pay the entire proceeds to the indorser. He does not collect his pro rata share of the net assets like the other creditors of the insolvent bank.

(5) CONDITIONAL INDORSEMENT. The indorser by *special indorsement* may wish to impose a condition precedent to the payment. In this event the indorsee may not receive payment until the condition is met. The condition, of course, is binding only between the indorser and subsequent purchasers. The maker of a note or the acceptor of a draft may disregard the condition and pay the holder. Should the instrument be dishonored by nonpayment, the holder must look to the indorsers. In this event, the condition must be met before collection from the indorsers is possible. If the party primarily liable does pay the holder before the condition

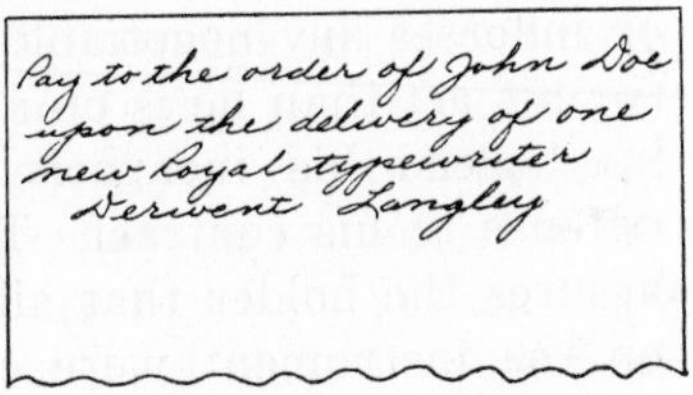
Pay to the order of John Doe
upon the delivery of one
new Royal typewriter
Derwent Langley

Conditional Indorsement.

is met, the holder must hold the money in trust for the indorser who imposed the condition until the condition is met. The maker or the acceptor cannot be sued for wrongful payment since the indorser cannot impose an additional obligation upon the one primarily liable.

Contract of an Indorser. Although each type of indorsement is a slightly different contract, all of these contracts have many provisions in common. The Negotiable Instrument Law writes out the terms of these contracts. An indorser, merely by signing his name, indicates his intention to be bound by the terms of the contract. These terms for all indorsers are as follows:

(1) The indorser warrants that the instrument, whether a check, note, or draft, is genuine and in all respects what it purports to be. If it purports to be a check for $500 drawn by Smith on the Bonner State Bank and payable to Danner, the indorser warrants that there has been no forgery, alteration, or other irregularity in the check. He warrants that it is exactly what it appears to be. If it is not, he can be sued by the holder for breach of warranty.

(2) The indorser warrants that he has good title to the instrument. This warranty is to provide the new holder with assurance that the person indorsing it to him did not steal the instrument, or find it, or come into possession of it in any unlawful manner.

(3) The indorser warrants that all prior parties had capacity to contract. If a minor, an insane person, or other incompetent person draws a check, executes a note, or indorses any negotiable contract, he is no more liable for his act than he is on any other type of contract. He may plead his incapacity to contract as an absolute defense to his contract. The indorser by this warranty assures the holder that all parties whose names appear on the instrument were competent to contract. If the maker of a note should avoid liability on the ground of

drunkenness at the time he signed the note, for example, the indorser would have to reimburse the holder.

(4) The indorser warrants that at the time he indorses the instrument, it is a valid and binding contract. Many contracts prove defective and void. Sunday contracts, illegal contracts, contracts entered into by a mistake as to the existence of the subject matter of the contract, and many others are void. A negotiable instrument given in payment of a gambling debt is no more binding on the primary party than any other type of contract for a similar payment. Also a negotiable instrument might be valid at the time it is accepted but subsequently become invalid. This warranty protects the holder against any of these infirmities in the contract.

(5) The indorser warrants that the instrument will be paid upon presentment at the proper time and place. Not all indorsers make this warranty, however. A qualified indorser makes the first four warranties. The purpose of his indorsement is to release him from this fifth warranty when the failure to pay is due merely to inability to pay. If the failure to pay is due to anyone of the conditions set out in the first four warranties, the qualified indorser is as fully liable as any other indorser.

One who makes a conditional indorsement does not unqualifiedly make this fifth warranty. After the condition set out in his indorsement has been met, he becomes fully liable on this fifth warranty.

It is well to note at this point that every indorser lays down two conditions which must be met by the holder before the indorser is liable on his indorsement: (a) that the instrument will be properly presented when due; and (b) that due notice of dishonor will be given to the indorser if it is not paid. These two conditions will be discussed more fully in Chapter 24.

Obligation of Negotiator of Bearer Paper. Bearer paper need not be indorsed when negotiated. Mere delivery passes title. One who negotiates a bearer instrument by delivery alone does not guarantee payment, but he is liable to his immediate purchaser only as a warrantor of the genuineness of the instrument, of his title to it, of the capacity of prior parties, and of its validity so far as he knows. These warranties are the same as those made by a qualified indorser, except that the warranties of the qualified indorser extend to all subsequent holders, not just to the immediate purchaser. But since negotiable instruments are not legal tender, no one is under any obligation to accept bearer paper without an indorsement. By requiring an indorsement even though not necessary to pass title, the holder protects himself by requiring the one who wishes to negotiate it to assume all the obligations of an indorser by indorsement.

- Dawson executed a negotiable note payable to bearer and delivered it to Adams, the payee. Adams transferred the note to Rainwater without indorsement. Rainwater by a blank indorsement transferred the note to Hurley. When Hurley presented it for payment, Dawson had become insolvent and was unable to pay. Hurley could sue Rainwater for indemnity, but he could not sue Adams; nor could Rainwater seek reimbursement from Adams.

Discharge of the Obligation. Negotiable instruments may be discharged by payment, by cancellation, or by alteration. Payment at or after the date of the maturity of the instrument by the party who is primarily liable constitutes proper payment. Cancellation consists of any act that indicates the intention to cancel the instrument. A cancellation is not effective, however, when it is made unintentionally or by mistake. A party to a negotiable instrument is discharged from liability if the instrument is materially altered without his consent. If such an instrument gets into the hands of a holder in due course, however, the holder in due course may collect according to the original terms of the instrument, and not according to its altered terms.

• Shea made a note payable to the order of Snow, who indorsed it to McCormick. The amount of the note was altered from fifty dollars to five hundred dollars. McCormick negotiated the instrument to Phillips, who was unaware of the alteration. The court held that Phillips could enforce payment from Shea to the amount of fifty dollars. Phillips could also recover damages from McCormick.

The obligations of the parties may be discharged in other ways, just as in the case of a simple contract. For example, the parties will be discharged from liability if they have been judicially declared bankrupt or if there has been the necessary lapse of time provided by a statute of limitations.

Frequently a negotiable instrument is lost or accidentally destroyed. This does not discharge the obligation. The party obligated to pay it has a right to demand the instrument's return if this is possible. If this cannot be done, then he has a right to demand security from the holder adequate to protect the payer from having to pay the instrument a second time. The security usually takes the form of an indemnity bond.

Questions

1. What is negotiation?

2. How may bearer instruments be negotiated?

3. Where should one indorse a negotiable instrument?

4. Name five kinds of indorsements and give an example of the proper use of each one.

5. Why is it usually undesirable to indorse a check in blank?

6. If an instrument that is payable to "bearer" is indorsed by special indorsement, what must the second holder do in order to pass title to it?

7. If a check is made payable to John Atkins, agent for the Branch Insurance Agency, when it should have been made payable to the agency, how should John indorse it when he delivers it to the agency? Why?

8. If one wishes to draw a check on his own account but include a condition in it without rendering the check non-negotiable, how may he do this?

9. What does the indorser warrant when he indorses an instrument?

10. How may negotiable instruments be discharged?

Case Problems

1. Paul Chapman, as the administrator of his uncle's estate, was required to collect all debts due the estate. One of the estate's debtors paid his debt of $1,100 by check made payable to Paul Chapman. Chapman indorsed this check as follows: "Pay to the order of Paul Chapman, Administrator of John Chapman's Estate. Paul Chapman." This check was never paid because the drawer had insufficient funds in the bank. Later demand was made on Paul Chapman that he pay this $1,100 out of his personal funds because of his special indorsement. Was he personally liable for it?

2. McDonald was the payee of a note for $3,500, signed by Garrard. He entered into a contract with Bell which provided that Bell was to accept the note by assignment so that McDonald would not be liable as an indorser. This was agreeable to Bell, but they were uncertain how to make the assignment. They decided to write on the note these words: "I hereby assign all my rights and interest in this note to John Bell. (Signed) Alex McDonald." Later Bell transferred the note by blank indorsement to Saye. The note was not paid by Garrard, and Saye sued McDonald as an indorser. He claimed he was only an assignor and therefore not liable under the warranties of an indorser. Was this contention correct?

3. Inez Katz owned and operated the Thrift Dress Shop, an exclusive dress shop. She sold an expensive gown to Mrs. Gene Shopen who paid for it by drawing a sight draft on Josiah Shopen for $1,100. Miss Katz sent this sight draft to Herman Shobelt, an attorney, for presentment for collection. She indorsed it as follows: "Pay to the order of Herman Shobelt. (Signed) Inez Katz." Shoblet collected the draft but, before he remitted the proceeds to Miss Katz, he was declared bankrupt. He had deposited the money in a special account, intending to remit by check from this special account. The question arose as to whether or not this

$1,100 was a part of Shobelt's estate to be taken over by the receiver in bankruptcy. What do you think?

4. Richards prepared the following note:

Ninety days after date I promise to pay to the order of Gene Vaughn $1,000 with 6% interest from date.

Signed: *E. J. Richards*

Richards lost this note before delivering it to Vaughn and Vaughn found it. Richards, before he lost it, had decided not to give the note to Vaughn. Was he liable on the note?

5. While the bookkeeper for the Simond Refining Company was on vacation, Miss Storey, the secretary, was to make the daily deposits. She made up her deposit slip, indorsed all checks in blank, and had them ready for deposit. On her way to the bank, she stopped to have a cup of coffee. While doing this, her pocketbook containing the deposit was stolen. Later some of the checks fell into the hands of innocent purchasers. Who must bear the loss on these checks, the innocent purchasers or the Simond Refining Company?

6. The Morrell Packing Company deposited checks totaling $4,000 in the Cedar Rapids National Bank. The checks were indorsed as follows: "Pay to the order of Cedar Rapids National Bank for deposit only. Morrell Packing Company." The Cedar Rapids National Bank in turn indorsed the checks in blank and mailed them through the usual channels for collection. Before any of them were collected, the Cedar Rapids National Bank went into receivership. The Morrell Packing Company immediately wired all drawers of the checks and asked them to stop payment. This they did. The receiver of the Cedar Rapids National Bank contended that the Morrell Packing Company had no right to do this. Do you agree?

7. The Matz Appliance Company received in payment of merchandise a check payable to "bearer." The transferor was Mayo, who did not indorse the check. The Matz Appliance Company transferred the check to the Comer Chevrolet Company and indorsed it in blank. The check was never paid, and the Comer Chevrolet Company sued both the Matz Appliance Company and Mayo. Mayo contended he was not liable since he had not indorsed the check. Was his contention correct? If the Matz Appliance Company paid it, could it in turn sue Mayo for reimbursement?

Chapter 24

Holders in Due Course

Holders in Due Course. Negotiable instruments would have no advantage over ordinary contracts if the remote parties could not be given immunity against many of the defenses which might be made against simple contracts. To enjoy this immunity, the holder of a negotiable instrument must be a *holder in due course.* The term "innocent purchaser" is also used to describe a person who is a holder in due course. Neither term can be used to describe any one but the holder of a negotiable instrument who has obtained it under these conditions:

1. The instrument must be complete and regular on its face.
2. It must not be past due at the time of the negotiation.
3. The holder must take the instrument in good faith and for value.
4. At the time the instrument is negotiated, the holder must have no notice of any infirmity in the instrument or any defect in the title of the person who negotiated it.

(1) INSTRUMENT REGULAR ON ITS FACE. Checks, notes, and drafts, the most common types of negotiable paper, are usually printed with blank spaces that are to be filled in by the person executing them. The instruments are regular when these spaces have been filled in properly and the instrument is signed. Any material deviation from this regular practice makes the instrument irregular and the holder takes it subject to all the defenses which the maker or acceptor can make against the original holder. If he has no defenses, the irregularity does not necessarily render the contract unenforceable.

Blank notes generally have a space for the rate of interest. If a note is non-interest-bearing, this space should be crossed out with x's. If this is done, and then "8%" is later written over the "x's," the note is not regular and the holder cannot be considered innocent. He is charged with notice that this may have been done subsequent to the delivery. If it later develops that the maker wrote the "8%" before delivering it, the contract is enforceable if there are no other defenses. The holder, however, cannot enjoy the privileges of an innocent purchaser. The irregularity is a warning signal to a prospective purchaser. If he does not heed the warning, he cannot claim immunity to any defenses.

(2) INSTRUMENT NOT PAST DUE. One who takes an instrument that is past due cannot be an innocent purchaser. If it is due and unpaid, there must be a reason. It is the duty of the prospective purchaser to ascertain that reason. If he fails or neglects to do so, he forfeits the privileges of a holder in due course. If the note is dated and payable in a fixed number of days or months, the instrument itself indicates whether or not it is past due.

If the instrument is transferred on the date of maturity, it is not past due but would be overdue on the day following the due date. If it is payable on demand, it is due within a reasonable time after it is issued. What is a reasonable time "depends upon the nature of the instrument, the usage of trade or business with respect to such instruments, and the facts of the particular case." For example, if a demand note is given in temporary settlement for merchandise purchased for which the usual terms are 2/10, n/60, a reasonable time would be approximately sixty days.

(3) FOR VALUE. This requirement does not mean that one must pay full value for a negotiable instrument in order to be a holder in due course. As a matter of fact,

one who purchases a negotiable contract at a discount can qualify as a holder in due course. The law states that he must take it "for value and in good faith." If the instrument is offered at an exorbitant discount, that fact may be evidence that the purchaser did not buy it in good faith. It is the lack of good faith that destroys one's status of a holder in due course, not the amount of the discount.

If the payee of a negotiable instrument for $3,000 offered to transfer it for a consideration of $2,700, and the purchaser had no other reason to suspect any infirmity in the instrument, he can qualify as a holder in due course. He took the instrument in good faith. If, on the other hand, the holder had offered to discount the note $1,000, the purchaser could not take it in good faith because he should suspect that there is some fatal infirmity in the contract.

As so often occurs, the purchaser pays for the instrument in cash and other property. The discount is concealed in the inflated value placed on the property taken in payment. The test always is: Were there any circumstances that should have warned a prudent man that the instrument was not genuine and in all respects what it purported to be? If there were, the purchaser did not take it in good faith.

• Tate held a note for $5,000 signed by Storey. Before maturity he sold the note to Aderhold for $3,000 cash and an old spinning wheel that formerly had been in the Tate family. When Aderhold attempted to collect from Storey, he refused to pay, claiming that there was no consideration since the note represented a gift.

Lack of consideration is not a good defense against a holder in due course. Buying a $5,000 note at a $2,000 discount would be sufficient notice to warn Aderhold that the note was not genuine. In this case, however, Tate placed a value of $2,000 on the old spinning wheel because of a sentimental attachment. For this reason, there was no circumstance to warn Aderhold that something was lacking in the genuineness of the obligation. Storey would have to pay Aderhold since he was a holder in due course.

(4) NO KNOWLEDGE OR NOTICE OF DEFENSE. The holder is considered to have knowledge or notice of facts that make the instrument defective if he has received from any source any information that would make a reasonably prudent man investigate the instrument before accepting it. He need not have actual knowledge of such facts. The title of a person who negotiates an instrument is defective when he obtains it by fraud, duress, or other unlawful means; or for an illegal consideration; or when he negotiates it in breach of faith or under circumstances amounting to fraud.

- Bell sold a secondhand truck to Sellers for $1,000 and guaranteed it to be in first-class condition. Bell had stolen the truck. The truck was in extremely poor condition, a fact which Bell knew. About a week after Sellers bought it, he sold it to Bodine for $1,500 and took a ninety-day negotiable note in payment. Sellers then offered to discount the note to Bell at 8 per cent. Bell accepted the offer. About two weeks later, the real owner of the truck repossessed it from Bodine. When the note came due, Bodine refused to pay it. At the time Bell took the note, he knew it had been given in payment of the truck sold to Sellers; therefore, he was not a holder in due course. He had knowledge of the infirmity.

The first holder in due course brings into operation for the first time all the protections which the law has placed around negotiable instruments. When these protections once accrue, they are not easily lost. Consequently, a subsequent holder may avail himself of them even though he himself is not a holder in due course. For example, Adams, without consideration, gives Bryce a negotiable note due in sixty days. Before maturity Bryce indorses it to Cordell under conditions which make Cordell a holder in due course. Ten days after maturity Cordell sells the note to Gray, but Gray is not a holder in due course since he did not obtain the note before maturity. If Gray is not a party to any wrongdoing or illegality affecting this instrument, he acquires all the rights of a holder in due course. This is true because Cordell had these rights, and when Cordell sold the note to Gray, he sold all of his rights, which include the right to collect the amount due and the right to be free from the defense of no consideration.

Duties of the Holder. As has been pointed out before, the prime significance of the Negotiable Instrument Law is that the purchaser of a negotiable instrument may obtain rights greater than the payee had. Even if he gets no greater rights, he may, and in most all cases does, obtain greater advantages.

Stevens purchases an automobile from Griffin for $900 and gives in payment this note: "Sixty days after date I promise to pay Archibald Griffin or order $900. Harold Stevens." What are Griffin's rights? If there was no fraud in the transaction or other infirmity in the contract, Griffin's simple right is to collect $900 on the due date of the note. Like all property rights this one may be sold. If Griffin, the payee, sells his rights to Comer, a holder in due course, does Comer obtain rights superior to Griffin? If Griffin's rights were perfect, Comer could obtain no greater rights. If Griffin, in order to sell the car, had made fraudulent representations about it, his right to collect $900 is reduced by the amount of damages which Stevens sustained. In this case Comer does get greater rights than Griffin had.

Under all circumstances Comer would obtain greater advantages than Griffin had. In order to collect the $900, Griffin could look only to Stevens. If Stevens is insolvent and unable to pay, Griffin's rights may prove to be worthless. Comer, however, has the right to look to both Stevens and Griffin for payment. His chances of collecting are twice as great as Griffin's, but through ignorance or lack of diligence, Comer may lose a substantial part of these rights.

The holder of a negotiable instrument has duties to perform in order to preserve his rights as an innocent purchaser of a negotiable instrument:

(1) He must present a bill of exchange for acceptance when its form requires an acceptance.

(2) He must present an accepted bill of exchange, a bill of exchange that need not be accepted, such as a sight draft or check, and a note for payment.

(3) If any of these contracts are dishonored either by nonacceptance or nonpayment, the holder must notify all indorsers and the drawer of bills of exchange of that dishonor.

The presentment and the notice of dishonor must both be done at the right time, at the proper place, and in the proper manner.

Proper Presentment for Acceptance. Not all drafts must be presented for acceptance, but all of them, except sight drafts, should be presented for acceptance. Presentment for acceptance must be made:

(1) When the draft is made payable a certain number of days after sight

(2) When the draft is made payable at some place other than the drawee's place of business or residence

(3) When the draft expressly stipulates that it must be presented for acceptance

The presentment for acceptance in these cases must be made at the proper time, which is a reasonable time after the bill is drawn. The courts interpret what constitutes a reasonable time depending on the circumstances in each particular case. Prudence, not the law, requires that the presentment be made at the next business day after the bill is received by the payee.

The presentment for acceptance must be made at the proper place, which is the drawee's place of business or his residence. If he cannot be found there, it may be presented anywhere he can be found. If he cannot be located with reasonable diligence, the failure to present it does not release the drawer and the indorsers, if any.

The bill must be presented by the payee or his agent to the drawee, his agent, or anyone else having the power to accept. If the drawee, for example, is dead, the administrator of his estate has the power to accept the bill.

Proper Presentment for Payment. All bills of exchange and all notes must be presented for payment. The law is even more exacting in this type of presentment than in the presentment for acceptance. This presentment must be made at the proper time, at the proper place, and in the proper manner.

The presentment for acceptance must be made within a reasonable time, but the presentment for payment must be made on the due date. It must not be done one day early nor one day late. If the due date falls on Sunday or a holiday, the presentment for payment must be made the following day. It not only must be made on that day, but it must be made during reasonable hours of that day. If the payer is a business firm, this will be during business hours.

Naturally sight drafts, checks, and demand notes do not have a due date. For demand notes the due date is a reasonable time after the date of issue. For all other instruments the presentment for payment must be made within a reasonable time after the last negotiation.

The presentment for payment must be made at the proper place. If a place of payment is stated in the instrument, presentment must be made at that place. If no place of payment is stipulated in the instrument, it must be presented at the payer's place of business if he has one. If he has no place of business, it may be presented anywhere he can be found.

The presentment for payment must be made in the proper manner. This means that the holder or his agent must present the instrument in person to the proper party. The holder must have the instrument in his possession and be able and willing to cancel it and to return it when payment is received.

When Presentment for Acceptance or Payment Is Excused. Sometimes the presentment for acceptance may be either delayed or excused. If the payee of a time draft, for example, learns before presentment that the drawee will not accept the draft, he may treat this knowledge as a dishonor and notify the drawer accordingly. The presentment for payment may be waived. This is usually done by inserting a provision in the instrument itself to this effect. If the drawee of a draft or the maker of a note cannot be located with reasonable diligence, either presentment for acceptance or presentment for payment may be excused or delayed. Mere inconvenience will not excuse a holder from presenting a negotiable instrument for payment at the proper time. Failure must be due to conditions beyond the holder's control.

Effects of a Failure to Present for Acceptance or Payment. The drawer of a draft is by his act assigning an amount of money due him to a payee in payment of a debt due the payee, unless the drawer and the payee is the same person, or the payee is the agent of the drawer. In these latter two instances the draft is a collection technique. When the draft is in payment of a debt, the presentment for acceptance is to notify the drawee that an assignment of the funds due the drawer has been made. Thereafter the drawee cannot safely pay the drawer. The drawer, however, remains fully liable to the payee until the draft is paid by the drawee if the payee properly presents the draft for acceptance and gives proper notice of dishonor if it is not accepted. The effect of a failure to present a draft for acceptance is to release the drawer from all liability to the payee or holder. If the instrument is a check, a failure to present it properly by the holder releases all indorsers absolutely, and it releases the drawer to the extent of his loss by reason of the improper presentment for payment.

The party primarily liable on a draft is the drawee and on a note, the maker. A failure to present a negotiable instrument for payment to the party primarily liable has no effect on his liability. The only exception to this rule is that when a draft or note is made payable at a particular place, a failure to present it properly at this place releases the party primarily liable from any payment of interest after the due date, provided he was able and willing to pay on that date.

Notice of Dishonor. If a negotiable instrument has been dishonored by nonacceptance or nonpayment, *notice of* this *dishonor* must be given to the drawer and to each indorser. The drawer or any indorser who has not been given notice will be discharged from liability. Notice is not required if the instrument is nonnegotiable.

The notice of dishonor for domestic instruments is not required to be in any special form; it may be in writing or it may be oral. The only requirement is that the notice must identify the instrument sufficiently and must indicate that it has been dishonored.

The notice of dishonor must be given within a reasonable time. It may be given personally or by mail. If the parties live in the same place, notice of dishonor must be given before the end of the day after the day of dishonor. When the parties live in different places, notice by mail must ordinarily be posted not later than the day after the day of dishonor. Proper mailing of the notice constitutes due notice, even if the notice is lost in the mail.

- Range was the holder of a check drawn by Pate and indorsed by Sawyer and Cross. The check was dishonored for nonpayment. Range gave notice of dishonor orally to Sawyer and an unsigned written notice to Cross. Both parties attempted to avoid payment because of improper form of the notice. Neither defense was good. A formal notice, although recommended, was not required. Had this been a foreign bill of exchange, a written notice of protest would have been required.

Protest. Notice of dishonor must sometimes be in the form of a protest. A *protest* is a formal declaration made in writing by a notary public in behalf of the holder of a negotiable instrument, attesting that it has been presented for acceptance or payment and that acceptance or payment was refused. The certificate of protest, signed and sealed by the notary, is accepted as evidence of the facts of presentment, demand, nonacceptance or nonpayment, and notice of dishonor. A protest must ordinarily be made on the day and at the place of dishonor.

Any negotiable instrument may be protested at the election of the holder. While it is not necessary to protest inland or domestic bills of exchange, such bills may be protested. Foreign bills of exchange (including checks), however, must be protested for nonacceptance or nonpayment. If a foreign bill is not protested, the drawer and the indorsers will be discharged from liability for payment.

The certificate of protest must be attached to the protested instrument or must contain a copy of the instrument. It must specify:

(1) The time and the place of presentment

(2) The fact that presentment was made and the manner in which it was made

(3) The demand made and the answer given, or the fact that the maker or the acceptor could not be found

(4) The cause of or the reason for the protest

Notice of Protest. Notice of the protest must be given to the parties not later than the day following the protest. No special form of notice is necessary. Any notice that informs the parties of the demand and the nonacceptance or the nonpayment is sufficient. The drawer or the indorser to whom notice of the protest is not given is ordinarily discharged from liability unless he has waived notice of protest.

It should be remembered, however, that the instrument may contain a clause in which the drawer and the indorsers waive presentment, notice of dishonor, protest, and notice of protest.

The State of SOUTH CAROLINA RICHLAND **County, ss.**

Columbia, June 1, *19*

Take Notice, *that a* check *for* $25.88

dated May 28, 19

drawn by M. R. French

in favor of L. C. Baldwin

on the South Carolina National Bank

~~*accepted by*~~

indorsed by L. C. Baldwin and the Peoples First National Bank

was this day presented for payment *which was refused, and therefore was this day Protested, by the undersigned Notary Public, for non* payment

The holder therefore looks to you for payment thereof, together with interest, damages, costs, etc., you being payee *thereof.*

H. J. Stevenson
Notary Public

To L. C. Baldwin, Charleston, S. Car.

A Notice of Protest.

Questions

1. Who is a holder in due course?

2. On a draft the term "60 days" is marked out and over it is written, "90 days." Can one become a holder in due course of this draft? Why?

3. When is a "demand note" past due?

4. What are the duties of a holder of a negotiable instrument?

5. When should a draft be presented for acceptance?

6. How long after a negotiable instrument has been dishonored either by nonacceptance or nonpayment does the holder have to notify the indorsers of the dishonor?

7. In what manner must the notice of dishonor be given?

8. What is the effect of a failure of an indorser to receive notice of dishonor?

9. What must a certificate of protest specify?

10. What procedure should be followed by the holder after a certificate of protest has been completed?

Case Problems

1. Lowe, manager for the Harper Building Supplies Corporation, received the following draft from Agnew, a customer, in payment of an account.

July 27, 19—

Two months after date pay to the order of J. W. Agnew
$2,104.52 and charge to the account of

Robert E. Finch

To: H. V. Kincaid
Memphis, Tenn.

This draft had been duly presented to Kincaid and accepted by him. It was indorsed by Agnew on September 26. Lowe presented this draft for payment the next day, and payment was refused. Lowe immediately notified Agnew and Finch of the dishonor. Both Agnew and Finch denied any liability on the instrument, pleading improper presentment for payment. Was their defense valid?

2. Miss Drew, secretary to the Barber Equipment Company, was sent to the office of the Bates Construction Company to collect a draft for $7,500, due that day. When she arrived at the office, she was told that Mr. Barber, the only man in the firm who had the authority to pay it, was out of town. The draft had these words on it, "Payable at the First National Bank of Dublin." Ten days later Miss Drew returned to the office and presented the draft to Mr. Barber for payment. He failed to pay it because of financial embarrassment. Six months later, when he was sued on the draft, he denied liability for both principal and interest, claiming the draft was not properly presented for payment. Was he liable for both the principal and the interest from the due date of the draft?

3. The Sparks Cordage Company sold merchandise to Sanderson amounting to $475. The terms called for a 60-day trade acceptance with bill of lading attached. After the merchandise was shipped, a 60-day trade acceptance was drawn, the bill of lading was attached, and the two sent to the Tri-State Bank with instructions to deliver the bill of lading to Sanderson upon his acceptance of the trade acceptance. When the bank presented the trade acceptance, Sanderson claimed the amount should have been only $425 and wanted to qualify his acceptance so as to obligate himself only for this amount. The bank claimed

such a qualified acceptance was in reality a dishonor of the bill and refused to deliver to him the bill of lading. Was the bank correct in its action? YES

4. The Standard Electric Company purchased merchandise from the Dow Fuse Company. The merchandise was guaranteed to be first class. The purchaser remitted his check for $2,500 although the invoice was $3,000. He showed on the margin of the check that the $500 deduction was for goods returned because they were defective. The Dow Fuse Company held the check six days so that it could check the accuracy of the deduction as well as the drawer's right to make it. During that six days the bank on which the check was drawn went into receivership, and the check was never paid. Was the drawer of the check released from liability because of this six-day delay in presentment? YES

5. Hipp, through fraud, induced Rocco to draw a draft on Hartman in favor of Hipp for $250. Hipp indorsed the draft to Morocco, an innocent purchaser. Morocco later sold the draft to Grant who knew of the fraud but was in no way a party to the fraud. When the draft became due, payment was refused because of the fraud. Did Grant have the privileges of a holder in due course? YES

6. The Mingo Lumber Company paid one of its accounts to the West Virginia Timber Company, indorsing a sight draft as follows: "Pay to the order of the West Virginia Timber Company (Signed) Mingo Lumber Company, by Dave Berle, President." The West Virginia Timber Company held this sight draft two weeks without presenting it to the drawee, the Hardin Coal Company, for payment. The Hardin Coal Company went bankrupt near the end of this two-week period. The draft was never presented, the holder claiming that it knew it was useless since it had learned that the drawee was bankrupt. The West Virginia Timber Company sued the Mingo Lumber Company on its indorsement. Was the indorser liable? No

Chapter 25

Defenses

Who May Make a Defense? There are both immediate and remote parties to negotiable instruments. The immediate parties to a note are the maker and the payee, and the remote parties are the indorsers. All the indorsers are liable on the note, and all of them may make a defense against paying it. In the case of a draft, the drawer, the payee, and the drawee, who later becomes the acceptor if it is a time draft, are the immediate parties. When the draft is accepted, the drawer assumes the legal status of an indorser if the draft is payable to a third party. The maker of a note or the drawee or acceptor of a draft is the one from whom the holder will first demand payment. If he refuses, the holder demands payment from one of the indorsers. We will discuss first the defenses which the maker or the acceptor may make against the holder.

Personal Defenses and Real Defenses. The defenses which the maker or the acceptor may make against the holder are classed as personal and real. If the holder is not an innocent purchaser or a holder in due course, either a real or a personal defense will bar recovery. He has no more privileges or immunities than the original payee. If he is a holder in due course or if he derives his title through a holder in due course, however, personal defenses are of no avail against him. He takes the instrument free from all personal defenses. The real defenses, however, are good against the whole world. If established, they are a complete bar to recovery regardless of one's status as a holder in due course.

Personal Defenses. *Personal defenses* are good against all holders except holders in due course. The one thing which makes this group of defenses peculiar to negotiable instruments is that they will not suffice to bar recovery even if true when made against an innocent purchaser. We have already discussed most of them in preceding chapters and found that any one of them renders a contract other than a negotiable instrument either void or voidable. It is this feature which gives negotiable instruments their privileged status among all other contracts. There are three links in the chain: the instrument must be negotiable; the holder must be an innocent purchaser; the defense must be personal.

The common personal defenses are:

1. Duress
2. Undue influence
3. Misrepresentation
4. Nondelivery of a completed instrument
5. Fraud
6. Lack of consideration
7. Payment or part payment
8. Setoff and counterclaim

(1) DURESS. Duress, as explained on page 48, is the act of obtaining one's consent to a contract by force or by the threat of force.

(2) UNDUE INFLUENCE. Undue influence, as explained on page 49, is a form of mental coercion or pressure brought to bear through the close personal relationship existing between the contracting parties.

(3) MISREPRESENTATION. *Misrepresentation* is an innocent misstatement or concealment of a material fact.

(4) NONDELIVERY OF A COMPLETED INSTRUMENT. If an instrument is stolen, lost, or otherwise wrongfully taken after it is completely filled out but before it is delivered

by the maker or the drawer, delivery is not considered to have been made. Nondelivery is a personal defense, and the instrument is therefore collectible in the hands of a holder in due course but not in the hands of others.

(5) FRAUD. Fraud relating to the formation of a negotiable instrument is a personal defense not good against a holder in due course.

- Crane offered to sell Yardley his car for $500 and stated that the car just recently had a complete overhauling of the engine and transmission. Yardley, relying upon this false statement, accepted the offer to his detriment. Crane suggested that Yardley sign a memorandum of the agreement pending final consummation of the sale. Crane, by trickery, substituted a negotiable note for $1,000 which Yardley signs.

  There was fraud in the sale which preceded the signing of the instrument. This type of fraud is a personal defense and is of no avail against a holder in due course.

We shall observe later that fraud which results in a mistake as to the nature of the agreement signed renders the agreement void and that such a defense is therefore valid against all holders. This type of fraud is covered under (4) of Real Defenses, page 261.

(6) LACK OF CONSIDERATION. Negotiable instruments, like all other contracts, must be supported by a consideration. In the hands of a holder in due course consideration is presumptive. A note made as a gift cannot be collected by court action by the original holder, but a holder in due course can collect it.

(7) PAYMENTS OR PART PAYMENTS. If the maker of a note or the drawee of a draft pays the full amount of the instrument, or any part of it, before maturity and, because of carelessness or neglect, fails to see that the proper notation is made on the instrument, he may be compelled to pay the instrument a second time. If the instrument is acquired by a holder in due course after

such a payment without the proper notation having been made, the defense of payment will not be good against that holder. A receipt for the payment will not be sufficient.

- The maker of a promissory note wished to pay it before it was due. The payee told the maker that the note was destroyed and gave the maker a receipt for the money paid. The payee had, however, previously negotiated the note to a holder in due course. The court held that the maker was obliged to pay it the second time.

(8) SETOFF AND COUNTERCLAIM. If the maker of a note or the acceptor of a draft given for the purchase of merchandise later returns a part of the merchandise, he has a right of setoff against the seller. The right is lost, however, if the seller transfers the instrument to a holder in due course.

- Tonne buys merchandise from Larson valued at $500 and later sells Larson merchandise valued at $100. He has a counterclaim against Larson for $100. If Tonne gave Larson a negotiable note for $500 and Larson transferred it to a holder in due course, Tonne could not make his counterclaim against the holder in due course.

Real Defenses. *Real defenses* are defenses of a somewhat unusual character that concern not the merits of the transaction, but rather the nature of the instrument itself. They are sometimes called absolute defenses because they are good against even a holder in due course. They are:

1. Personal incapacity to make an enforceable contract
2. Illegality
3. Forgery and alteration
4. Fraud in the inception
5. Lapse of time under a statute of limitations
6. Nondelivery of an incompleted instrument
7. Usury
8. Mistakes which render a contract void

(1) PERSONAL INCAPACITY TO MAKE AN ENFORCEABLE CONTRACT. This defense relates to minors, insane persons, and all other persons legally incompetent to contract.

(2) ILLEGALITY. If statutes have declared certain instruments void, no enforeable rights under them can be acquired against the maker, drawer, or acceptor. This rule applies especially when statutes have declared void negotiable instruments given in payment of gambling transactions. General indorsers of such instruments must pay damages for breach of the warranty of validity.

(3) FORGERY AND ALTERATION. A forgery is an absolute defense. It is quite evident that a person cannot be compelled to pay a negotiable instrument that he did not sign. If a material alteration has been made in a negotiable instrument, the party who made the alteration will not be permitted to recover. A holder in due course who received the instrument after it was altered may recover the amount due on the original instrument. A material alteration is one that affects:

(a) The sum payable, either principal or interest
(b) The time, the place, or the date of payment
(c) The number or the relationship of the parties

In the case of both forgery and alteration, the bank is liable to the drawer of checks if through the bank's negligence the forgery or alteration is not detected. In the absence of negligence, the depositor sustains the loss. Even when the bank is negligent, the depositor must notify the bank within a reasonable time after the forgery or alteration is discovered. What is a reasonable time is fixed by statute in many states and by court decisions in others. The time varies from two months to one year.

(4) FRAUD IN THE INCEPTION. Fraud in the inception, which is one of the mistakes that render an agreement

void, is a real defense. It exists when a person is induced by fraud, without negligence on his part, to sign a negotiable instrument that he believes is an instrument of some other character. Since the party primarily liable has no intention of creating a negotiable instrument, none is created.

- Westfall agreed to sign a contract for the purchase of a car from Robinson. Robinson used a trick type of paper which contained the correct terms of the contract to sell. The paper was such that when the true contract was lifted up, it revealed a note for $5,000 and the signature of Westfall was to the note, not the contract to sell. This was fraud in the inception or execution and constituted a real defense, good against the whole world, provided the maker was not negligent. When a trick or device such as this is used, there is no negligence if an ordinary person could not detect the trick.

(5) LAPSE OF TIME UNDER A STATUTE OF LIMITATIONS. This defense relates to instruments that have been outlawed by the expiration of a statutory period.

(6) NONDELIVERY OF AN INCOMPLETED INSTRUMENT. If the negotiable instrument is incomplete and is not delivered, no contract is ever formed and even a holder in due course cannot collect. To be a real defense, the instrument must be both incomplete and nondelivered. If it is incomplete but still is actually delivered, the defense is personal, not absolute.

If the maker or the drawer of a negotiable instrument that is incomplete—that is, one on which blanks have been left—delivers it to another, he gives the holder implied authority to fill in the blanks and to complete the instrument in accordance with his directions. The signer is bound on the instrument if the blanks are filled in accordance with the authority given. The signer is liable even though the instrument was completed in a manner contrary to his directions, however, if the instrument is negotiated to a holder in due course.

(7) USURY. *Usury* is charging an interest rate in excess of the maximum rate fixed by law. The law on this point is not uniform, but in most states usury at the inception of the note is a real defense. New York makes an exception to this rule in the case of banks. If a bank accepts a negotiable instrument under conditions which make it a holder in due course, usury at the inception of the instrument is a personal defense, not a real defense.

(8) MISTAKES WHICH RENDER A CONTRACT VOID. In Chapter 5, pages 41 to 44, we discussed the mistakes that render a contract void. These mistakes made in the execution of a negotiable instrument constitute a good defense against even a holder in due course.

Defenses of the Indorsers. The preceding discussion of defenses relates to the defenses which only the maker of a note or the acceptor of a draft may make against a holder in due course. When the holder presents a negotiable instrument for payment and is refused, his next step is to demand payment from the indorsers. He can demand payment from them, either individually or jointly, regardless of the reason which the maker or the acceptor may give for not paying it. One or more of the indorsers, however, may have a tenable defense to make.

> *On June 26, 19—, I promise to pay to John Doe or order $500.*
>
> *Richard Roe*

This note was indorsed as follows:

Pay to the order of Adam Smith.
John Doe

Pay to the order of Henry Ratcliffe.
Adam Smith

Pay to the order of Bernard Funk.
Henry Ratcliffe

I IS THE INSTRUMENT NEGOTIABLE?	II IS THE PARTY A HOLDER IN DUE COURSE?	III WHAT IS THE NATURE OF THE DEFENSE?
The instrument must: 1. Be in writing and signed by the party executing it. 2. Contain either an order or a promise to pay. 3. Make the order or the promise unconditional. 4. Provide for the payment of a sum certain in money. 5. Be payable on demand or at a fixed or determinable future time. 6. Be payable to the order of a payee or to the bearer of the instrument. 7. Designate the payee and the drawee with reasonable certainty.	1. The instrument must be complete and regular on its face. 2. It must not be past due at the time of the negotiation. 3. The holder must take the instrument in good faith and for value. 4. The holder must have no notice of any infirmity in the instrument or any defect in the title of the person who negotiated it.	PERSONAL DEFENSES: 1. Duress. 2. Undue influence. 3. Misrepresentation. 4. Nondelivery of a completed instrument. 5. Fraud. 6. Lack of consideration. 7. Payment or part payment. 8. Setoff and counterclaim. REAL DEFENSES: 1. Personal incapacity to contract. 2. Illegality. 3. Forgery and alteration. 4. Fraud in the inception. 5. Lapse of time under a statute of limitations. 6. Nondelivery of an incompleted instrument. 7. Usury. 8. Mistakes which render a contract void.

Important Features of the Law of Negotiable Instruments.

On June 26, Bernard Funk presents the note to Richard Roe for payment, and payment is refused. Funk can now look to any one or all of the indorsers for payment. To do this, however, he has the note duly protested, and notice of dishonor and protest is given to each of the indorsers. Let us assume that Ratcliffe reimburses Funk. Ratcliffe then demands and receives payment from Smith; and Smith in turn goes back to Doe for reimbursement.

If Funk serves notice of dishonor, or notice of protest on Ratcliffe only, then Ratcliffe, in order to preserve his right to proceed against Smith and Doe should give notice to them. If Funk gives the notice to Smith and Doe, Ratcliffe need not do so.

If we assume the same facts except that Funk gave Doe and Smith notice of dishonor and protest but not Ratcliffe, then Ratcliffe would be the one to plead no notice as a defense. This would be a good defense for him, but it would not release Smith and Doe from liability since their rights were in no way jeopardized by Funk's failure to give notice to Ratcliffe.

The note may provide for a waiver of presentment for payment, as well as protest and notice of dishonor and protest, by the maker and all indorsers. In such event, the law as described above would not apply.

If notice of dishonor and protest is impossible, and the holder exercises all due diligence in an effort to give notice, then a failure to receive the notice is not a good defense. The last indorser is known to the holder, but his address may be unknown. The holder may not know any of the other indorsers or their addresses. In this event he is required only to use due diligence in trying to notify them.

Questions

1. Who are the immediate parties to a note?
2. Name the immediate parties to a draft.
3. Who is the one primarily liable on a note? On a draft?

4. What is the difference between a real defense and a personal defense?

5. Name and explain three personal defenses.

6. Who may collect a completed instrument that has been lost or stolen before it is delivered?

7. Name and explain three real defenses.

8. When does fraud in the inception exist?

9. What is the effect upon a holder in due course if the instrument is incomplete and is not delivered?

10. When the holder presents a negotiable instrument for payment and is refused, what is his next step?

Case Problems

1. Caroline Debbs was a private secretary to General Neal W. Butter. One of her duties was to reconcile his personal bank account each month. One month three checks had been clearly altered, but she delayed reconciling his statement. She was not exactly sure how to make a reconciliation and had not been able to make one for the two preceding months. The law in her state provided that all forgeries and alterations must be reported to the bank in 60 days. She did not report them for 95 days, and would not have discovered them then had it not been for the fact that General Butter gave a check in payment of his Country Club dues that was returned as a bad check. This mortified General Butter and he threatened to sue the bank. Must the bank or General Butter bear this loss?

2. A note dated July 8 for $1,200 and due four months from date was transferred by blank indorsement on September 12 to the Rock Island Implement Company in payment of the indorser's account. At the time the bookkeeper for the Rock Island Implement Company received the note, he was aware that A. W. Stout, the maker, was going to plead fraud when the note came due. On November 8, a representative of the Rock Island Implement Company presented the note to Stout for payment and payment was refused. The holder called J. W. Holsinger, the indorser, by telephone, and notified him of the dishonor. Stout now denied liability because of fraud, and Holsinger denied liability because the note was not presented for payment on the due date and also because he did not receive proper notice of dishonor. Were any of the defenses valid against the Rock Island Implement Company? YES

3. Cooper leased a house for one year to Runey for $90 a month. Runey was to sign the lease in triplicate. Through a clever device one of the signatures was made on a note for $5,000. Cooper then sold the note to Chavez, an innocent purchaser. When the note came due, Runey refused to pay, claiming fraud. Was this a good defense against an innocent purchaser?

4. Tatum, a young man twenty years of age, gave the Lamont Motor Company some cash and a note for the purchase of an automobile. The Lamont Motor Company transferred the note to a finance company. When the note became due, Tatum refused to pay, claiming infancy as a defense. Was this a good defense? Why?

5. Garrett gave Brooks the following note:

> *December 15, 19—*
>
> *60 days after date I will pay E. Brooks, or another party if he so orders, $500.*
>
> *A. Garrett*

Brooks induced Garrett to give him this note through fraud. He sold the note to Smith, an innocent purchaser. Smith, in turn, sold it to Jones who knew of the fraudulent nature of the transaction, but was not himself a party to it. Jones sued Garrett for the note, and Garrett attempted to plead fraud as a defense. Would the court permit him to offer this defense?

6. Davis filled out a note payable to Mullins. It was completed in every respect except that the amount was omitted pending a determination of the exact amount. Mullins stole the note, filled in the amount spaces for $1,000 and then sold it to Fortune, an innocent purchaser. Could Fortune collect the note from Davis?

What would your answer be if it had been completed before Mullins obtained possession of it?

7. Allen signed a note on June 1 payable on demand for $100 at 10 per cent interest. The maximum rate of interest in that state is 6 per cent and the penalty for usury is rendering the whole contract null and void. On December 1, Dodge, the payee, sold the note to Ford for value. Allen refused to pay the note on demand. Ford waited one month and then notified Dodge that the note had been dishonored. He later sued both Allen and Dodge for the value of the note. What defense, if any, could either defendant offer?

Cases for Review of Part V

1. Stevens executed the following instrument:

> New York, Aug. 17th, 1865. I certify that James Smilie, Jr., has deposited with me five hundred dollars, payable to his order on demand with interest from February 15, 1864, on the return of this certificate and my guarantee of his note to his brother, John Smilie, dated February 15, 1864, for the sum of five hundred dollars.
>
> Simon Stevens

This instrument was sold for value to an innocent purchaser. Stevens contended that the instrument was not negotiable in form, and therefore he could raise personal defenses even against an innocent purchaser. (Smilie vs. Stevens, 39 Vt. 315) Was the instrument negotiable?

2. Robbins executed a negotiable promissory note payable to Angie Daggett. Robbins did not deliver the note to Daggett but instead gave it to Hattie Ray, her own maid, to hold pending her directions as to delivery. Before the note was ever delivered to the payee, Daggett, the maker died. After the maker's death, Hattie Ray delivered the note to Daggett. Simonds, the executor of Robbins's estate, refused to pay the note on the ground there had never been a true delivery. (Daggett vs. Simonds, 53 N. E. 907) Was there ever a legal delivery?

3. Emmons Davis executed the following note:

> "For value received, I promise to pay to Elizabeth Gamble, or order, the sum of $1,500 in twelve months after I shall become the legal owner of one hundred and fifteen acres of land conveyed to me by my father, H. V. Davis, reserving to him, H. V. Davis, a life estate in said land.
>
> Emmons Davis

Gamble indorsed this note to McClenathan, an innocent purchaser. At the time the note was made Emmons Davis was absolutely certain to obtain title to the real estate although he did not have title at that time. Emmons Davis contended that the note was not payable at a definite and determinable future time, and therefore it was not negotiable. (McClenathan vs. Davis, 243 Ill. 87) Was this note negotiable?

4. Keel and Hoover executed a note to Day. The date of the note was erroneously omitted and the bank subsequently filled in the date, December 30, when actually the true date was December 1. Day, as an indorser, claimed that he was released from liability because of this improper date. (Bank of Houston vs. Day, 145 Mo. App. 410) Do you agree with Day?

5. Frank and Sophie Jackson executed a promissory note in favor of George Tribble. Sophie Jackson being unable to write, signed her name by a mark. When Tribble sued on the note, the Jacksons contended they were not liable because the notes were not properly signed. (Jackson vs. Tribble, 156 Ala. 480) Do you agree?

6. Under the laws of Kentucky a bet or a wager is said to be "vicious, illegal, and void." In that state a note was given in payment of a gambling debt. The note was transferred to a holder in due course. (123 Ky. 677) Would the holder in due course be permitted to collect the note from the maker?

7. Johnson Buford drew a draft on John H. Crutchfield for $202, payable to Jasper S. Martin. The draft was duly accepted when presented. When Martin brought suit against Crutchfield, the latter raised as a defense the fact that the drawer was a minor. (Crutchfield vs. Martin, 27 Okla. 764) Was this a valid defense?

8. Linnick signed his name to a blank check and later the incompleted check was stolen, the blank spaces filled in, and then indorsed over to Nutting & Company. Nutting & Company later cashed the check. Linnick sued Nutting & Company for reimbursement on the ground that they never had rightful title to the check. (125 N. Y. S. 93) Do you agree?

9. Clukey was the treasurer of the Belgrade Silver Black Fox Ranch Company. In this capacity it was his duty to draw checks on the company's bank account. He drew checks without authority on the company's account, payable to a personal creditor. One of these checks was to the Lewiston Trust Co. to whom he owed money. Later the Belgrade Silver Black Fox Ranch Company went bankrupt and the receiver sued the bank for a return of this money. (Boyle vs. Lewiston Trust Company, 126 Me. 74) Was the trust company a holder in due course?

10. Easly was the holder by negotiation of a certificate of deposit payable on demand, with a provision that no

interest would be paid after twelve months. Easley acquired the certificate considerably more than a year after its date. (Easly vs. East Tennessee National Bank, 138 Tenn. 369) Was Easley a holder in due course?

11. Samuel and Annie Jacobson executed a promissory note for $4,500, payable to Frank and Angelo Sarandrea. At the time of executing the note the Jacobsons lived in apartment 55 A of an apartment house of several apartments. The Sarandreas sold the note to Luis J. Cuddy and his wife. When the note became due, it was placed with Edwin C. and Henry Potter for collection. The Jacobsons moved before maturity and left no address. The Potters, not being able to find the makers to present the note for payment, notified the indorsers of the nonpayment. The indorsers contended that the holders did not make proper presentment. (Cuddy vs. Sarandrea, 52 R. I. 465) Do you agree?

12. Hall had very poor eyesight and had to rely upon someone to read for her. She was asked to sign a note in favor of Ferguson and Barnes. She never intended to sign this particular note, but through the fraud of her own attorney, she signed the note not realizing it was a note she was signing. The note was later sold to the First National Bank, a holder in due course. Hall refused to pay on the ground of fraud. (First National Bank vs. Hall, 169 Iowa 218) Was Hall liable on the note?

13. During Wright's absence from his office, a thief appropriated a note made payable to bearer. The thief negotiated the note to Clark for value. (54 Ill. 296) When the note was due, would Wright be obliged to pay Clark?

14. Bullock fraudulently induced Costello to make a note payable to Bullock's order. Bullock transferred the note to Ratcliff, a holder in due course. Ratcliff immediately sold the note to his father, and later repurchased it. At the time he repurchased the note, Ratcliff had notice of the fraud. (117 Va. 563) Would Costello have a good defense if he set up the fraud of Bullock as a defense to the suit brought by Ratcliff?

Part VI
AGENCY AND EMPLOYMENT

Chapter 26

Creation of an Agency

The Nature of Agency. When one party, known as a *principal,* appoints another party, known as an *agent,* to enter into contracts with third parties in the name of the principal, a contract of *agency* is formed. By this definition at least three parties are involved in every contract which an agent negotiates, the principal, the agent, and the third party. This feature of agency distinguishes it from all other types of employment relationships. The principal, the agent, or the third party may be a person, a partnership, or a corporation.

Importance of Agency. Because of the magnitude and the complexity of our modern industry, many of the important details pertaining to business transactions must be delegated by the owners of businesses to agents for performance. The relation creating this delegation of powers is governed by the general principles of law pertaining to contracts.

The underlying principles of partnerships and joint-stock companies are dependent upon an application of the law of agency; and the business of a corporation can be carried on only through the medium of agents. Much of the business of banks, manufacturing enterprises, and similar businesses is carried out by agents.

Even in the performance of ordinary routine matters by individuals, agents are necessary in order to bring one person into a business contractual relationship with other persons. Thus a farmer who sends an employee to town to have a piece of machinery repaired gives the latter the authority to enter into a contract that binds the farmer to the agreement. This case is an application of the maxim that "whatever a person does through another, he does himself."

What Powers May Be Delegated to an Agent? Generally speaking, all those things that one has the right to do personally he may do through an agent. There are, however, certain acts which are of such a personal nature that the courts will not permit them to be delegated to others. The law insists that if these acts are performed at all, they must be performed by the one who, because of the personal nature of such acts, should do them. Some of the acts that are considered personal and that may not be performed by an agent are: voting in a public election, executing a will, making an affidavit, painting a portrait, and representing a client in a lawsuit.

What one may not lawfully do himself may not be done through another. Thus no person can authorize an agent to commit a crime, to publish a libelous statement, to perpetrate a fraud, or to do any other act that is illegal, immoral, or opposed to the welfare of society. For example, an agreement to act as an agent to help another to secure a public office through improper means or to defraud the public cannot be enforced.

• Bibbs was an agent of the Magnolia Paint Company. His contract with this company provided that, in order to make sales, he might pay bonuses to parties unknown to the paint company. In making sales, Bibbs paid between $500 and $600 as bonuses. The paint company refused to reimburse Bibbs, and he brought suit to collect. The court held that if these bonuses were intended to be paid as bribes to purchasing agents, the agreement was illegal and Bibbs could not enforce the contract. Such an agreement is contrary to public policy and is opposed to honesty in business.

Other Types of Employment Relationships. There are two other types of employment relationships:

1. Independent contractors
2. Employer and employee, originally referred to in law as master and servant

Harold M. Lambert

Construction Contracts May Involve Laws Pertaining to Principals and Agents, Employers and Employees, and Independent Contractors.

(1) INDEPENDENT CONTRACTORS. A vast amount of work and many business transactions are performed for others by independent contractors. Probably the most common type of work performed by an independent contractor is that performed by building contractors. Services of newspaper carriers and delivery services are other examples of work preformed by independent contractors. In this type of employment relationship the contractor is not subject to the routine discipline of an agent or an employee. He need only fulfill his duties according to contract, but his hours of employment and tempo of work are fixed by him, not the employer. The chief need for making the distinction is to comply with the tax laws and labor legislation.

With but few exceptions every employer must pay social security taxes on the wages of his employees and agents, meet the minimum wage laws, pay time and a half for overtime and Sunday employment, and bargain with his workers collectively when they properly demand it. The employer need not comply with these laws in his dealings with independent contractors. The problem is complicated by the fact that many agents are neither employees nor independent contractors. Examples are lawyers, real estate agents, and in most cases, insurance agents. Must a life insurance company for example bargain collectivley with its agents? Most courts have said no, but the question is by no means finally settled.

(2) EMPLOYER AND EMPLOYEE. The chief difference between an employee and an agent is that an employee does not have the power to bind his employer on a contract while an agent does have that power. Furthermore, an employee does not owe his employer the same degree of loyalty and good faith required of an agent. For this reason an agent may be sued by his employer, the principal, for all damages due to a lack of good faith; while under identically the same circumstances, a mere employee would not be liable.

• Vaughn employed Pearson to fix his automobile. While Pearson was working on it, a prospective purchaser, thinking Pearson was the owner, offered him $2,000 for the car. Pearson bought the car from Vaughn for $1,800 and then sold it immediately to the interested party. As an employee, Pearson would not have to account to his employer for this profit. Such an act, however, would be a breach of good faith on the part of an agent.

Classification of Agents. Agents may be classified as follows:

1. General agents
2. Special agents

(1) GENERAL AGENTS. A *general agent* is one who is authorized to carry out all of his principal's business of a particular kind, or all of his principal's business at a particular place even though it is not all of one kind. A

purchasing agent and a bank cashier are examples of general agents who perform all of the principal's business of a particular kind. A manager who is in full charge of one branch of a chain of shoe stores is a general agent who transacts all of his principal's business at a particular place. In this capacity he buys and sells merchandise, employs help, pays bills, collects accounts, and performs all other duties. He has a wide scope of authority and the power to act on his own initiative.

(2) SPECIAL AGENTS. A special agent is one who is authorized by his principal to transact some specific act or acts. He is invested with only limited powers which he may use only for a specific purpose. The authorization may cover just one act, such as buying a house; or it may cover a series of acts which are mere repetitions, such as selling admission tickets to a movie.

Special Types of Agents. There are several special types of agents. In general these are special agents, but because of the nature of their duties, their powers may exceed those of the ordinary special agent.

1. Factors
2. Factors del credere
3. Brokers
4. Attorneys in fact

(1) FACTORS. A *factor* is one who receives possession of another's property for sale on commission. The commission merchant is the largest class of factors. He may sell in the name of his principal, but the usual practice is for him to sell in his own name. When he collects, he deducts his commission or factorage and remits the balance to the principal. The third party as a rule is aware that he is dealing with an agent by the nature of the business or by the name of the business. The words "Commission Merchant" usually appear on all stationery.

He has the power to bind the principal for the customary terms of sale for the type of business he is doing. In this regard his powers are slightly greater than those of the ordinary special agent.

(2) FACTORS DEL CREDERE. A *factor del credere* is a commission merchant who sells on credit and guarantees to the principal that these accounts are good. This is a form of contract of guaranty but the courts have ruled that the contract need not be in writing as required by the Statute of Frauds since it is a primary obligation of the factor.

(3) BROKERS. A *broker* is a special agent whose task is to bring the two contracting parties together. Unlike the factor, he does not have possession of the merchandise. In real estate and insurance he generally is the agent of the buyer rather than the seller. If his duty is merely to find a buyer, or sometimes a seller, he has no authority to bind the principal on any contract.

(4) ATTORNEYS IN FACT. An *attorney in fact* is a general agent who has been appointed by a formal contract. Of all types of agents, he has the greatest authority. A real estate agent can enter into a contract of sale that binds his principal but he does not have the power to execute the deed and sell the land, but an attorney in fact may be empowered to execute the deed as well. Some types of business, such as American Lloyds Insurance companies can act only through attorneys in fact. Their powers are coextensive with the principal's. The appointment of an attorney in fact must be by formal contract.

Extent of Authority. An agent's authority is from its very nature somewhat indefinite. There are many borderline acts which are difficult to determine as to whether or not they come within an agent's authority. These acts are a fruitful source of litigation.

Generally speaking, a general agent has authority to transact two classes of acts: those clearly within the scope of his actual or contractual authority, and those outside of this scope which appear to third parties to be apparently within the scope of the agent's actual authority.

As to innocent third parties, the powers of a general agent may be far more extensive than those granted to him by his principal. Secret limitations upon a general agent's authority are not necessarily binding upon a third party who has no knowledge of them.

• The owner of a radio shop employed a general agent to sell radios and instructed him to sell for cash only. If the agent disregarded this instruction and sold a radio on credit at reasonable terms of payment, the contract would have been binding upon the principal. Since it is the custom of radio shops in general to sell on credit, the purchaser had a right to presume that this agent had authority to sell on credit. This is frequently called *customary authority*.

If the salesman had taken a car in payment of the radio and had agreed to pay the purchaser $150 for the difference in value, the principal would not have been bound. This would clearly have been beyond even the apparent scope of the agent's authority, and the purchaser would have had no right to assume that the agent had such authority.

The foregoing rules apply only to general agents. Almost the opposite is true of special agents. The third party is required (1) to ascertain if the party is in fact a special agent and (2) to determine the powers of the agent. If a man represents himself to be the agent of another for the purpose of selling the car of that other person, the very nature of the transaction indicates that he is at most a special agent. The prospective purchaser must seek assurance from the principal as to the agent's authority.

Furthermore, where it is admitted that the agent has such authority and that the prospective customer is aware of it, the agent has no apparent authority to sell any other property of his principal. The very nature of the transaction notifies the customer that the agent is empowered to sell only the car. This leads to the conclusion that a special agent can bind his principal only when he has been expressly empowered to do so, unless the principal is present and by his silence implies additional authority.

Who May Appoint an Agent? Every person who is legally competent to act for himself may act through an agent. This rule is based upon the principle that whatever a person may do for himself, he may do through another. Hence corporations, partnerships, unincorporated clubs and societies, as well as individuals, may appoint agents.

In general the appointment of an agent by a minor is considered void; some states, however, have broken away from this strict rule and hold that the appointment of an agent by a minor is merely voidable, as in the case of the minor's ordinary contracts.

Who May Act as an Agent? Ordinarily any person may be appointed to act as an agent, provided he has sufficient intelligence to carry out his principal's orders. An idiot or a very young child could not act as an agent. Although a minor is limited in his power to contract for himself, he may act for an adult principal and bind the latter by his acts.

There are some types of transactions which cannot be performed by an agent unless he meets certain requirements. For example, in many states a realtor must possess certain definite qualifications and must, in addition, secure a license to act in this capacity. Unless he does this, he is disqualified to act as an agent in performing the duties of a realtor. Nor can anyone act as an agent if he also has an interest in the subject matter which is adverse to that of his principal, unless, of course, the principal is aware of the agent's interest.

Creation of an Agency. There are several ways in which the relationship of agency may be created. They are usually created by:

1. Appointment
2. Ratification
3. Estoppel
4. Necessity

(1) APPOINTMENT. The usual way of creating an agency is by appointment. The contract may be oral or written, formal or informal. There are some instances, however, where the appointment must be made in a particular form. The contract appointing an agent must be in writing if the agency is created to transfer title to real estate. Also, if an agent's authority is to extend beyond one year from the date of the contract, the contract is required by the Statute of Frauds to be in writing. If an agent is appointed to execute a formal contract, such as a mortgage, the contract appointing the agent must likewise be formal.

A written instrument indicating the appointment of an agent is known as a *power of attorney.* If a power of attorney is to be recorded, it must also be acknowledged before a notary public or other officer authorized to take acknowledgments. An ordinary form of power of attorney is shown on page 282.

(2) RATIFICATION. The approval by one person of an act previously done by another in the former's name without authority is known as *ratification.* The unauthorized act may have been done by an assumed agent who purported to act as an agent without real or apparent authority, or it may have been done by a real agent who exceeded his apparent authority. The supposed principal in such a case is not bound by the act unless and until he ratifies it. The effect of the ratification is that the ratification relates back to the date of the act done by the assumed agent; hence the assumed agent is put in the same

Power of Attorney

Know All Men By These Presents: *that* I, Gene Dorsey of Boise, Idaho

have *made, constituted and appointed and by these presents do make, constitute and appoint*

James Turner

my *true and lawful attorney for* me *and in* my *name, place and stead to*

represent me in the operation of my lumber mill in the State of Idaho

Hereby giving and granting unto my *said attorney full and whole power and authority in and about the premises; and generally to do all and every act and acts, thing and things, device and devices, in the law whatsoever needful and necessary to be done in and about the premises, for* me *and in* my *name to do, execute and perform as large and amply, to all intents and purposes, as* I *might or could do, if personally present; and an attorney or attorneys under* him *for the purpose aforesaid, to make and substitute, and the same to remove and revoke at* his *pleasure, hereby ratifying and confirming as good and effectual, in law and in equity, all that* my *said attorney or* his *substitute shall lawfully and legally do by virtue hereof.*

In Witness Whereof, I *have hereunto set* my *hand and seal the* tenth *day of* March *in the year of our Lord one thousand nine hundred and* fifty-seven

Sealed and Delivered in Presence of

Glenn Gordon

Travis Taylor

Gene Dorsey (SEAL)

(SEAL)

A Power of Attorney

position as if he had had authority to do the act at the time the act was done by him.

The essential elements of a valid ratification are:

(a) The one who assumed the authority of an agent must have acted for the party who attempts to ratify the act.

(b) The unauthorized act must have been committed in the name of the alleged principal.

(c) The one attempting to ratify must have been capable of authorizing the act at the time the act was done. Thus an act of a promoter cannot be ratified by a corporation that is formed subsequently. Since the effect of the ratification is that the ratification is thrown back to the day the act was done, the corporation cannot ratify the act of the promoter because it was not in existence at the time of the act.

(d) The one attempting to ratify must be capable of authorizing the act at the time he gives his approval of the act.

(e) The one attempting to ratify must have knowledge of all material facts.

(f) The one attempting to ratify must approve the entire act.

(g) A valid ratification once made cannot later be withdrawn.

(h) The act that is ratified must be legal.

(3) ESTOPPEL. Agency by ratification and agency by estoppel are often confused. In agency by ratification the principal is bound because he intended to be bound; otherwise he would have refused to ratify the act of the person who assumed to act as his agent. In *agency by estoppel* the principal is bound regardless of the fact that there was no intention to be bound. This liability arises when a person by words or conduct leads another person to believe that a third party is his agent. The principal is held liable for the purpose of preventing an injustice to parties who have been mislead by the acts or the conduct of the principal.

• Slaughter was permitted access to the stationery, forms, seal, and authenticating certificates of the Maxsted Surety Company. In addition, it was customary for the surety company to permit Slaughter to deliver bonds and other instruments on which the company was liable and to collect the initial premiums. Persons calling up the surety company to apply for bonds were customarily referred to Slaughter, whose office was in the offices of the surety company. Slaughter stole some of the bonds and sold them to Kahn, an innocent purchaser for value. Kahn sued the surety company, and the company was held liable on the forged bonds. The court held that the surety company had so clothed Slaughter with apparent authority to act for it that the surety company was estopped from denying his authority to deliver and collect on the forged bonds.

(4) NECESSITY. The relationship of agency may be created by necessity. A husband is bound to support his wife and minor children. If he fails to provide them with necessaries, the wife may pledge the husband's credit, even against his will. Agency by necessity may also arise from some unforeseen emergency. Thus the driver of a bus operating between distant cities may pledge the owner's credit in order to have needed repairs made, and may have the cost charged to the owner.

Questions

1. What is an agency?

2. Name the parties who are involved in a contract which an agent negotiates?

3. Why are most business transactions carried on by agents?

4. What acts can never be delegated to an agent?

5. How does an independent contractor differ from an agent?

6. What is the difference between an employee and an agent?

7. What is a general agent?

8. What is the difference in the authority of a special agent and a general agent?

9. (a) Who may appoint an agent?
(b) May a minor act as an agent?

10. What are the essential elements of a valid ratification?

Case Problems

1. McDowell was business manager for the WTUW radio station. Philips, representing himself as the agent of the Hartsfield Oil Company, presented to McDowell an advertising program to run for two weeks over the station. The charge agreed upon was $800. After the program was completed, McDowell sent a bill to the Hartsfield Oil Company.

The company denied liability on the ground that Philips did not have the authority to place advertising contracts with the station. The facts showed that Philips' actual authority was to call on stations selling the Hartsfield products, to recruit new agents for the company, and to build goodwill for the oil company whenever possible. Was this authority broad enough to empower him to contract for advertising campaigns?

2. The Kinsey Machine Tool Company shipped by its own truck a truck load of machine tools from its plant in New Jersey to Jacksonville, Florida. On the way the truck driver had several flat tires and one tire blew out because the truck was overloaded. He stopped in Richmond and purchased twelve new heavy duty tires and tubes, a complete set for the truck, and had the tire company install them. He charged the tires to the Kinsey Machine Company. When the bill was received the company refused to pay it, claiming the truck driver was only an employee, not an agent. Was the purchaser liable for the tires?

3. Dalton, a real estate broker, was asked by Hallahan to find him some business property of a particular description. Dalton, through advertisements and other means, located a property that was acceptable to Hallahan. Dalton acted as intermediary between Hallahan and the owner until an agreement that was satisfactory to both parties was reached. This called for a binder payment of $1,000. Hallahan made this payment to Dalton. Dalton then disappeared. Hallahan and the owner of the real estate each insisted that Dalton was the other's agent. Who must bear this $1,000 loss, Hallahan or the owner of the real estate?

4. Hill invested all his savings in the Hill Top Service Station and began operations in high hopes of an improved income. He purchased gasoline and oil from the Rife Distributors. After about $2,C00 worth of products had been delivered, the driver presented Hill with a statement and a request for payment. Hill paid the bill in cash. The truck driver disappeared, and Rife Distributors demanded that Hill pay again. Must he do so?

5. Flannigan, a secondhand car dealer, promised Fugate 20 per cent commission if he, Fugate, would sell Flannigan's cars for cash. Fugate sold one to Pepper for $100 cash and $50 a month until the balance was paid. Flannigan refused to abide by the contract. Was he bound by it?

6. McClannahan was a washing machine salesman for the Home Appliance Company. He was instructed to sell for 20 per cent down and the balance in 12 months. He sold one machine and gave the buyer 18 months to pay the balance. The buyer knew that McClannahan was not supposed to allow more than 12 months. Was the principal liable?

7. The Lee Mercantile Company employed Parker, a young man nineteen years of age, as their purchasing agent. Parker entered into an agreement with the White Motor Company to buy a delivery truck. Would the firm be bound by this act if they felt that their purchasing agent had made an unwise purchase?

8. Johnson promised his neighbor, Dennis, a 20 per cent discount if he would sell Johnson's car for cash. Dennis sold the car to Smith for $800, took an old car valued at $300 as a down payment, and agreed to let Smith pay the balance at the rate of $40 a month. Johnson refused to be bound by the agreement. Was he within his rights?

9. Johnson, in the presence of Elliott, said to Black, "Elliott has made me his agent to sell his stock of merchandise in bulk. I would like to talk to you about it." Elliott made no comment. Shortly thereafter Johnson entered into a written contract with Black whereby Black agreed to buy the stock in bulk for $6,000. Was Elliott bound by this contract?

10. Mrs. Fred Berry, without her husband's knowledge or consent, bought necessaries from a merchant on her husband's credit.

(a) In this case was Mrs. Berry really an agent?

(b) Could Fred Berry be held for the contract price or for the reasonable value of necessaries furnished to his family? Explain.

Chapter 27

Operation and Termination of an Agency

Operation of Agency. Every contract creates rights, duties, and obligations on the part of all the contracting parties. These rights, duties, and obligations are set out in the contract. In a contract of agency, the law imposes upon the agent certain duties even though they are not set out in the contract. Likewise, the relationship of agency creates specific duties and obligations which the principal owes to his agent even though these are not specifically enumerated in the contract. In turn, the same relationship imposes upon both principal and agent certain duties and obligations to third parties. An examination of these duties and obligations will reveal the importance of the relationship of agent and principal as well as the necessity for each party in the relationship to be fully cognizant of both his rights and his duties.

Agent's Duties to His Principal. An agent owes the following important duties to his principal:

1. Loyalty and good faith
2. Obedience
3. Skill and diligence
4. Accounting

(1) Loyalty and Good Faith. The relationship of principal and agent is fiduciary in nature; that is, the principal must trust the agent to perform his duties according to contract. The relationship of agent and principal calls for a higher degree of faith and trust than do most contractual relationships. For this reason the law imposes upon the agent the duty of loyalty and good faith, and deprives him of his right to compensation,

reimbursement, and indemnification when he proves disloyal to his principal or acts in bad faith. The interests of the principal must be promoted by the agent to the utmost of his ability.

● James DeFoe was the manager of Smith's Super Market, acting as general agent of the owner. Without the knowledge or consent of Smith, the principal, DeFoe purchased a half interest in a competing firm. When Smith learned of this act, he discharged DeFoe and refused to pay him the commission which had accrued for the past three months. Smith was justified in this action because DeFoe had not acted with loyalty and good faith toward Smith. In addition, Smith could sue DeFoe for any damages which he may have sustained by reason of the breach of trust.

(2) Obedience. An agent may have two types of instructions from his principal: one is routine and the other is discretionary. In all routine instructions the agent must carry them out to the letter. An illustration is an instruction not to accept any payments made by check. The agent is liable for any losses incurred by reason of disobeying instructions. He is not justified in disobeying such instructions under any conditions.

If the instruction is a discretionary one, the agent must use the best judgment of which he is capable. For example, if the agent is instructed to accept checks, he is not liable for a bad check when in his judgment the drawer of the check was solvent and reliable. If he accepts a check, however, which he has reason to believe is bad, he will be liable for any loss which the principal sustains by reason of this act.

(3) Skill and Diligence. One who acts as an agent must possess the skill required to perform his duties and must be diligent in performing the skill. There is an implied warranty that the agent has such skill and will exercise such diligence in the contract of agency. Any breach of this warranty subjects the agent to a liability for damages for the loss by reason of the breach.

● Johnson, a certified public accountant, prepared an income tax return for his client, The Madras Textile Company. Because of a lack of knowledge of the tax laws, errors were made in the return which were later discovered by the Internal Revenue Bureau investigator.
The interest and penalty for the erroneous amount of tax was $150. Johnson was liable for this extra expense because of his implied warranty that he had the skill required to make out the return correctly.

(4) ACCOUNTING. The duties of an agent include the keeping of a record of all money transactions pertaining to the agency. He must account to the principal for any money and property of the latter that may come into his possession. Money should be deposited in a bank in the name of the principal, preferably in a bank other than that in which the agent keeps his own personal funds. If the deposit is made in the name of the agent, any loss that may be caused by the failure of the bank will fall on the agent. The agent must keep personal property belonging to the principal separate from his own. If the agent commingles the property of both of them in such a manner that it cannot be separated, the principal will have the right to the entire mass.

● Edenfield sold for cash merchandise for his principal in the amount of $1,800. He made out a deposit ticket in favor of his principal and sent the money by a hotel messenger boy to be deposited in the bank. The messenger boy absconded with the money. Edenfield was liable for the loss because he had not properly accounted for the collections. The funds had to be imparted to the control of the principal before the agent's liability ceased.

Principal's Duties to His Agent. The principal has three important duties in respect to his agent:

1. Compensation
2. Reimbursement
3. Indemnification

(1) COMPENSATION. The compensation due the agent is determined by the contract of employment. As in most other contracts, this provision may be either express or

implied. If the amount is clearly and expressly stated, disputes seldom arise. If one is asked to serve as agent but no amount of compensation is stated, the customary rules apply. This is especially true when one acts as an attorney or an accountant. If there are no customary rules, a reasonable rate will be fixed by the court according to the character of the services rendered. Frequently, the compensation is on a contingent basis, such as a percentage of the selling price, provided a sale is made. In such a case, no matter how much time is expended by the agent, he cannot collect compensation unless a sale is made.

• The Devon Motor Company promised Fletcher a reasonable commission on all sales of cars which Fletcher might make. Fletcher sold one for $2,400 and then demanded a 33⅓ per cent commission. So long as this agreement remained executory, it was void because the offer was not specific enough to accept. After a car was sold, however, the Devon Motor Company had to pay a customary commission for the sale. If the commission in that locality was 20 per cent, then Fletcher could collect this amount but no more.

(2) Reimbursement. Any expenses incurred or disbursements made by the agent from his personal funds as a necessary part of the agency is the liability of the principal. The agent is entitled to reimbursement. If, for example, the agent had to pay from his personal funds a $100 truck repair bill before he could continue his mission, he would be entitled to reimbursement. If, on the other hand, he had to pay a $50 fine for speeding, the principal would not be required to reimburse him. Any expense incurred as a result of an unlawful act must be borne by the agent.

• Burbank instructed his agent, Edison, to buy 1,000 shares of U. S. Steel stock. Edison, from his own funds, purchased through an error, 1,000 shares of Bethlehem Steel stock. Edison was not entitled to reimbursement because of his negligence. He could, however, resell the stock and reimburse himself since the stock actually belonged to him because Burbank refused to accept it.

(3) INDEMNITY. A contractual disbursement made by the agent for the principal is an expense of the principal. If the payment is made by the agent, not by reason of a contract but as a result of a loss or damage due to an accident, the principal must indemnify the agent. He reimburses him for expenses and indemnifies him for losses and damages. If an agent is fined for an act done at the request of the principal and the agent is ignorant of the illegal nature of the act, then the principal must indemnify the agent.

- Cooper, at the express instruction of his principal, the Adams Aggregate Company, contracted to supply all the aggregate needed for the construction of a certain building, the total cost to be $7,000. Cooper lost $1,500 on the project. The Adams Aggregate Company had to indemnify him.

Agent's Liabilities to Third Parties. Ordinarily whenever an agent performs his duties, he thereby binds the principal but not himself. In his relations with third parties, however, an agent may make himself personally liable in several ways:

(1) If an agent contracts in his own name and does not disclose the name of the principal, he becomes liable to the same extent as though he were the principal.

(2) An agent may make himself personally liable to the third party by an express agreement to be responsible.

(3) If a person assumes to act for another without authority, or if one exceeds or materially departs from the authority that he was given, he is personally liable to those with whom he does business. The latter situation may arise when an agent is overzealous in effecting what he may think is a desirable contract.

(4) If an agent signs a contract in his own name, he will be held liable. He will not escape this liability by writing the word "Agent" after his name or by signing his name and then indicating that he is the agent for a certain person. Such words merely describe the agent.

(5) An agent is personally liable for fraud or any other wrongdoing, whether it was caused by disobedience, carelessness, or malice, or whether it was committed on the order of the principal.

Principal's Duties and Liabilities to Third Parties. The principal is ordinarily liable to third parties for contracts made within the apparent scope of a general agent's authority, and within the actual scope of a special agent's authority. When the agent enters into an unauthorized contract that is not within the apparent scope of his authority, the principal is not bound unless he subsequently ratifies the contract.

The enforceability of any contract may be denied, not because the agent did not have the authority to make the contract, but on the ground that he exceeded his authority or violated his instructions. In such a case the test is: Did a reasonably prudent man have a right to believe the agent had the authority to make a contract with these provisions? If the answer is in the affirmative, the principal is bound by the contract. For example, if the manager of a furniture store sells a suite of furniture on credit contrary to the authority granted to him, the principal is bound to fulfill the contract with the third party, provided the latter did not know of the limitation upon the agent's authority. The agent is then liable to the principal for any loss sustained.

The principal, as well as the agent, is liable for an injury to the person or the property of a third party that was caused by the negligence or the wrongful act of the agent in the course of his employment. When the agent steps aside from the business of his principal and commits a wrong or injury of his own to another, the principal is not liable unless he ratifies the act.

Termination by Acts of the Parties. Agencies may be terminated by acts of the parties or by operation of law.

The chief ways by which an agency may be terminated by acts of the parties are by:

1. Original agreement
2. Subsequent agreement
3. Revocation
4. Renunciation by the agent

(1) ORIGINAL AGREEMENT. The contract creating the agency may specify a date for the termination of the agency. In that event, the agency is automatically terminated on that date. Most special agencies, such as a special agency to sell an automobile, are terminated because their purpose has been accomplished.

(2) SUBSEQUENT AGREEMENT. An agency may be terminated at any time by a mutual agreement between the principal and the agent.

(3) REVOCATION. The principal may revoke the agent's authority at any time, thereby terminating the agency. One must distinguish between the right to terminate the agency and the power to do so. The principal has the right to terminate the agency any time the agent breaches any material part of the contract of employment. If the agent, for example, fails to account for all money collected for the principal, the agent may be discharged and the principal incurs no liability for breach of contract. The principal, on the other hand, has the power, with one exception, to revoke the agent's authority even though the agent has complied fully with his part of the contract. Under these circumstances, however, the principal becomes liable to the agent for all damages which he sustains by reason of the unjustifiable discharge. This is the agent's sole remedy because he cannot insist upon the right to continue to act as an agent even though he has done nothing to justify a termination before the end of the contract period. The only exception

to this rule is an agency coupled with an interest, illustrated below.

● Bradshaw owned a house which he wished to sell for $15,000. He also owed Grant $4,500. He appointed Grant his agent to sell the house, agreeing to pay Grant five per cent commission for selling the house, out of which Grant would have to pay all advertising and other expenses incidental to selling the house. Grant was also to deduct the $4,500 from the selling price and remit the balance to Bradshaw.

After Grant had spent $25 advertising the house for sale, Bradshaw attempted to revoke Grant's authority to sell the house. This was an agency coupled with an interest, namely the right to collect the $4,500 from the selling price. Bradshaw had neither the right nor the power to terminate the agency here by unilateral action. Grant could enter into a binding contract of sale in spite of Bradshaw's attempted revocation.

To constitute an agency coupled with an interest, the interest must be substantial, not trivial. The expenditure of $25 for advertising was not in itself sufficient to constitute this an agency coupled with an interest.

(4) RENUNCIATION. Like the principal, the agent has the power to renounce the agency at any time. If the agent abandons the agency without cause before the contract is fulfilled, he is liable to the principal for all losses due to the unjustified abandonment.

Termination by Operation of Law. An agency may be terminated by operation of law. The chief ways in which this may occur are:

1. Subsequent illegality
2. Death or incapacity
3. Destruction
4. Bankruptcy
5. Dissolution

(1) SUBSEQUENT ILLEGALITY. Subsequent illegality of the subject matter of the agency terminates the agency.

(2) DEATH OR INCAPACITY. Death or incapacity of either the principal or agent terminates the agency. For

example, if the agent loses his power of speech so that he cannot perform his principal's business, the agency is automatically terminated.

(3) DESTRUCTION. Destruction of the subject matter, such as the destruction of a house by fire that was to be sold by the agent, terminates the agency.

(4) BANKRUPTCY. Bankruptcy of the principal terminates the agency. In most cases bankruptcy of the agent does not terminate the agency.

(5) DISSOLUTION. Dissolution of a corporation terminates an agency. This is equivalent to death since a dissolution of a corporation is a legal death.

Notice of Termination. When an agency is terminated by an act of one party, the principal must give notice to third parties with whom the agent has previously transacted business and who would be likely to deal with him as an agent.

When an agency is terminated by the operation of law, notice need not be given either to the agent or to third parties. Since the law has put a stop to the agency, it also relieves the parties from the necessity of giving notice.

Questions

1. What duties does an agent owe his principal?

2. What two types of instructions may a principal give his agent?

3. What does an agent warrant when he accepts his job?

4. How should an agent deposit his principal's money in a bank?

5. If the agent and the principal do not set the amount of the agent's compensation at the time the contract is performed, how is the amount determined if the agent and the principal cannot agree?

6. If an agent must pay agency expenses out of his personal funds in order to complete his mission, what is the liability of the principal?

7. If an agent grossly exceeds his authority when contracting with a third party, who is held liable on the contract?

8. If an agent commits a fraudulent act on the instructions of the principal, who is liable to the third party for damages?

9. What is the principal's liability in regard to third parties for injuries caused by the negligent acts of his agents?

10. How may an agency be terminated?

Case Problems

1. Simpson was the office manager for the Yellow Leaf Cigar Corporation. The corporation borrowed $10,000 from the bank. Simpson was duly authorized to borrow the money and to sign the note. He signed the note as follows:

Yellow Leaf Cigar Corporation,
James Simpson, Agent

The corporation went bankrupt and the bank sued Simpson on the note. Was Simpson liable for its payment?

2. Gordon's, Inc. was a national organization with a large field force of salesmen supervised by district sales superintendents. The head office prepared a Salesman's Manual, a copy of which was given to each salesman when he was employed. He was told to obey all instructions in the manual. One of these instructions read as follows: "Each day the salesman must deposit all collections before closing hours of the bank, make out a duplicate deposit slip, and mail one of these to the Main Office." One week one of the district sales superintendents met one of his salesmen each day about noon, had lunch with him, and inquired as to how much money the salesman had collected that day. Then he said, "I am returning to the head office as soon as we finish lunch. You let me have the money, and I'll take it in with me." Five of the salesmen did this, and the sales superintendent never returned to his office. The salesmen were sued by Gordon's and the bonding company for the amount of money embezzled by the supervisor. Must each salesman make good the loss to the extent of his collections?

3. The Scott Investment Company owned a housing project consisting of about 200 private dwellings. Langdon was the manager for this project. One of his duties was to keep each property properly insured. He was a secret partner in an insurance agency with his mother-in-law. He placed all insurance with this agency. There was no evidence that he purchased any more insurance than was necessary nor was there any excessive charge of any kind. When the principal learned of Langdon's ownership of the agency, it demanded his share of the profits on all policies placed on the 200 dwellings. Was the Scott Investment Company entitled to these profits?

4. Ogletree was a collecting agent for the Benson Realty Company. He deposited $3,200 of the company's money in his personal account in the Planters National Bank. He then remitted to his principal by personal check. Before this check was cleared, the creditors of Ogletree levied upon his bank account with the Planters National Bank. The court awarded the money to Ogletree's creditors. The Benson Realty Company sued Ogletree, claiming he had not accounted for the money he had collected for them. Had Ogletree properly accounted for these funds?

5. Larson, agent for the Cronin Fuel and Supply Company, had instructions to sell nothing on credit unless he was convinced that the customer's credit was good. Tarpley, a new customer, was given credit to the extent of $400. Larson extended this credit to Tarpley because Tarpley looked honest and he had no information that Tarpley's credit was not good. The local credit bureau kept an up-to-date record of the town's residents relative to their credit rating. This bureau had information which showed that Tarpley was a very poor credit risk. This information would have been supplied to Larson had he requested it. Larson claimed he was not aware that there was such an organization in town. The principal sued Larson for the $400. Was he liable?

6. Worsham was appointed an exclusive agent to sell the Old Dominion Motel for $175,000 at a 3 per cent commission. He had two or three prospective buyers who had made appointments to inspect the property. To impress them, Worsham issued to dozens of people tickets entitling them to one night's free lodging. Worsham paid for these guests out of his personal funds but with the full knowledge of the owner of the Motel. Monroe purchased the Motel and then learned of Worsham's action. He sued Worsham personally

for the damages he sustained because of the fraud. Worsham contended that as an agent he was not liable even if fraud was used. Was this a good defense for Worsham?

7. A paper mill was situated on the bank of a river in a state where it was a violation of law to dump raw waste material in the river. Kilgore was the manager of the plant for the absentee owners. He personally ordered waste material dumped in the river, and because of its poisonous nature many fish were killed. Kilgore was fined $2,500 for this act. He then demanded that his employer indemnify him. Must the principal do so?

8. Amoss was the agent for the Bolivar Hardware Company. One of his duties was to collect all time drafts and notes of the company as they came due. Twenty days after one note for $500 came due, he presented it for payment, but it was dishonored. After another two weeks, he notified the indorsers of the dishonor. As a result of these delays the indorsers were released and the maker of the note became bankrupt. Amoss's employer then demanded payment from Amoss. Was he liable?

9. Drake acted in the capacity of a general agent for the D & E Grocery Company. One of Drake's duties was to collect each week from the company's charge customers. Drake was discharged. Without the knowledge of the company, he made several collections after his discharge and failed to account for the money. The D & E Grocery Company demanded that its customers pay a second time. Must they pay again if they had already paid Drake?

Chapter 28

Employer and Employee

Nature of the Employment Contract. The vast majority of workers are employees, not agents. They are hired to perform certain specified tasks but do not deal with third parties as agents of their employers. They have no implied authority to bind the employer on contracts. The common law very definitely sets forth the rights, duties, and responsibilities of both the employer and the employee. In the early days these laws were slanted heavily in favor of the employer. Modern legislation has modified much of this common law, but many well-established principles of the common law are still in force. Modern labor legislation is set out in Chapter 29. This chapter will deal primarily with the remnants of the common law as it relates to employers and employees.

Creation of Employer and Employee Relationship. The relationship of employer and employee arises from the contract of employment, either express or implied. As a rule, the relationship arises only from an express contract. The common law was jealous of the right of the employer to hire whom he pleased and of the right of the employee to choose freely his employer. The relationship of employer and employee could not be imposed upon anyone without this assent. Thus, if one voluntarily performs the duties of a servant, he cannot by that act subject the employer or householder to assume the liability of a master. But if a man accepts the proffered services of another in such a way as to imply a willingness to hire him, he will be bound as an employer even though the contract is implied.

In all but a few instances the contract of employment may be oral. If the contract of employment cannot be performed within one year from the date of making, the contract must be in writing as required by the Statute of Frauds.

Union Contracts. As indicated in a preceding paragraph, the employer-employee relationship can come into existence only as the result of a contract, express or implied. Formerly the employer contracted individually with each employee. Under this condition two employees doing the same kind of work might receive radically different rates of pay. The contract of employment came into existence by an offer and an acceptance. Theoretically it was a personal matter with each employee whether he was willing to work for less money than a fellow employee doing the same work. Men with large families and great responsibilities tended to be meek in direct ratio to their responsibilities. This tended to hold wages in general down. Out of this and other economic factors grew the union movement and collective bargaining or contracting in many industries. An agent of the employees speaks and contracts for all the employees collectively. As a general rule a contract is still made individually with each employee, but the union contract binds the employer to pay certain wages and work each employee only a certain number of hours. In other words, the union contract binds the employer to include certain minimum features in each employee's contract.

Duties and Liabilities of the Employer. The employer under the common law had five well-defined duties:

1. Duty to exercise care
2. Duty to provide a reasonably safe place to work
3. Duty to provide safe tools and appliances
4. Duty to provide competent and sufficient employees for the task
5. Duty to instruct employees with reference to the dangerous nature of employment

(1) Duty to Exercise Care. The employer under the common law is not an insurer of the employee's safety. He is liable for negligence in the care of his employees. He must exercise that degree of care which the nature of the business demands. He is not liable, however, for injuries resulting from the hazardous nature of the business itself. The courts generally use two tests to determine if the employer has used the degree of care required. First, did he use that degree of care which an ordinary prudent man under similar circumstances would use? Second, did he act under the particular circumstances as an ordinary prudent man? If the anwer is "yes" in both instances, then the employer is not liable for the resulting injuries to the employees. If the nature of the business is highly hazardous, then the employer must exercise a high degree of diligence to prevent accidents.

(2) Duty to Provide a Reasonably Safe Place to Work. The employer is required to furnish every employee with a reasonably safe place to work. What is a safe place depends upon the nature of the work. A coal mine is a dangerous place; but if it is made as safe as the nature of coal mining permits, the employer is not liable for accidents under the common law. Most states have statutory laws supplementing and modifying the common law for hazardous industries. When one of these statutory laws and the common law conflict the statutory law prevails.

● Smith and Jones were painters. The Mathis Construction Company supplied them with adequate scaffolding material to build all necessary scaffolds. Smith and Jones negligently built the scaffold in such a way that it fell injuring both of them. The Mathis Construction Company was not liable because it fulfilled its duty by making possible a safe working place. It was not liable to the employees when their injuries were the result of their own negligence. Under the workmen's compensation laws, a covered employee may, however, collect insurance for injuries caused by his own negligence.

The safe place to work includes not only the particular spot where the worker performs his duties, but the whole premises which the employee may use in the course of his employment.

(3) Duty to Provide Safe Tools and Appliances. The tools furnished the employees by the employer must be reasonably safe. This rule applies also to the machinery and appliances. Safe does not mean, of course, free from all danger. Some types of machinery and appliances are dangerous even under the best working conditions possible. The employer is required to use only ordinary care, relative to the nature of the work, in providing safe tools and machinery. He is not bound to discard old tools in order to install the latest and safest devices. If experience has shown that certain appliances or devices are dangerous and that newer devices have eliminated or greatly minimized the hazardous nature of the tool or device, then an employer must provide the safer method.

(4) Duty to Provide Competent and Sufficient Employees for the Task. Both the number of employees and their skill and experience affect the hazardous nature of many jobs. A task which is safe when performed by four men may be highly hazardous when only three men attempt it. Futhermore, the task may be safely performed by three men who are competent, but the same task may be very hazardous when one of the men is inexperienced. The employer is liable for all injuries to employees when the direct cause is due either to an insufficient number of workers or to the lack of skill of some of the workers. The employer is required to know the safe number of men required for each task. He also must have knowledge of the skill required to perform the task in a safe manner and make sure that each employee actually possesses that skill.

The Employer Has the Duty to Provide Safe Tools and Equipment.

Ewing Galloway

• The Open Spaces Trucking Company employed Mullins as a truck driver. Mullins had the use of only one eye and could not see too well out of that one. As a result of Mullin's defective vision, the truck was wrecked and Dennis, the helper on the truck, was killed. The employer was liable for the fatal injury because of his failure to provide competent employees. It was the duty of the Open Spaces Trucking Company to determine the status of Mullin's vision before hiring him.

(5) DUTY TO INSTRUCT EMPLOYEES. All new employees must be instructed as fully as necessary to familiarize themselves with their duties. When new machinery or devices are installed, all employees who must work with the machinery must be instructed as to the nature of the operation and the dangers involved. If the employees are experienced in the use of the appliances, no additional instruction need be given them. Also, there is no need to instruct employees about the dangerous nature of machines when the danger is very evident for all to see, such as a moving saw or meshing gears.

Liabilities of the Employer to Third Parties. The employer is liable under certain circumstances for injuries to third parties which are caused by his employees. To be liable, the employee must have committed the injury in the course of his employment. If the employee, on his own initiative, injures a third party, and the injury was not a result of his work on his job, then the employee is personally liable but the employer is not. The employer will be liable, however, if he ordered the act which caused the injury, or if he had knowledge of the act and assented to it. Finally, the employer is liable for the torts of his employees when these torts are due to his own negligence in not enforcing safe working procedures or in not employing competent employees.

• The Benten Wrecking Company instructed its employees not to throw timbers from the roof of the building it was wrecking unless one employee was on the ground to see that no one was in danger. The employees ignored this instruction and threw a large timber from the roof, injuring a man walking along beside the building. The company was liable for this injury even though the employees ignored their instructions.

Termination of Employment. When the relation of employer and employee is based upon a contract of employment, the relation may be terminated in the same manner as any other ordinary contract. When the relation exists for an indefinite period, either party may terminate the relation at any time by giving the notice required by law. In such a case the party terminating the relation will not incur any liability.

Justifiable Discharge. An employer may discharge an employee for cause before the end of his term of employment. When an employee is thus discharged, he has no legal right of action against his employer for damages. In the event of a discharge of an employee without cause before the end of his term of employment, however, the employer is liable for damages. Justifiable causes for discharge may be summarized as follows:

(1) The willful disobedience of any reasonable and lawful order

(2) Gross moral misconduct, defrauding the employer, or revealing trade secrets

(3) Incompetency, serious illness, or permanent disability

(4) Habitual neglect in the performance of duties

Justifiable Abandonment. When an employee abandons his employment without cause before the end of his term of employment, he is liable for damages. There are certain circumstances, however, under which an employee may rightfully abandon his employment and not be held liable for a breach of contract. These causes may be summarized as follows:

(1) The nonpayment of wages

(2) The wrongful assault of the employee by the employer

(3) The performance of services not contemplated in the agreement

(4) Injurious conditions of employment due to the negligence or the acts of the employer

Common-Law Defenses of the Employer. While the common law imposed many duties upon the employer to protect the worker on the job, it allowed several defenses that were sufficient to defeat practically all claims for compensation for injuries sustained on the job. The four most common ones were:

1. Contributory negligence rule
2. The fellow-servant rule
3. The assumption of the risk rule
4. The nonsurvivorship rule

(1) CONTRIBUTORY NEGLIGENCE RULE. Under the common law if a worker sustains an injury on the job, he can sue his employer for damages. To establish liability, he must prove breach of duty on the part of the employer, namely that he failed to provide safe working conditions, or one of the other duties set out on page 300. The employer can escape liability for this breach of duty if he

can establish the fact that the employee's own negligence contributed to the accident. If the employee could have avoided the injury by the exercise of due diligence, he is not entitled to damages.

(2) THE FELLOW-SERVANT RULE. If an employee is injured on the job and he himself was in no way negligent, the employer may still avoid being held liable by proving that the injury was caused by a fellow servant. A *fellow servant* is an employee who has the same status as the injured worker and is working with him. A foreman is not a fellow servant, nor is an employee in a different department even though he has the same status as the injured worker. The justification of this rule is that the employees assume this risk when they accept employment.

(3) ASSUMPTION OF THE RISK RULE. Every type of employment in industry has some normal risks. Employees assume these normal risks by voluntarily accepting employment. This does not excuse the employer from the duty of providing safe working conditions; but even after this is done, many types of jobs, such as coal mining, are hazardous. If the injury is due to the hazardous nature of the job, the employer cannot be held liable. Even when the employer fails to provide the safe tools or safe conditions of employment, the employer is not liable if the employee could easily see the hazardous condition and did not protest. He is assuming to have waived his right to demand safe working conditions.

(4) THE NONSURVIVORSHIP RULE. The three preceding rules apply when the worker receives a nonfatal injury. If the injury is fatal, suit cannot be maintained by a surviving heir or spouse. This rule simply states that the right to damages, after all, is the loss of future wages. If a worker sustains a nonfatal injury that incapacitates him for six months, his damages are six months' wages.

The nonsurvivorship rule is based on the theory that if a worker is fatally injured, he has not lost any future wages. This rule has now been repealed in all states. The other three rules have been partially repealed. In every state some workers are still covered by the common law. These defenses are repealed for all workers covered by workmen's compensation laws.

Modern Laws Dealing with Industrial Accidents. The federal government and all the states have passed laws repealing or modifying materially the common law relative to industrial accidents. The chief laws of this class are:

1. Federal Employers' Liability Act
2. State Workmen's Compensation Laws

(1) Federal Employers' Liability Act. Advances in technology brought about by the Industrial Revolution made it necessary for society to modify the common law to eliminate much injustice and hardship. One of the earliest acts along this line was the Federal Employers' Liability Act to govern the liability of common carriers engaged in interstate commerce. This act has been amended several times, the provisions of the present act being:

(a) An employee of a common carrier may collect damages caused by the injury of a fellow employee or from any defect in the equipment that is due to the negligence of the carrier. This greatly modified the common-law fellow-servant rule.

(b) The contributory negligence of the injured worker does not bar recovery as under the common law, although such negligence may diminish the amount of damages.

(c) If an employee is fatally injured, the right to sue for damages survives to the next of kin. Under the common law the right to sue lapsed with the death of the worker.

(d) Contracts by the employer to limit or circumscribe the carrier's liability under the Act are void.

In addition to this act a few other federal laws deal with safety regulations and compensation for injuries. The most important of these are the Federal Coal Mine Safety Act, the Federal Safety Appliance Act, and the Longshoremen's and Harbor Workers' Act, a workman's compensation law to cover maritime workers who are not covered by a state workmen's compensation law.

(2) STATE WORKMEN'S COMPENSATION LAWS. The state workmen's compensation laws deny the employer the three common-law defenses of contributory negligence, fellow-servant rule, and assumption of the risks of the industry rule. The theory back of them is that the cost of an injury to a worker should be borne by society in general, regardless of the cause, provided the injury arises in the course of his employment. In a few states willful negligence and intoxication bar recovery if these acts are the direct cause of the injury.

The general nature of the workmen's compensation laws is to fix a sum to compensate for every type of injury, such as the loss of an eye, a limb, or a life. The worker or his next of kin in case of death, need only prove that a particular injury was received in the course of employment. The law, itself, fixes the amount due. No formal trial is necessary, only an informal hearing before an examiner. In most cases, it is not necessary to employ counsel. Even though the amount allowed for the injury is often pitifully small, yet the net amount received by the worker is considerably higher than under the old law where court costs and attorneys' fees consumed a large share of all awards.

Some states make the laws apply only to hazardous jobs; others make them cover all employees except domestic servants, farm help, government workers, and casual workers. The common-law rules apply to all workers in the state except those specifically covered by these laws.

Questions

1. In what important respect are employees distinguished from agents?

2. Are contracts of employment ever required to be in writing? If so, when?

3. How has collective bargaining affected the employer-employee relationship?

4. If a mine owner fails to brace the slate roof of the mine properly and, as a direct result of this failure, a miner is injured, who is liable for the injury?

5. What is the duty in regard to the safety of the tools the employer furnishes?

6. What is the employer's liability concerning the number of competent employees he must provide for each task?

7. If an employee in the course of his employment negligently injures a third party, who is liable?

8. When may an employer justifiably discharge an employee?

9. When may an employee justifiably abandon his employment?

10. What is the purpose and nature of the workmen's compensation laws?

Case Problems

1. Dennis employed Sisk as a truck driver and gave him strict orders not to drive over 30 miles an hour. Sisk, while driving at 45 miles an hour, injured a pedestrian. The injury was clearly the result of Sisk's negligence. The injury could have easily been avoided had Sisk been driving at 30 miles an hour or less. Was Dennis liable for damages in this case?

2. The House Truck Company employed Davis as a truck driver and furnished him with a truck with faulty brakes. Davis, after his first trip, called this matter to the attention of House, owner of the company. No action was taken. Later during the day Davis wrecked the truck when the brakes failed to hold, and he was seriously injured. He brought suit against House for damages. Was he entitled to collect?

3. Justice was a miner for the Carter Coal Company. While working in the mine, he was seriously injured by falling slate. According to the law in his state he had the option of collecting under the workmen's compensation act or suing the employer under the common law. If he sued the employer, could Justice collect damages?

4. Lane was employed by the Acme Grocery Company to make deliveries for the firm. After making the required deliveries in a nearby village, he drove to another town on personal business that interested him alone. While doing so, he negligently and carelessly drove the automobile and thus caused an injury to a pedestrian. The injured man brought a suit for damages against the Acme Grocery Company. Who, in your judgment, was liable? Why?

5. The Duane Lumber Company employed Dunnaway to cut timber with a motor saw. Dunnaway had never before cut timber nor used this type of saw. He was shown how to start the motor and turn the saw but otherwise was not instructed in its use. As a result of his inexperience he was seriously injured by the saw. He was not covered by the state workmen's compensation law. Could he recover from the employer?

6. The Lavine Scrap Iron Company operated a crane to pick up scrap iron. While operating the machine, the operator negligently injured a pedestrian by dropping a load of scrap iron near him without warning. Was the company liable for this injury?

7. Hill, an elevator operator in an apartment house, left his elevator door open while he went on an errand. While he was gone, someone entered the elevator and took it to the next floor above. Hill returned and without observing that the elevator had been moved, stepped into the elevator shaft, fell two floors, and was seriously injured. The owner of the apartment house was not covered by the workmen's compensation law. Could Hill collect under the common law?

8. Sirmans, who owned and operated a drugstore, employed Stine, a registered pharmacist, to fill prescriptions. Stine filled one for Hamilton incorrectly and, as a result, Hamilton became seriously ill. He brought suit against Sirmans. Was Sirmans liable?

Chapter 29

Modern Labor Leglislation

Types of Labor Legislation. To avoid confusion, the labor legislation of recent years should be classified as that dealing primarily with unions and that dealing with the labor force as a whole.

THE LAWS DEALING WITH UNIONS

Norris-La Guardia Act. Prior to 1932 the law with regard to labor unions was primarily the common law of conspiracy and restraint of trade. *Conspiracy* is any combination of two or more persons to accomplish by concerted action some unlawful act or some lawful act by unlawful means. If a labor union under this rule had as its aim to injure the employer by denying him free access to the labor market, it was a conspiracy and therefore illegal. Under the common-law doctrine of *restraint of trade,* this rule was extended to cover injury or inconvenience to the public by being cut off from the normal access to the commodity market.

Under these two doctrines the courts were free to declare most collective actions of employees illegal. To restrain them from engaging in collective action to increase wages and improve working conditions, the employers obtained an injunction to restrain the workers from engaging in an illegal act such as a strike. An *injunction* is a court order commanding a person to refrain from committing a contemplated act. This was the means used by employers to prevent a strike or other union activity.

The Norris-La Guardia Act sets forth certain acts of labor which could not be enjoined by an injunction provided the workers were using lawful means. The acts are (a) ceasing to work, that is, to strike; (b) joining a union even though they had contracted not to; (c) paying strike benefits to strikers; (d) aiding a striker who is involved in a court action; (e) giving any publicity to the facts of any labor dispute by any means whatsoever, peaceful or otherwise; (f) peaceable assembly during a labor dispute; (g) notifying any person of an intention to do any of these things; (h) urging others to do any of these things. All of these acts by labor had been enjoined prior to 1933 through the process of an injunction. The Norris-La Guardia Act attempts to remove these acts as a justification for obtaining an injunction.

The Management Relations Act. In 1935 Congress passed the National Labor Relations Act. This act was designed primarily to protect labor in its union and collective bargaining activities. In 1947 the National Labor Management Relations Act, better known as the Taft-Hartley Act, replaced the National Labor Relations Act, although many of the features of the former act were retained. The act consisted of five main provisions:

1. The National Labor Relations Board
2. A declaration as to the rights of employees
3. A declaration as to the rights of employers
4. A prohibition of employers' unfair labor policies
5. A prohibition of certain unfair labor practices

(1) THE NATIONAL LABOR RELATIONS BOARD. The Labor Management Relations Act provides for a National Labor Relations Board of five members appointed by the President. This board hears complaints of unfair labor practices of employers and also complaints made by both employers and employees of unfair union practices. If the board finds that an unfair practice exists, it has the power to seek an injunction to enjoin the practice. In strikes affecting the national welfare, the board is empowered to seek an injunction postponing the strike for

eighty days. The board conducts investigations, supervises elections among employees for union recognition and for the union shop, and receives union financial reports. In addition to the board's function, a general counsel is appointed by the President. This general counsel is entirely independent of the board in prosecuting complaint cases, but in most other matters he acts as the chief legal advisor to the board.

(2) A DECLARATION AS TO THE RIGHTS OF EMPLOYEES. The Labor Management Relations Act, like the National Labor Relations Act, sets forth the following list of rights which the employees have:

(a) To organize

(b) To bargain collectively through their own chosen agents

(c) To engage in concerted action; that is, strike, for their mutual aid and protection

(d) Of an individual employee to join or not to join a union as he wishes unless a majority of all workers vote for a union shop

(3) A DECLARATION AS TO THE RIGHTS OF EMPLOYERS. The Labor Management Relations Act gives the employer many important rights which he did not have under the National Labor Relations Act. The most important of these rights are:

(a) To petition for an investigation when he questions the union's rights to speak for the employees

(b) To refuse to bargain collectively with foremen and other supervisory employees

(c) To institute charges before the board of unfair labor practices by the unions

(d) To sue unions for breaches of the union contract whether the breach is done in the name of the union or as an individual union member.

(e) To plead with his workers to refrain from joining the union provided no threats are used. These provisions were included to "equalize" the rights of the employer and the employee on the assumption that the National Labor Relations Act gave the workers an undue advantage.

(4) A PROHIBITION OF UNFAIR LABOR PRACTICES BY EMPLOYERS. The chief acts which are declared to be unfair practices by employers are:

(a) Interfering in the exercise of the rights granted employees

(b) Refusing to bargain collectively with employees when they have legally selected a representative

(c) Dominating any labor organization or contributing financial support to it.

(d) Discriminating against or favoring an employee in any way because of his membership or lack of membership in the union

(e) Discriminating against an employee because he has filed a complaint against his employer

All of these unfair practices were also prohibited under the National Labor Relations Act. The board, when it finds the employer guilty of any of these acts, usually issues a "cease and desist order." If this order is not effective, an injunction may be obtained.

(5) A PROHIBITION OF UNFAIR UNION PRACTICES. The National Labor Relations Act did not list any unfair union practices. The new act listed seven specific acts which unions and their leaders may not engage in:

(a) Any coercion or restraint of workers in the exercise of their legally expressed rights

(b) Interference with the employer in his selection of a bargaining agent

(c) Refusal to bargain collectively with the employer

(d) Charging excessive initiation fees and discriminatory dues and fees of any kind

(e) Barring a worker from the union for any reason except the nonpayment of dues

(f) Secondary boycotts or strikes in violation of law or the contract

(g) Attempts to exact payment for services not rendered

These are the abuses which the advocates of a new labor law to replace the National Labor Relations Act claimed were widespread. The board, as well as the general counsel, was empowered to investigate all charges that any of these abuses existed and to take the necessary legal action to abate them. The most effective method of dealing with them is an injunction.

LABOR LEGISLATION DEALING WITH THE WHOLE LABOR FORCE

Federal Social Security Act. The four main provisions of the Federal Social Security Act are:

1. Old-age and survivors insurance
2. Old-age assistance
3. Unemployment compensation
4. Taxation to finance the plan

(1) OLD-AGE AND SURVIVORS INSURANCE. The Social Security Act, originally passed in 1936, has been amended several times. At present practically everyone is covered by the act. The only major groups specifically excluded are self-employed medical doctors, at their request, and all other self-employed people who earn less than $400 in one year.

Self-employed farmers are covered; but if their gross income is less than $1,800, they may elect to compute net earnings as 66 2/3 per cent of gross earnings in lieu of actual net earnings. If their gross earnings are over $1,800 but net earnings are less than $1,200, they may use either actual net earnings or $1,200. Farm laborers who have cash wages of $150 a year from one employer or who work for twenty or more days for cash wages on a time basis, not a piece-rate basis, are covered.

Specifically excluded from coverage are certain types of work for close relatives, such as a parent for his children, work by a child under 21 for his parents, employment of a wife by her husband, and coversely employment of a husband by his wife.

Most employees of state and local governments can be brought under federal old-age and survivors insurance by means of agreements between the state and the federal government. Before employees in positions under state and local retirement systems can be included in a state-federal agreement, a majority of the eligible employees must vote in favor of having old-age and survivors insurance coverage in special referendum on the question.

Eligibility for Social Security Benefits. To be eligible for retirement benefits, one must meet three requirements: (a) be fully insured; (b) be 65 years of age for men, 62 years for women; and (c) have after reaching 65 (or 62) applied for retirement benefits. To be eligible for retirement benefits one must be fully insured at the time he retires. He is fully insured if when he reaches retirement age, he has one quarter of coverage (earned any time after 1936) for each two full calendar quarters after 1950. At least 6 quarters of coverage are necessary in every case. When he has earned 40 quarters of coverage, he is fully insured for life. In this case it is not necessary that he be working at the time he applies for retirement benefits. If he is not fully insured at retirement age, he may continue to work until he has enough quarters to be fully insured.

When a worker dies before he achieves a fully insured status, his family is entitled to survivors benefits if he was currently insured at the time of his death. One is currently insured if at the time of his death he has at least 6 quarters of coverage during the 13-quarter period ending with the quarter in which he dies or the quarter in which he becomes entitled to old-age insurance benefits.

Calculating Retirement Benefits. The first step in calculating one's retirement benefits, his average monthly income from the time he was first covered by social security to the time of retirement must be calculated. Before this is done, there are two adjustments that may need to be made. First, the insured may request that five years of his employment be excluded in calculating his average monthly wage. The higher this wage the higher the retirement income. If one as a college student earned $80 a month while in college but earned $350 a month or more after that, he can have this $80 a month excluded and the months during which he earned it also excluded. This will give him a higher average monthly income and consequently a higher retirement income than he would have without the exclusion.

Second, the law allows a worker what is called a "disability freeze." If at any time during one's working career he is disabled and unable to earn any income for a considerable period, his average monthly income would be reduced. This is true because his earnings would be listed as zero for the months of disability, but the months would not be excluded in calculating the total number of months covered. If you are totally disabled for six months or more, you may ask that this entire period of disability be ignored in calculating your average monthly income.

Survivors Benefits. If the insured dies before reaching 65, his widow, dependent children, and dependent parents may be eligible for survivors benefits. The insured's primary benefit is calculated as though he had retired. Then the widow draws three fourths of the husband's benefit if she has a child under 18 years of age.

If the deceased's widow has only one child under 18, the child draws three fourths of the father's primary benefit. If there is more than one child under 18, each child draws one half of the father's primary benefit plus an equal share in an additional one fourth, with the provisions that the benefits for the family do not exceed $200 a month or 80 per cent of the father's average monthly income, whichever is less.

If there is no widow or childen under 18, the parents of the deceased may draw three fourths of his primary benefit. For the parents to draw these benefits, however, the son must have been fully insured when he died and the parents must be dependent.

In addition, a lump sum payment of $255 or three times the deceased's primary benefit, whichever is less, is paid to the widow.

The 1956 amendment to the Social Security Act provides for disability payments under certain conditions. When one becomes so severely disabled that he is unable to work after age 50, he can qualify for disability payments if (a) he is both fully and currently insured at the time of disability, and (b) he has 20 quarters of coverage in the 40 calendar quarters before the beginning date of his disability. The disability benefits are calculated exactly as though the disabled worker had reached 65 and retired. The disability must be so severe that it prevents any substantial gainful employment, must have continued for 6 months, and must be expected to continue indefinitely.

(2) Old-Age Assistance. Since many people for various reasons are not covered by the insurance feature of the Federal Social Security Act, other means of assistance are provided for people over 65. Each state was left to adopt its own pension system and the federal government agreed to match any state pension up to 75 per cent of the first $20 and 50 per cent of the remainder, with a top limit of $50 for each pension. This is a noncontributory system. Need is the only test, whereas with the old-age insurance feature need is not considered.

(3) Unemployment Compensation. In handling unemployment compensation, the federal government cooperates with the states, which set up their own rules for the payment of unemployment benefits. Payments of un-

employment compensation are made by the states and not by the federal government.

Federal Law. Every employer of four or more persons (except employers of the exempted classes) must pay a federal tax on his payrolls. No tax is levied on the employee.

Under the provisions of the federal act, no payment of benefits can be made to any individual with regard to unemployment that occurs within two years after the beginning of the time when contributions were required by the state in which he lived. Twenty-two states began the payment of unemployment compensation benefits in January, 1938; most of the other states began the payment of these benefits by January, 1939.

State Laws. Naturally the unemployment compensation laws of the various states differ in many respects. They are alike, however, in providing for raising funds by levies upon employers.

The state unemployment compensation laws apply in general to workers in commerce and industry. Agricultural workers, domestic servants, governmental employees, and the employees of nonprofit organizations formed and operated exclusively for religious, charitable, literary, educational, scientific, or humane purposes are not included under the laws.

Prior to World War II the maximum benefit under the act was $15 a week and the maximum number of weeks for which unemployment would be paid was twenty-six weeks. Since the War most states have liberalized both these provisions.

In order to be eligible for benefits, a worker must meet the following requirements:

(a) He must be available for work and registered at an employment office.

(b) He must have been employed for a certain length of time within a specified period in an employment covered by the state law.

(c) He must be capable of working.

(d) He must not have refused employment for which he is reasonably fitted.

(e) He must not be self-employed.

(f) He must not be out of work because of a strike or a lockout still in progress.

(g) He must have served the required waiting period.

(4) TAXATION TO FINANCE THE PLAN. To pay all social security benefits, except unemployment compensation, both the employer and the employee are taxed an equal per cent of all wages up to $4,200 a year. Self-employed persons pay one and a half times the rate for an employee on all income up to $4,200 a year.

Fair Labor Standards Act. The Fair Labor Standards Act was passed by Congress in June, 1938, and amended in 1949 for the purpose of protecting the health, efficiency, and general well-being of workers. The Act provides for the regulation of child labor and for the regulation of minimum wages and maximum hours for all employees in industry who are engaged in interstate commerce. Exempted employees include executives, professional men, agricultural employees, seamen and fishermen, and employees whose hours are fixed by the Interstate Commerce Act.

The important provisions of the act are:

(1) The wages of all employees under this act must meet the minimum of $1.00 an hour, effective in March, 1956.

(2) Maximum working hours are limited to 40 hours a week, with additional time permitted provided payment is made at the minimum rate of time and a half for overtime work.

(3) Oppressive child labor is prohibited by this act; however, the act applies only to child employees engaged in interstate commerce. No goods worked on by children under 16 years of age (except children working for

their parents in occupations other than manufacturing or mining) may be shipped in interstate commerce without special permission from the Children's Bureau of the United States Department of Labor. The Children's Bureau also has the power to restrict the types of interstate employment in which children between the ages of 16 and 18 may engage, and to permit the employment of minors between the ages of 14 and 16 in occupations other than manufacturing or mining that will not interfere with their well-being or with their education and schooling.

(4) The administrator of the Fair Labor Standards Act presides over the new Wage and Hour Division of the Department of Labor that was created by the act. The Court of Appeals may be petitioned to review any disputed orders under the Fair Labor Standards Act and may affirm, modify, or set aside any order.

Walsh-Healey Act. The Walsh-Healey Act, or as it is known, the Public Contracts Act, sets a basic 8-hour day and a basic 40-hour week for workers in establishments of private employers who fill government orders. Neither this Act nor the Fair Labor Standards Act fixes a maximum-hour week for male employees. Both Acts simply state that time and a half must be paid for all hours over the basic 40-hour week.

Questions

1. (a) What was a conspiracy as that term was applied to labor unions under the common law?

(b) How did conspiracy relate to restraint of trade?

2. What act of Congress limited the right of courts to issue injunctions in labor disputes?

3. What was the main purpose of the National Labor Relations Act of 1935?

4. What are some of the duties of the National Labor Relations Board?

5. Under the National Labor Management Relations Act of 1947, what power does the board have in a strike affecting the National welfare?

6. (a) If an employer refuses to bargain collectively with his employees, is this an unfair labor practice?
(b) Name some unfair labor practices by employers.

7. What are the unions rights in regard to initiation fees and dues?

8. What workers or income recipients in America are not covered under the old-age retirement part of the Social Security Act?

9. Who may benefit if the insured dies before reaching 65?

10. How does the Fair Labor Standards Act regulate the labor of children in industry?

Case Problems

1. Dubinsky, a seamstress, agrees with a suit manufacturer to sew buttons on the vests on a piece-rate basis. The manufacturer delivered the vests to her home and picked them up when they were completed. After Mrs. Dubinsky had worked 45 weeks, during which time she worked fifty hours a week and earned only $28 a week, she quit and demanded more money under the minimum wage law for the 45 weeks she had worked. The manufacturer contended, first that she was an independent contractor and not entitled to minimum wages; and secondly, that workers on piece rate work cannot claim a minimum wage of $1.00 an hour. Was either or both of these contentions correct?

2. Davis operated a laundry near a service camp. The army commander gave him a contract to do a large amount of laundry work for the camp. Davis worked his employees ten hours a day for $5.00 a day. He was notified that he would have to pay them $1.00 an hour and time and a half for overtime. Davis contended that since his laundry was intrastate business, he did not have to pay these wages. Was his contention correct?

3. Mosteller was the assistant to the president of the Florence Bakery. While Florence was away on an extended trip, Mosteller was left in charge. During this time three of the bakery's employees engaged in a determined effort to organize the workers into a union. Mosteller, in an attempt to protect his employer's interest, fired the three employees. They brought an action before the National Labor Relations Board to compel the Florence Bakery to restore them to their jobs and to pay them for all wages lost pending the settlement of their complaint. Were they entitled to this relief?

4. The Norris Freezer Locker Company's employees were on strike. Norris went into a state court and obtained a general injunction against the union prohibiting among other things: (1) paying strike benefits to the strikers; (2) giving any aid or comfort to the strikers or their families; (3) broadcasting any information about the strike to the members of the union. What remedy did the union or its members have if they thought such an injuncton illegal?

5. A college fraternity hired a cook for $12 a week and two meals a day. After she had worked for the same fraternity for several years, she became ill and could work no longer. She applied for unemployment compensation. List the reasons why she might not be permitted to draw unemployment compensation.

6. The workers in the Hub Linen Company met to exchange ideas on the desirability of forming a union. One of the workers, dubbed a "stooge' by his fellow workers, reported the names of the leaders of this movement to the personnel office. The three main leaders were then fired for their union activities. What remedy did the discharged workers have?

Cases for Review for Part VI

1. Burnett was one of several joint owners of some land. They contracted with Potts to sell land, and agreed to give Potts as his share of the proceeds of the sale any amount received in excess of $35,000. Potts obtained a contract to sell the land for $37,000 with $1,000 paid down at the time. The prospective purchaser did not fulfill the contract and thus forfeited the $1,000. Potts contended that he was entitled to a share of the $1,000 because by the contract he became a part owner of the land and therefore of the $1,000. (Burnett vs. Potts, 236 Ill. 499) Do you agree?

2. A man represented himself to Heyn that he was the agent of O'Hagen. Upon this representation Heyn sold goods on credit to the man whom he did not know and shipped the goods to O'Hagen's former place of business. O'Hagen learned of the fraud when he was billed for the goods but did not immediately notify Heyn of the fraudulent nature of the transaction. Soon thereafter, Heyn sold additional goods at the agent's request and charged them to O'Hagen. O'Hagen then denied all liability for the acts of this unauthorized agent. (Heyn vs. O'Hagen, 60 Mich. 150) Did O'Hagen's silence ratify the agency?

3. Bronson through his agent, Bostwick, sold some real estate to Chappell. The agent was expressly authorized to receive the first payment from Chappell. Bostwick was the general agent for Bronson. In this capacity he received future collections from Chappell. Having become insolvent, Bostwick failed to pay over to Bronson some of the money collected from Chappell. Bronson sued Chappell for the payments, contending that they should not have been made to Bostwick. (Bronson's Executor vs. Chappell, 12 Wall. [U. S.] 681) Must Chappell pay a second time?

4. Frederick and Adelaide McFerren were man and wife, though separated. While thus separated, the Goldsmith-Stern Company sold Mrs. McFerren some merchandise, mostly clothing, and then sued Frederick McFerren for the price on the ground that Mrs. McFerren was agent by necessity. There was no evidence that Frederick McFerren had failed to supply his wife with necessities because they were separated. (McFerren vs. Goldsmith-Stern Company, 137 Md. 573) Was Frederick McFerren liable?

5. Green, an architect, was employed by McMicken, a special agent of Litchfield. Green was employed for one job only—to draw plans for a tower. Litchfield did not authorize McMicken to enter into a contract of this nature. (Litchfield vs. Green, 43 Ariz. 509) Was Litchfield liable?

6. Leary was a general agent of the Spokane Amateur Athletic Club. Leary hired Francis for a period of twenty-six weeks, although Francis knew that Leary did not have the authority to employ and discharge employees. Francis contended that since this is within the apparent scope of a general agent's authority, the club was bound by the contract. (Francis vs. Spokane Amateur Athletic Club, 54 Wash. 188) Do you agree?

7. Heath employed Spencer to deliver a piano to Stoddard. Stoddard had previously agreed with Heath to purchase the piano if it were satisfactory. Spencer himself was a dealer in pianos. Spencer without authority from Heath persuaded Stoddard to buy the piano at the time Spencer's truck drivers delivered it to Stoddards's home. The purchase price was paid to Spencer, but Spencer failed to turn the money over to Heath. Heath then brought suit against Stoddard to collect the price of the piano, claiming that Spencer was not his agent, and therefore he had no right to pay him. (Heath vs. Stoddard, 91 Me. 499) Could Heath collect?

8. Heard and Company were purchasing agents for Heinemann and Payson. The agents were instructed to buy silk at a certain price for the principals. Heard and Company had information which they felt would cause the price of silk to fall. Consequently, they delayed buying the silk at the price stated by the principals, thinking they could save their principals money by the delay. Instead of the price declining as they expected, it rose and they were thus unable to buy at the price fixed by Heinemann and Payson. The principals sued their agents for the loss sustained by their failure to obey instructions. (Heinemann vs. Heard, 50 N. Y. 27) Were the agents liable?

9. Jones was employed by the West End Consolidated Mining Company as a miner. The mine in which he worked was a shaft mine about one hundred feet deep. The miners entered the shaft by means of a bucket hoist which lowered and raised the workers by a machine operator. Jones entered the hoist preparatory to being lowered to the mine to begin work. Because of a defect in the hoist engine, he dropped to the bottom of the shaft, receiving serious injuries. The employer denied liability for the injury claiming that this was a risk which Jones assumed when he accepted employment. (Jones vs. West End Consolidated Mining Company, 36 Nevada 149) Was the company's defense valid?

10. A telegraph operator in a railway station was asleep when a freight train passed by his station. Because of this, the operator did not hear the train. Later he was called by another operator to inquire if the freight train had passed his station and he assured the operator that it had not. On the basis of this assurance, a train was dispatched over a single track line, heading toward the station the train had passed. The two trains later had a head-on collision causing the death of Dixon, the fireman. Dixon's estate sued the railroad for damages because of Dixon's death. (Northern Pacific Railroad Company vs. Dixon, 194 U. S. 338) Was the railroad company liable?

11. The Industrial Commission, of Arizona, awarded James Whalen a judgment for $2,514.15 for damages sustained by personal injury while working for Six Companies, Inc. Before Whalen collected the lump sum claim, he died and payment was denied. The Commission and the Six Companies, Inc. refused payment to Whalen's administrator on the ground that the claim was for future wages lost by reason of the injury and since Whalen died, he could not have earned the future wages even had he not been injured. (Sorenson vs. Six Companies, Inc. 53 Ariz. 83) Was this defense valid?

12. The Industrial Commission, of Wisconsin, awarded unemployment compensation to Marie Rybacki. Rybacki had for the past ten years worked each spring for the Slocum Straw Works as a seamstress. The work was highly seasonal so that Rybacki worked only a couple of months each year. The Slocum Company brought an action to prevent the Commission from paying unemployment compensation to Rybacki on the ground that she was not an employee, but self-employed, and therefore ineligible. (Slocum Straw Works vs. Industrial Commission, 232 Wis. 71) Do you agree with this contention?

Part VII

PARTNERSHIPS

Chapter 30

Formation of a Partnership

What Is a Partnership? A *partnership* is an association of two or more competent persons who have combined their money, property, or labor and skill, or some or all of them, for the purpose of carrying on some lawful business for their joint profit.

The partnership must be formed for the purpose of operating a lawful business. If the business is unlawful, the attempt to form a partnership to operate such a business is void. Furthermore, a partnership may not be formed for the purpose of conducting a lawful business in an illegal manner.

Since the purpose of a partnership must be to conduct a trade, business, or profession for profit, a hunting club, a sewing circle, a trade union, a chamber of commerce, or other nonprofit association cannot be treated as a partnership.

Advantages of the Partnership. By the operation of a partnership, capital and skill may be increased, competition may be lessened, labor may be made more efficient, the ratio of expenses per dollar of business may be reduced, and management may be improved. It is not certain that all these advantages will accrue to every partnership, but the prospect of greater profits by reason of them is the incentive which leads to the formation of a partnership.

Disadvantages of the Partnership. The most important disadvantages are:

(1) The unlimited liability of each partner for the debts of the partnership

(2) The relative instability of the business because of the danger of dissolution by reason of the death or withdrawal of one of the partners

(3) The divided authority among the partners, which may lead to disharmony

Classification of Partnerships. Partnerships may be classified as follows:

1. Ordinary partnerships
2. Limited partnerships
3. Trading and nontrading partnerships

(1) ORDINARY PARTNERSHIPS. When two or more persons voluntarily contract to pool their capital and skill to conduct some business undertaking for profit, with no limitations upon their rights and duties, an *ordinary partnership* is created. This is the oldest type of business combination and is still widely used today. This type of business organization is governed by the common law except in those states which have adopted the Uniform Partnership Act. The purpose of this act is to bring about uniformity in the partnership laws of the states. The following states and Alaska have thus far adopted the act:

> Alaska, Arkansas, California, Colorado, Delaware, Idaho, Illinois, Indiana, Kentucky, Maryland, Massachusetts, Michigan, Minnesota, Missouri, Montana, Nebraska, Nevada, New Jersey, New Mexico, New York, North Carolina, Ohio, Oregon, Pennsylvania, South Carolina, South Dakota, Tennessee, Utah, Vermont, Virginia, Washington, West Virginia, Wisconsin, and Wyoming.

(2) LIMITED PARTNERSHIPS. A *limited partnership* is one in which one or more of the partners have their lia-

bility for the firm's debts limited to the amount of their investment. This type of partnership cannot operate either under the common law or the Uniform Partnership Act. Such a partnership cannot be formed without a specific state statute prescribing the conditions under which it can operate. If the limited partnership does not comply strictly with the enabling statute, the courts hold it to be an ordinary partnership.

(3) TRADING AND NONTRADING PARTNERSHIPS. A *trading partnership* is one engaged in buying and selling merchandise. A *nontrading partnership* is one devoted to services, such as accounting, medicine, dentistry, law, and similar professional services. The chief reason for making the distinction is that the members in a nontrading partnership usually have considerably less apparent authority than the partners in a trading partnership. For example, one partner in a nontrading partnership cannot borrow money in the name of the firm and bind the firm. One dealing with a nontrading partnership is charged with considerably more responsibility in ascertaining the actual authority of the partners to bind the firm than is a person dealing with a trading partnership.

Who May Be Partners? Since a partnership is based upon a contract, any person who is competent to make a contract is competent to be a partner. A minor may become a partner to the same extent to which he may contract about any other matter. His contracts are voidable by him; but since he is the agent of the other partner or partners, he can bind the partnership on contracts within the scope of the partnership business. On the other hand, the adult partners cannot as a rule bind the minor if he wishes to avoid personal liability. If the partnership has incurred debts, all the assets of the partners, including those of the minor, are subject to application on these debts. This is an exception to the minor's right to disaffirm his contracts.

Kinds of Partners. The members of a partnership may be classified as follows:

1. General partners
2. Silent partners
3. Secret partners
4. Dormant partners

(1) GENERAL PARTNER. A *general partner* is one who is actively and openly engaged in the business and is held out to everyone as a partner. He has unlimited liability in respect to the partnership debts. He holds himself out to the public as a full fledged partner, assumes all the risks of the partnerships, limits none of his rights, and assumes all the duties of an owner. This is the usual type of partner.

(2) SILENT PARTNER. A *silent partner* is one who takes no active part in the management of the business. He limits his rights as a partner to the sharing of the profits in the ratio agreed upon. As a general rule the other partners offer him two inducements to invest his money but take no active part in the management. These inducements are: limited liability and no share of the losses. To have his liability limited, he must make known to all creditors the extent of his limitations, and the creditors must contract with the firm with notice of such limitations. He performs more the function of an investor than that of an entrepreneur.

(3) SECRET PARTNER. A *secret partner* is an active partner who attempts to keep his status as a partner concealed from the public. His motives are to escape the unlimited liability of a general partner and at the same time to take an active part in the management of the business. Should his relationship to the firm become known to the public, however, he would not escape unlimited liability. He differs from the silent partner in two respects: (1)

He is unknown to the public; and (2) he takes an active part in the management of the business. He may feign the status of an employee or he may work elsewhere; but he meets frequently with the other partners to discuss management problems.

(4) DORMANT PARTNER. A *dormant partner* (sometimes referred to as a *sleeping partner*) usually combines the characteristics of both the secret and the silent partner. He is usually unknown to the public as a partner, and he takes no part in the management of the business of the firm. When he becomes known to the public as a partner, he is liable for the debts of the firm to the same extent as a general partner. He foregoes his right to participate in the management of the firm. In return he receives a limitation on his liability so far as the other partners are able to effect it. He may, in addition, agree to limit his income to a reasonable return on his investment, since he contributes no services.

Creation of a Partnership. A partnership is the result of a contract, express or implied, just as all other business commitments result from a contract. The partnership contract must meet the five tests of a valid contract as set out in Chapter 3, pages 25-26.

Articles of Copartnership. In the absence of a statute to the contrary, a written contract providing for the formation of a partnership need not be in a particular form. The written agreement is commonly known as *articles of copartnership*. Partnership articles may vary according to the needs of a particular situation, but ordinarily they should contain the following information:

(1) The date
(2) The names of the partners
(3) The nature and the duration of the business
(4) The name and the location of the business

(5) The individual contributions of the partners
(6) The sharing of profits, losses, and responsibilities
(7) Keeping of accounts
(8) The duties of the partners
(9) The amounts of withdrawals of money
(10) Unusual restraints upon the partners
(11) Provision for dissolution and division of assets
(12) Signatures of partners

Implied Partnership Agreements. Under certain circumstances a partnership may be implied by the acts of the individuals. The parties may not intend to form a contract of partnership, but the court may infer such an intention under these circumstances:

(1) If the contracting parties agree to share net profits and losses in a specific business undertaking, the presumption is that they intended to form a partnership.

(2) If the parties agree to share net profits only, with no mention of losses, the implication of an intention to form a partnership still prevails, though it is a weaker implication than when both net profits and losses are to be shared.

Either of the contracting parties may overcome this implication by showing that the profits are shared for one of these purposes:

(a) To pay a debt
(b) In lieu of wages
(c) In lieu of a fixed rent
(d) As an annunity to the widow of a deceased partner
(e) As interest on a loan
(f) To create good will for the business

(3) If two or more individuals agree to share gross returns from community property, the courts may imply that a partnership exists. This is not conclusive evidence and may be overcome by proving a contrary intention.

Estoppel Partnerships. A partnership may be inferred from the acts of the parties. This is commonly known as a *partnership by estoppel.* In this case, the parties have no intention of forming a partnership but behave in such a manner as to lead a third party to believe that a partnership exists. In that event, the courts will impute to them an intention to form a partnership. The parties are "stopped" from denying the relationship.

- Lloyd Campbell, a man of considerable wealth was present when Shuler said to Miller:

  "Mr. Campbell and I are partners in this cotton gin. We would like to buy this machinery from you for $5,000 and will pay for it in ninety days."

  Campbell did not deny this statement. Miller, knowing of Campbell's wealth and relying upon the truth of Shuler's statement, sold the machine on credit. When Shuler defaulted, Miller sued both him and Campbell as partners. Campbell was held liable because he was estopped to deny that he was a partner.

Partnership Firm Name. A firm name is not a legal necessity or requirement for a partnership, but it is useful as a matter of convenience and for the purpose of identification. Any name that does not violate the rights of others or that is not contrary to law may be adopted by the firm and may be changed at will by agreement. In some states it is not permissible to use the name of a person who is not a member of the firm, or to use the words "and Company" unless the term represents a partner. Many of the states permit the use of fictitious or trade names.

A partnership cannot bring a suit at law or be sued in the name of the firm. A suit must be brought in the names of the individual members. Under the common law real property must be held in the names of the partners, but under the Uniform Partnership Act it may be held and conveyed in the name of the firm.

Joint-Stock Companies. A *joint-stock company* is in some respects similar to a partnership, but the ownership is indicated by shares of stock, as in a corporation. The ownership of these shares may be transferred without dissolving the association, thus overcoming one of the chief disadvantages of the general partnership. The joint stockholders are still liable, jointly and severally, for the debts of the firm while they are members, and for this reason, joint-stock companies do not offer the safeguards of a corporation. These joint-stock companies are permitted to operate in some states by special statutes authorizing them, or in some states, without statute, as a common-law association.

Questions

1. For what purpose may a partnership be formed?

2. (a) What are the advantages of a partnership?
(b) What are the disadvantages of a partnership?

3. What are the different classes of partnerships?

4. Are partnerships in your state governed by the common law or by the Uniform Partnership Act?

5. (a) Who may be a partner?
(b) May a minor be held to his contract creating a partnership?

6. (a) What are the classifications of partners?
(b) How is a partnership formed?

7. How can two or more parties form a partnership when they have no intention to form one?

8. What are articles of copartnership?

9. What is a partnership by estoppel?

10. (a) Is it necessary for a partnership to have a firm name?
(b) Under the common law could a partnership own real estate in the name of the firm?

Case Problems

1. Howard was an experienced neon light technician. Smith entered into an oral contract with Howard whereby they were to operate Smith's neon light business, pay all expenses, and divide the balance on a fifty-fifty basis. If Howard's share was not $75 a week, Smith guaranteed to make up the deficit from his share. The business continued for about five years under this arrangement. Once during that period Smith "fired" Howard, but after two or three days they resumed the relationship. The business became insolvent, and the creditors sued Howard as a partner. Was this a partnership?

2. Holliday was a salaried accountant in the CPA firm of Boling and Bond. Bond asked Holliday to loan the firm $5,000. This he did and received a note signed as follows.

Boling and Bond
By: *G. L. Bond*

There was no evidence that Boling knew of the transaction or had any part in it. Before the note was due, the firm dissolved. Bond had used the money to pay a personal debt and was bankrupt. Boling refused to pay any part of the note. Could Holliday compel Boling to pay it?

3. Perry, store manager for one of a chain of supermarkets, secretly entered into a partnership with Allen to operate an independent supermarket. He invested half the capital but took no part in the management of the firm. He was to receive 8 per cent on his investment guaranteed, and one fourth of any additional profits. The firm became insolvent, and the creditors learned of Perry's status. Perry claimed he was a limited partner, while the creditors contended he was a dormant partner. What was the significance of making this distinction?

4. Dince, Strahorn, and Gilbert operated an ordinary partnership. Gilbert died leaving a wife but no children. The two surviving partners agreed to employ Mrs. Gilbert at $200 a month and to give her the share of profits which Mr. Gilbert would have received had he lived. At the end of five years, the firm was to belong solely to Dince and Strahorn. Mrs. Gilbert, during this five years, was to have all the powers of a partner, and the name, Dince, Strahorn, and Gilbert Clothiers was to remain unchanged. At the end of two years, the firm was insolvent and the creditors sued Mrs. Gilbert personally for the debts of the firm. Was she liable?

5. Lenoir, Lorenz, and LeConte were general partners in an insurance and real estate agency. LeConte died and Lenoir and Lorenz purchased the widow's share. They agreed to pay her one third of the net profit until the purchase price was paid. Mrs. LeConte took no part in the business and her name was never used in any way. The partnership became insolvent and the creditors attempted to hold Mrs. LeConte liable as a partner. Was she liable?

6. Taffell and Taylor jointly own a building that rents for $800 a month. They pay all expenses and divide the balance evenly. Taylor has an automobile wreck in which two people are killed. Suit is brought against him and Taffell for $100,000, alleging that a partnership existed. Was this a partnership?

7. Watford owned, as a sole proprietor, a hardware store. He had three sons who had helped him in the business when they were not in school. After they finished school, they devoted full time to the business. No salaries were ever paid, but each one was permitted to withdraw a stipulated amount each week. This arrangement continued for five years, and then the sons sued in a court of equity for an accounting and a dissolution of the partnership. Other than the use of the three sons as helpers, no change in the operation or management of the business was ever made. Was this a partnership?

8. Randall, Hodgson, and Carlton each invested $6,000 in an auto parts store. They agreed to take shares of stock valued at $100 each for their investments. They further agreed that each one could sell any or all of his shares without dissolving the business. The business became bankrupt and Carlton claimed that his personal estate was not liable for the firm's debts. Was this contention correct?

9. Rich operated the Home Radio Shop and employed Smith as a clerk. A salesman for the Plymouth Radio Manufacturers took the shop's order for $1,500 worth of radios. Rich, in an effort to boost his credit standing, introduced Smith as his partner in the business. The seller had previously sold goods to Smith and knew his credit was good. Smith did not deny the statement of Rich that they were partners. The Home Radio Shop became bankrupt, and the seller sued Smith for the $1,500. Were Rich and Smith partners?

Chapter 31

Operation of a Partnership

Duties of Partners. Someone has said that our partnership laws reflect everything noble in our society. The truth of this statement is evident when one lists the duties which the law says each partner owes to his copartners. These duties leave no room for sharp practices in the partners' dealings with each other. The law imposes upon each partner the utmost fidelity in all his relationships with his fellow partners. If any partner is remiss in his duty, the other partners have ample legal recourse to redress the wrong.

The four most common duties which the partner owes to the others are:

1. Duty to observe good faith
2. Duty to use care and skill
3. Duty to conform to the partnership contract
4. Duty to keep records

(1) DUTY TO OBSERVE GOOD FAITH. Partners owe each other and the firm the utmost good faith. Since each partner is the agent of the firm, the relationship of principal and agent prevails. This relationship is a fiduciary one so that strict fidelity to the interests of the firm must be observed at all times. No partner may take unfair advantage of his copartners. Any personal profits earned directly as a result of one's connection with the partnership must be considered profits of the firm. If the personal interest or advantage of the partner conflicts with the advantage of the partnership, it is the duty of the partner to eschew the personal advantage.

● Bailey, Baker, and Barlow entered into a partnership agreement to sell an expensive piece of real estate and were to receive a commission of 5 per cent of the selling price. They tried to find a purchaser over a period of twelve months but failed to consummate a sale. The partnership then dissolved, and a new partnership of Bailey and Baker was formed. Soon thereafter, the new partnership sold the property for $1,200,000 to a prospect who was found before the old partnership was dissolved. Barlow demanded one third of the commission of $60,000. He was entitled to it. Bailey and Baker had profited from information that was ascertained during the term of the old partnership. Good faith demanded that they account to Barlow for his share of the profits.

(2) Duty to Use Care and Skill. Each partner must use good care and skill in conducting the firm's business. Any loss resulting to the firm because of a partner's failure to use adequate care and skill in transacting business must be borne by that partner. If the partnership supplies expert services, such as accounting services and engineering services, then each partner must perform these services in a manner that will free the firm from liability for damages for improper services. However, honest mistakes and errors of judgment do not render a partner liable individually nor the partnership liable collectively.

● Reed was a partner in the engineering firm of Reed and Dudley. Because of carelessness, as well as incompetency, Reed miscalculated the dimensions of steel piers for a bridge. As a result of this lack of care and skill, the firm was held liable for a $30,000 loss. Reed in turn was personally liable to the firm for the loss.

(3) Duty to Conform to the Partnership Contract. Anyone who enters into a contractual relationship with another has a duty to abide by the terms of the contract. The partnership contract must be observed scrupulously because of the fiduciary status of the partnership type of business organization. Each partner has the power to do irreparable damage to his copartners should

he choose to betray their trust in him. For this reason, the law holds each partner to the utmost fidelity to the partnership agreement. Any violation of this agreement gives the other partners at least two rights: First, they can sue the offending partner for any loss resulting from his failure to abide by the partnership agreement; second, they may elect also to ask the court to decree a dissolution of the partnership. A trivial breach of the partnership agreement will not justify a dissolution, however.

- Hanks, Haley, and Friddle formed a partnership to conduct a jewelry store. The articles of copartnership stipulated that Hanks was to have the exclusive right to do all the buying for the firm. Contrary to this agreement, Haley purchased $20,000 worth of jewelry for the firm. Hanks had previously bought an adequate stock of merchandise. Because of a rapid drop in prices, the firm lost $5,000 on the merchandise that Haley purchased. Haley was liable to his partners for this loss.

(4) Duty to Keep Records. Each partner must keep such records of partnership transactions as are required for an adequate accounting. If the articles of copartnership provide for the type of records to be kept, a partner's duty is fulfilled when he keeps such records, even though they may not be fully adequate. Since each partner must account to the partnership for all his transactions for purchases, sales, commission payments, receipts, and all other business transactions, this accounting should be based upon written records.

Rights of Partners. Every partner, in the absence of an agreement to the contrary, has four well-defined rights:

1. Right to participate in management
2. Right to inspect accounts
3. Right to contribution
4. Right to withdraw advances

(1) Right to Participate in Management. In the absence of a contract limiting his rights, each partner has the right by law to participate equally with the others in the management of the partnership business. Because the exercise of this right often leads to disharmony, it is considered as one of the basic disadvantages of the partnership type of business organization; but it deserves to stand as a prime advantage because the investor maintains control over his investment, even though his control may often be exercised in a foolish manner. The right of each partner to a voice in management does not mean a dominant voice. In all routine day to day mangerial decisions, the views of the majority are decisive. The major decisions, however, must be by unanimous consent.

• Cowen, Reynolds, and Shapiro formed a partnership. Reynolds and Shapiro put up all the capital, and Cowen contributed only his skill. Cowen contended that because of his superior skill and experience, he should be made manager and allowed to run the firm without interference from the other partners. This position was unsound since Reynolds and Shapiro had equal rights in the management unless the articles of copartnership limited their rights.

(2) Right to Inspect Accounts. The partnership records must be kept at the firm's place of business, and each partner has the right to inspect these records at any time. Any partner also has the right to inquire of any other member as to the significance of any entry that is not clear since it is the duty of the partners to render on demand full information on all matters affecting the partnership.

(3) Right of Contribution. If one partner pays a firm debt from his personal funds, he has the right to demand a pro rata contribution from each of the other partners. Such payments made by one partner must be for the ordinary and proper conduct of the business.

(4) Right to Withdraw Advances. No partner is entitled to withdraw any part of his original investment without the consent of the other partners. If one partner, however, makes additional advances in the form of a loan, he has a right to withdraw this loan at any time after the due date. Also, he is entitled to interest on this loan unless there is an agreement to the contrary. A partner is not entitled to interest on his capital account. It is therefore desirable to keep each partner's capital account separate from his loan account.

Liabilities of Partners. A partner's liabilities are of two kinds:

1. Contractual liabilities
2. Liability for torts

(1) Contractual Liabilities. Every member of a general partnership is liable individually for the debts of the firm. If one partner incurs a liability in the name of the firm that is beyond both his actual and implied authority, however, he is personally liable but the firm is not. The firm also is not liable for illegal contracts made by any member of the firm since everyone is charged with knowledge what is illegal. Thus, if a partner in a wholesale liquor firm contracted to sell an individual a case of whiskey, the contract would not be binding on the firm in a state where individual sales are illegal for wholesalers.

(2) Liability for Torts. The partnership is liable for all torts committed by each partner if the tort is committed in the course of his services to the partnership. If the tort is due to the gross negligence of the partner, he may be required to indemnify the other partners, but this does not bar the injured party from suing the partnership.

• The widow Jones left some bearer bonds and other valuables with the partnership firm of Flannagan and Boyd for safekeeping. Boyd cashed some of the bonds and used the money for his personal benefit. The partnership was liable to Jones for the injury even though Boyd in turn would be liable to reimburse Flannagan for any loss which he sustained.

Nature of Partnership Liabilities. The partners are jointly liable on all partnership contractual liabilities unless the contract stipulates otherwise. They are jointly and severally liable on all tort liabilities. For joint liabilities the partners must be sued jointly. If the firm's assets are inadequate to pay the debts, the partners are, of course, liable individually for the full amount. If all the partners but one are insolvent, the remaining solvent partner must pay all the debts even though the judgment is against all of them. The partner who pays the debt has a right of contribution from the other partners but he may lack the power to collect it because of their insolvency.

Withdrawing partners are liable for all partnership debts incurred up to the time they withdraw unless these partners are expressly released from liability by the creditors. New partners admitted to the firm under the common law are liable only for the debts incurred after admission unless they agreed otherwise. Under the Uniform Partnership Act and the Bulk Sales Laws each incoming partner is liable for all debts as fully as if he had been a partner when the debt was incurred, except that this liability for old debts is limited to his investment in the partnership. Withdrawing partners may contract with incoming partners to pay all old debts, but this is not binding on creditors.

Implied Powers of a Partner. In the absence of an agreement providing otherwise, each partner has the implied authority to bind the firm, and with it the individual members and the property of the firm, by any act committed within the scope of the partnership business in a transaction with a third party. If the authority of the partners is restricted by an agreement, notice of the restriction must be given to third parties to be effective. If that is not done, a third party may hold the partners liable on a contract made with one of them. Among the implied powers of a partner are the following:

(1) To compromise and release a claim against a third party.

(2) To receive payments and to give receipts in the name of the firm.

(3) To employ agents and employees whose services are needed in the transaction of the partnership business, or to discharge them.

(4) To draw and indorse checks, to make notes, and to accept drafts.

(5) To insure the property of the partnership, to cancel insurance policies, or to give proof of loss and to collect the proceeds.

(6) To buy goods on credit or to sell part or all of the stock of the partnership, provided this is done in the regular course of business.

Powers Not Implied. Among the acts that a partner does not have the implied power to do and for which he must obtain the unanimous consent of all the partners in order to bind the firm are the following:

(1) To assign the assets of the firm for the benefit of creditors.

(2) To indorse a negotiable instrument as an accommodation.

(3) To submit a partnership controversy for arbitration.

(4) To discharge a personal debt by agreeing that it will be set off against one due the firm.

(5) To dispose of the goodwill of the business, or to do any other act that would make impossible the continuance of the business.

This restriction covers such items as the admission of a new partner, the addition of a new line of business, the dropping of an old line, changing the locations of the business, or any other act that might result in an adverse effect that would make the continuance of the business impossible. Any partner can block any of these major changes.

Sharing of Profits and Losses. The articles of copartnership usually specify the basis upon which the profits and the losses are to be shared. This proportion cannot be changed by a majority of the members of the firm. If the partnership agreement does not fix the ratio of sharing the profits and the losses, they will be shared equally and not in proportion to the contribution to the capital. In the absence of an agreement to the contrary, the majority of the partners may order a division of the profits at any time.

Questions

1. What duties does each partner owe his copartner?

2. If one partner, as a result of his membership in the firm, is able to make a personal profit, must he share this profit with the other partners?

3. If *A* and *B* form a partnership for the purpose of operating a public accounting office, who is personally liable if *A*, through his ignorance of accounting principles, loses $1,000 of the firm's money?

4. What records must a partner keep of the transactions he performs for the partnership?

5. Is the right of each partner to participate in management equally with the other partners an advantage or disadvantage of the partnership type of business?

6. Does a partner have the right to inspect firm records at all times?

7. If one partner makes a loan to the firm, when may he withdraw this money without the consent of the other partners?

8. What are a partner's liabilities?

9. What are the implied powers of a partner?

10. If the partnership contract does not set out the method of dividing profits and sharing losses, how are these distributed?

Case Problems

1. Hacket, Hammond, and Harper each invested $15,000 in an insurance agency. Each one was to handle a specified function of the business. Salaries of $500 each were to be drawn at the end of each month. After the partnership had operated for two years, during which time the net profits after salaries were $15,000, Hacket and Hammond wanted to retain all profits in the business and add a real estate agency. They would then enter into an ambitious real estate suburban development program. Hacket and Hammond were to handle these added duties and receive an additional $500 a month salary. Harper was to receive no increase. Harper refused to agree to these proposals. Hacket and Hammond insisted that the majority should rule and attempted to ignore Harper's objections. Could these changes be undertaken without Harper's consent?

2. Day, Dolwin, and Farmer operate a partnership engaged in the laundry and dry cleaning business. Each one has $40,000 invested in the business. In addition Day has loaned the business $10,000. At the end of the year the net profits are $25,000. Day and Farmer want to use the profits to install new machinery although the machinery they now have is good. The new machinery has a few modern gadgets which they think will tend to improve their profits. Cash equal to their reserve for depreciation account has been invested in common stock of various corporations. Dolwin insists this stock should be sold and used to purchase new machinery when necessary. He claims he needs his share of the profits to send his four sons to school and insists upon withdrawing his profits and his $10,000 loan. Does he have the right to do so?

3. Metcalf and Mallary were partners, operating a cafeteria. Metcalf, without Mallary's knowledge, was also a secret partner in a grocery store. Metcalf bought meat and groceries from his own grocery store, paying considerably higher prices than were charged elsewhere. Was Metcalf acting in good faith?

4. Gotesky and Grant were partners in a public accounting firm. Gotesky audited a firm's books in such a careless and negligent manner that the firm lost $4,000 by relying on the inaccurate audit. The partnership was required to pay damages of $4,000. Was Gotesky required to reimburse Grant?

5. Collins and Conwell were partners in a men's clothing store. Each invested $12,000. At the end of the first year the profits were $10,000 and each partner drew out $3,600. The balance of the profits were distributed equally to their capital accounts. The following year Collins wished to draw out the remaining $1,400 of his profits plus $1,100 of his original investment. Was he able to do this without Conwell's consent?

6. Pringle and Whyte were partners in a drug business. The articles of copartnership provided that each partner might draw $50 each week as his share of the profits of the business. Pringle became seriously ill, and as a result Whyte was compelled to work overtime to take care of the business. Because of the extra work he performed, Whyte drew a larger amount of money each week.

(a) Did Whyte have the right to draw a larger sum?

(b) If Whyte found it necessary to employ another person, would the wages of this person be considered an expense of the firm or would they be deducted from the amount Pringle drew?

(c) While Pringle was ill, was he entitled to as much of the profits as though he had worked all the time?

7. Hahn, Brown, and Comer were partners in the operation of a gasoline station. Hahn and Brown authorized Comer to buy a delivery truck for use in the business. Comer bought a truck and then presented a bill to the firm for a commission. Was Comer entitled to be paid a commission? Explain.

8. Kirk and York, general partners operating a grocery store, had an agreement that neither would sign a note without the other's consent. Kirk disregarded this instruction and gave the firm's note for $5,000 from the Grundy National Bank. He then used the money for his personal affairs. York contended that he was not liable for any part of the note. Was he correct in this contention?

Chapter 32

Dissolution of a Partnership

Dissolution and Termination of a Partnership. If one member of a going partnership withdraws for any reason, the partnership relation is dissolved but the business may continue to operate. This change is called a dissolution. If, because of the dissolution, the partners wind up their affairs and cease all operations, the partnership is terminated. All business transactions except liquidation then cease, and the partners abandon their rights and duties under the articles of copartnership.

Dissolution by Acts of the Parties. A partnership is dissolved by act of the partners in the following ways:

1. Agreement
2. Withdrawal or alienation
3. Expulsion

(1) AGREEMENT. At the time the partnership agreement is formed, the partners may fix the time when the partnership relation will cease. Unless the agreement is renewed or amended, the partnership is dissolved on the agreed date. If no date for the dissolution is fixed at the time the partnership is formed, the partners may by mutual agreement dissolve the partnership at any time. Even when a definite date is fixed in the original agreement, the partners may dissolve the partnership prior to that time. The agreement to dissolve under this condition must be by unanimous consent.

Sometimes no date is fixed for terminating the partnership, but the agreement sets forth the purpose of the partnership, such as the construction of a building. In this event the partnership is terminated as soon as the purpose has been achieved.

(2) WITHDRAWAL OR ALIENATION. The withdrawal of one partner at any time and for any reason dissolves the partnership. In a partnership for a definite term, any partner has the power to withdraw at any time, but he does not have the right to withdraw. He is liable for any loss sustained by the other partners because of his withdrawal. If no termination date is fixed in the articles of copartnership, a partner may withdraw at will without liability unless a sudden withdrawal would result in an irreparable damage to the firm. The withdrawing partner is entitled to receive his capital, undistributed profits, and any loan upon his withdrawal.

If a termination date is fixed in the articles of copartnership or by subsequent agreement, the withdrawing partner breaches his contract by withdrawing prior to the agreed date. He is then not entitled to demand immediate reimbursement for his capital investment. The remaining partners may offset any damages sustained as a result of the withdrawal against the withdrawing partner's capital.

Closely related to the withdrawal of a partner is the alienation of his interest either by a voluntary sale or an involuntary sale to satisfy personal creditors. If the sale is voluntary, it does not of itself dissolve the partnership. The purchaser does not become a partner by purchase since the remaining partners cannot be compelled to accept as a partner anyone who might be "persona non grata" to them. The buying partner has a right to the capital and profits of the withdrawing partner, but he has no right to participate in the management.

If the sale of one partner is involuntary and is made to satisfy creditors, the sale dissolves the partnership.

(3) EXPULSION. The articles of copartnership may and should contain a clause providing for the expulsion of a member, especially if there are more than two members. This clause should spell out clearly the acts for

which a member may be expelled and the method of settlement for his interest. In the absence of a proviso to this effect in the original agreement, no member of a partnership may be expelled for any reason. The expulsion of a member dissolves the partnership but does not terminate the business since the remaining members can continue operation under a new name. This is very desirable for firms enjoying good profits.

Dissolution by Court Decree. Under certain circumstances the court may issue a decree dissolving a partnership. The chief reasons justifying such a decree are:

1. Insanity
2. Incapacity
3. Misconduct
4. Futility

(1) Insanity of a Partner. If a partnership is formed for a specified period of time and one member becomes insane before the termination of that time, the other members of the partnership may petition a court of equity to dissolve the partnership. It cannot be dissolved by agreement since this agreement must be by unanimous consent, and the insane member is incompetent to enter into a binding contract of dissolution.

If the other members dissolve the partnership without the insane member's consent, he can sue them for breach of contract upon regaining his sanity. The sane members avoid this liability by obtaining a court decree dissolving the partnership because of the insanity of one member. The dissolution is made under the superivsion of the court so as to protect the insane member's rights. Such a dissolution may or may not result in a termination of the business also. If the sane members of the firm desire to continue the business of the firm under a new name, and the interest of the insane member is not jeopardized thereby, the court may order a dissolution but not a termination.

(2) Incapacity of a Partner. Insanity, as described in the preceding section, is one type of incapacity which always justifies a dissolution of a partnership by decree of the court. There are other types and degrees of incapacity. Each incapacity must be considered upon its merits as to whether or not it justifies a dissolution. The test is whether or not the incapacity makes it impossible for the partner to perform the services to the partnership which the original partnership agreement contemplated. A member of an accounting firm who loses his eyesight would probably be incapacitated for his work to the extent of justifying a dissolution. The court, not the partners, must be the judge in each case as to whether or not the partnership should be dissolved.

The incapacity as a rule must be permanent, not temporary. A temporary inability of one partner to perform his duties is one of the risks which the other partners assumed when they formed the partnership and does not justify a court decree in dissolving the partnership.

(3) Misconduct. If one member of a partnership is guilty of misconduct that is prejudicial to the successful continuance of the business, the court may, upon proper application, decree a dissolution of the partnership. Typical illustrations of such misconduct are habitual drunkenness, dishonesty, persistent violation of the partnership agreement, irreconcilable discord among the partners, and abandonment of the business by a partner.

- McClannahan and O'Quin were partners in a retail coal business. Their wives were constantly bickering and feuding, and this often led to cross words between the partners. This was held to be trifling misbehavior and insufficient to justify a dissolution.

(4) Futility. All business partnerships are conducted for the purpose of making a profit. When it is clear that this objective cannot be achieved, the court may decree a dissolution. One partner cannot compel the other mem-

bers to assume continued losses after the success of the business becomes highly improbable and further operation appears futile. A temporary unprofitable operation does not justify a dissolution. It is only when the objective reasonably appears impossible to attain that the court will issue a decree of dissolution.

• Matney and Waldron formed a partnership to operate a skating rink and other recreational facilities on a river island. Soon after operation began, a flood changed the course of the river and practically destroyed the island. The court decreed a dissolution of the partnership because the original objective became impossible to achieve.

Dissolution by Operation of Law. Under certain well-defined circumstances, a partnership will be dissolved by operation of law. No decree of the court is necessary to dissolve the partnership. The law itself achieves this purpose. The most common examples are:

1. Death of a partner
2. Bankruptcy
3. Illegality

(1) DEATH OF A PARTNER. The death of one member of a partnership automatically dissolves the partnership. A representative of the deceased may act to protect the interest of the heirs, but he cannot act as a partner. This is true even when the articles of copartnership provide that the partnership is not to be dissolved by the death of a member. A dead man cannot be a partner, nor can he appoint an agent to act for him because death also terminates the relationship of principal and agent.

The articles of copartnership can provide for an orderly process of dissolution upon the death of a member. Thus, a provision that the surviving partners shall have twelve months in which to liquidate the firm and pay over the deceased partner's share to the heirs is binding. This is not, however, a continuation of the partnership.

(2) BANKRUPTCY. When an individual is declared a bankrupt, he is discharged from most of his debts, including those connected with the partnership. Thus bankruptcy dissolves the partnership. The rule in equity could not be otherwise. If a partner could be adjudicated a bankrupt for his personal estate and remain solvent in his partnership estate, his creditors could be defrauded. The trustee in bankruptcy has the right to assume control of the bankrupt partner's share of the partnership business. The trustee is not, however, a partner. The trustee merely stands in the place of the partner to see that the creditors' interests are protected.

(3) ILLEGALITY. Many types of business are legal when undertaken, but because of a change in the law later become illegal. This is particualrly true in the alcoholic beverage field. If a partnership is formed to conduct a lawful business and later this type of business is declared illegal, then the partnership is automatically dissolved. If a partnership is formed for the purpose of operating an insurance underwriting business, the partnership is dissolved by a law restricting this type of business to corporations.

- Smith, Combs, and Dennis formed a law partnership to act as counsellors at law. Smith was later appointed judge. The partnership was automatically dissolved under the law that bars a judge from membership in a law partnership.

Effects of Dissolution of a Partnership. Dissolution of a partnership does not necessarily mean the liquidation of the business. The firm may continue to operate as a new partnership, as a sole proprietorship, or as a corporation. Until the new business is formed, a partnership that has been dissolved for any reason cannot engage in any new business unless that is necessary to liquidate the firm. If a part of the assets of the firm are goods in process and additional raw materials must be purchased before the goods in process can be converted into finished goods, these raw materials may be purchased.

Anyone who extends credit to the partnership after he has received notice of the dissolution cannot look to partnership assets for collection. The liquidating partner becomes personally liable for these debts. The liquidating partner or partners are trustees of the firm's assets and must account for all funds in existence at the time of liquidation. As a general rule the partner in charge of liquidation is entitled to reasonable compensation for his services.

Notice of Dissolution. When a partnership is dissolved, a new firm is frequently established. Such a change may not become known to creditors and other third parties who have done business with the old firm. For the protection of these third parties, the law requires that in certain cases they must be given actual notice of the dissolution. If notice is not given, every member of the old firm may be held liable for the acts of the former partners that are committed within the scope of the new business.

Notice is usually given to former creditors by mail. The withdrawing partner or partners must be prepared to prove that this notice was actually received by the creditors. As a means of proof, a registered letter with a return receipt attached is the safest form of notice. It is sufficient to give the general public notice by publication. This would be adequate also for former creditors if it could be established that they read

LEGAL NOTICE

Notice is hereby given that Henry Masterson and Sons, Realty Specialists, a partnership consisting of Henry Masterson, Louis Masterson, and Robert Masterson, and conducting its business at 4325 Main Street, Tucson, Arizona, has this day been dissolved because Henry Masterson has retired from the firm. Louis Masterson and Robert Masterson will continue the business at the same address, under the firm name of Louis and Robert Masterson, Realtors.

A Newspaper Notice of the Dissolution of a Partnership.

the publication. If the name of the firm included the name of the withdrawing partner, he should, of course, have his name removed from the firm name and from all stationery.

In the following instances notice is usually not deemed necessary:

(1) To those who were partners

(2) When the partnership was dissolved by the operation of law

(3) When the partnership was dissolved by a judicial decree

(4) When a dormant or a secret partner retired

Distribution of Assets. After the termination of a solvent partnership, the partners are entitled to participate in the assets remaining after the debts are paid to creditors. The distribution of the remaining assets among the partners is usually as follows:

(1) Partners who have advanced money to the firm or have incurred liabilities in its behalf are entitled to reimbursement.

(2) Each partner is next entitled to the return of the capital that he contributed to the partnership.

(3) Any assets remaining are distributed equally, unless there is an agreement in the partnership contract that provides for an unequal distribution.

When a firm sustains a loss, the loss will be shared equally by the partners, unless there is an agreement to the contrary.

Questions

1. What is the difference between a termination of a partnership and the dissolution of the partnership business?

2. If no time is fixed for the duration of the partnership in the articles of copartnership, how long will the partnership extend?

3. If the articles of copartnership provide for a ten-year term for the business, does any partner have the power to withdraw at any time?

4. What are the rights of a person who buys a partner's interest in the firm?

5. In the absence of a specific provision in the partnership contract, may one partner be expelled by the other members?

6. If one member of a firm becomes ill and cannot perform his share of the work, what recourse do the other partners have?

7. What is the remedy for the innocent partners if one of their members conducts himself in such a way that the good name of the business is seriously damaged?

8. One member of a partnership dies. What effect does this have on the partnership?

9. If a partner is declared personally bankrupt, what effect has this upon the partnership?

10. After the termination of a solvent partnership, how are the assets divided?

Case Problems

1. Andrews and Averitt operated a shoe store as a partnership. Andrews became seriously ill, and the court decreed a dissolution and a liquidation. The Snow Shoe Company, sold $3,000 worth of shoes to the firm upon Averitt's order even though its manager, Henry Griffith, had notice of the dissolution. The account was never paid, and the Snow Shoe Company insisted upon the right of sharing in the firm assets along with other partnership creditors. Was it entitled to do so?

2. Kelley, Love, and Marler form a partnership to operate a men's clothing store. The firm operates several years and is very profitable. Marler becomes insane and appears to be beyond hope of recovery. Mrs. Marler enters into a contract with Kelley and Love to dissolve the partnership. Kelley and Love pay her Marler's share of the partnership assets. Kelley and Love operate the new partnership for three years during which time their net profits are $36,000. Marler, having regained his sanity, now demands one third of these profits. Is he entitled to them?

3. Coleman and Hanson formed a partnership for the purpose of operating a hardware store. Coleman contributed $4,000 and Hanson contributed $2,000 of the capital. Both gave their entire time to the business. The agreement did not specify the manner in which the profits were to be divided. At the end of a year, the partners agreed to dissolve the partnership. They had on hand at that time $2,000 of undivided profits.

(a) To how much of the undivided profits was Coleman entitled?

(b) To how much of the undivided profits was Hanson entitled?

(c) How much of the invested capital was each entitled to recover?

4. Adams and Diehl conducted a printing establishment as a partnership under the name of The Economy Print Shop. Diehl withdrew and Miss Haley, the secretary-bookkeeper, was instructed to send notices of dissolution to all creditors. She did so but overlooked one paper company from which the partnership had in the past bought a considerable quantity of paper on credit. About two weeks after the dissolution, Adams ordered $1,000 worth of paper from the paper mill that had not received notice of dissolution. The order was made on a new type of order blank from which Diehl's name had been removed. Other than this, there was nothing to indicate any change in the business. The account was never paid and the paper mill sued Diehl personally. Was Diehl liable?

5. Sirmans and Barton form a partnership for ten years to engage in the sale and servicing of air conditioning systems. Their profits average about $3,000 after salaries. Barton becomes personally bankrupt, owing $40,000 in excess of his personal estate assets. His creditors, through the trustee in bankruptcy, demand that the partnership be liquidated and the proceeds of Barton's share of the assets be applied to Barton's debts. Must the partnership be liquidated?

6. Holmes and Horton, formed a partnership to operate a livestock auction barn. Holmes invested nothing except his skill; Horton invested $14,000. Profits and losses were to be shared equally. In a few years the firm liquidated. After all debts were paid, there remained $14,000. How would this be distributed among the partners?

Cases for Review of Part VII

1. The three Myles brothers operated a meat shop as a partnership. They owned as a part of the partnership property some beef cattle which were to be slaughtered and sold through their meat shop. One of the partners, R. A. Myles, became personally indebted to the A. D. Davis Packing Company. The Packing Company levied upon ten steers belonging to the partnership and sold them for R. A. Myles's personal debts. The partnership sued to recover the value of these assets. (R. A. Myles & Co. vs. A. D. Davis Packing Company, 17 Ala. App. 85) Was the partnership entitled to recover?

2. The L. Katz and Company was a partnership consisting of Katz and Brewington. Katz kept control of the books and refused to allow Brewington to inspect them. He also insisted upon managing the business, and refused to permit Brewington to have access to the business or have a voice in its management. Katz did this because he supplied all the capital, even though profits were to be divided equally. Brewington brought an action to compel Katz to give him access to the books. (Katz vs. Brewington, 71 Md. 70) Was Brewington entitled to have access to the books?

3. Yost, Campbell, and Sewell formed a partnership operating under the name of the Independent Lumber Company. Freeman purchased Campbell's interest in the firm. At the time of the purchase there were many debts outstanding. Freeman knew of these debts but did not agree to become liable for them. New debts were incurred after the date of purchase. Freeman denied liability for both the old debts and the new debts on the ground that he never intended to become a partner, but intended to form a corporation with Yost and Sewell. (Freeman vs. Hutting Sash & Door Company, 105 Texas 560) Was Freeman liable for both the old and the new debts?

4. Green, Casey, and James were partners. Casey died. His personal estate was insolvent at the time of his death. Emanuel, a partnership creditor, brought an action against Casey's estate to collect the partnership debt. Casey's individual creditors claimed they had priority over Emanuel. Prior to Emanuel's action the partnership became insolvent and the remaining partners were also personally insolvent. (Emanuel vs. Bird, 19 Ala. 596) Was Emanuel entitled to share in the personal estate of Casey?

5. Heckard, Martin, and James, a general partnership operating as Heckard & Sons, sold paving bricks to H. D. Dougherty, in reality a partnership consisting of Dougherty and Martin. Heckard & Sons sued Dougherty and Martin as a partnership for the debt. Martin contended that he was not liable since the only name ever used for their alleged partnership was H. D. Dougherty. (Dougherty vs. Heckard, 189 Ill. 239) May a partnership operate under the name of one of the partners?

6. J. D. Brown owned a farm. He entered into an agreement with Pelkey to operate the farm on shares, that is "to the halves." Brown and Pelkey interpreted the expression "to the halves" to mean that expenses were to be paid and the remainder divided equally. Pelkey bought seed from the Farmers' Exchange and charged it to Brown and Pelkey. Brown refused to pay his share and the Farmers' Exchange brought suit, alleging that a partnership existed between Brown and Pelkey; therefore, Pelkey had the power to bind Brown. (Farmers' Exchange vs. Brown, 106 Vt. 65) Was this a partnership?

7. W. M. Brown was a partner in a partnership firm. This firm purchased from the High Smith Brothers a horse and executed a promissory note in payment. This note was duly negotiated to the Green River Deposit Bank. W. M. Brown later purchased from the bank a one-half interest in the note at a reasonable discount. The other partners contended that Brown must share the discount with the other partners. (Deavenport vs. Green River Deposit Bank, 138 Ky. 352) Was this discount a partnership profit?

Part VIII
CORPORATIONS

Chapter 33

Nature of a Corporation

What Is a Corporation? A *corporation* is "an association of individuals united for some common purpose, and permitted by law to use a common name and to change its members without dissolution of the association." This definition was given in an early decision by the Supreme Court of the United States and is still considered a satisfactory definition of the term "corporation." Unlike a partnership, a corporation need not be organized for the purpose of making and sharing profits. It may be organized for any lawful purpose, whether that purpose is for pleasure or profit.

A corporation is known in law as an "entity," that is, something that has a distinct existence separate and apart from the existence of its individual members. Chief Justice Marshall defined a corporation as "an artificial being, invisible, intangible, and existing only in contemplation of law."

A corporation is considered an artificial person that has been substituted for the natural persons who are responsible for its formation and who manage and control its affairs. Hence, when a corporation makes a contract, the contract is made by and in the name of this legal entity, the corporation, and not by and in the name of the individual members. It has all the rights and powers of an individual. It can sue and be sued, it can be fined for violating the law, it has recourse to the constitution to protect its liberties, and in most other respects it enjoys the same prerogatives as an individual.

Importance of Corporations. Corporations have been in existence for a long time, but essentially they are the product of the last century. The rapid expansion of industry from small shops to giant enterprises required large amounts of capital. Few men had enough money of their own to build a railroad or a great steel mill, and men hesitated to form partnerships with any but trusted acquaintances. In addition, even though four or five men did form a partnership, insufficient capital was still a major problem. The need was for hundreds or even thousands of men, each with a few hundred or a few thousand dollars, to pool their capital for concerted undertakings. The corporate form of business was well adapted to meet this need. It not only provided the necessary capital, but also freed the investors from the risks and restraints of partnerships by limiting each investor's liability to his original investment.

It is evident that our mass-production enterprises could not have expanded to their present size except through corporate financing. Small enterprises still offer opportunities; but experience has demonstrated that certain businesses that require much capital, such as a steel mill, an automobile manufacturer, or a railroad, can best be operated by a corporation.

Differences Between Partnerships and Corporations. There are many differences between the law governing partnerships and that governing corporations. For the investor particularly, these differences are extremely important. For example, three men with $20,000 each can form a partnership with a capital of $60,000. We saw, however, in the chapters on partnership, how each partner risks losing not only this $20,000 but also everything else he may own since he is personally liable for all partnership debts. If a corporation is formed and each investor contributes $20,000, this amount is the maximum he can lose since he is not liable for the corporate debts beyond his investment.

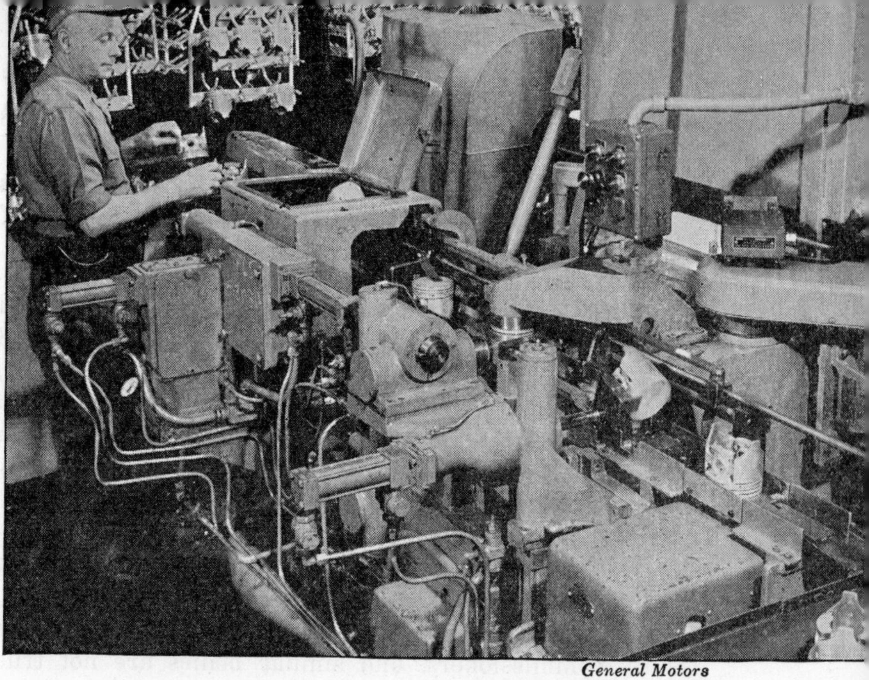

General Motors

Expensive Equipment Required by a Large Manufacturer Can Be Provided by the Corporate Form of Business.

This advantage of the corporation over the partnership is offset by at least one important disadvantage. In a partnership each partner has an equal voice in the management of the business. Furthermore, he is the sole judge as to whether or not his share of the profits should be withdrawn or left in the business. In a corporation the men who own or control a majority of the common stock have not merely a dominant voice in management but the sole voice. If there are fifteen stockholders but one owns 51 per cent of the common stock, he is free to run the corporation as he sees fit. He alone decides whether or not profits are to be paid out as dividends or retained in the business. He must not act in an arbitrary and capricious manner, but otherwise there are but few restraints on him. The owners of the minority stock have no right to employment in the business, in fact they may even be prosecuted for trespassing if they enter upon the corporate property. The person who invests his savings in a business in the hope of becoming "his own boss" may not find the corporate type of business organization the most desirable unless he can be sure of controlling a majority of the common stock.

Public Corporations. Corporations may be classified as public and private. A *public corporation* is one formed to carry out some governmental function, such as a city, a state university, or a public hospital. The powers and functions of public corporations are not comparable with private corporations conducted for profit. Public corporations are created by the state primarily for the purpose of facilitating the administration of governmental functions. They are an excellent device for fixing the limit of any public administrator's authority.

Some public bodies, such as school boards, board of county commissioners, and similar bodies are not true public corporations but have many similar powers, such as the right to sue and be sued, own, buy, and sell property, and to sign other contracts as an entity. They are called *quasi corporations,* quasi meaning "as if."

Private Corporations. *Private corporations* are those formed by private individuals to perform some nongovernmental function. They in turn are classified as:

1. Nonstock corporations
2. Stock corporations

(1) NONSTOCK CORPORATIONS. A *nonstock corporation* is one formed by private individuals for the purpose of conducting some charitable, educational, religious, social, or fraternal service. These corporations are not organized for profit, nor is membership in them evidenced by stock ownership. There is no stock issued. The corporation, however, is a legal entity like any other corporation, and can sue and be sued as a corporation, can buy and sell property, and otherwise operate as any other corporation. Membership in these corporations is acquired by agreement between the charter members in the

beginning and between the present members and new members thereafter.

A nonstock private corporation that has for its sole purpose some charitable undertaking may be called an *eleemosynary corporation.*

(2) STOCK CORPORATIONS. In terms of number and importance stock corporations organized for profit constitute the chief type discussed in this text. Membership in a *stock corporation* is represented by shares of stock. The extent of one's rights and liabilities is determined by the number of shares of stock owned and by the charter and the bylaws of the corporation.

Other Classes of Corporations. Corporations may be classified in other ways depending on the purpose of the classification. Thus we may need to classify them as domestic or foreign corporations. A corporation is a *domestic corporation* in the state where it received its initial charter; it is a *foreign corporation* in all other states. If it is incorporated in another country, it may be referred to as an *alien corporation.*

Corporations may also be classified as de jure and de facto. A *de jure corporation* is one that has fulfilled every requirement of the state corporation laws where it received its charter. It is a corporation in both fact and law. A *de facto corporation* is one in fact but not in law. It has failed to comply with some minor requirement of the law governing the formation of corporations, but otherwise acts as a corporation. Only the state can question the status of a de facto corporation. Its contract with the state is not complete, and the state may bring an action to cancel its charter.

Formation of a Corporation. A group of individuals, usually not less than three, subscribe a predetermined sum of money to the proposed corporation, and file with the secretary of the state in which the corporation is to be formed *articles of incorporation* in which are set forth:

(1) The name of the proposed corporation
(2) The purpose for which the incorporation is formed
(3) The amount of the capital stock and the nature of the shares to represent this stock
(4) The location of the principal business office
(5) The duration of the proposed corporation
(6) The number and the names of the persons selected as directors for the first year

After the articles of incorporation have been filed, if the instrument is satisfactory and all requirements have been met, a charter is granted.

The Charter. The *charter* is a written document setting forth the facts prescribed by law for the issuance of a charter and asserting that the corporation has complied with these legal requirements. This charter is the base on which rests all the authority of the corporation. It is a contract between the corporation and the state. So long as the corporation complies with the terms of the contract, the state cannot alter the charter in any material way without the consent of the stockholders.

Some courts have further held that a charter is a contract between the corporation and the stockholders, as well as between the stockholders and the state. This makes the charter a three-way contract. When the incorporators meet, elect a board of directors, and begin business, acceptance of the charter is presumed and all parties are bound by it.

Powers of a Corporation. The powers which the corporation has are granted to it expressly or impliedly by the state.

The charter sets out the nature of the business to be undertaken by the corporation. The corporation's power is limited by this scope of the undertaking. The charter further sets forth the type and the amount of stock to be sold.

Incidental Powers. Certain powers that are always incidental to a corporate existence are:

1. To have a corporate name
2. To have a continous existence
3. To buy, sell, and hold property
4. To make bylaws and regulations
5. To sue and be sued in the corporate name
6. To have and use a corporate seal

(1) CORPORATE NAME. A corporation must have a corporate name. The members may select any name they wish, provided it is not contrary to the statutes or is not already used by another firm or corporation within the state. Many of the states have statutes regulating corporate names, for example, by requiring the name to begin with "The" and to end with "Company," or to be followed by the word "Incorporated" or an abbreviation thereof.

(2) CONTINUOUS EXISTENCE. During the period for which the charter was granted, the existence of the corporation is continuous. This is one of the features of a corporation that makes this form of organization valuable. The death of a member does not dissolve the organization. Some times this characteristic is referred to as perpetual or continuous succession.

(3) PROPERTY RIGHTS. A corporation has the right to buy, sell, and hold property that is necessary in its functioning as a corporation and that is not foreign to the purpose for which it was created. Such power is usually given by statute or by the charter.

(4) BYLAWS AND REGULATIONS. Rules and regulations are necessary to govern and to determine the future con-

duct of the organization. They must conform to the statutes and must not be contrary to public policy.

(5) Legal Actions. Another power that has long been considered incidental to corporate existence is the power to sue in the corporate name. Since a corporation may be composed of hundreds or thousands of stockholders, it would be a very cumbersome task, if not an impossible one, to secure the consent of all the stockholders each time a suit was to be brought by a corporation. A corporation may likewise be sued in the corporate name.

(6) Corporate Seal. A corporation has the incidental power to have and to own a seal. Under the common law the corporation was required to use its seal in most of its transactions. The rule now is that a corporation need not use its seal except (a) in executing deeds and other written instruments that require the use of a seal when executed by natural individuals or (b) in carrying out transactions where the use of the seal is required by special statutory requirements.

Implied Powers in General. In addition to the powers that are incidental to or expressly conferred upon all corporations, a corporation has also the implied power to do all acts that are reasonably necessary for carrying out the purpose for which the corporation was formed. A corporation may borrow money and contract debts if such acts are necessary for the transaction of the corporate business. It may make, indorse, and accept negotiable instruments. It has the power to acquire and convey property, and to mortgage or lease its property in case such transactions are necessary for carrying on its business.

As a general rule a corporation does not have implied power to enter into a contract of partnership or into a contract of guaranty.

Ultra Vires Contracts. Any contract entered into by a corporation that is not authorized by any of its three classes of powers (charter powers, incidental powers, and implied powers) is an *ultra vires contract.* These contracts are called ultra vires because they go beyond the powers of a corporation. If the contract is wholly executory or wholly executed, most courts do not disturb them. They will not enforce wholly executory utlra vires contract for either party, nor permit a rescission by either party if the contract is wholly executed. If the contract is executed by one party but executory to the other party, most courts permit the performing party to recover a reasonable amount for his performance.

A stockholder may obtain a court order, an injunction, to bar a corporation from undertaking a contemplated ultra vires act. The stockholders cannot intervene, however, if the act has already been executed. The state may revoke the charter of a corporation for an ultra vires act, but this is merely a penalty and in no way affects the rights of the parties to the ultra vires contract.

● The Ritter Lumber Company was organized to cut, grade, and sell lumber. The board of directors voted to use corporate funds to publish a newspaper. Woolem, a stockholder claiming that the publication of a newspaper was an ultra vires act, sought to obtain an injunction against it. The court held that the corporation could publish the newspaper because it would serve as an advertising medium for its products.

Questions

1. What is a corporation?

2. What is meant by the expression that a corporation is an entity?

3. What are the rights of the stockholders in a corporation who control a majority of the common stock of the corporation?

4. If one person owns 49 per cent of the stock in a corporation, does this fact automatically give him a right to work for the corporation?

5. (a) What is the purpose of forming a public corporation?

(b) Give three examples of public corporations.

6. Give three examples of nonstock private corporations.

7. When may the state alter the charter of a corporation?

8. What information is usually included in the articles of incorporation?

9. What powers does a corporation have other than those expressly set out in its charter?

10. What action may the state take if a corporation engages in an ultra vires act?

Case Problems

1. A state fixed a minimum of $5,000 paid-in capital before a corporation could begin business. The East End Coal Corporation began business with only $4,500 paid-in capital. Soon after the corporation began business, it entered into a contract with the Carter Coal Company to purchase 10,000 tons of coal a month at $4.50 a ton. Later the Carter Coal Company refused to deliver the coal, claiming the contract was invalid because the East End Coal Corporation was not a real corporation on account of its failure to comply with the state law. Was this a valid defense?

2. A corporation organized in New Jersey was issued a charter authorizing it to engage in highway construction. Soon after the corporation's organization, it was lowest bidder on a state road construction job and the contract was duly let to the corporation. Later the state attempted arbitrarily to avoid the contract, claiming a corporation was not entitled to the protection of the Federal Constitution protecting individual citizens against the abridgement of their contractual rights. Do corporations enjoy the same constitutional protections as individual citizens?

3. Childs, Clyatt, and Collins formed a partnership dealing in antiques. Each invested $20,000 in the business. It was a very profitable enterprise but was endangered by the constant bickering among the three partners. As a solution to their problem, they incorporated, each taking $20,000 worth of stock in the corporation. In addition, the corporation was authorized to sell an additional $21,000 worth of stock, $7,000 worth for each stockholder. When Clyatt and Collins

refused to buy any more stock, Child's mother-in-law bought the other shares. In electing a board of directors each of the original stockholders put up a separate slate. Child's slate won all places. The board of directors discharged Clyatt and Collins from their jobs and denied them all access to the business. From Clyatt's and Collins' point of view, did the corporate type of business organization overcome the so-called weaknesses of the partnership type?

4. A local chapter of a national fraternity was incorporated under the state law of its location. The local chapter entered into a contract to purchase a house for the use of the local fraternity. The contract called for a $20,000 mortgage on the property to be paid at the rate of $125 a month. Would the individual members of the local fraternity be personally liable for this mortgage in the event of default by the corporation?

5. Donaldson, who owned two large farms devoted to the production of livestock, had two sons, John and Henry. He wanted to take them into business with him in such a way that he would keep one of the farms exclusively for himself and operate the other one as a partnership or corporation. He was told that under a partnership arrangement both farms could still be subjected to liability for the debts of the partnership. To avoid this, the three of them drew up a corporation type of contract, providing for shares of stock, a board of directors, and all the other requirements of a corporation. They did not obtain a charter, however, nor did they attempt to comply with the state corporation laws. They did file a federal and state corporation income tax return each year. The firm, due to the bad management of the two sons, became heavily indebted and the creditors brought suit to collect. The firm's assets were wholly inadequate to pay the firm's debts. The creditors then sought to hold the father personally liable for these debts. Was he liable?

6. A group of fifty dairy farmers formed a corporation for the purpose of marketing milk and other dairy products. The charter stipulated that it was authorized to bottle and market whole milk in the city of Auburn. Soon the question arose as to whether or not the corporation could do any of these acts: (a) Buy milk from farmers other than the fifty members; (b) make and sell ice cream; (c) make and sell butter and cheese; (d) buy and operate a freezer locker plant in conjunction with its milk plant; (e) buy a dairy farm in the name of the corporation to produce milk for sale by the corporation; (f) to operate a feed store for the convenience of the stockholders in purchasing dairy feed; (g) to own and operate the Dairy Queen, a restaurant, selling only dairy products such as ice cream, milk shakes, and other dishes consisting mainly of milk or milk products. Which of these acts were permissible either under the charter, the incidental, or the implied powers of the corporation?

7. A corporation was formed for the purpose of manufacturing and selling jewelry. It owned its own building. The directors found that they had more space than was needed for their business, and they decided to rent one of the floors for office purposes. One of the stockholders opposed the idea, contending that such an act would be ultra vires. Was the stockholder right in his contention in this case? Why?

8. Dempsey, Carpenter, and Rhinehart owned all the stock in the Mathis Lumber Company. They voted unanimously to authorize the board of directors to guarantee the faithful fulfillment of a construction contract by the Dade Construction Company. Did the corporation have the power to do this?

9. The Blue Stone Coal Company, a corporation, voted through its board of directors to use its surplus to construct a hotel to be operated for a profit. After the hotel was completed and in operation, a stockholder brought an action to compel the board of directors to sell the hotel. Was this the proper action?

10. The Big Ben Railroad, a corporation, signed a contract with the Hodgsen Fertilizer Corporation to run an experimental farm to test the various types of fertilizer manufactured by Hodgsen. The Hodgsen Corporation sued the railroad for $10,000, the amount owed for fertilizer bought for the experiments. The railroad claims it is not liable because the contract was an ultra vires act. Was this defense valid?

Chapter 34

Membership in a Corporation

Capital Stock. The *capital stock* of the corporation is the amount authorized by the charter and the articles of incorporation. This stock is subscribed and paid for by the members. It generally is not necessary that all the capital stock of a corporation be subscribed and paid for before the corporation begins operation. The amount of capital stock authorized in the charter cannot be altered without the consent of the state and the stockholders.

The capital stock is divided into units called *shares.* These shares may have a set value of one dollar, ten dollars, one hundred dollars, or any other amount not prohibited by law.

Membership. Membership in a corporation is acquired by the ownership of one or more shares of stock. The members are known as *stockholders.* The shares of stock may be obtained by subscription either before or after the corporation is organized, or they may be obtained by gift or purchase from another stockholder. The amount of ownership, that is, the number of shares owned, is evidenced by a stock certificate.

Stock Certificate. A *certificate of stock* is the owner's receipt for the money he has invested in the corporation. It is not considered as property in itself, but only as evidence of the owner's rights in the corporation. It shows on its face the number of shares represented, the par value of each share if there is a par value, and the signatures of the legally authorized officers.

Kinds of Stock. Stock is divided into many classes. The classes are determined by the laws under which the corportion is organized. The two principal classes of stock are:

1. Common stock
2. Preferred stock

(1) COMMON STOCK. *Common stock* is the simplest form of stock issued. The owners of common stock are entitled to a pro rata share of the profits after prior claims have been satisfied. If a corporation has issued 5,000 shares of common stock, the owner of 100 shares is entitled to 1/50 of the profits that are made available to the common stockholders. Unlike the partners in a partnership, the owners cannot receive the profits until they have been made available, in the form of a dividend, declared by the board of directors.

The common stockholders generally have full right to manage and operate the corporation, but they cannot perform this function as individual stockholders or as a group. They must elect agents or directors, who in turn appoint the managers, usually though not necessarily from the stockholders. The stockholders who are not employed by these managers to work for the corporation have no more rights in determining the operating policies of a corporation than has an outsider.

(2) PREFERRED STOCK. *Preferred stock* differs from common stock in that some sort of preference is granted to the holder of this stock. The preference may pertain to voting, to the division of profits, to the division of assets upon dissolution, or to any two or more of these preferences in combination. The most valuable preference is the preference as to profits.

The fact that particular stock is called preferred stock does not tell much about what preference the holder really has. It may be preferred as to assets only, which gives the holder no advantage except in the event of liquidation. It may be preferred as to dividends only, but not as to assets in the event of liquidation. The most common type is that which gives preference both as to dividends and assets; but even here the stock may be either first preferred, second preferred, or third preferred. In this event the first preferred is given preference in the payment of dividends before the second preferred is entitled to anything. Likewise the second preferred must be paid before the third preferred is entitled to receive a dividend.

The two rights usually given up by the preferred stockholders are the right to vote in stockholders' meetings and the right to participate in profits beyond the percentage fixed in the stock certificate. A few states prohibit any restriction upon any stockholder's right to vote.

When the stock is preferred as to dividends, this right may be cumulative or noncumulative. This fact is significant if the corporation operates at a loss about as often as it does at a profit. For example, a corporation that has $1,000,000 outstanding common stock and $1,000,000 outstanding 7 per cent preferred stock operates at a loss for two years, and then earns 21 per cent net profit the third year. If *noncumulative preferred stock* has been issued, it is entitled only to one dividend of 7 per cent and the common stock is entitled to the remaining 14 per cent. If *cumulative preferred stock* has been issued, it is entitled to three preferences of 7 per cent, or 21 per cent in all before the common stock is entitled to any dividend. Or if the company earns a net profit each year equal only to 7 per cent on the preferred stock, the directors could, if the preferred stock is noncumulative, pass the dividend the first year, and declare a 7 per cent dividend on both the common and the preferred stock for the second year. Since the directors are elected by the common stockholders, the common stockholders could easily defraud the preferred stockholders. For that reason the law is that preferred stock is cumulative unless specifically stated to be noncumulative. This is true only, however, when the corporation earns a profit but fails to declare a dividend. Unless the stock expressly states that it is cumulative, the preference does not cumulate in the years during which the corporation operated at a loss.

Preferred stock may also be participating or nonparticipating. Thus 7 per cent *participating preferred stock* may pay considerably more than 7 per cent annually; but if it is *nonparticipating preferred stock,* 7 per cent annually would be the maximum to which the preferred stockholders would be entitled no matter how much the corporation earned. If the preferred stock is to participate in any profits beyond the rate fixed in the stock, this right must be expressly stated in the stock certificate or articles of incorporation. The law presumes it is nonparticipating in the absence of a contract to the contrary. If it does participate, it can do so only according to the terms of this contract. The contract may provide that the preferred stock shall participate equally with the common stock, or it may provide that the preferred stock is entitled to an additional 1 per cent for each additional 5 per cent the common stock receives.

Par-Value Stock and No-Par-Value Stock. Stock to which a face value, such as $25, $50, or $100, has been assigned is *par-value stock.* Stock to which no face value has been assigned is *no-par-value stock.* Preferred stock usually has a par value, but common stock may be either par-value or no-par-value stock. It is ordinarily assumed that par-value stock is issued at par value; but after the business is operating, the price at which the stock can be sold may be either more or less than the par value. No-par-value stock may be issued at any price, although some states do set a minimum price, such as $5, for which it can be issued.

If par-value stock is sold by the corporation at a discount, the purchaser is liable to subsequent creditors for the amount of the discount. No-par-value stock was intended to overcome this weakness of par-value stock.

Treasury Stock. If a corporation purchases stock that it has sold, this stock is referred to as *treasury stock.* When stock is first offered for sale, there may be less sales resistance encountered if the prospective purchaser can be assured that the corporation will repurchase the stock upon request. Treasury stock may also be reacquired by donation. The corporation then sells the stock and places the proceeds in a donated surplus account. This is generally done when the corporation is in financial difficulties and the stockholders agree to this plan of building up the working capital.

Treasury stock can be repurchased only out of surplus. If the corporation resells it, the directors may fix any price which they deem feasible. Until it is resold, no dividends can be paid on it.

Watered Stock. When par-value stock is issued as fully paid up but the purchase price is paid with property of inflated values, it is said to be *watered stock.* If real estate actually worth $10,000 is paid for in stock having a par value of $100,000, it is watered to the extent of $90,000. In most instances, watering stock is not prohibited outright, but it cannot be used to defraud creditors. In the event of insolvency, the creditors may sue the owners of watered stock for the difference between the par value and the actual purchase price. This is not true, of course, if the creditors knew the stock was watered or if the holder of the stock purchased it from the one to whom it was orginally issued. Except for creditors, most state statutes do not prohibit the watering of stock by corporations other than public utility companies.

If the payment for stock is in overvalued real estate, the extent of the watering can be determined with reasonable accuracy. If the payment is in the form of patents, trade marks, blueprints, or other similar assets, it may be difficult to fix the extent of the watering. The extent of the watering is not one of law, but one of fact, and is to be fixed by the jury based upon the evidence presented in each case.

Transfer of Stock. A stock certificate indicates the manner in which the stock may be transferred to another party. On the back of the certificate is a blank form which the owner may use in executing an assignment. The signature of the previous owner gives to the new holder full possession and the right to exchange the certificate for another made out to himself by the corporation. The new owner should have the certificate exchanged for a new one in his own name so that he will be registered as a stockholder on the books of the corporation. Unless he is so registered, he is not entitled to the rights and privileges of a stockholder, and he will not receive any dividends when they are declared.

Dividends. The profits of a corporation belong to the corporation until the directors set them aside for distribution as *dividends*. Dividends may be paid in cash, stock, or other property.

A cash dividend usually can be paid out of earned surplus only, but there are two exceptions. A cash dividend may be paid out of donated or paid-in surplus. Also for corporations with depleting assets such as coal mines, oil companies, lumber companies, and similar industries, cash dividends may be paid out of capital to the extent of the depletion.

Stock dividends are usually paid out of earned surplus, but they may usually be paid out of any surplus account. A stock dividend cannot be declared if there is no surplus of any kind for this would result in stock watering. Dividends also may be paid in the form of property which the corporation manufactures, but this is seldom done.

The right to declare a dividend on either common or preferred stock depends entirely upon the discretion of the directors. The directors, however, must act reasonably and in good faith; otherwise the stockholders may invoke the aid of a court in compelling them to do so. There is no absolute rule as to when a dividend should be declared. If profits have accumulated but dividends have not been declared, the profits become part of the assets of the corporation and may be used in improving the property or in extending the business.

If a dividend is illegally declared and paid, either the stockholders or the directors may be sued by creditors for its return.

When a cash dividend is declared it cannot later be rescinded. It becomes a liability of the corporation the minute it is declared. A stock dividend on the other hand may be rescinded at any time prior to the issuance and delivery of the stock.

Blue-Sky Laws. The purpose of the so-called blue-sky laws is to regulate the sale of securities and to prevent fraud through the sale of worthless stocks and bonds.

• The term *blue-sky laws* is applied to all security laws because of a remark made in connection with the passing of the first statute of this nature, that some companies tried to "capitalize the blue sky."

These security laws usually stipulate that before a salesman may offer stocks or bonds for sale, a statement of the responsibility of the seller, the general financial condition of the corporation, and the nature of the stocks or the bonds that are for sale must be furnished to a designated state official or a commission. Criminal penalties are provided for violation of these laws, and there is a civil liability on the part of the seller to purchasers.

Federal Securities Act, 1933. Because the state blue-sky laws apply only to intrastate sales of securities, in 1933 the federal Congress passed the Federal Securities Act to regulate the sale of securities in interstate commerce. Any corporation offering a new issue of securities for sale to the public must register them with the Commission. This act does not apply to the sales of securities under $100,000 by corporations, nor does the act regulate the sale or purchase of securities by individuals.

In addition to the registration and the information contained in it, the proposed prospectus must be filed and approved by the Securities and Exchange Commission before the securities can be offered for sale. Full information must be given relative to the financial structure of the corporation. Information filed must also include the types of securities outstanding, if any, the terms of the sale, bonus and profit-sharing arrangements, options to be created in regard to the securities, and any other data which the commission may deem relevant.

The registration statement must be signed by the company, its principal officers, and a majority of the board of directors. If either the registration statement or the prospectus contain misstatements or omissions, the commission will not permit the securities to be offered for sale. If they are sold before the false information is ascertained, an investor may rescind his contract and sue any individual who signed the registration statement for damages he has sustained. Any failure to comply with the law also subjects the responsible officials to criminal prosecution.

Federal Securities Exchange Act, 1934. The chief markets for the sale of securities are the security exchanges and over-the-counter markets. In 1934 Congress passed the Securities Exchange Act to regulate such transactions. The act declares it unlawful for any broker, dealer, or exchange to use the mails for the purpose of using the exchange facilities in making a sale unless the exchange is registered with the Securities and Exchange Commission.

All the securities exchanges must declare definite rules for the regulation of members of the exchange. The bylaws of every security exchange must provide for the expulsion or disciplining of any member who violates the rules of the exchange or who engages in conduct contrary to the rules of the trade. No exchange can sell securities until it is registered with the commission and this registration may be withdrawn if the exchange violates the requirements of the statute. Individuals making misleading statements or contracts in violation of the Act may be punished by a fine and imprisonment.

Questions

1. Must all of the authorized stock of a corporation be sold before the corporation can begin business?

2. What evidence does one have that he owns stock in a corporation?

3. What are the two principal classes of stock?

4. How do the stockholders of a corporation manage the corporation?

5. Explain the difference between par-value stock and no-par-value stock.

6. What is treasury stock?

7. What is stock watering?

8. In what ways may dividends be paid?

9. Who may declare a dividend on stock?

10. What is the major purpose and function of the Securities and Exchange Commission?

Case Problems

1. Mrs. Dixon used the proceeds of her deceased husband's life insurance policies to purchase $50,000 worth of noncumulative 7 per cent preferred stock in the belief that the $3,500 annual income from this investment would be adequate to support her. Over a ten-year period the corporation averaged 14 per cent on its preferred stock, but during four years it earned no net profits and paid no dividends. Mrs. Dixon sued the corporation to compel it to pay these dividends. Was she entitled to dividends for the four years which the corporation operated at a loss?

2. Parrish, Mosteller, and Garrard operated a very profitable partnership in the wholesale meat business. Garrard died. Parrish and Mosteller persuaded Mrs. Garrard to enter the partnership as a general partner. She accepted their offer, and her share of the profits gave her a very nice income. Parrish and Mosteller proposed that the partnership incorporate. Soon after the corporation was formed, Parrish and Mosteller decided not to pay any dividends and to use them instead to open up a new plant in another city. Mrs. Garrard protested so vehemently that they voted to discharge her as bookkeeper. She was then without any source of income. She brought suit to compel the directors to declare a dividend and also to restore her to her position as bookkeeper for the firm. Was she entitled to these remedies?

3. Madison purchased 1,000 shares of 7 per cent preferred stock at $120 a share. The salesman assured him that it was participating stock and pointed to the word "participating" written in bold letters in the stock certificate. The salesman assured him that it was possible to make 20 per cent on his investment. A careful reading of the certificate revealed that the preferred stock was to participate equally with the common stock after the dividends on the common stock equaled the par value of the stock. Madison sued the corporation for a return of his money alleging fraud on the part of the salesman, an agent of the corporation. Was he legally entitled to a return of his money?

4. Konter was the owner of 1,000 shares of stock for which he had paid only about 10 per cent of their true value at the time the stock was issued. Later he sold 500 shares to Raul who paid full value for the stock. The corporation became insolvent and the creditors sued Raul, claiming that since his stock was 90 per cent watered, he was personally liable. Was this correct?

5. The profits and surplus of a corporation are equal to the capital stock. The corporation is ten years old and has never paid a dividend. The board of directors decide again this year not to pay a dividend but to use 80 per cent of the accumulated profits to build an extension to the factory. A stockholder owning 20 per cent of the stock brings suit to compel the directors to declare a dividend. Who will win the suit?

Chapter 35

Management and Dissolution of a Corporation

Nature of Corporate Management. Since a corporation is an artificial being, existing only in contemplation of law, it can perform business transactions only through actual persons, acting as agents. The directors are both trustees and agents. To the corporation, they are trustees and are chargeable for breaches of trust. To third parties, directors are agents of the corporation.

The board of directors elects the chief agents of the corporation, such as the president, the vice-president, the treasurer, and other officers, who perform the managerial functions. The board of directors is primarily a policy-making body. The chief executives in turn appoint subagents for all the administrative functions of the corporation. These subagents are agents of the corporation, however, not of the appointing executives.

It is evident from this summary of the managerial scheme of a corporation that a stockholder cannot, merely by reason of his membership in the corporation, act as an agent or exercise any managerial function. His only control is in electing a board of directors.

Even if a stockholder owned 49 per cent of the common stock of a corporation, he would have no more right to work or participate in the management of the corporation than a stranger would have. Under the partnership law, if a man owns even 1 per cent of the partnership, he has just as much right to work for the partnership and to participate in its management as any other partner. In a corporation the only way one can be sure that he can have employment with his own company is to own 51 per cent of the stock.

THE CINCINNATI SHOE COMPANY

Notice of Annual Meeting of Shareholders
MARCH 22

The annual meeting of the shareholders of The Cincinnati Shoe Company will be held at the Main Office of the Company, 170 East Main Street, Cincinnati, Ohio, on Thursday, March 22, at 10:00 o'clock A. M., Eastern Standard Time, for the purpose of electing directors, receiving reports of officers, and transacting such other business as may properly come before the meeting.

The Board of Directors has fixed the close of business, February 15, as the record date for determining shareholders entitled to notice of the meeting and to vote.

Proxy Statement accompanies this Notice.

T. L. LAWSON, Secretary.

By Order of the Board of Directors.
February 22.

You are requested to sign and return, as soon as possible, the attached Proxy.

A Notice of a Stockholders' Meeting.

Stockholders' Meetings. In order to make the will of the majority binding, the stockholders must act at a duly convened and properly conducted stockholders' meeting. These meetings must ordinarily take place in the state in which the corporation was organized, regardless of the number of states in which the corporation maintains branch offices or factories.

A regular meeting is usually held at the place and the time specified in the charter, and notice of the meeting is ordinarily not required. A special meeting may, however, be called by the directors of the corporation or in some instances by a particular officer or a specified number of stockholders. Notice of such a meeting is ordinarily required.

These meetings of the stockholders are theoretically a check upon the board of directors. If the directors do not carry out the will of the stockholders, a new board can be elected that will be amenable to the stockholders' wishes. This procedure is, in the absence of fraud or bad faith on the part of the directors, the only legal means by which the investors can exercise any control over their investment.

Quorum. A stockholders' meeting, in order to be valid, requires the presence of a quorum. At common law a *quorum* consisted of the stockholders actually assembled at a properly convened meeting. A majority of the votes cast by those present expressed the will of the stockholders. It is now ordinarily required by statutes, by-laws, or charters, that a majority of the outstanding stock be represented at the stockholders' meeting in order to constitute a quorum. This representation may be either in person or by proxy as described on page 389.

If the stockholders wish to oust the present board of directors, the first step is to acquire the proxies of those stockholders who cannot attend the stockholder's meetings in person. If there are a million stockholders, this is a very expensive undertaking. The present board of directors will also conduct a campaign to acquire proxies, but with few exceptions this expense is paid from corporate funds. If the dispute between the "ins" and the "outs" is over operating policy, the law permits the board of directors to charge to the corporation all expenses necessitated by the proxy war. If the only issue involved is that the "ins" wish to stay in and the "outs" want in, each side must pay the expenses from its personal funds.

Voting. The right of a stockholder to vote is his most important right because this is the only way in which he can exercise any control over his investment. The right to vote is limited to the bona fide stockholders, as evidenced by the stockholders' record book. An owner of stock purchased from an individual does not have the right to vote until he has the transfer made on the corporate books. Subscribers who have not fully paid for their stock are not as a rule permitted to vote.

The right to vote is controlled by the state corporation laws. There may be issued, if the law permits, voting and nonvoting common stock. The laws in all the states permit the charter of a corporation to restrict the right of preferred stockholders to vote. If the charter is silent in this regard, then the preferred stockholders have equal voting privileges with the common stockholders.

There are two major classes of elections in which the stockholders vote: the annual election of directors, and the elections to approve or disapprove some corporate policy which only the stockholders can authorize. Examples of some of these acts are consolidating with another corporation, dissolving, increasing the capital stock, and changing the number of directors.

Methods of Voting. Each stockholder has one vote for each share of stock that he holds. In the election of a board of directors, the candidates receiving a majority of the stock actually voting wins. In corporations with 500,000 stockholders, control of 10 per cent of the stock is often sufficient to control the election. In all cases the owners of 51 per cent of the stock can elect all the directors. This leaves the minority stockholders without any representation on the board of directors. To alleviate this situation, two legal devices are in existence which may give the minority stockholders a voice, but not a controlling voice, on the board of directors:

1. Cumulative voting
2. Voting trusts

(1) CUMULATIVE VOTING. In some states the statutes provide that in the election of directors a stockholder may cast as many votes in the aggregate as are equal to the number of shares held by him multiplied by the number of directors to be elected. This method of voting is called *cumulative votng.* Thus, if a stockholder owns ten shares and ten directors are to be elected, he can cast ten votes for each of the ten directors or one hundred votes for one director. As a result, under this plan of voting the mi-

nority stockholders may have some representation on the board of directors, although it is a minority.

(2) VOTING TRUSTS. Under a voting trust stockholders give up their voting privileges entirely by transferring their stock to the trustee and receiving in return *voting trust certificates.* This is not primarily a device to give the minority stockholders a voice on the board of directors; but it does do that, and often in large corporations it gives them a controlling voice. Twenty per cent of the stock always voted as a unit is more effective than individual voting. State laws severely restrict the use of voting trusts. Most of these laws require the trustee to be a stockholder and limit the life of the trust to ten years.

Proxies. Under the common law a stockholder was not permitted to vote unless he was present in person. Under the statutory law, the charter, or the bylaws, a member who does not wish to attend a meeting and vote in person may authorize another to vote his stock for him. This right is called *voting by proxy;* the person who is authorized to vote for another is known as a *proxy.*

THE CINCINNATI SHOE COMPANY

PROXY

ANNUAL MEETING MARCH 22

KNOW ALL MEN BY THESE PRESENTS, That the undersigned shareholder of THE CINCINNATI SHOE COMPANY hereby constitutes and appoints O. W. PRESCOTT, A. B. BROWN, and GEORGE CONNARS, and each of them, the true and lawful proxies of the undersigned, with several power of substitution and revocation, for and in the name of the undersigned, to attend the annual meeting of shareholders of said Company, to be held at the Main Office of the Company, 170 East Main Street, Cincinnati, Ohio, on Thursday, March 22, at 10:00 o'clock A. M., Eastern Standard Time, and any and all adjournments of said meeting, receipt of the notice of which meeting, stating the purposes thereof, together with Proxy Statement, being hereby acknowledged by the undersigned, and to vote for the election of a Board of nine directors for the Company, and to vote as they or he may deem proper upon all other matters that may lawfully come before said meeting or any adjournment thereof.

Signed the 10th day of March

L. S. Simms

A Proxy.

If a stockholder should sign more than one proxy for the same stockholders' meeting, the proxy having the later date would be effective.

Rights of Stockholders. The stockholders of a corporation enjoy several important rights and privileges. Three of these rights have been discussed. They are:

(1) A stockholder has the right to receive a properly executed certificate as evidence of his ownership of shares of stock.

(2) He has the right to attend corporate meetings and to vote unless this right is denied him by express agreement, the charter, or statutory provisions.

(3) He has the right to receive a proportionate share of the profits when profits are distributed as dividends.

In addition, each stockholder has the following rights:

(4) He has the right to sell and transfer his shares of stock.

(5) He has the right, when new stock is issued by the corporation, to subscribe for new shares in proportion to the shares that he owns. For example, if a stockholder owns 10 per cent of the original capital stock, he has a right to buy 10 per cent of the shares added to the stock. If this were not true, stockholders could be deprived of their proportionate share in the accumulated surplus of the company. Only stockholders have the right to vote to increase the capital stock.

(6) He has the right to inspect the corporate books in the absence of a statute to the contrary. He also has the right to have the corporate books inspected by an attorney or an accountant. This right is not absolute since most states have laws restricting the right. The tendency is for these laws to be drawn, not to hamper a stockholder in his right, but to protect the corporation from indiscriminate inspection.

There are two sets of corporate books, one called the *corporate books* and the other the *financial books*. The corporate books, which may be inspected by stockholders, contain a detailed record of all stock transactions and minute books for stockholders' meetings and directors' meetings. The other set, which in some states may not be inspected by stockholders, contains a record of the financial operations of the corporation.

(7) He has the right, when the corporation is dissolved, to share pro rata in the assets that remain after all the obligations of the company have been paid.

Directors. Every corporation is managed by a board of directors elected by the stockholders. The law requires every board to consist of at least three members; but if the number is in excess of three, the number, together with qualifications and manner of election, is fixed by the charter and the bylaws of the corporation.

The directors, unlike the stockholders, cannot vote by proxy. Nor can they make corporate decisions as individual directors. All decisions must be made collectively and in a called meeting of the board.

The functions of the directors can be classified as:

1. Powers
2. Duties
3. Liabilities

(1) POWERS. The powers of the board of directors are limited by law, by the charter, and by the bylaws. The directors have the power of general agents, and in this capacity may do any act reasonably necessary to achieve the purpose of the corporation so long as this power is not expressly limited. Unless authorized by statute, they do not have the power to divert corporate assets for charitable purposes. By law they are barred from using corporate funds directly for political purposes. As general agents they have the power to do only what they are expressly authorized to do or what may reasonably be implied as necessary to carry out their function.

(2) DUTIES. The directors are charged with the duty of establishing policies that will achieve the function of the corporation, selecting executives to carry out these policies, and supervising these executives to see that the policies are efficiently executed. They must act in person, not by proxy, in exercising all discretionary power. The directors also must act as a group, not as individuals; and in the absence of authority to the contrary, a majority of the directors must be present before any binding discussions can be made. The directors may delegate ministerial and routine duties to subagents, but the duty of determining all major corporate policies, except those reserved to the stockholders, must be assumed by the board of directors.

(3) LIABILITIES. As trustees of the corporation, the directors are liable for bad faith and for gross negligence. They are not liable for losses when they act with due diligence and reasonably sound judgment. Countless errors of judgment are made annually by directors in operating a complex business organization. Only when these errors are due to a breach of good faith can a director be held personally liable.

- Everette Wadley was a director for the Central Publishing Company. He was also secretly a large stockholder in a competing firm. Wadley, as director, sponsored and voted for measures detrimental to the Central Publishing Company and beneficial to the competiting firm in which he held stock. This was not an error of judgment but a breach of trust. He was liable for the resulting damages to the Central Publishing Company.

In the above case, the other directors who voted and approved the same measures as Wadley would not be liable if they acted in good faith and with reasonable skill and care. The error of judgment must be traceable to some ulterior motive to establish a breach of trust.

Some of the more common acts, besides negligence and bad faith, for which directors have been held personally liable are:

(a) Losses on loans of corporate funds to officers and directors of the corporation

(b) Purchase of treasury stock out of capital instead of surplus

(c) Dividends declared out of capital instead of earned surplus

Dissolution. A corporation may terminate its existence by paying all its debts, distributing all remaining assets to the stockholders and surrendering its charter. The corporation then ceases to exist, and its dissolution is complete. This action may be voluntary on the part of the stockholders, or it may be involuntary by action of the court or state. The state may ask for a dissolution for any one of the following reasons: (1) forfeiture or abuse of the corporate charter, (2) violation of the state laws, (3) fraud in the procurement of the charter, and (4) failure to pay taxes for a continuous period of three or more years.

When a corporation dissolves, it is legally dead. It is then incapable of suing, owning property, or forming contracts except for the purpose of converting its assets into cash and distributing the cash to the creditors and stockholders. The distribution of the cash must be in this order:

(1) All taxes due all governmental units must be paid first.

(2) Secured liabilities must be paid next after taxes.

(3) All unsecured debts are paid after taxes and secured claims are met in full. Any payments out of this order subject the stockholders and the directors to personal liability for losses sustained by the state or by the creditors because of improper distribution.

(4) Stockholders that are preferred as to assets are paid.

(5) Any remaining cash is distributed to the common stockholders.

In the event that there are not enough assets to pay all creditors, the stockholders are not held personally liable. This is one of the chief advantages of a corporation over a sole proprietorship or partnership. It is an advantage from the stockholder's standpoint, but a disadvantage from the creditor's standpoint.

Questions

1. What is the only way that a corporation can perform business transactions?

2. What is the function of the board of directors?

3. How many stockholders must be present at a stockholders' meeting to constitute a quorum?

4. How does the corporation determine who is qualified to vote at a stockholders' meeting?

5. How many votes does each stockholder have?

6. What is cumulative voting?

7. If a stockholder cannot attend a stockholders' meeting, how may he vote?

8. (a) Does every stockholder have the right to vote?
(b) If there are three members of a board of directors and all three agree to buy a certain piece of real estate, can they do so without formally calling a director's meeting?

9. When are directors liable to the stockholders for errors of judgment that result in financial loss?

10. (a) Under what conditions may the state order a dissolution of a corporation against the stockholders' consent?
(b) In the event of the dissolution of a corporation, how are the corporate assets distributed?

Case Problems

1. The Hardin Textile Company promoted a stock purchase plan among its employees. Every worker purchased at least one share, and many purchased as many as 50 shares. The workers as a group owned about 10 per cent of the stock. Because some of the workers became annoying to the management over policy decisions, they were discharged and nonstockholding workers were employed to replace them. The discharged workers claimed that since they owned stock in the corporation, they were entitled to jobs in their own company. Was this contention correct?

2. Rooney was the president of the Frozen Food Lockers, Inc. The three-man board of directors loaned Rooney $15,000 from the corporate funds. Later Rooney became bankrupt, and the corporation lost the entire loan. The stockholders brought suit against the board members personally for the loss. Were they liable?

3. Dawson, who owned 10 shares of common stock in a corporation, was very much dissatisfied with the management because of its failure to pay dividends. There was a movement to line up proxies to elect a new board of directors. Dawson received a letter from Carlton James who expressed great dissatisfaction also and asked Dawson to send him a proxy so that he could vote Dawson's shares. Dawson did this. After the election, he learned that James was the corporation's attorney and used this ruse to inveigle Dawson to send a proxy actually to be voted in favor of the present board. Dawson brought suit to have the election of the board of directors nullified and a new election held. Was he entitled to this relief?

4. O'Malley was the bookkeeper for the Quitman Corporation, which had capital stock common outstanding of $100,000 and an earned surplus of $3,500. The board of directors declared a 2.5 per cent dividend and instructed O'Malley to calculate the amount due and mail each stockholder a check. O'Malley, through an error, calculated the dividend at 25 per cent instead of 2.5 per cent. This resulted in a payment of dividend out of capital. Later the judgment creditors sued the directors personally for the amount of the dividend in excess of earned surplus. Were they liable?

5. There were five directors in the National Auto Finance Corporation. A meeting of the board of directors was called

for the specific purpose of accepting an offer to buy a very desirable piece of real estate for the corporation's own use. Three directors could not be present but sent proxies instead. One of the two members present was strongly opposed to the purchase, but the other member voted to accept the offer and also voted the three proxies to accept. The owner of the property later decided not to sell and contended there was no binding contract because a majority of the board of directors were not personally present at the time the contract was signed. Was this contention correct?

6. Carson, the father, Mrs. Carson, the mother, and their son, John, own all the stock in the Carson Enterprises, Inc. One night at the supper table they unanimously agreed to merge with another corporation upon the terms proposed by the other corporation. Was this the proper procedure?

7. There were thirty stockholders in the Southern Gum Products Corporation. At a regular stockholders' meeting, three stockholders owning 60 per cent of the stock were present. A new board of directors was elected. Later a stockholder challenged the authority of the board, contending it was not legally elected because a quorum was not present when it was elected. Was this contention sound?

8. There are fifteen stockholders in the Young Men's Shop, Inc. The corporate charter provides for cumulative voting for the members of the board of directors, consisting of five members. The majority stockholders were anxious to elect all five members of the board, while the minority members attempted to elect only a majority. If the majority stockholders owned 600 shares and the minority stockholders owned 500 shares, which group would elect its slate?

9. Henderson was a director on the board of directors of the Watson Corporation. Henderson also was a large stockholder in a competing firm. In a board of director's meeting Henderson voted for a measure that was highly detrimental to the Watson Corporation but highly profitable for the competing firm. A stockholder in the Watson Corporation sought to make Henderson personally liable for the loss. Was he liable?

Cases for Review of Part VIII

1. The Citizens' Ice and Cold Storage Company's charter contained this provision: "to issue bonds secured by mortgage." The company purchased machinery on credit and executed two mortgages to secure the payment contracted for this machinery. These mortgages were in favor of Anna Ballingall. Ballingall assigned these mortgages to Brown. When Brown brought an action to foreclose the mortgages, the question arose as to whether or not executing these mortgages was an ultra vires act. (Brown vs. Citizens' Ice and Cold Storage Company, et al., 17 N. J. Eq. 437) Was this an ultra vires act?

2. Tower subscribed to some stock in a proposed corporation, The Hudson Real Estate Co. The subscription to the stock was made under some definite assurances given by the salesman of the stock. Later these assurances were broken and Tower withdrew his subscription. This was before the corporation was formed. After the charter was granted, the Hudson Real Estate Company brought suit to enforce the subscription. Tower contended that his subscription was only an offer, and could be withdrawn any time prior to acceptance. (Hudson Real Estate Company vs. Tower et al. 156 Mass. 82) Could Tower withdraw the offer before the corporation came into existence?

3. Van Slyke owned 151 shares of stock in the Metropolitan National Bank. The capital stock of this corporation increased from $300,000 to $500,000 Van Slyke was given sixty days in which to exercise his right to purchase his prorata share of the new stock. He did not exercise this right, and after the expiration of the sixty days, Norris and other stockholders purchased the stock to which Van Slyke was entitled. Van Slyke brought suit against Norris and others for damages which he alleged were sustained by his being deprived of his proportionate share of the new stock. (Van Slyke vs. Norris, 159 Miss. 63) Was Van Slyke entitled to damages?

4. The Knight & Wall Company held a claim against the Tampa Sand Lime Brick Company but was unable to collect. Upon investigation it found that the Sand Lime Brick Co. had issued $30,000 in bonds, and with each bond purchase one share of stock was issued to the purchaser free. The Knight & Wall Company brought an action to collect from the stockholders to the extent of their bonus stock since their credit was extended after the bonus stock was issued. (Knight & Wall Company vs. Tampa Sand Lime Brick Company, 55 Fla. 728) Was Knight & Wall Company entitled to collect from the stockholders?

5. Hyatt owned some stock in a corporation. He sold this stock to Allen, but reserved a right to all profits and dividends on the stock until the following January 1. The corporation earned considerable profits prior to January 1 but did not declare a dividend until the following April 9. This dividend was paid to Allen since he had registered his stock with the corporation. Hyatt sued Allen to recover the dividend since he had reserved the right to all profits and dividends to January 1. (Hyatt vs. Allen, 56 N. Y. 553) Was Hyatt entitled to recover this dividend?

6. The Nauss Brothers Company was a New York corporation. Its profits had been substantial but not excessive. These profits were transferred to surplus. Adam Nauss, a stockholder, brought an action to compel the board of directors to declare a dividend out of surplus. There was no convincing evidence that the board of directors was acting in bad faith. (Nauss vs. Nauss Brothers Company, 187 N. Y. S. 165) Did the directors have to declare the dividend?

7. J. E. Lawshe was a stockholder in the Royal Baking Powder Company. He was anxious to buy stock from any other stockholder who was willing to sell. In order to contact the other stockholders to offer to buy their stock, he called at the corporation office and asked to have access to stockholders' ledger. He was refused access to this record, and he brought an action to compel the corporation to permit him to see these records. (Lawshe vs. Royal Baking Powder Co., 104 N. Y. S. 361) Did Lawshe have a right to see the stockholders' ledger?

8. A stockholder in the Chicago City Railway Company sought to inspect the books of the company for the purpose of obtaining the names of the stockholders. He planned to use this list of names to solicit votes for his election as a director. He was refused the right to inspect the books of the company. (246 Ill. 170) Was the company justified in refusing the stockholder permission to inspect the books?

Part IX

RISK-BEARING DEVICES

Chapter 36

Nature of Insurance

Definition of Insurance. It is the function of insurance to reduce uncertainty to a certainty. Life is full of unfavorable contingencies. The possibility of any one of these contingencies happening is ever present. A home owner is faced with the constant possibility that his home will burn with a large loss to him. By accepting an absolutely certain annual loss in the form of a fire insurance premium, he can shift the uncertainty, that is, the possibility of a large loss, to the insurance company. Not every peril in life can be shifted by insurance, but many of the most common perils can be shifted, or at least the burden can be shifted. *Insurance* can be defined then as a contract whereby a party transfers a risk of financial loss for a fee to the risk bearer, the insurance company.

Terms Used in Insurance. The company agreeing to make good a certain loss is known as the *insurer,* or sometimes as the *underwriter;* the person protected against the loss is known as the *insured,* or the *policyholder.* In life insurance the person who is to receive the benefits or the proceeds thereof is known as the *beneficiary.*

Whenever a person takes any kind of insurance, he enters into a contract with the insurance company, just as in the case of other business agreements. The written contract is commonly called a *policy.* The amount that the insurer agrees to pay in case of a loss is known as the *face* of the policy, and the consideration the insured pays for the protection is called the *premium.* The danger of a loss of, or injury to, property, life, or anything else, is called a *risk* or *peril;* when that danger may be covered by insurance, it is known as the *insurable risk.*

Although the uncertainty is called the "risk," this term by common usage, now also applies to the property itself. In this sense one speaks of a brick house as being a "good risk." The factors, such as fire, floods, and sleet, that contribute to the uncertainty are called *hazards.*

Types of Insurance Companies. There are two major types of insurance companies:

1. Stock companies
2. Mutual companies

(1) STOCK COMPANIES. A *stock insurance company* is a corporation organized for the purpose of making a profit. Like all other corporations the stockholders elect the board of directors and receive the profits as dividends. The original capital is raised through the sale of stock, either common or common and preferred. Unlike other corporations, insurance companies must place a major portion of their original capital in a reserve account. As the volume of business increases, the reserve must be increased by setting aside a part of the premiums.

(2) MUTUAL COMPANIES. In a *mutual insurance company* the policyholders are the members and owners and correspond to the stockholders in a stock company. In these companies the policyholders are both the insurer and the insured, but the corporation is a separate legal entity. If a person takes a $10,000 fire insurance policy in a mutual company that has $100,000,000 insuance in force, he owns 1/10,000 of the company and is entitled to share the profits in this ratio. He also may have to share losses in the same ratio if it is an assessment mutual. A policyholder in a stock company never shares the losses.

A Construction Contractor Has an Insurable Interest in a House Which He Is Building for a Fixed Price.

Keystone View Co.

In a nonassessment mutual insurance company, the policyholder's liability is limited to the amount of premium which he contracts to pay. If his pro rata share of the losses for any year exceed his premium, he cannot be assessed for the excess. In this case the insured is as fully protected as a stockholder in a stock company. In an assessment mutual insurance company, however, the insured is liable for his pro rata share of the losses of the corporation without reference to the premium he agrees to pay. If this premium is inadequate to pay all losses, the insured can be assessed for his pro rata share of the losses in excess of his premium.

Who May Be Insured. To become an insured, one must first of all have an insurable interest. The insurance contract is in its entirety an agreement to assume a specified risk. If the insured has no interest to protect, there can be no assumption of risk, and hence no insurance. The law covering an insurable interest is different for life insurance and for property insurance. Consequently, this law will be treated fully in the chapters dealing with these types of insurance.

To become an insured, one must also be competent to contract. Insurance is not a necessity; thus, a minor is not bound on his insurance contracts if he wishes to disaffirm them. A minor who disaffirms a contract may demand the return of his money, but he must return any goods which he still possesses. Since insurance contracts provide protection only, this cannot be returned. Many states hold that because of this a minor cannot demand a refund of his insurance premium except the unexpired portion. Most states hold, however, that he may demand a return of the entire premium.

Some Legal Aspects of the Insurance Contract. The laws applicable to contracts in general apply to insurance contracts. There are five principles, however, that have special significance for insurance contracts:

1. Concealment
2. Representation
3. Warranty
4. Subrogation
5. Estoppel

(1) CONCEALMENT. The nature of insurance is such that the insurer must rely upon the information supplied by the insured. This places upon the insured the responsibility of supplying all pertinent information. A willful failure to disclose this pertinent information is known as *concealment.* The concealed facts must be material; that is, they must materially increase the risk assumed by the insurer. The willful concealment of material facts renders the contract voidable. The rule of concealment does not apply with equal stringency to all types of insurance contracts. In fire insurance where the agent has ample opportunity to inspect the property, the court may consider the concealed hazard as waived. Also, the concealment must be willful. In ocean marine insurance the concealed hazard is never waived, and the concealment need not be willful.

• A forest fire was raging in the neighborhood of Duncan's house. He hurried to town and took out in-insurance on his house. He concealed the fact of the forest fire. The contract was voidable because of concealment.

(2) REPRESENTATION. A statement of fact made by the insured as a basis for obtaining insurance is known as a *representation.* It must be substantially correct. The representation must be made as an inducement to the insurer to enter into a contract. It is collateral to the contract, not a part of the contract. The significance of this distinction will be shown under warranties. A false representation, though innocently made, avoids the contract if the fact is material.

Misrepresentation is more easily established than concealment, which in a sense is a misrepresentation by silence. In concealment the insurance company must prove that the insured had an intent to defraud before it can avoid the contract. No intent to defraud need be shown in misrepresentation. An innocent misrepresentation of a material fact gives the insurance company the right to avoid the contract only. If the misrepresentation is both material and willful, it is a tort and gives the insurance company the right to avoid the contract and also to sue for damages if it cares to do so. The company must of course prove actual damages in order to hold the insured liable.

- Weddell in applying for a fire insurance contract on his house was asked, "Is your home encumbered?" Weddell answered, "No." There was a delinquent tax claim against the house which, legally interpreted, is an encumbrance. The representation was false, though substantially true because of the immateriality of the tax claim, and thus the contract was valid. Had the representation been material, the contract would have been voidable even though Weddell was ignorant as to what constituted an encumbrance.

(3) WARRANTY. A *warranty* is a part and parcel of the contract itself. Representations are made to induce the other party to contract, but a warranty is incorporated into the contract. If one states, in applying for fire insurance, that his house has fire stops in the framework, this is a representation. If the same statement is incorporated into the written contract itself, it is a warranty.

The significance is this: A warranty must be absolutely true whether material or not. A representation must be only substantially true and is not of significance unless it is material.

It is customary for insurance companies to attach the written application for insurance to the policy and to stipulate that the application is made part of the contract. Many states have amended the law of warranty so that the fact warranted must be material before it renders the contract voidable.

- West insured his house with the Southern Fire Insurance Company. The contract stipulated that the house was occupied by the insured. The house was actually unoccupied at the time. This was a warranty and rendered the contract voidable, since the warranty must be literally true. A few states have modified this strict rule.

(4) SUBROGATION. In insurance, *subrogation* is the right of the insurer under certain circumstances to "step into the shoes" of the insured. Subrogation is particularly applicable to some types of automobile insurance. If the insurer pays a claim to the insured, under the law of subrogation the insurer is entitled to any claims which the insured had because of the loss. For example, *A* has a collision insurance policy on his car. *B* negligently damages *A's* car. The insurance company will pay *A* but then has the right to sue *B* for reimbursement. If *A* commits any act after the accident which releases *B*, then the insurance company is released from liability to *A*. This is often referred to as the law of substitution. It is not applicable either to life insurance or to health and accident insurance.

(5) ESTOPPEL. If one by word or act admits a fact, he is estopped to deny the truth of the fact. If the insurer, in order to induce the insured to enter into the contract, waives some provision in the contract, the company is estopped to plead this fact as a defense to

payment. *Waiver* is the abandonment of a right and when a right is lawfully waived, one cannot later insist on the right. Insurance agents are severely restricted as to their power to waive provisions of the contract, but the company itself may waive most provisions.

Estoppel arises when one by his acts leads another to believe that certain facts are true when they are untrue, thereby leading the other person to act to his detriment. Waiver, on the other hand, may be either an expressed or an implied abandonment of a right, usually the waiving of a provision in the written contract. The one doing the waiving must of course have the authority to waive. One cannot waive a provision in an insurance contract that is required by law to be in it. The insurance company cannot waive, for example, the legal requirement that the insured must have an insurable interest in the property insured.

• Bates, in applying for a fire insurance policy, stated that he owned the house being insured, but he was merely a tenant under a thirty-year lease of the lot on which the house was situated. The contract stipulated that the insured owned both. The company countersigned the policy and thus waived this requirement. It was then estopped to insist on this provision.

Questions

1. What is the function of insurance?

2. What is an insurable risk?

3. Explain the difference between a stock insurance company and a mutual insurance company.

4. Who may be insured?

5. May a minor disaffirm his insurance contracts?

6. If someone has twice in the past week attempted to burglarize your home, should you reveal that fact to the insurance company when you apply for burglary insurance?

7. On an application for health and accident insurance, you are asked, "Have you had any serious illness in the past two years?" You answer "no," although you have spent six months in the hospital during that time. What is the effect of this false representation on the contract?

8. What is the difference between a warranty and a representation?

9. Briefly define subrogation and illustrate its application to insurance.

10. May the insurance agent waive any provisions of the contract?

Case Problems

1. Thomas, who owned and operated a storage business carried fire insurance to cover about 50 per cent of its value. Someone called him and told him that smoke was coming from the gable end of the building and that he believed it was on fire. Thomas before going to the building saw his insurance agent and placed another $50,000 fire policy on it but made no mention of the smoke and possible fire. It developed that there was no fire. About two weeks later, however, the building was destroyed by fire, and the company refused to pay on the second policy because it had learned of the circumstances under which it was purchased. Was the insurance company liable on this policy?

2. A fire insurance policy contained a clause that no provision of the policy could be waived by the agent except in writing and attached to the policy. One provision in the policy stated that manuscripts were not covered unless specifically named in the policy. Mitchell, an author, had a manuscript about completed for a novel which he felt would be a best seller. He called his agent and asked that the manuscript be named in his household effects policy. The agent said that was not necessary and that the company would insure it. A fire destroyed Mitchell's home and the manuscript was burned up. The company refused to pay for it. Was Mitchell entitled to collect for the value of the manuscript?

3. Morrison who owned three houses asked his secretary to call the insurance agent and place a fire insurance policy on the one at 256 Cloverhurst. The agent asked her, "Is the house brick or frame?" She was not sure but thinking it made no difference, replied, "It is a brick building." It was in fact a frame building. The house was destroyed by fire, and the company refused to pay for the loss. Was Morrison entitled to collect?

4. A fire insurance policy on a sawmill contained this clause: "The insured warrants that a watchman will be on duty at all times while the mill is not operating." The mill caught fire during the day and was completely destroyed. The previous night the night watchman was ill and could not work. He called Brewer, the superintendent, and informed him he could not report for work. Brewer did not get anyone to take the watchman's place and the mill was without a watchman for that one night only, but the fire was in no way remotely related to this fact. The insurance company refused to pay for the loss. Could the owner of the mill collect on this policy?

5. Schools, a minor, insured his house against loss by fire, and his automobile and jewelry against loss by either fire or theft. Eleven months later he demanded a return of his entire premium. Was he entitled to a refund?

6. A provision in a life insurance policy stated that the applicant was not eligible for insurance if he was a pilot on an airplane. The application for insurance showed that the applicant's occupation was that of an airplane pilot. The policy was issued. One month later the insured was killed in a plane crash and the insurance company refused to pay. Was the insurance company justified in its action?

7. Mozark's jewelry worth $10,000 was stolen. She obtained a theft insurance policy on the jewels, but did not disclose the fact that the jewels were missing. About one week after the policy was written, Mozark reported the loss. Was she able to recover?

8. Harmon's and Carmichael's cars collide, seriously damaging Harmon's car but doing only slight damage to Carmichael's. The accident was Harmon's fault; but since Carmichael had insurance, he agreed to assume the blame so that the insurance company would have to pay for the damage to Harmon's car. What effect did this act have upon the insuance company's liability?

Chapter 37

Life Insurance

Nature of Life Insurance. A man with dependents is faced with the risk of an untimely death, leaving his dependents without a source of income. A *life insurance* policy is a contract whereby the underwriter agrees for a price, known as the premium, to assume the responsibility of providing the dependents with a source of income. Additional features which the life insurance contract may contain are numerous.

The life insurance contract, unlike most other types of insurance, is not a contract of indemnity. This means that no attempt is made to place a value upon a human life so that the beneficiary, the one who is to receive the benefits, may be indemnified for the loss. The amount to be paid is fixed by the contract itself.

Types of Life Insurance Contracts. Although there are many different types of life insurance policies and annuity contracts, the following are the most important:

1. Term insurance
2. Straight life insurance
3. Limited payment life insurance
4. Endowment insurance
5. Annuity insurance

(1) TERM INSURANCE. *Term life insurance,* as the name implies, provides protection for a stipulated term of one, five, ten, twenty, or any other number of years. It is the cheapest type for two reasons. First, it covers only a possible loss to the insurer, not a certain one. Second, there are no savings features in term insurance. The policy provides protection only.

(2) Straight Life Insurance. A *straight life insurance* contract is one whereby the insured agrees to pay the premium throughout life. When he dies, his named beneficiary collects the face of the policy. If the insured is still living at age 100, however, he can collect the face of the policy. If one buys this policy at age 20, the rate is relatively low because of the long life expectancy of the insured. This rate cannot be raised as the insured gets older.

Under the level premium plan whereby the insured pays the same premium throughout life, the rate is sufficient to pay all death claims, operating expenses, sales commissions, and profits. The excess payment during the earlier years the policy is in force is the basis of the *cash surrender value* of the policy. If the policy is dropped after the third year, this value may be paid to the insured.

(3) Limited Payment Life Insurance. If one does not wish to pay a relatively small premium for his whole life, he may pay a larger premium for a limited number of years and have his insurance paid up for life. From the mortality table the insurance company calculates the life probability for the applicant. If this probability is thirty-eight more years for a man thirty years of age, he would pay a premium based on this probability. If he wishes to pay for twenty years, he will pay approximately the same amount in twenty payments as he would have in thirty-eight payments on a straight life insurance policy. This makes the rate much higher.

(4) Endowment Insurance. The premiums for *endowment insurance* are paid for a limited period of ten, twenty, or thirty years, and if the insured is still living at the end of that period, the face amount is paid to him. This type of insurance is primarily for the benefit of the insured, and secondarily for his dependents. If the insured under a twenty-year endowment policy dies eighteen

years after the date of the policy, the beneficiary receives only the face amount of the policy.

(5) ANNUITY INSURANCE. In pure *annuity insurance* contract the underwriter assumes no risk, only an obligation to return the payments with interest. If the annuitant pays $5,000 into the company over a period of ten years, the insurance company contracts to return this amount to him with interest. The payments are generally made to the annuitant on either a monthly or an annual basis.

In most annuity insurance contracts sold today, however, the insurance company assumes a risk by guaranteeing the annuitant a fixed monthly payment for life. The cost of the annuity is determined to a large extent by the life expectancy of the annuitant. If he lives far beyond this age, the insurance company loses money on him. They make a profit on those who die before the end of their life expectancy.

Comparative Costs. The following table gives a comparison of the premiums on a $1,000 policy for a man thirty years of age:

Term insurance—twenty years	$ 6.81
Straight life insurance	18.60
Limited payment life—twenty years ...	29.84
Endowment insurance—twenty years ..	46.38

If the insured should die within the twenty-year period, the beneficiary would collect the same amount under all four policies, that is $1,000.

Payment of Premiums. The premiums must be paid within the time specified by the policy. If they are not paid when due, the policy may lapse. The policy or a statute of the state may provide that after a certain number of premiums have been paid, the policy will be extended for a specified time in case of the nonpayment of a premium. Under such a condition a paid-up policy is sometimes issued for the term of the insurance but for a

NUMBER

The Franklin
LIFE INSURANCE COMPANY
Springfield, Illinois

NAME OF INSURED	Benjamin Franklin
AGE OF INSURED	30
PRINCIPAL SUM INSURED	Five Thousand Dollars
ANNUAL PREMIUM	$237.60
PREMIUMS PAYABLE DURING	20 YEARS OR UNTIL PRIOR DEATH OF THE INSURED
FIRST POLICY YEAR BEGINS	January 2, 1952
BENEFICIARY	Deborah Franklin, wife

The Franklin Life Insurance Company agrees to pay the Principal Sum Insured under the conditions hereof to the Beneficiary upon receipt of due proof of the death of the Insured.

RETURN PREMIUM BENEFIT: In the event of the Insured's death occurring before the end of the twentieth policy year and if no premium is in default beyond the grace period, in addition to the Principal Sum Insured there will be payable a Return Premium Benefit, so that the total amount payable upon receipt of due proof of the death of the Insured will be the sum specified in the Table on page 7 hereof for the policy year in which death occurs. Said Table sets forth the total amount payable in event of the death of the Insured for each One Thousand Dollars ($1000) of the Principal Sum Insured hereunder. If this Policy is continued in force after the end of the twentieth policy year in accordance with Option 2, page 8 hereof, the amount payable in event of the death of the Insured will be the Principal Sum Insured.

This Policy is issued and accepted subject to all the conditions, benefits and privileges set forth on the subsequent pages hereof, which are hereby made a part of this Contract.

In Witness Whereof, THE FRANKLIN LIFE INSURANCE COMPANY has caused this Policy to be executed at Springfield, Illinois, January 2, 1952.

George E. Hatmaker
SPECIMEN
SECRETARY

SPECIMEN
PRESIDENT

COUNTERSIGNED:
SPECIMEN
REGISTRAR

20 Payment Life—Participating—Annual Dividends.
Guaranteed Coupons—Return Premium Benefit during first 20 years.
Premiums payable for 20 years or until prior death of Insured

Form 919

A Limited Payment Life Insurance Policy.

smaller amount. Sickness is no legal excuse for the non-payment of premiums. In such a case the company may, if it so elects, extend the time of payment or take a promissory note for the amount of the premium.

Limitation on Risks. Life insurance companies may limit the risk they assume by making a provision in the policy that the insurer is not liable if death is due to certain stated causes. The most common of these restrictions are:

1. Suicide
2. Death resulting from the commission of crime
3. Execution

(1) SUICIDE. Most life insurance policies today contain a clause excluding the insurance company from liability if death is due to suicide. This clause is usually limited to two years. In most states this limitation is enforceable. Some courts have held that if the insured is insane at the time of his self-destruction, the exclusion is not enforceable. The exclusion clause may be made effective, however, by adding the words "while sane or insane." Even if there is no suicide clause, the contract is not enforceable if the company can prove that the policy was purchased with the intent to commit suicide. This would be a clear case of fraud.

(2) DEATH CAUSED BY THE COMMISSION OF A CRIME. Life insurance policies contain a clause exempting the company from liability if death is due to the commission of a crime. The mere act of violating the law at the time of death is not sufficient. If one is driving an automobile without a license, he is committing a crime. If he is killed in a collision, this does not invalidate the policy because the crime is not the proximate cause of death. If he is attempting to escape in an automobile after committing a crime, the policy is voidable, in most states. The crime must be the proximate cause of the death.

(3) EXECUTION. Most life insurance contracts contain a clause excluding the company from liability if death is brought about by execution by the state. This clause is effective in most states. Even in the absence of this clause some states hold that it is contrary to public policy to enforce the contract when death is due to execution. Other courts hold that it is contrary to public policy not to compel payment in the absence of such an exclusion because his dependents might become public charges.

Incontestability. Life insurance policies are made incontestable, either by statutory law or by the policies themselves, after a certain period of time, usually two years. After the expiration of the period of contestability, the insurance company usually cannot contest the validity of a claim on any ground except nonpayment of premiums.

Insurable Interest. In most states every person can take out a life insurance policy on his own life and make any person he pleases the beneficiary. The beneficiary need not have an insurable interest in the insured's life.

When one person insures another's life, however, and makes himself or someone else whom he selects beneficiary, he must have an insurable interest in the life of the insured at the time the policy is taken out. This interest, however, need not be based upon a legal right as in the case of fire insurance. It is sufficient if it is based upon a reasonable expectation of benefit. For example, an employee cannot take out a fire insurance policy on the property of the business for which he works. He has no legal right to expect continued employment; therefore, he has no insurable interest. He can, however, take out a life insurance policy on his employer since he has a reasonable expectation of continued employment.

A person has an insurable interest in the life of another when such a relationship exists between them that a direct pecuniary benefit will be derived from the continued existence of the other person. These are the relationships most frequently giving rise to an insurable interest: parents and children, husband and wife, employer and employee, principal and agent, partner and copartner, and a creditor in the life of the debtor to the extent of his debt. This list is not exhaustive, as there are numerous other relationships which give rise to an insurable interest. A sister may have such an interest in her brother if she has a reasonable expectation that he will support her.

A life insurance policy will remain enforceable after the insurable interest ceases to exist. In this respect life insurance differs from fire or other insurance. An insurable interest need not exist in fire insurance at the time the insurance is effected, but it must exist at the time the loss occurs; an insurable interest must exist in life insurance at the time the insurance is effected, but it need not exist at the time the policy is payable.

- A creditor insured the life of a debtor for the amount due him. Before the death of the insured, the debt was paid in full. The court held that the insurable interest which existed at the time the policy was taken out supported an action to recover against the insurance company after the death of the insured.

Change of Beneficiary. If a man takes out insurance on his own life and makes another his beneficiary, he cannot later change the beneficiary unless he reserved the right to do this. If the beneficiary pays the premiums, the insured does not have the right to change the beneficiary. There are both advantages and disadvantages in reserving the right to change the beneficiary, but most modern life insurance policies reserve this right to the insured. If a man takes out a life insurance policy on his life and makes his wife the beneficiary but later divorces her, he cannot change the beneficiary unless he reserved the right to do so. If he does reserve the right, his creditors can attach the surrender value of the policy for his debts. If he does not reserve the right, then the creditors of the beneficiary can attach the surrender value of the policy for her debts. Exemption statutes may limit the right of creditors to attach benefits of an insurance policy.

If the beneficiary dies before the insured, it frequently is highly desirable to change the beneficiary, which is impossible unless the right to change has been reserved. The rights of such a beneficiary are vested and, upon his death, pass to his personal representative. Since this rule may cause unintended results, some courts hold that if the beneficiary dies before the insured, the beneficiary's interest terminates and reverts to the insured.

Assignment of the Policy. Any claims under an insurance policy may be assigned unless the contract specifically prohibits an assignment. This prohibition is applicable only to the insured, not to the beneficiary. If the insured reserves the right to change the beneficiary, he has title to the cash surrender value or the loan value of the policy. He may assign this right as security for a loan. It is not necessary to notify the insurance company if there is no prohibition against assignment, but it is wise to give notice. The beneficiary may assign any of his rights under the policy freely. His chief right is the right to collect the face of the policy upon the death of the insured. Since this is merely a claim for money, there is no bar to its assignment.

Other Types of Insurance. There are several other types of insurance closely related to life insurance. They are health and accident insurance, hospitalization insurance, and group medical insurance. These types of insurance differ from life insurance in a number of particulars. In the first place, the beneficiary is always the insured. The purpose is to protect the insured against cessation of earning power or burdensome expenses rather than to protect someone who depends upon the insured for support.

Questions

1. What risk does a life insurance company assume in a life insurance policy?

2. Name the important types of life insurance and briefly describe each type.

3. If one wishes to pay premiums for a limited number of years, what kind of life insurance should one buy?

4. What risk do most annuity insurance policies assume?

5. What may an insurance company do for one who becomes sick and cannot pay the life insurance premium on the date it is due?

6. What are some limitations on risks that a life insurance company may provide?

7. What is the nature of the incontestability clause in a life insurance contract?

8. When does a person have an insurable interest in the life of another?

9. Under what circumstances may the insured change the beneficiary of a policy?

10. Name other types of insurance closely related to life insurance.

Case Problems

1. Pilson applied for a life insurance policy. On the application was this question: "Has any member of your immediate family died of tuberculosis in the past five years?" Pilson answered no. He did not know that his aunt, whom he had never seen, had died from tuberculosis in the past year. The company would not have issued a policy to him had it known this. The life insurance policy contained a clause which read: "The application for insurance is made part of this contract, and all statements therein are deemed to be warranties." Pilson died about 18 months after the policy was issued. The company, having learned of the death of Pilson's aunt, refused to pay the beneficiary the face of the policy. Must the company pay?

2. Miss Terry was engaged to marry Richard Spencer. She procured insurance on his life and paid the premiums.

Spencer died before the marriage took place. The insurance company refused to pay Miss Terry the amount of the policy on the ground that she had had no insurable interest in the life of her fiancé. Was Miss Terry entitled to collect from the insurance company? Why?

3. Johnson was told by a cancer specialist that he had a cancer of the stomach in an early stage. He immediately applied for a $50,000 life insurance policy but did not reveal to the insurance company what the specialist had told him. The doctor who made the physical examination for the policy did not discover the cancer. Johnson died one year later and the insurance company refused to pay the $50,000. Could the beneficiary compel payment?

4. (a) Holliday, a married man with a family, was thirty years old. He bought a twenty-year term insurance policy for $10,000, the premium being $94 a year. He died nineteen years later. How much money did the beneficiary collect?

(b) How much had been paid for premiums for the nineteen years?

(c) If, instead, he had bought a twenty-year endowment policy, premium $503.20 a year, what would be your answers to (a) and (b)?

5. Rowan failed to pay the premium on his policy until ten days after it was past due. Three months later he died and the insurance company resisted payment of the policy. Was the insurance company liable? Why?

6. Jacob Doolittle owed James Stiles $2,000. Since he had no security for the payment of the debt, Stiles decided to insure Doolittle's life for the amount of the debt. Might Stiles do so? Explain.

7. Madray took out a $15,000 twenty-year endowment policy on himself and made his wife the beneficiary. Madray, however, reserved the right to change the beneficiary. After paying on the policy fifteen years, Madray became insolvent and his creditors sought to obtain the cash surrender value of the policy?

(a) Could the creditors take this for Madray's debts?

(b) If Madray had not reserved the right to change the beneficiary, what would your answer be?

(c) If Madray did not reserve the right to change the beneficiary, and his wife was involved in an automobile accident for which she became liable for $10,000, could these creditors take the cash surrender value of the policy?

Chapter 38

Property Insurance

Nature of Property Insurance. *Property insurance* is a contract whereby the insurer, in return for a compensation, agrees to reimburse the insured for loss or damage to specified property that is caused by the hazard covered. A contract of property insurance is one of indemnity that protects the policyholder from actual loss.

If a building actually worth $10,000 is insured for $15,000, the extra premiums paid are to no avail since $10,000, the actual value, is the maximum that can be collected in case of total loss. On the other hand, if the building is insured for only $8,000 and it is totally destroyed, the insurance company must pay only $8,000. It will be seen from this that the maximum amount to be paid is fixed by the policy when the insurance is less than the value of the property. If the property is fully insured, the value of the property fixes the maximum.

Fire Insurance. Fire is the greatest source of loss to property. Originally this was the only risk covered by insurance. For this reason all the early laws and court decisions dealing with property insurance covered loss by fire. As the additional types of property insurance developed, the same laws were applied to them that had been applied to fire insurance. Consequently, a thorough understanding of the laws of fire insurance will be adequate in the main in understanding the laws governing all types of property insurance.

Insurable Interest. One must have an insurable interest in the property at the time of the loss to be able to

The Face Value of a Fire Insurance Policy Fixes the Limit of Liability of the Insurance Company.

Harold M. Lambert

collect on a fire insurance policy. Since fire insurance is fundamentally indemnity insurance, there must be some loss before there can be indemnity. Ownership is, of course, the clearest type of insurable interest; but there are many other types of insurable interest. The most common types of insurable interest other than ownership are:

(1) The mortgagee has an insurable interest in the property mortgaged to the extent of his mortgage.

(2) A lien creditor has an insurable interest in the property on which there is a lien. An unsecured creditor, however, does not have an insurable interest in the property of his debtor.

(3) When property is sold on the installment plan and title is retained as security for the unpaid purchase price, the seller has an insurable interest in the property.

(4) The bailee has an insurable interest in the property bailed. The insurance on the bailed goods should protect the bailee for loss due to his own negligence or to that of his employees.

(5) A partner has an insurable interest in his firm to the extent of his possible loss.

(6) An administrator or an executor has an insurable interest, in his fiduciary capacity, in the property of the estate.

Any change of either title or possession of the insured property may render the contract void because the insurable interest ceases. This interest must exist at the time of the loss. If the change in the title or possession does not terminate the insurable interest, as when the insured executes a mortgage on the insured property, the insurance policy remains in effect. If the mortgagor insures the property for the benefit of the mortgagee, a sale of the property cancels the policy. If the mortgagee purchases a policy, a sale of the mortgaged property does not cancel the policy.

- Greely insured an automobile on which he held a chattel mortgage. The mortgage was paid in full. About two months later, Greely purchased the automobile. The car was later destroyed by fire. Greely sought to collect on his insurance. He could not collect on his insurance because of no insurable interest when the chattel mortgage was extinguished. A void policy cannot be revived.

The Fire Insurance Policy. The type of fire insurance indicates the nature of the risk assumed. There are the *valued policy* and the *open policy*. On certain types of property, such as works of art and antiques, the face of the policy is its value. In the event of the destruction of such property, the insurer cannot raise the question of value. Seldom will an insurance company write a valued policy on homes, business, and personal property. The open policy merely sets the limit of the risk assumed. The insurer is liable only for the actual loss up to, but never exceeding, the face of the policy.

● Jones insured his house for $20,000. The house was totally destroyed by fire. The actual cash value of the house at the time of its destruction was $15,000. The insurer was liable only for this amount.

Insurance policies also may be specific, blanket, or floating. A *specific policy* applies to one item only, such as one house. A *blanket policy* covers many items of the same kind in different places or different kinds of property in the same place, such as a building, fixtures, and merchandise in a single location. *Floating policies* are used for trucks, theatrical costumes, circus paraphernalia, and similar items which are not kept in a fixed location. A floater policy is also desirable for items that may be sent out for cleaning, such as rugs or clothes. Articles of jewelry and clothes that may be worn while traveling are also covered in a floater policy. A fire insurance policy on household effects covers for loss only at the named location. The purpose of the floater policy is to cover the loss no matter where the property is located at the time of the loss.

Description of the Property. Both personal and real property must be described with reasonable accuracy. This description applies both to the nature of the property and its location. A description of a house as brick, when it is actually asphalt brick siding, is a misrepresentation. Personal property should be so described that in the event of loss its value can be determined. One "piano" does not indicate the value of the piano as does "one baby grand piano—new." Also, the general description "living room furniture" may make it difficult to establish the value and the number of items. A complete inventory should be kept and preferably one copy filed with the insurance company. In this event, such description as "household furniture" is adequate.

The location of the property is important because the location affects the risk. If personal property used in a brick house on a broad paved street is moved to a frame house on an out-of-the-way dirt road, the risk may be increased considerably. Express permission must always be obtained when property is moved except under a "floating" policy.

- West applied for a fire insurance policy on his house and gave the address as 817 S. Elm Street. The real address was 817 N. Elm Street, a clay dirt street which became impassable during rainy weather. The error was innocently made. The rate was considerably higher on property in the north section of Elm Street than in the south section. This was a misrepresentation of a material fact and rendered the contract voidable.

Risk and Hazard. The insurance company assumes the risks caused by normal hazards. The insured must not commit any act which increases the risk. Negligence by the insured is a normal hazard unless so gross as to indicate a criminal intent. When a fire occurs, the insured must use all due diligence to minimize the loss. He is not held responsible for an increased risk over which he has no control or knowledge. The insured must remove household effects from the building if this can safely be done. Loss due to theft, however, is not covered.

- Mullin's house was on fire. Both the house and the furniture were insured. Part of the furniture was damaged while it was being removed, and while the furniture was piled in the street, a part of it was stolen and sparks damaged a part of it. The insurance company was liable for the breakage and the damage caused by sparks, but not for the loss due to theft. Yet, if the insured had not removed the property, he would have increased the risk to the company and thus rendered the policy voidable.

Coinsurance. Under the principle of *coinsurance* the insured assumes a portion of the risk. Simply stated, coinsurance permits the insured to recover for a loss in the same ratio as his insurance bears to the amount of insurance which the company requires. Many policies contain an 80 per cent clause. This clause means that the insured may carry any amount of insurance he wishes up to the value of the property, but that the company will not pay the full amount of a partial loss unless he carries insurance for at least 80 per cent of the value of the property. If a building is worth $20,000 and the insured buys a policy for $8,000, the company under the 80 per cent coinsurance clause will pay only half of the damage and never more than $8,000. The 80 per cent clause requires the insured to carry $16,000, or 80 per cent of $20,000, to be fully protected. Since he carries only half of this amount, he can collect only half of the damage.

Repairs and Replacements. Most insurance contracts give the insurer the option of paying the amount of loss or repairing or replacing the property. If the property is repaired or replaced, materials of like kind and quality must be used. The work must be completed within a reasonable time. A house thirty years old could not be replaced with materials of like kind since new material would have to be used. For this reason, the option to replace is seldom exercised by the insurer. He may also usually have the option of taking the property at an agreed valuation and then pay the insured the full value of the damaged property. Under no circumstances can the insured abandon damaged property to the insurer. The owner must do everything possible to minimize the loss by protecting the property from further damage from the elements. Any expense involved in doing this is recoverable as a part of the loss.

If the insurer pays a sum equal to the damage and the insured restores the property to its original status, new insurance must be obtained to cover the replaced part, unless there is an automatic restoration clause in the contract. Such a clause is frequently provided in insurance policies covering residential property where the loss is limited to a relatively small amount. Policies covering large industrial plants, hotels, apartment buildings, and similar structures seldom contain a restoration clause.

• Funk had a $30,000 insurance policy on his warehouse. A fire destroyed a portion of the building and the insurance company paid him $10,000 for the damage. The warehouse was fully repaired. Before the expiration of the policy, the entire building was destroyed by fire. The court held that the insured could recover only $20,000 since he had already collected $10,000 on the policy. No new insurance had been taken out on the repaired portion of the building, nor was there an automatic restoration clause in the policy.

Cancellation and Termination of the Policy. Fire insurance policies permit each party to cancel by giving the other party notice. If a policy is canceled by the insured, a refund is made on the premium at the short-term rate. If the insured cancels a three-year policy costing $600 at the end of six months, he is not entitled to a refund of $500. The short term rate for six months is considerably higher than one-sixth of a thirty-six month policy.

When the insured sells property, he may either cancel and get a refund or let the purchaser assume the policy and pay the seller a pro rata part. This is more advantageous to the seller. The policy can be transferred only with the written consent of the insurer.

An insurance policy is automatically terminated on the expiration date of the policy. The standard form calls for termination at noon standard time on the expiration date. The policy may be renewed simply by calling the insurance agent before the expiration date and receiving oral assurance that the policy will be renewed. Even if the property is destroyed before the new policy is written, the loss is recoverable.

• Hipps had a $15,000 insurance policy on his house, the policy expiring on August 5. At 12:55 p.m. daylight saving time on that date, the house caught fire and was totally destroyed. Since the policy called for expiration at noon standard time, which is one o'clock daylight saving time, the policy was still in effect at the time the fire started. The fact that most of the loss occurred after the expiration date is immaterial. Hipps was allowed to recover the $15,000.

Questions

1. What is meant by the statement that a property insurance contract is one of indemnity?

2. If one insures a fur coat for $2,000 against theft when its actual value is only $800, how much may the owner collect if the coat is stolen?

3. When must one have an insurable interest before he can collect under a fire insurance policy?

4. If *A* sells a house to *B* and at the time of the sale *A* has a $20,000 fire insurance policy on the house, what effect does the sale have on the insurance policy?

5. What is the difference between a valued fire insurance policy and an open policy?

6. What is the purpose of a floating insurance policy?

7. How must one identify his household furniture when he purchases household effects fire insurance?

8. When one insures property located at 256 Hope Street, what is the effect on the policy if the owner moves to a new location without notifying the insurance company?

9. If a house that is fully insured for $30,000 is damaged to the extent of $5,000 and then restored, how much may the owner collect if later during the same year the house is totally destroyed?

10. How is a fire insurance policy terminated?

Case Problems

1. John gave his young bride, Josephine, a fur coat as an anniversary present. The cost of the coat was $2,500. John and Josephine had a fire insurance policy on their household effects in the amount of $2,000. Realizing that this amount was too low, especially since the value of their effects had been increased by $2,500, they increased the face of their policy to $5,000 and paid the additional premium. While visiting relatives, the relatives' home was destroyed by fire and the fur coat was burned up. Could Josephine collect for this loss on her insurance contract?

2. Paul and Nancy purchased a bungalow from Carson for $12,000. Carson had a fire insurance policy for $10,000 on the house that did not expire for eight months after the sale. Carson agreed to transfer the policy to Paul and Nancy. Before the eight months expired, the house was totally destroyed by fire. The insurance company refused to pay anything, contending that the policy became void as soon as Carson sold the house. Was this contention correct?

3. Bohling insured his house for $25,000. The actual cash value was only $15,000. The house was totally destroyed by fire. How much was Bohling entitled to collect?

4. Simmons entered into a contract to purchase a house and lot for $15,000, delivery of the deed and possession of the property to be made in sixty days. Simmons immediately took out an insurance policy on the house. Before the sixty days expired, the house was destroyed by fire. The insurance company denied its liability for the loss. Was it correct in its interpretation?

5. Turner insured his household goods, which were located in a building at 1011 Cedar Street. Later he moved them to a new location without the knowledge or the consent of the insurance company. When the goods were destroyed by fire, the insurance company refused to pay for the loss. Turner brought a suit against the company. Was Turner entitled to collect from the insurance company? Why?

6. Donaldson owned a business building actually worth $20,000. His fire insurance policy contained an 80 per cent coinsurance clause. His policy was for $8,000. If there was $4,000 fire loss, how much could Donaldson collect?

7. Walston owned a brick building valued at $20,000. He carried an $18,000 fire insurance policy on it. The building was damaged by fire to the extent of 50 per cent of its value. A city ordinance required Walston to demolish the rest of the building because it was a hazard to pedestrians. For what sum was the fire insurance company liable?

Chapter 39

Automobile Insurance

The Nature of Automobile Insurance. The laws dealing with automobile insurance can best be understood by discusssing the major classes of insurance and their risks. These two classes of insurance are direct damage insurance, including fire, theft, and collision; and public liability, including bodily injury and property damage. To understand the law one must know what specific risk is assumed by the insurance carrier and the terms of the policy covering that specific risk.

Direct Damage Insurance. As the name implies, *direct damage insurance* covers the risks of injury or damage to the car itself. It includes:

1. Fire insurance
2. Theft insurance
3. Collision insurance
4. Comprehensive coverage

(1) FIRE INSURANCE. Much of the law of fire insurance discussed in the preceding chapter applies to automobile insurance. There are many differences, however, between automobile fire insurance and other types of fire insurance. If the car is damaged or destroyed by the collision, sinking, stranding, or burning of any conveyance upon which the car is being transported, such as a barge, boat, or train, the fire policy covers this loss.

There are many exclusions in this type of policy, the most important ones being:

(a) If the fire occurs while, with the permission of the owner, the car is being driven by one who is barred by law from driving, the loss is not collectible. Drivers without a driver's license, intoxicated people, and minors under sixteen years of age are prohibited either by law or by the policy from driving.

(b) If the fire occurs while passengers are being transported for hire, the company is not liable. Trips on which passengers share the cost do not constitute "passengers for hire" if such trips are only occasional and not done for the purpose of making a profit.

(c) If the car is driven in violation of law, such as with illegal license tags, the loss is not collectible.

(2) THEFT INSURANCE. A theft insurance policy usually includes pilferage of tools, carburetors, and other removable items. Theft does not include packages, wearing apparel, and similar items left in the car. If someone other than the owner gets possession of the car rightfully but converts it to a wrongful use, this is not theft and the owner cannot collect under a theft policy.

• Wells permitted Sellers, a prospective buyer of his car, to drive it a few miles to see if the car met his approval. Sellers never returned with the car. Wells sued to collect under his theft policy. He could not collect because the act was not considered theft. Many policies now have a "trick or device" clause to cover this situation. In the absence of this clause, one cannot collect under a theft policy unless the thief gets possession of the car without permission and unlawfully.

Some theft policies today cover loss of the use of the car in addition to its actual cash value.

(3) COLLISION INSURANCE. Practically all policies now are written to include upsets and collisions with any object or any part of the roadbed. The collision policy does not cover damage to a trailer drawn by the car. Most policies provide that the policy shall become void if any trailer is attached. The policy must expressly cover the

This Is the Type of Damage Covered by Collision Insurance.

National Safety Council

trailer-drawing car to be enforceable. The risk is greater for this type of car, and the insurance rate is higher.

If a car covered by collision but not by fire insurance is wrecked and as a direct result of the wreck the car burns, some courts would hold the insurance company liable for the collision loss alone, and not for the fire loss. However, other courts would hold the collision insurance company liable for the entire loss since the collision is the proximate cause of the fire. If the car were covered by a fire policy and not a collision policy, the fire insurer would be liable only for the loss by fire.

Where both the perils of fire and collision are insured against and the damage caused by each can be determined, each insurer bears his share of the loss.

If, for example, a car overturns denting the fenders and the body but doing no serious injury to the motor and chassis, the company issuing the collision policy would pay for this damage. If, in addition, the car caught fire by reason of the wreck and was totally destroyed by fire, the fire insurance company would be liable for the value of the car after the collision damage.

Most collision insurance policies have a deductible clause. It is possible to buy policies without any deductible clause, but the rates are high. It is cheaper for one to assume some of this risk.

If the insurance company pays the insured a claim for collision damage, under the law of subrogation the company has the right to sue the other party to the collision if he was at fault.

(4) COMPREHENSIVE COVERAGE. Insurance companies will write automobile insurance covering almost every conceivable risk to a car. A partial list will show the extent of the coverage: windstorm, earthquake, flood, strike, spray from trees, malicious mischief, submersion in water, acid from battery, riot, glass breakage, hail, and falling aircraft. Any one of these risks can be transferred to the insurance company for a fee. All companies today write what is called a *comprehensive policy* which may include all of these risks plus fire and theft. A comprehensive policy covers only the hazards enumerated in the policy.

Public Liability Insurance. The second major division of automobile insurance law is the public liability for damage to the property and the life of other people. This type of insurance is logically divided into:

1. Bodily injury insurance
2. Property damage insurance

(1) BODILY INJURY INSURANCE. Insurance covering the risk of bodily injury to the insured's passengers, pedestrians, or the occupants of another car is correctly designated public liability insurance. The insurance company obligates itself to pay any sum not exceeding the limit fixed in the policy for which the insured may be personally liable. If he is not liable for damages, the insurance company has no liability except the liability for defending the suit in court. This type of insurance does not cover any injury to either the person or the property of the insured. Such damage is covered under other types of policies.

The driver of a car that is not his own is liable for injury to others even though he does not own the car he is driving. The owner of the car is liable for all injuries to the person and property of others if he is personally driving in a negligent manner, or if any member of his family is so driving, or if any other person is driving the car with the owner's permission.

Under the "defense clause" the insurer agrees to defend the insured against any claim for damages. The insurer reserves the right to accept or reject any proffered settlement out of court.

● Graham had a public liability policy covering both bodily injury and property injury to others. In a collision with another car the driver of the other car was seriously injured and his car wrecked. Graham's policy provided for coverage up to $15,000 for bodily injury and $5,000 for property damage. The injured driver offered to settle the claim out of court for $14,000. The insurance company rejected the offer and defended the claim in court. The court gave judgment against Graham for $30,000. He, Graham, had to pay all over and above his insurance. Had the insurance company settled out of court, Graham would not have had to pay anything. The insured has unlimited liability, but the insurer's liability is limited by the terms of the policy.

A bodily injury insurance policy does not cover accidents occurring while the car is being driven by a person who is under the age designated by state law. It does not cover accidents occurring while the car is rented or leased, while the car is used to carry passengers for a consideration, while the car is used for any purpose other than that named in the policy, or while it is used outside the United States and Canada. Some policies exclude accidents while the car is being used for towing a trailer or any other vehicle used as a trailer. These are the ordinary exclusions. Some policies may have additional exclusions of various kinds.

In the event of an accident resulting in bodily injury or death, the insured must give immediate written notice to the insurer. He must also furnish the fullest information obtainable at the time of the accident and must promptly forward any legal papers or summons served on the policyholder. It is also his duty to help secure information, evidence, and the presence of witnesses, and to cooperate to the fullest extent with the insurer. The insured is not permitted to settle claims or to incur expenses other than those for immediate surgical help. In the event that the insurance company pays a loss, it is entitled to be substituted to any rights that the insured may have against others because of such losses.

(2) PROPERTY DAMAGE INSURANCE. In automobile property damage insurance the insurer agrees to pay, on behalf of the insured, all sums that the insured may be legally obligated to pay by reason of the liability imposed upon him by law for damages because of injury to or the destruction of property, caused by accident and arising out of the ownership, the maintenance, or the use of the automobile. The liability of the insurer, however, is limited to the amount stated in the policy.

In the event of an accident, it is the duty of the policyholder to give the insurer written notice respecting the damages resulting from the accident. The notice must identify the insured and give the name and the address of the owner of the damaged property and those of any available witnesses. It is also necessary to give information relative to the time, the place, and the circumstances of the accident.

If a claim is made or a suit is brought against the insured, he must immediately forward to the insurance company every demand, notice, or summons received in order that the insurer may be able to make the proper legal defense.

The policy usually provides that the insurer will not be liable in the event that the car is being operated, maintained, or used by any person in violation of any state or federal law as to age or occupation. The insurer is not liable for damage to property owned by, leased to, transported by, or in charge of the insured.

Questions

1. What are the two main classes of automobile insurance?

2. If John, the owner of a car, and four other young men drive to Jacksonville to attend a football game and each is to pay one fifth of the cost of the trip, is the insurer liable if the car is destroyed by fire during the trip?

3. What is covered by theft automobile insurance?

4. What effect does attaching a trailer to an automobile have on collision insurance?

5. Why do most automobile collision insurance policies have a deductible clause?

6. Name several causes of damage that may be covered by comprehensive insurance.

7. What two kinds of losses are covered by public liability insurance.

8. Who is liable for property damage if the owner is not driving the car?

9. What must one do with reference to his insurance when he has an accident?

10. If *A* has in his possession a watch worth $100 belonging to *B* and as a direct result of an automobile accident the watch is destroyed, who must pay for the loss?

Case Problems

1. A car owned and driven by John collided with a car owned and driven by Henry. The damage to John's car was $1,100 and that to Henry's car was $800. Henry carried collision and public liability insurance, but John carried no insurance. The collision was clearly the result of John's negligence. John and Henry were fraternity brothers, and Henry agreed to admit it was his fault. Miss Vaughn, secretary to the agent who serviced Henry's insurance policy, overheard the agreement between John and Henry and reported it to her employer. As a result, the insurance company refused to pay either for the damage to John's car or Henry's. Was the company within its rights?

2. John and Janet Kettle hooked their car to their house trailer and set out to tour the country. They carried full insurance on the car but none on the trailer. While crossing a mountain in West Virginia, John lost control of the car and it plunged over the mountainside, completely demolishing both the car and the trailer. The insurance company refused to pay the damage for either of the car or the trailer. Must the company pay for the car?

3. Bennett, a truck driver for the Beck Bakery, struck a child. The child was not hurt and the police exonerated Bennett for the accident. Consequently Beck did not notify the insurance company of the accident. Six months later the boy's father sued the bakery for $10,000, alleging the boy suffered internal injuries. It cost Beck $800 to defend the suit even though he won it. Was the insurance company liable for the $800?

4. Clevenger was an automobile dealer. A prospective customer selected a secondhand car and agreed to buy it if a trial run proved satisfactory. He was allowed to try the car out but never returned. Was the insurance company liable under a theft policy?

5. Robinson had a fire insurance policy on his automobile but no collision insurance. As a result of a collision the car was damaged and then caught fire and was destroyed. Did the company have to pay for the value of the car?

6. Hardy had a bodily injury policy of $10,000 on his car. As a result of a collision, Sandlin was injured and demanded that Hardy pay to him $20,000. Hardy's insurance company refused to pay, and Sandlin offered to compromise and settle for $4,000. The insurance company still refused. Sandlin then sued and obtained a judgment for $16,000. Was the insurance company required to pay the full $16,000?

7. Porterfield, the owner of the car, had a public liability and collision policy. Three fellow college students arranged to ride home with him at Christmas time and agreed to pay $10 each for the ride. This was considerably more than the cost of the trip. On the way the car was wrecked. Was the insurance company liable on the policy?

8. Winters was sued for a loss from bodily injuries caused by his automobile while it was being driven by his son, who was sixteen years of age. There was an ordinance in that city making it unlawful for anyone under eighteen years of age to operate an automobile. Who would be liable for the loss?

Chapter 40

Guaranty and Suretyship

Nature of the Contract. The peculiarity of the contract of guaranty or suretyship is that it is founded on another contract. Without a primary obligation there can be no occasion for a contract of guaranty or suretyship. It is from its very nature a contract to ensure or guarantee that someone else will perform his contract. It could not come into existence without this other contract since it is an agreement whereby one party promises that he will be responsible for the debt, default, or obligation of another. Such contract generally arise when one person assumes responsibility for the extension of credit to another, as in buying merchandise on credit or in borrowing money from a bank.

A person who is entrusted with money of another, such as a cashier, a bank teller, or a county treasurer, may be required to have someone guarantee the faithful performance of his duties. This, too, is a contract of suretyship, although it is commonly referred to as a *fidelity bond.*

Parties. There are three parties to a contract of guaranty or of suretyship. The party who undertakes to be responsible for another is the *guarantor* or the *surety;* the party to whom the guaranty is given is the *creditor;* and the party who is primarily liable is the *principal debtor,* or simply the *principal.*

Distinctions. The words "surety" and "guaranty" are often used interchangeably. Sometimes such usage is correct and sometimes it is incorrect. In a contract of suretyship the liability of the insurer is coextensive with that of the principal debtor. The surety renders himself directly and primarily responsible for the debt or obligation as though he were the primary debtor himself. His obligation, then, is identical with the one for whom he assumes the responsibility.

A guarantor's obligation is collateral to that of the principal debtor. He promises to pay only in the event that the principal defaults. The guarantor's obligation does not arise simultaneously with the principal's. His obligation is contingent upon the happening of another event, namely, the failure of the principal to pay. The surety's obligation, on the other hand, arises the instant the contract is formed.

Buffalo, N. Y., Dec. 4, 19

Mr. John J. Johnson
Elmira, New York

Dear Sir:

In consideration of the letting of the premises located at 221 Main Street, this city, to Mr. Henry H. Hansen for a period of two years from date, I hereby guarantee the punctual payment of the rent and the faithful performance of the covenants of the lease.

Very truly yours,

S. S. Samuels

A Letter of Guaranty.

Importance of Making a Distinction. There are three reasons why it is important to distinguish between a contract of guaranty and a contract of suretyship. These reasons pertain to:

1. Form
2. Remedy
3. Notice of default

(1) FORM. Contracts of guaranty and suretyship have many similarities, but it is the dissimilarities which it is particularly important to recognize. All the essential elements of a contract must be present in both. If the nature of the contract is such that it falls within the description of a contract of guaranty, it must be in writing; most contracts of suretyship may be oral.

The Statute of Frauds provides: "The promise to answer for the debt, default, or obligation of another must be in writing and be signed by the party to be charged, or by his authorized agent." It is held, however, that this provision applies only to a promise that creates a secondary obligation, that is, an obligation of guaranty, not to a promise that creates a primary obligation, that is, suretyship. One must first classify the obligation as primary or secondary before he knows whether or not the contract must be in writing.

(2) REMEDY. In the case of suretyship, the surety takes upon himself an original obligation. He binds himself to pay if the other party does not. The reason that the other party does not pay is immaterial. He is liable as fully and under the same conditions as if the debt were his from the beginning. The rule is different in many contracts of guaranty. If the guaranty is conditional, the guarantor is liable only if the other party cannot pay.

Arnold writes, "Let Brewer have a suit; and if he is unable to pay you, I will." This guaranty depends upon Brewer's ability to pay. Therefore, the seller must make all reasonable efforts to collect from Brewer before he can look to Arnold. If Arnold had said, "Let Brewer have this suit, and I will pay you," he would have created an original obligation for which he would have been personally liable. Therefore, Arnold would be deemed a surety if the understanding was that Brewer was to pay for the suit, but the merchant could look to Arnold if Brewer merely did not pay, rather than if Brewer could not pay.

(3) NOTICE OF DEFAULT. Since the surety is primarily liable for the debt, it is not necessary to notify him if the debt is defaulted. He is charged with a knowledge of the principal's default. The guarantor, on the other hand, must be notified by the creditor. Failure to give notice does not of itself discharge the guarantyship. If the guarantor is damaged by the failure to receive notice, he may offset the amount of the damage against the claim of the creditor.

- Defoe was the guarantor of a debt of $1,000 for Dione. Dione defaulted in the payment, and King, the creditor, did not give notice of default to Defoe until sixty days after the default. Dione was then insolvent. Defoe was able to prove that he could have collected from Dione had he been notified immediately of the default. Since Defoe was damaged to the extent of $1,000 by the unreasonable delay in giving notice, he was discharged from the obligation of guarantyship.

Rights of the Surety and the Guarantor. A guarantor and a surety have the following rights:

1. Indemnity
2. Subrogation
3. Contribution

(1) INDEMNITY. If the guarantor or the surety pays the debt or the obligation of the principal, he is entitled to be reimbursed for the amount paid. This right is known as the right of *indemnity.* The guarantor or the surety can collect only the amount he has paid; he cannot recover for damages suffered or sacrifices made because of the default of the principal. If he has paid part of the debt, he is a creditor for that amount and is entitled to reimbursement. The guarantor or the surety may be induced to pay the debt when it becomes due in order to avoid the accumulation of interest and other costs.

(2) SUBROGATION. When the guarantor or the surety pays the debt of his principal, he is entitled to all prop-

erty, liens, or securities that were held by the creditor to secure the payment of the debt. This right of subrogation does not arise until the creditor has been paid in full, but it does arise if the surety or the guarantor has paid a part of the debt and the principal has paid the remainder.

- Hardwick, Ellis, and Cook jointly and severally guaranteed the payment of a debt for $3,000 owed by Grant to Graves. When the debt became due Grant defaulted. Hardwick paid the entire claim and then received, by way of subrogation, collateral worth $1,200 which Grant had deposited with Graves. Hardwick then demanded that Ellis and Cook each contribute $1,000, or one third of the claim, since he paid the entire amount. The right of subrogation inures to the benefit of all guarantors. Therefore, Ellis and Cook had to contribute only two thirds of $1,800, or $600 each.

(3) CONTRIBUTION. When two or more persons are jointly held liable for the debt, default, or obligation of a certain person, they are known as *coguarantors* or *cosureties*. When one of two or more guarantors or sureties has paid more than his proportionate share of the debt, he is entitled to recover from the other guarantors or sureties the amount in excess of his pro rata share of the loss. This right is known as the right of *contribution.* It does not arise until the surety or the guarantor has paid the debt in full or has otherwise settled the debt.

Discharge of a Surety or a Guarantor. Both a surety and a guarantor may be discharged from their obligation by the usual methods of discharging any obligation, including performance, impossibility, voluntary agreement, and bankruptcy. There are, however, some additional acts that will discharge the surety or the guarantor. These are:

1. Extension of time
2. Alteration of the terms of the contract
3. Loss or return of collateral by the creditor
4. Varying the surety's or guarantor's risk

(1) EXTENSION OF TIME. If the creditor extends the time of the debt without the consent of the surety or the guarantor and for a consideration, the surety or the guarantor is discharged from further liability. This extension of time, however, must be such that the creditor waives his rights. So long as he reserves his right to sue at any time, his leniency is not penalized. Such an extension does not jeopardize the surety's or the guarantor's rights because he can pay the debt and then sue the principal immediately. It is only when the extension of time debars an immediate prosecution of the claim that the surety or the guarantor is released. The courts in a few states hold that a paid guarantor, such as a bonding company, is released by an extension of time only if it can be proved that the guarantor has been damaged by the extension.

• Thompson guaranteed a loan of $10,000 from the First National Bank to Talmadge. When the principal defaulted, the bank did not sue for three months. During this time Talmadge kept the interest paid up and there was a "gentleman's agreement," but not a contract, that the claim would not be pressed for three months. This did not release Thompson since the extension of time was a mere indulgence, not a contract.

(2) ALTERATION OF THE TERMS OF THE CONTRACT. Any material alteration of the contract by the creditor discharges the surety or the guarantor. The change must be prejudicial to the surety or the guarantor. A reduction in the interest rate has been held not to discharge the surety, while a change in the place of payment has been held to be an act justifying a discharge of the surety. Even though the change is made for the convenience or the benefit of the surety, his obligation is discharged if the change is material. A material change in a contract is in fact substituting a new contract for the old. The surety guaranteed the payment of the old contract, not the new one, even though the new one is less onerous than the old one.

• Parrish purchased a suit for $100 from the Ideal Clothing Store. Since Parrish was a minor, the seller required Searberry to guarantee the debt before he would extend credit. One week later Parrish executed a 50-day noninterestbearing note for the account. This discharged Searberry since the account receivable was replaced by a note receivable.

(3) LOSS OR RETURN OF COLLATERAL BY THE CREDITOR. If the creditor through negligence loses collateral security given to secure the debt, a surety or a guarantor is discharged. The same is true if the creditor returns to the debtor any collateral security. This collateral must be held for the benefit of the surety until the debtor pays the debt in full.

• Askew loans Bonner $5,000. To secure the loan Bonner deposits with Askew $2,500 in stock as collateral. In addition, Tate guarantees the repayment of the loan. Bonner pays $3,000 on the loan and Askew returns the collateral. Bonner fails to pay the remaining $2,000 and Askew sues Tate. The return of the collateral released Tate from any further liability.

(4) VARYING THE SURETY'S OR THE GUARANTOR'S RISK. If an act of the creditor varies the risk of the surety or the guarantor, the liability of the latter ceases. This variation need not necessarily increase the risk. The act might even be beneficial to the surety or the guarantor. The following acts have been held sufficient to discharge the surety or the guarantor:

(a) A tenant leased only a part of a building. He later leased all of it. This released the guarantor of the rent payments.

(b) The mortgagee accepted an additional guarantor in consideration of extending the time of payment. Since this altered the contract, the original guarantor was released.

(c) The creditor accepted a note for an open account. The guarantor of the open account was released even though the note was more collectible than the open account.

(d) A teller at a bank, whose financial integrity was vouched for by a surety, was promoted to assistant cashier. This increase in responsibilities of the principal released the surety.

Bonding Companies. In recent years *bonding companies* have taken over most of the business of guaranteeing the employer against losses due to the dishonesty of his employees. These bonding companies are known as paid sureties to distinguish them from accommodation or unpaid guarantors. In some instances the courts have held that paid sureties must prove damages before they are released from their contract by reason of some act of the creditor. If the bonding company's risk is not increased by the creditor's act, the guaranty will be enforced. For the most part, however, the law of suretyship and guaranty apply with equal force to both paid sureties and accommodation sureties. The bonding company's obligation arises from its written contract with the employer. This contract of indemnity sets out in detail the conditions under which the surety will be liable.

Questions

1. What is the nature of a contract of guaranty or suretyship?

2. Name the parties to a contract of guaranty or suretyship.

3. When does the obligation of a surety arise?

4. When does the obligation of a guarantor arise?

5. What must be the form of a contract of guaranty? Of suretyship?

6. If the guarantor or the surety pays the debt of the principal, what is his right to reimbursement called?

7. When does the right of subrogation of the guarantor or surety arise?

8. What is the right of contribution?

9. If the creditor through negligence loses the collateral put up by the debtor, what is the guarantor's liability?

10. Name some acts that would be sufficient to discharge the surety or the guarantor.

Case Problems

1. Chapman was bookkeeper and credit manager of the Rowe Lumber Company, from which Mason purchased building materials amounting to $750. Reece, Mason's brother-in-law, entered into an oral contract of suretyship whereby he promised to be fully responsible for the debt. The original credit period was for 90 days. When the account came due, Mason paid $150 and asked to be allowed to give his 60-day note in payment of the balance. Chapman accepted the note and about two weeks later notified Reece of the new arrangement. Mason never paid the note, and the Rowe Lumber Company sued Reece. Reece denied liability for four reasons: first, oral contract; second, an extension of time; third, improper notice of default; and fourth, discharge of the debt which he had guaranteed. Where any of these defenses valid?

2. Coulter leased the Parkview Apartment Hotel for $1,500 a month. Denton deposited with the owner stock valued at $18,000 to be held as collateral to guarantee the payment of the rent by Coulter. When the lease was renewed at the end of the first year, the rent was increased to $1,850 a month, but Denton was not notified of this increase. Coulter defaulted in the payment of the rent, and demand was made upon Denton as guarantor to pay the rent. Was Denton liable for the rent?

3. Flannagan entered into a contract with WGAU Radio Broadcasting Company to carry on an advertising campaign over a period of 60 days. The total cast was $6,000. The radio station required Flannagan to provide some guaranty of payment of the $6,000 before the advertising campaign could start. Gill, a wealthy friend of Flannagan, orally agreed "to be personally responsible for this debt if for any reason Flannagan fails to pay it." There was three witnesses to this oral contract. Flannagan failed to pay any part of the $6,000, and the radio corporation demanded that Gill pay. Was Gill liable for this debt?

4. Holdnak became a guarantor on a debt for $5,000 which Cooley owed to Lanier. Cooley deposited $2,000 worth of stock with Holdnak at the time the guaranty was made. Cooley defaulted in the payment but Lanier never notified Holdnak of the default. About one month after the debt was due Cooley asked Holdnak to return the stock, and Holdnak complied, thinking the debt was paid. Later Lanier demanded that Holdnak pay the entire $5,000. Was he liable for this amount?

5. Faulkner guaranteed the payment of a $1,200 debt which Ronald owed to Byck. When Ronald defaulted, Byck sued Faulkner immediately. At the trial Faulkner proved that Ronald possessed an automobile worth $2,000, owned a house and lot worth $12,000, and had a job paying him $80 a week. Were these facts relevant in the case?

6. Hoover guaranteed a $525 debt for Grant in favor of Joel. The debt called for the payment of 6 per cent interest from date. A few days later Joel agreed to reduce the interest rate to 5 per cent if Grant would agree to pay the debt thirty days sooner than he had previously agreed to do. What effect did this have on Hoover's liability?

7. Phelps was the surety on a note given by Boone to Doak. Phelps later learned that Boone had given Doak several shares of stock in a corporation to hold as security for the payment of the note. After Phelps paid the note, did he have a right to the shares of stock? Why?

8. Lane, Blank, and King were sureties for the payment of Doll's promissory note. When the note became due, the holder brought suit against King, one of the sureties, and collected the full amount from him. What remedy did King have? Explain.

9. Rich and Good were cosureties on a $10,000 note for Poor. Poor deposited with the lender $4,000 worth of negotiable government bonds as additional security. Poor defaulted, and Rich paid off the entire debt. Poor had assets, other than those pledged as security for the loan, worth $4,000, and Good had assets worth $2,000. Explain in detail Rich's rights under these circumstances.

Cases for Review of Part IX

1. Alexander died insolvent, but he left an insurance policy of which his wife was beneficiary. His creditors sought to show that the money used to pay the premiums on this policy was money that actually belonged to the creditors because of the insured's insolvency and that the proceeds should not go to the beneficiary but should go to the deceased's estate from which his debts could be paid. (Irving Bank vs. Alexander, 280 Pa. 466) Did Alexander's widow have a right to the proceeds of the policy free from her husband's debts?

2. Ross took out automobile collision insurance with the Michigan Mutual Auto Insurance Company. Ross, while trying to pass a truck, collided with an object on the opposite side of the road. He did this to avoid colliding head-on with a car coming in the opposite direction. The evidence indicated that he might have avoided any accident had he dropped back behind the truck when he realized he could not pass. His policy contained a clause excusing the insurance company from liability if the car "is driven contrary to the rules of the road." The insurance company denied liability because of this clause. (Ross vs. Michigan Mutual Auto Insurance Company, 224 Mich. 263) Do you agree?

3. Fludd took out a life insurance policy on his own life and made his wife the beneficiary. Before the policy was delivered, the insurer, the Equitable Life Assurance Company, learned of certain misrepresentations in the application. The company delivered the policy anyway to Fludd even though it had the right to refund the premium and refuse to issue the policy. When Fludd died the insurance company refused to pay Mrs. Fludd the proceeds. (Fludd vs. Equitable Life Assurance Company, 75 S. C. 315) Was the company liable?

4. Remley took out an insurance policy on his own life, payable to "his executors, administrators, or assigns." Under the state law creditors were barred from attaching the proceeds of a life insurance policy taken out for the benefit of the insured's wife. (Remley vs. Travelers Insurance Company, 108 Minn. 31) Were the creditors of Remley entitled to the proceeds of this policy?

5. Samuel Morgan took out a fire insurance policy on certain property owned by him. A fire destroyed the property and Morgan brought suit to collect for the loss. The insurance company denied liability on the ground of a breach of warranty. Morgan admitted that certain warranties were not true but sought to show that they were not material to the risk. (Virginia Fire and Marine Insurance Company vs. Morgan, 90 Va. 290) Was Morgan's contention sound?

6. Williams took out a life insurance policy of his own life in favor of his wife, Christine, as beneficiary. He reserved the right to change the beneficiary. Williams later assigned the policy to a bank as collateral security for a debt. (102 Fla. 214) Upon the death of Williams, who was entitled to the proceeds of the policy?

7. An automobile truck belonging to Adams was damaged when the loaded scoop of a steam shovel used in loading the truck fell upon it. (181 N. W. 1007) Was the insured entitled to indemnity under a policy of collision insurance?

8. Ranson was the surety on Black's note in favor of the City Bank. On the date that the note was due, Black procured from the bank an extension of time for thirty days. (39 Iowa 290) How did this extension affect the surety and the maker?

9. Erwin, a minor twenty years of age, made a contract with Patterson. Weare became surety to Patterson for Erwin. Erwin broke his contract, and Patterson brought suit against Weare, the surety. Weare contended that Erwin was not bound by his contract because of his minority, and that therefore he, the surety, could not be bound. (177 W. Va. 256) Was Weare's contention correct?

Part X
PROPERTY

Chapter 41

Nature of Property

Definition of Property. *Property* is anything which may be owned, possessed, used, or disposed of for a price. Law is concerned with both property and property rights. After all, it is the use of property, not property itself, which has value. The right to use property is broader than ownership because one may enter into a contract with another to use property which does not belong to him. The law protects not only the right to own property but also the right to use it. In law property is defined in such a way as to include not only physical property but such things as money, notes, and bonds which give the right to acquire either physical property or the use of such property.

Property may be classified according to its movability. In this sense all property falls into one of two classes, real property and personal property.

Real Property. *Real property* consists of land, timber, minerals under the soil, buildings, and all permanent attachments to the land, such as fences, walls, and other man-made property. Through court interpretations we have accumulated a definite set of rules to guide us in distinguishing real property from personal property. The most important of these rules pertain to:

1. Trees and perennial crops
2. Rivers and streams
3. Fixtures

(1) Trees and Perennial Crops. Trees that are growing on the land, orchards, vineyards, and perennial crops, such as clovers, grasses, and others that are not

Growing Trees Are Real Estate; but When the Trees Are Cut and Made into Lumber, the Lumber Becomes Personal Property.

planted annually and cultivated, are classed as real property. When land is sold, if there is any doubt as to whether or not a particular item belongs to the land, the parties should agree before the sale is completed just how the item is to be classed. If one sells land and does not mention the clover crop, for example, the buyer gets the clover.

Many disputes arise between neighbors over fruit trees growing on the boundary line. The fruit from the trees and plants belong to the one on whose land the tree or plant stands. If the limb of an apple tree, for example, hangs across the line of an adjacent property owner, the fruit still belongs to the owner of the tree. If the fruit falls to the ground, the title to the fruit is not lost. If the adjacent property owner will not permit the owner to cross the line to harvest his fruit, the owner may obtain a warrant and have the sheriff get the crop. The adjacent property owner may, however, cut off all limbs or vines that extend over his property.

(2) Rivers and Streams. If a nonnavigable river flows through a man's land, he owns the river bed but not the water that flows over the bed, nor the fish that swim in the water. He cannot impound or divert the water to his own use in such a way as to deprive his neighbor of its use. If the river or the stream forms the boundary line, then each owner owns the land to the middle of the river bed.

Where navigable rivers form the boundary, the owner of the adjoining land owns the land to the low-water mark.

(3) FIXTURES. Movable property attached to the land is known as a *fixture*. If it is permanently attached so that its removal would mar or damage the property, the fixture becomes real property and is acquired by the one who purchases the real estate to which the fixture is attached. If the fixture is not securely attached to the real estate, then the intention of the party installing it may be the controlling factor. If stones are piled on each other in such a way as to form a wall and actually serve as a wall, the stones become real property. The same stones brought to the land and placed on it in such a way as to indicate an intention to keep them movable, remain personal property. Stone naturally found on the land is real estate.

Store fixtures and trade fixtures, when installed by a tenant, clearly indicate an intention to keep them as personal property unless they are so attached that the real property will be damaged by the removal of the fixture. If the tenant surrenders possession of the premises before first removing the fixtures, he is presumed to have considered them to be real estate. He may, however, expressly reserve the right to remove them. Such items as built-in cabinets cannot be removed since they become real property as soon as they are attached.

Personal Property. *Personal property*, often referred to as chattels, is any property or property right which is not classified as real property. Personal property includes movable physical property and notes, stocks, bonds, and all written evidences of debt. Personal property is divided into two classes:

1. Tangible
2. Intangible

(1) TANGIBLE PERSONAL PROPERTY. *Tangible personal property* consists of all physical items which are not real estate. The property itself can be seen, touched, and possessed. Animals, merchandise, furniture, annual growing crops, clothing, jewelry, and similar items are all classified as tangible personal property.

(2) INTANGIBLE PERSONAL PROPERTY. Many important property rights consist merely of evidences of ownership of personal property. Contracts, copyrights, checks, stocks, savings account certificates, and other evidences of rights give us the power to acquire tangible personal property or other intangible personal property.

Estates. An *estate,* strictly speaking, is an interest or a right in real estate. This interest may be classed as real property or personal property, depending upon the nature of the right. One's title to an estate not only indicates the extent of ownership but also its nature, that is, whether it is real or personal property.

Real Property Estates. The following titles are classed as real estate:

1. Estate in fee simple
2. Life estate

(1) ESTATE IN FEE SIMPLE. A *fee simple estate* is the largest and most complete right which one may possess in real property. It gives the owner the right to the surface of the land, the air above the land "all the way to heaven," and the subsoil beneath the surface all the way to the center of the earth. The courts have held, however, that the right to the air above the land is not absolute. One cannot prevent an airplane from flying over his land unless it flies too low.

One can own the surface of the land only, but not the minerals, oil, gas, and other valuable property under the top soil. One may also own the soil but not the timber.

(2) LIFE ESTATE. One may have the right to use land as long as he lives but not the right to sell the land. This is known as a *life estate.* At the death of the owner, the title either reverts to the one who conveyed the life estate to the deceased, the interest of the grantor being called a *reversion,* or the property goes to someone other than the grantor, such interest being called a *remainder.*

- John Dotson conveyed to his wife, Minnie, a life estate in all his real estate. At her death the property was to go to his three sons in equal parts. This was a remainder. Had the property at Minnie's death returned to her husband or to his estate, it would have been a reversion. In either case, the property right is real property, not personal property.

Personal Property Estates. The following interests in real property are classed as personal property: *estate for years,* such as leases for one month, one year, fifty years, or any other definite time; and *estates at will or by sufferance,* which are leases for no definite period of time. Although these estates give one the exclusive right to use real estate for the period fixed by the grant, the property right is classed as personal property.

Methods of Acquiring Ownership. The title to property may be acquired by (1) purchase, (2) will, (3) gift, (4) descent, (5) accession, (6) confusion, (7) creation, and (8) original possession.

Acquiring ownership of property through purchase is a common occurrence. The process of acquiring property through a will or a gift is also well known. Since the other methods are less common and in most cases less important, they are not so well known and understood.

One of these less common methods is *descent.* If a man dies *intestate,* that is, without leaving a will, his heirs acquire, as a matter of law, title to his personal property according to the law of descent existing in the decedent's state, and to his real property according to the law of descent in the state where the land is located.

When a river is the boundary between two pieces of real estate and the line is not designated by "metes and bounds" but merely follows the river, one may acquire real estate by *accession.* The line shifts with the river. This shifting may be by a slow process or it may suddenly shift during a flood. By either process one property owner may obtain real estate by accession. This will be the land lying between the new river bed and the location of the old river bed at the time he purchased the land. He may lose it in the next flood.

Confusion is the mixing of the goods of different owners so that the parts belonging to each owner cannot be identified and separated. Grain, lumber, oil, and coal are examples of the kinds of property that are susceptible to confusion. The property, belonging to different owners, may be mixed by common consent, by accident, and by the willful act of some wrongdoer.

When confusion of the property is brought about by common consent or by accident, each party will be deemed the owner of a proportionate part of the mass. If the confusion is willful, the title to the total mass passes to the innocent party, unless the one causing the confusion can clearly prove how much of his property was mingled with that of the other person; if he fails, the whole mass belongs to the other person.

One may acquire personal property by *creation.* This is particularly true of inventions, paintings, musical compositions, and other intellectual productions. Title to these is made secure by means of patents and copyrights.

The one who first applies for and obtains a patent gets title to the production. Creation alone does not give absolute title; it gives only the right to obtain absolute title by means of a patent. This is not true for songs, books, and other compositions that are copyrighted. This

Page 1

FORM A

CLASS	REGISTRATION NO.
A	DO NOT WRITE HERE

Application for Registration of a Claim to Copyright
in a published book manufactured in the United States of America

Instructions: Read the information provided on page 4 before completing the form. Fill in applicable items on all pages. Follow the instructions which accompany each item. The application should give the facts which existed at the date of publication. Pages 1 and 2 should be typewritten or printed with pen and ink. Pages 3 and 4 may be carbon copies. Mail all pages to the Register of Copyrights, Library of Congress, Washington 25, D. C., together with 2 copies of the best edition of the work and the registration fee of $4. Make your remittance payable to the Register of Copyrights.

1. Copyright Claimant(s) and Address(es): Give the name(s) and address(es) of the copyright owner(s). Ordinarily the name should be the same as in the notice of copyright on the copies of the work deposited.

Name South-Western Publishing Company

Address 5101 Madison Road, Cincinnati 27, Ohio

Name

Address

2. Title: Give the title of the work as it appears on the copies. College Law, Fifth Edition

3. Authors: The citizenship of the author and information concerning domicile must be given. If an organization is the author and was formed under the laws of the United States or one of the States, citizenship may be stated as U. S. A. Authors may be editors, compilers, translators, illustrators, etc., as well as authors of original text. In the case of a work made for hire, the employer is the author. If the claim is based on new matter (see item 5 (*a*)), give information about the author of the new matter. If the author's pseudonym appears on the copies rather than his legal name, the pseudonym should be given in the application, and the legal name may be included if desired; e. g., John Doe, pseudonym of Richard Roe.

Name A. Aldo Charles Citizenship U. S. A. (Name of country)

Domiciled in U. S. A. Yes X No Address University of Georgia, Athens, Georgia

Name Citizenship (Name of country)

Domiciled in U. S. A. Yes No Address

Name Citizenship (Name of country)

Domiciled in U. S. A. Yes No Address

4. Date and Place of Publication:

(*a*) Give the date (month, day, and year) when copies were first placed on sale, sold, or publicly distributed.

February 15, 1957

(*b*) Give the name of the country in which the work was first published.

U. S. A.

5. Previous Publication:

(*a*) *New matter in this version:* If any part of this work has been previously published, in the United States or elsewhere, give a brief general statement of the nature of the new matter in this version. New matter may consist of compilation, translation, abridgment, editing, and the like, as well as additional text or pictorial matter.

Additions and revisions

(*b*) *United States edition of a work subject to the ad interim provisions of the law:* If the work is in the English language and all or part was previously first published outside the United States, and copyright was not secured under section 9 (c) of title 17, U. S. C., by virtue of the Universal Copyright Convention, give the year date of first publication outside the United States and state whether or not a claim to ad interim copyright was registered.

Year date of first publication outside the United States. Claim to ad interim copyright registered. Yes ☐ No ☐

16—63324-2 *See next page*

An Application for a Copyright.

is a holdover from the common law which gave absolute title to one's mental creation but not to one who invented a new device. After one publishes a book, a song, or a painting, he must apply for and obtain a statutory copyright to replace his common-law right or he loses all right to his creation. A statutory copyright is superior to a common-law right because it fixes the date of the creation; thus it settles the question of priority when there are two or more contenders for the title.

Original possession results in the ownership of personal property. For example, wild animals and fowls belong to no one so long as they are in the state of nature. But if a man captures a wild bird, it belongs to him as soon as he brings it under his control.

Lost and Abandoned Property. A person who discovers and takes possession of property that has been abandoned and has never been reclaimed by the owner acquires a right thereto. The prior owner, however, must have completely relinquished his ownership.

Property is considered to be *abandoned* when the owner actually discards it with no intention of reclaiming it. Property is considered to be *lost* when the owner, through negligence or accident, unintentionally leaves it somewhere. The difference between abandoned and lost property lies in the intention of the owner to part with the property. If the relinquishment is intentional, the property is abandoned; if the relinquishment is unintentional, the property is lost.

The finder of lost property has a right of possession against all but the true owner; he does not have the right of possession against the true owner except in those instances when the owner cannot be found through reasonable diligence on the part of the finder and when certain statutory requirements are fulfilled. The finder of abandoned goods, however, has an absolute right to possession.

Questions

1. What is property?

2. Give several illustrations of real property other than land.

3. If an apple tree stands on *A's* land but within a few feet of the boundary line between *A* and *B,* who owns the fruit on the limbs hanging over on *B's* side?

4. If a nonnavigable stream is the boundary line between two pieces of property owned respectively by Smith and Sampson, who owns the river bed?

5. If a tenant who has installed trade fixtures on the property moves away without removing the fixtures, to whom do the fixtures belong?

6. Name three types of personal property that are intangible.

7. What is the name of the largest estate or title to which one can have in land?

8. If a man dies intestate, how may his heirs obtain title to his property?

9. If Young willfully mixes 1,000 pounds of his low-grade rice with 3,000 pounds of high-grade rice belonging to Harris, who owns the mixture?

10. What is the difference between lost and abandoned property?

Case Problems

1. Lawson rented a cotton farm to Cherry on a share-crop basis whereby Lawson and Cherry would divide the cotton fifty-fifty. Cherry was to do all the work in planting, growing, and picking the cotton. The lease terminated December 31. At that time about five bales of cotton remained unpicked. Cherry moved away. Winefree, a neighbor, thinking the cotton was abandoned, went on the land, picked the cotton, and sold it. Both Lawson and Cherry sued him, Lawson claiming all the cotton, and Cherry contending half of it belonged to him. What were the rights of the parties?

2. Walker sold a farm to Hollison. At the time the contract to sell was entered into, there were 1,000 fence posts that had been set in the post holes but had not yet been

tamped in. There was also about $1,000 worth of wire stacked on the farm ready to be put up as soon as the posts were tamped and braced. Nothing was said about the posts and wire. Before the deed was made, Walker removed the posts and wire, contending that they were not a part of the farm. Hollison contended that they went with the land. Who was entitled to the posts and wire, Walker or Hollison?

3. Rice and Troelson owned adjoining farms. The dividing line was a nonnavigable stream. Troelson attempted to prevent Rice from fishing in the stream, claiming that since his own title was older than Rice's, his line extended to the far side of the stream. Was this contention correct?

4. A pecan tree stood on Divan's lot just two feet from the line separating Divan's and Spratlin's lots. About half of the pecans grew on the limbs overhanging Spratlin's lot. Spratlin insisted that the pecans on the limbs overhanging his lot belonged to him. Was this contention correct?

5. Carmeron owned a mink farm on which he had minks valued at $10,000. A truck crashed into the fence surrounding the mink cages and about half the minks escaped. Wade, a neighbor, caught ten of the minks about thirty minutes after they escaped, and Cameron demanded that Wade return them to him. To whom did the minks belong?

6. Holland, on April 15, sold his farm to Dillard for $15,000. At the time of the sale the land consisted of sixty acres of wheat. Nothing was said about the wheat. After the deed was delivered, Holland insisted that the wheat belonged to him. Was this contention correct?

7. Dorothy Hummingbird composed a song, both words and music, and many of her friends complimented her on it and urged her to publish it. Since Miss Hummingbird was not sure the song had merit, she sent it to a radio crooner and asked him to sing it on one of his programs to see if the public liked it. The crooner liked the song very much and recognized its great merit. He made a few slight alterations and improvements, and had the song copyrighted in his own name. He wrote Miss Hummingbird that the song was without merit. The song was a hit, and the crooner received several thousand dollars in royalties. Miss Hummingbird sued him, claiming the song was hers as she had title to it by creation. Who had title to this song?

Chapter 42

Transfer of Real Property

Transfer of Real Property. The three common ways of transferring title to real estate are by:

1. Sale
2. Will or descent
3. Adverse possession

(1) Sale of Real Estate. The most common way of transferring title to real estate is by sale. If the entire interest in the estate is sold, the contract of sale is followed by delivery of a deed. One may transfer a leasehold title giving the rights to the use and possession of land for a limited period by means of a lease. The extent of the interest conveyed is determined by the provisions of the deed or the lease.

Even when title to real property is conveyed as a gift, the transfer must be evidenced by a deed. As soon as the gift is fully executed, that is, the deed is prepared, signed, acknowledged, and delivered, title vests fully in the donee. An executory promise to make a gift is unenforceable.

(2) Transfer by Will or Descent. The owner of real estate may convey title to another by will. Title is not absolute until the will is probated and the executor of the will transfers title under the approval of the court. If the owner dies without leaving a will, title to his property is inherited by his heirs. An administrator is appointed by the court to transfer the title to the heirs. The heirs inherit the right to obtain the deceased's estate, not the estate itself.

(3) ADVERSE POSSESSION. One may lose possession to his real estate by permitting someone else to occupy the land for a statutory period of years, varying from seven years in some states to twenty years in others. For one to obtain title to real property by *adverse possession,* one must have actual possession of the land, and the possession must be visible, exclusive, hostile, and continuous.

Deeds. A *deed* is a formal contract conveying title, other than a lease, to real property. The law sets forth the form which the deed must have and this form must be observed lest one's title prove defective. The parties to the deed are the *grantor* or seller and the *grantee* or buyer. There are two principal types of deeds:

1. Quitclaim deeds
2. Warranty deeds

(1) QUITCLAIM DEEDS. A *quitclaim deed* is just what the name implies. The grantor quits any claim which he may have to the real property. He makes no warranty that he has any claim, although a few states prohibit the use of a quitclaim deed unless the grantor has some interest in the property.

Unless it is prohibited by law, there is no reason why a quitclaim deed may not be used in making all conveyances of real property. The grantor's full and complete interest is as effectively transferred by a quitclaim deed as with a warranty deed. When one buys real property, however, he does not always want to buy merely the interest which the grantor has. He wants to buy a perfect and complete interest so that his title cannot be questioned by anyone. A quitclaim deed conveys only the interest of the grantor and no more. It contains no warranty that the grantor's title is good. The buyer in an ordinary sale is justified in refusing to accept this type of deed.

A quitclaim deed should be used only in making a sale of some minor right or claim to real property.

● Clevinger sold Chambers a farm containing 700 acres. Clevinger reserved "all the timber growing on the farm at the time of the sale." Later Chambers wished to sell the farm to Dudley, but Dudley refused to buy the farm because it appeared that Clevinger still owned all the growing timber. Clevinger had, prior to the sale to Chambers, cut all the marketable timber. Chambers contended that Clevinger had no more interest in the land, and Clevinger agreed with this interpretation. Consequently, Clevinger, for a consideration of $1, sold Chambers all the interest which he had in the land. He conveyed this right by a quitclaim deed since he did not wish to warrant that he had any right. His act merely removed the cloud from Chamber's title so that he could sell to Dudley.

(2) WARRANTY DEEDS. A *warranty deed* not only conveys the grantor's interest in the real property, but in addition warrants that he has a right to sell. The two types of warranty deeds are general warranty deeds and special warranty deeds.

A *general warranty deed* not only warrants that the grantor has good title to the real property, but further warrants that the grantee "shall have quiet and peaceable possession, free from all encumbrances, and that the grantor will defend the grantee against all claims and demands from whomsoever made." This warranty, then, warrants that all prior grantors had good title and that there are no defects in any prior grantor's title. The grantee is not asked to assume any risks.

A *special warranty deed* warrants that the grantor has the right to sell the real property. He does not warrant the genuineness of any prior grantor's title. This type of deed is used by trustees and sheriffs who sell land at a foreclosure sale. It is also used by executors and administrators. There is no reason why these officials should warrant anything other than that they have the legal right to sell whatever interest the owner has.

Requirements of a Deed. Since a deed is a contract, the requirements applicable to contracts in general apply

WARRANTY DEED THE McGREGOR CO., PRINTERS, ATHENS, GA.

STATE OF GEORGIA,

Clarke County

THIS INDENTURE, Made this first day of February in the year of our Lord One Thousand Nine Hundred and fifty-seven between Marvin Flemming of the State of Georgia and County of Clarke of the first part, and David Smith of the State of Georgia and County of Bartow of the second part,

WITNESSETH: That the said part___ of the first part, for and in consideration of the sum of Ten Thousand (10,000)-- DOLLARS in hand paid at and before the sealing and delivery of these presents, the receipt whereof is hereby acknowledged, has granted, bargained, sold and conveyed, and by these presents does grant, bargain, sell and convey unto the said party of the second part, his heirs and assigns, all that tract or parcel of land lying and being in Bartow County and being fully described by plat recorded in Plat Book No. 3, page 56 of Bartow County, Georgia, reference to which plat is hereby made for full description, being the same land conveyed to me by Harley Dotson by deed dated June 1, 1939 and recorded in Deed Book No. 84, page 356 in Bartow County, Georgia.

TO HAVE AND TO HOLD the said bargained premises, together with all and singular the rights, members and appurtenances thereof, to the same being, belonging or in any wise appertaining, to the only proper use, benefit and behoof of___ the said party of the second part, his heirs and assigns forever, IN FEE SIMPLE.

And the said party of the first part, for his heirs and executors and administrators will warrant and forever defend the right and title to the above described property unto the said party of the second part, his heirs and assigns, against the lawful claims of all persons whomsoever.

IN WITNESS WHEREOF, The said party of the first part has hereunto set his hand and affixed his ~~our~~ seal___, the day and year above written.

Signed, sealed and delivered in the presence of

Glenn Turner

Charles Wright

Lola Sutton, Notary Public

Marvin Flemming (SEAL)

(SEAL)

(SEAL)

(SEAL)

(SEAL)

A Warranty Deed.

to deeds. Unless statutes provide otherwise, a deed should fulfill the following requirements:

1. Parties
2. Consideration
3. Covenants
4. Description
5. Signature
6. Acknowledgment

(1) PARTIES. The contract must have proper parties, the grantor and the grantee, and they must be named in the deed. If the grantor is married, his name and that of his wife should be written in the deed. If the grantor is unmarried, this fact should be indicated by the term "bachelor" or "spinster," as the case may be; if he is divorced, this fact should be indicated by the terms "divorced and unmarried."

(2) CONSIDERATION. The amount paid to the grantor for the property is the consideration. The payment may be in money or in money's worth. A statement of the consideration must be made in the deed, although the amount specified need not be the actual price paid. In some localities the practice is to name a nominal amount, as one dollar, although a much larger sum was actually paid. The reason for stating a nominal amount as the consideration is to prevent a subsequent purchaser from learning the actual price paid for the property in the previous sale.

(3) COVENANTS. One of the most important parts of a deed includes the covenants. These include the assertions of the grantor that he has good title to the land and that the grantee and his heirs shall have quiet and peaceable possession. There may be as many additional covenants as the grantor and the grantee wish to include. Some of these are *affirmative covenants* whereby the grantee is obligated to do something, such as maintaining a driveway used in common with adjoining property.

Others are *negative covenants* whereby the grantee agrees to refrain from doing some event. Such covenants are very common in urban residential developments. The more common ones prohibit the grantee from using the property for business purposes and setting forth the types of homes that can or cannot be built on the property. Covenants, both affirmative and negative, go with the land and are binding upon all future purchasers.

(4) DESCRIPTION. The property to be conveyed must be correctly described. Any description that will identify the property will suffice. Ordinarily, however, the description that was used in the deed by which the present owner acquired the title should be used if it is correct. The description may be by lots and blocks if the property is in a city; or it may be by metes and bounds, section, range, and township if the property is in a rural district.

(5) SIGNATURE. The deed should be signed by the grantor in the place provided for the signature. If the grantor is married, his wife also should sign for the purpose of giving up her dower right. Her signature should be written below that of her husband. In some states the signatures must be attested by a witness or witnesses. If the grantor is incapable of signing his name, he may execute the deed by making his mark, thus:

James Smith
Witness of the mark of
Henry Hoe

Henry $\left\{\begin{matrix}\text{His}\\ \text{X}\\ \text{Mark}\end{matrix}\right\}$ Hoe

(6) ACKNOWLEDGMENT. The statutes in practically all the states require that the deed be formally acknowledged before a notary public or other officer authorized to take acknowledgments. The purpose of the acknowledgment is to make it possible for the deed to be recorded. After a deed has been recorded, it may be used as evidence in a court without further proof of its authenticity being given. Recording is not essential to the validity of

the deed, but it is invaluable as security of the title of the grantee.

The *acknowledgment* is a declaration made by the properly authorized officer, in the form provided for that purpose, that the grantor has signed and sealed the instrument in his presence; that the grantor has knowledge and understanding of its contents; and that the grantor is personally known to the officer. These facts are attested by the officer, who affixes his official seal, and are further evidenced by his certificate.

Delivery and Acceptance. A deed is ineffective until it has been both delivered and accepted. *Delivery* consists of giving up possession and control over the deed. So long as the grantor maintains control over the deed and reserves the right to demand its return before the deed is delivered to the grantee, then there has been no legal delivery. If the grantor executes a deed and leaves it with his own attorney to deliver to the grantee, there has been no delivery until his attorney delivers the deed to the grantee. Since the attorney is the agent of the grantor, he, the grantor, has the right to demand that his own agent return the deed to the grantor. If the grantor, however, delivers the deed to the grantee's attorney, then there has been an effective delivery.

The mere delivery of the deed to the grantee or the grantee's agent does not pass title. The grantee must by word and act accept the deed. If, however, after reading it, the grantee is not satisfied with the provisions of the deed, the grantee may reject it.

• Woolard signed and acknowledged a deed conveying all his real property to his son, Roger. Woolard gave the deed to his brother with instructions to deliver the deed upon the death of the grantor. When the grantor died, the three brothers who were disinherited brought suit to set the deed aside. The court held that the deed was void. Since the grantor died prior to the moment when title passed to Roger, the real estate became a part of the decedant's estate and had to be distributed according to the law of descent.

Recording. A deed need not be recorded in order to complete one's title. Title is complete as soon as the deed is delivered and accepted. Recording the deed protects the grantee against a fraudulent second sale by the grantor, and against any liens which may accrue against the property while it is still recorded in the grantor's name.

• Wheeler sold his house and lot to Davis for $30,000. Davis held the deed twenty days before having it recorded. Five days after the sale, a creditor of Wheeler's obtained a judgment for $20,000 against Wheeler. This judgment was recorded in the Judgment Lien Docket Book twelve days before Davis put his deed on record. The minute the judgment was recorded it became a lien on all the real estate which the deed books showed that Wheeler owned at the time of the judgment. Davis, then, had to pay the $20,000 judgment since it was a lien against the house and lot. His only remedy was to attempt to recoup his loss from Wheeler.

The recording official should stamp the deed immediately upon receipt to show the date, the hour, and the minute the deed was received for recording. The exact minute of receipt is important. A judgment recorded one minute before the deed is received becomes a lien against the real estate. The recording official may hold the deed several days before it is actually recorded. This is immaterial, since it is the date the deed is received to be recorded which determines the priority.

Abstract of Title. Before one buys real estate, it is advisable to have an abstract of title prepared. This may be done by a title abstract company or it may be done by an attorney. The *abstract of title* gives a complete history of the real estate, showing an unbroken line of transfers. It also shows whether or not there are any unpaid taxes and assessments, mortgages, or deeds of trust still outstanding, and any unpaid judgments or other unsatisfied liens of any type against the property.

If an abstracting company makes the abstract, it is advisable to have an attorney read the abstract to see if it reveals any flaws in the title.

Many defects in the title to real estate cannot be detected by an abstract. Some of the most common of these defects are forgery of signatures in prior conveyances; claims by adverse possession; incompetency to contract by any prior party; fraud; duress; undue influence; defective wills; loss of real property by accretion; errors by title examiner, tax officials, surveyors, and many other public officials. A title insurance policy will cover most of these defects. The policy may expressly exclude any possible defects which the insurance company does not inure to the benefit of a subsequent purchaser as long as the insured owns the property. The policy does not inure to the benefit of a subsequent purchaser or to a mortgagee. The policy does not insure a perfect title but it does insure the individual named in the policy against a financial loss because of a defective title.

Questions

1. If Hale wishes to transfer title to his land to his son by gift, what must he do?
2. If one obtains title to real estate by will, what must be done before the title is absolute?
3. How is it possible to obtain title to real estate by adverse possession?
4. What are the advantages and disadvantages of a quitclaim deed?
5. Define a warranty deed.
6. Who are the parties that must be named in a deed?
7. What is the difference between an affirmative covenant and a negative covenant?
8. When does a deed become effective?
9. (a) Is it necessary to record a deed in order to complete one's title to the land?

   (b) What does recording a deed do?
10. What is an abstract of title?

Case Problems

1. Abney had three sons at the time of his death. They inherited jointly Abney's home. The three sons sold the property to Penker for $30,000. The three grantors were not individually named in the deed but simply stated, "We, the heirs of Howard Abney." Each one signed the deed, and each one separately had it notarized. Later the question arose as to whether or not this violated the rule that the grantor must be named in the deed. Would you be willing to accept a deed with the grantors thus designated?

2. Donaldson purchased a house and lot. In a prior deed the grantor had inserted a covenant that the grantee would never use the property for commercial or business purposes. Such covenants were included by the original owner in the deeds for all the houses in that residential section. Donaldson wished to set up a dry-cleaning establishment in the basement of his house. A neighbor brought an equity suit to enjoin him from doing so. This action was based upon the original restrictive covenant. Was Donaldson bound by this covenant?

3. Morris, as a notary public, was authorized to acknowledge deeds. A man brought Morris a deed to be acknowledged. He represented himself as Sullivan, the grantor named in the deed, whereby Sullivan conveyed to William Peyton a valuable tract of real estate. Morris did not know Sullivan, the grantor, but he acknowledged the deed and certified that Sullivan personally appeared before him and signed the deed of conveyance. The man who claimed to be Sullivan was actually not Sullivan but William Peyton, the grantee. Peyton immediately sold the land to Ashby for cash. When Sullivan, the true owner, learned of Ashby's claim to the land, he denied him access to it and notified him that he had never signed the deed of conveyance to Peyton. Ashby produced an abstract of title that had been prepared by an attorney. Point out the mistakes the various people made in these transactions and show how they might have been avoided.

4. Tucker, who had two sons, owned two homes of about equal value. In an attempt to avoid the expense of a will or other costs incident to the transfer of this property to his two sons after his death, he executed two deeds, leaving each of the sons one of the houses. He gave the deeds to his sister and instructed her to "keep the deeds in a safe

place and under no circumstances part with them during my life. After my death give each son his deed." This request was followed to the letter. One son, John, was dissatisfied with the house he received, claiming the other house was worth twice as much as his. He refused to record his deed and brought a suit to have both of them set aside. Were these deeds valid?

5. Riley sold to the Ruark Lumber Company, "all the timber now on my farm." The timber was cut, and about ten years later Riley contracted to sell his farm to Greeley. Greeley refused to complete the purchase, claiming that Riley did not own the timber. Thereupon Riley obtained a letter from the Ruark Lumber Company stating that it did not claim to own the timber. Was this adequate to clear the title?

6. Stewart sold Stern a house and lot, executing a special warranty deed. About a year later Sprouse sued Stern to recover the property, claiming that the signature of the grantor of the property ten years earlier was forged. The man who sold the property to Stewart was not a party to the forgery. Must Stewart make good the loss to Stern? Would your answer be different if he had made a general warranty deed?

7. Holcomb executed a deed to his home, conveying all the property to his son, John. The deed was delivered to John but before he had it recorded, a brother, Roger, found the deed and burned it up. Before Holcomb could make another deed, he died and John sought to have the court declare him the rightful owner of the house and lot. Was John entitled to the property?

8. Stillman purchased some land from Cope. He held the deed one week before having it recorded. In the meantime, Cope's creditors obtained judgments against Cope and had these recorded before Stillman's deed was recorded. Were these judgments a lien against Stillman's land?

9. Munson purchased lot "A" from Pepper. Through an error the deed actually conveyed title to lot "B." Munson built a house on lot "A" and lived on it for twenty-one years. Pepper's heirs attempted to dispossess Munson and take possession of lot "A" and the house on it. Were they entitled to the property?

Chapter 43

Real Estate Mortgages

Definition. A *mortgage* is a lien given upon property to secure a debt. The mortgage is not the debt itself but only the security for the debt. Without a debt or potential obligation the mortgage would lack a consideration. Land or any interest in land may be mortgaged. Land may be mortgaged separately from the improvements, or the improvements may be mortgaged apart from the land. Growing crops may be mortgaged for the purpose of securing a loan. In fact, all kinds of property and property rights may be mortgaged.

Under the common law a real estate mortgage was an absolute transfer of both title and possession of real property to the mortgagee. The mortgagor received in substance an option to repurchase the real estate, that is, the right to regain both title and the possession upon the payment of the debt. Under the modern plan the mortgagor does not give up possession of the property, although he may contract to do so. The common law rule was rather harsh because one might lose a $10,000 piece of property because of one's inability to repay a $1,000 loan. Since a modern mortgage does not give the mortgagee an absolute title, he must sell the mortgaged property at a foreclosure sale. If the property brings more than the debt and the costs, the mortgagor is entitled to receive the balance.

The Mortgage Contract. A mortgage that makes a contingent sale of the land, subject to reacquisition upon fulfilling the obligation secured, must be in writing. The contract, as a rule, must have the same form as a deed; that is, it must be acknowledged and must be under seal.

A Mortgage Makes It Possible for a Family to Acquire a Home Before the Full Purchase Price Has Been Saved.

H. Armstrong Roberts

The mortgage, like all other contracts, sets forth the rights and the duties of the contracting parties. Over the years, however, courts have built up a body of court decisions interpreting these rights and duties. For this reason, one must look to these decisions as well as the contract for a full understanding of the nature of the mortgage contract.

A mortgage is usually given to raise money for the purchase price of real estate, but may be given for other reasons. One may borrow money for any reason and secure the loan by a mortgage. One may assume a contingent liability for another, such as going on his bond, and receive a mortgage as security. The debt must be in existence at the time a mortgage is foreclosed, but not necessarily at the time the mortgage is given.

Recording. The mortgage gives the mortgagee a lien in a definite order of priority according to the time it is recorded. Recording the mortgage protects the mortgagee against subsequent creditors since the public record is notice to the whole world as to the mortgagee's rights. There may be both a first mortgage and a second mortgage. Since the second mortgage recites the fact that a first mortgage exists, the second mortgage does not achieve priority over the first even though it is recorded first. The mortgage is also recorded to notify subsequent purchasers that the purchase price, or as much as is necessary, must be paid to the mortgagee.

Duties of the Mortgagor. The mortgagor assumes three definite duties and liabilities when he places a mortgage upon his real estate. These pertain to:

1. Interest and principal
2. Taxes, assessments, and insurance premiums
3. Security of the mortgagee

(1) INTEREST AND PRINCIPAL. The mortgagor must make all payments of interest and principal as they become due. Most mortgages call for periodic payments, such as monthly, semi-annual, or annual payments. These payments are used to pay all accrued interest to the date of payment, and the balance is applied on the principal. Other mortgages call for periodic payment of interest and for the payment of the entire principal at one time. In either case, a failure to pay either the periodic payments of interest and principal, or of interest only, is a default and gives the mortgagee the right to foreclose.

If the mortgagor wishes to pay off the mortgage debt before the due date so as to save interest, he must reserve that right at the time the mortgage is given. He can pay off the debt at any time, but the interest must be paid till the due date in the absence of an agreement to the contrary.

(2) TAXES, ASSESSMENTS, AND INSURANCE PREMIUMS. The mortgagor must pay taxes, assessments, and insurance premiums. The mortgagor is required by law to pay taxes and special assessments. If he does not do so,

the mortgagee may pay them and compel a reimbursement from the mortgagor. If the mortgage contract requires the mortgagor to pay these charges, a failure to pay them becomes a default the same as not paying a periodic payment of principal and interest.

The law does not require the mortgagor to keep the property insured. This duty must be imposed on the mortgagor by contract. Both the mortgagor and the mortgagee have an insurable interest in the property to the extent of each one's equity or maximum loss.

(3) SECURITY OF THE MORTGAGEE. The mortgagor must keep the security of the mortgagee unimpaired. The mortgagor must do no act that will materially impair the security of the mortgagee. Cutting timber, tearing down buildings, and all acts that waste the assets impair the security and give the mortgagee the right to seek legal protection. Some state statutes provide that any one of these acts is equivalent to a default. This gives the mortgagee the right to foreclose. Other statutes provide only that the mortgagee may obtain an injunction in a court of equity enjoining any further impairment. Many state laws also make it a criminal offense to impair willfully the security of mortgaged property.

Rights of the Mortgagor. The mortgagor has four well established rights. These rights pertain to:

1. Possession of the property
2. Rents and profits
3. Cancellation of lien
4. Redemption

(1) POSSESSION OF THE PROPERTY. The mortgagor usually has the right to retain possession of the mortgaged property. In practically all states the mortgagor now has this right, either as a matter of law or by contract. A few

states provide that in the event of default by the mortgagor, the mortgagee has the right to possession provided he is in possession at the time of the default or obtains such possession lawfully.

(2) Rents and Profits. The mortgagor is entitled to rents and profits. In the absence of an express agreement to the contrary, the mortgagor has the right to all rents and profits realized from the mortgaged property. If the mortgagor cuts timber from the mortgaged property, which can be done only with the consent of the mortgagee, the value of the timber must be applied on the mortgage lest the security be impaired. The mortgagor may retain the profits. This rule or any other rule may, of course, be superseded by a contract providing otherwise.

(3) Cancellation of Lien. The mortgagor has the right to have the lien canceled on final payment. As soon as the mortgage is delivered to the mortgagee, it becomes a lien upon the mortgaged real estate. As a practical matter, a mortgage must be recorded since an unrecorded mortgage is void as to subsequent purchasers, mortgagees, or judgment creditors who have no notice of the mortgage. A mortgage lien is canceled by having the clerk in the recorder's office enter a notation, usually on the margin, certifying that the debt has been paid and that the lien is canceled. The mortgagee, not the mortgagor, must have this done. If he fails or refuses to do so, the mortgagor may institute court action to have this cloud removed from his title.

(4) Redemption. The mortgagor is entitled to the right of redemption. In the event of default, the mortgagee may institute foreclosure proceedings. If the payments in arrears are paid in full by the mortgagor, and all court costs are paid, his right in the property is redeemed. This right is a statutory right, and each statute

sets forth exactly what the mortgagor must do to exercise the right of redemption. Some statutes provide that if one installment is in arrears, the whole debt becomes due and must be paid in full before the mortgagor can redeem his interest. This duty may be imposed by contract rather than by law.

If the property has been sold at a foreclosure sale, the mortgagor has in many states a definite period of time to redeem his interest. To do so he must pay the full purchase price, plus all court costs and commissions, plus any unpaid balance of the mortgage debt.

Foreclosure. If the mortgagor fails to pay the debt secured by the mortgage when it becomes due, or fails to perform any of the other terms set forth in the mortgage, the mortgagee has the right to foreclose for the purpose of collecting the debt. *Foreclosure* usually consists in a sale of the mortgaged property made under an order of a court and generally by an officer of the court.

Foreclose literally means a legal proceeding to shut out all other claims. A first mortgage may not necessarily constitute a first claim on the proceds of the sale. The cost of foreclosure and taxes always take precedence over the first mortgage. People who furnish materials for the construction of a house and workers who work on it have a claim, under what is known as a *mechanics lien,* that takes precedence over a first mortgage. The foreclosure proceedings establish the existence of all prior claims and the order of their priority. Foreclosure proceedings are fixed by statutory law and therefore vary in different states.

If the proceeds of the sale of mortgaged property are greater than the amount of the debt and the expenses of foreclosure, the surplus must be given to the mortgagor. If a deficiency results, however, the mortgagee may secure a deficiency judgment for this amount. In that case the unpaid balance of the debt will stand as a claim against the mortgagor until the debt is paid.

Trust Deed. A trust deed is often used as a substitute for the ordinary form of mortgage for the purpose of securing a debt. A *trust deed* (sometimes called a *trust mortgage*) conveys the property to a disinterested third party, called a *trustee,* to be held in trust for the benefit of the creditor or creditors. If a default in payment occurs, the trustee must foreclose the property and apply the proceeds to the payment of the debt. The proceedings in the foreclosure of a trust deed are similar to those in the foreclosure of an ordinary mortgage. The right to redeem under a trust deed, when it exists, is similar to that under a mortgage.

There are several advantages in the use of a trust deed as a method of securing an obligation. For instance, a trust deed can be used more conveniently than an ordinary mortgage to secure an indebtedness owed to a large number of persons. A bank or a loan agency that has made a large loan receives as evidence of the indebtedness bonds or notes usually for amounts that are multiples of $1,000. The bonds or notes are acompanied by a trust deed. They may then be sold to small investors. The purchaser of one of these bonds or notes becomes a mortgagee to the extent of his purchase.

In the event that the mortgagor defaults in his payments, the mortgagee who holds an ordinary mortgage can foreclose, that is, have the mortgaged property sold to satisfy the debt. In most states, however, he must go into court and have a judicial court foreclosure. In some states the trustee in a trust deed may sell the mortgaged property on the mortgagor's default outside of court without going through a time-consuming court foreclosure. Hence, the property can be more quickly sold at a trustee's sale.

Buying Mortgaged Property. It is a common practice to buy property on which there is a mortgage or a trust deed. The purchaser may agree to "assume the mortgage," that is, to be primarily liable for its payment. He should understand the difference between "assuming" the mortgage and buying the property "subject to the mortgage." In the first case he binds himself to be liable for the mortgage obligation as fully as if he had been the original mortgagor. If he takes the property "subject to the mortgage," he may lose the property but no more. Observe how a knowledge of this point of law may be worth several thousand dollars:

- Ratcliffe sold Hurley a farm for $20,000, Hurley agreeing to pay $5,000 down and "assume a $15,000 mortgage." He held the farm a few years during which time the value of farm land declined considerably. The mortgagee foreclosed on the mortgage and sold the farm for $9,000. This left an unpaid balance of $3,000. Hurley was compelled to pay that. Had he purchased the property "subject to the mortgage," he would not have had to pay the balance of $3,000.

The original mortgagor is not automatically released when he sells mortgaged property whether the purchaser assumed the mortgage or bought it subject to the mortgage. He remains fully liable in both cases. He may be released by the mortgagee by novation, that is, the mortgagee agrees to release the mortgage by extending the time of payment without the mortgagor's consent. Courts have held that the acceptance of interest payment after the principal of the mortgage has become due constitutes an extension of the mortgage. If this is done without the mortgagor's consent, he is fully released from all liability under the mortgage.

Assignment of the Mortgage. The mortgagee may assign his rights under the mortgage agreement. The assignee, that is, the purchaser, obtains no greater rights than the assignor had. To protect himself, the assignee should require the assignor to produce an estoppel certificate signed by the mortgagor. This certificate should acknowledge that the mortgagor has no claims of any kind in connection with the mortgage. This would bar him from subsequently claiming the right of offset.

Questions

1. (a) Define a mortgage.

(b) Does the mortgagor lose possession of the mortgaged property at the time the mortgage is executed?

2. If two mortgages are executed on the same land, which mortgagee has priority?

3. When one executes a twenty-year mortgage on his home, what must he do if he wishes to prepay the mortgage at some future date?

4. If there is a street assessment against mortgaged property for $1,000, who must pay this, the mortgagor or the mortgagee?

5. If the mortgagor tears down a garage worth $800, does this give the mortgagee the right to foreclose?

6. When the mortgage is paid in full, how is this fact indicated in the record books in the county clerk's office?

7. How may the mortgagor redeem his property after it has been sold under a foreclosure sale?

8. If the proceeds of a foreclosure sale of property is not enough to pay off the mortgage, how is the balance of the debt canceled?

9. Name two characteristics that distinguish a trust deed from a mortgage.

10. What is the difference in the liability of the purchaser when he buys mortgaged property "subject to the mortgage" and "assuming the mortgage"?

Case Problems

1. Johnson owned a farm, which included 10 acres of growing cotton. He borrowed $5,000 from Dupree and executed a real estate mortgage on his farm to secure the debt. The mortgage contained the usual clause that the mortgagor must not commit any act that would decrease the mortgagee's risk. It also provided that if the mortgagor sold any timber, pulpwood, or any other part of the real property, the net proceeds must be applied on the $5,000 note. Johnson later sold the cotton for $1,500 but spent the money for living expenses. Dupree brought suit to foreclose on the mortgage because Johnson had violated his contract. Was Dupree entitled to foreclose?

2. Jensen, who had some extra money to invest, agreed to lend Bowen on a first mortgage $15,000 with which Bowen was to build a house on a lot he owned. Jensen agreed to let Bowen have $3,000 to start, and $3,000 a month as the construction progressed, the balance of the $15,000 to be loaned when the building was completed. About 30 days after the home was completed, Jensen and Bowen learned that the contractor had purchased on credit about $3,500 of materials for the house and had not paid for these materials out of the money Bowen paid him for building the house. In addition he owed $1,200 for labor that he had not paid. The materials supplier and the workers demanded that Bowen pay them. He had no money and could not pay. They threatened to sell the house unless Jensen paid them. Jensen contended his first mortgage took precedence over these items. Was this correct?

3. Dennison owned the timber on 1,000 acres of land but did not own the land or any other interest in the land. He borrowed $10,000 from Swanson and executed a first mortgage to Swanson on the timber as security for the loan. He sold about half of the timber to the Logan Lumber Company for $12,000 but did not pay any part of the proceeds on the $10,000 mortgage. Swanson indicted Dennison for willfully impairing the security of his loan, and he brought an action to foreclose the mortgage. Was he legally justified in taking these actions?

4. Barbara and Donald Shea bought a home for $20,000 and financed it by paying $4,000 down and giving a 20-year first mortgage for $16,000 at 5 per cent. Donald wished that in the event of his premature death, Barbara have the home free of debt. Consequently he purchased a mortgage life insurance policy whereby the insurance company agreed in event of Donald's death to pay off the balance of the principal of the mortgage plus accrued interest. Donald died one year later. At that time there was a balance of $15,860 principal and accrued interest on the loan. The life insurance company paid this. The mortgagee refused, however, to cancel the mortgage, claiming an additional $7,200 for interest for the next 19 years since the mortgage did not contain an acceleration clause. Must Barbara pay this $7,200?

5. Billy and Yvonne Rogers owned 80 acres of land with a modern dwelling. There was a first mortgage on the property for $12,000. The entire property was worth about $14,000. Yvonne's father was retired on a pension of $80

a month. Billy and Yvonne deeded him and his wife two acres of land so that he could take what cash he had and build himself a modest house for $6,000. Soon after the father-in-law completed his house, the country experienced a rather serious recession. Real estate values declined about 25 per cent. Billy lost his job and was unable to keep up his payments on the mortgage. The mortgagee foreclosed on the 78 acres and sold it at public auction. It brought only $9,000, leaving a balance on the mortgage of $3,000. The mortgagee threatened to sell the father-in-law's two acres and house if the father-in-law did not pay the $3,000. Was Billy's mortgage also a lien on the father-in-law's property?

6. Holleran borrowed $10,000 from Carswell and executed a first mortgage on his home as a security for the loan. Carswell later purchased a restaurant from Holcomb for $20,000 and, as part payment, assigned to Holcomb the first mortgage which he held on Holleran's home. At the time of the assignment Holleran had a claim against Carswell for $3,000 as a result of an automobile accident caused by Carswell's negligence. Holcomb did not know of this claim at the time he sold his restaurant to Carswell. When the mortgage came due and Holcomb demanded payment, Holleran contended he did not owe $10,000, but only $7,000 after taking credit for the $3,000 damage claim. May Holleran offset his claim of $3,000 against Holcomb's claim for $10,000?

7. Cook wished to borrow his neighbor Fleeman's truck to haul cotton to the gin. Fleeman, fearing that Cook might have a wreck which would subject Fleeman to a suit for damages, had Cook execute and deliver to him a mortgage on Cook's farm for $5,000. Was this a valid mortgage?

8. Mr. and Mrs. North purchased a home and agreed to pay $18,000 for it. They paid $3,000 down and assumed a $15,000 mortgage, which was to be paid off at the rate of $100 a month. The company for which Mr. North worked moved away, and Mr. North therefore lost his job. As a result he was unable to keep up the payments on the mortgage. The property was foreclosed and sold. The purchaser paid $10,000. This left an unpaid balance of $2,000. Were Mr. and Mrs. North liable for the payment of this $2,000?

9. Rankell had a ten-year mortgage on his home, to be paid at the rate of $75 a month. He was discharged from his job and defaulted on two monthly payments before he obtained another job. The mortgagee foreclosed immediately upon the first default. What were Rankell's rights?

Chapter 44

Landlord and Tenant

Relation of Landlord and Tenant. The relation of landlord and tenant is created by a contract, written or implied, whereby one person agrees to lease land or a building to another. No special words or acts are necessary to create such an agreement. The possession of the premises and the payment of rent for its use are the chief characteristics that determine the relation of landlord and tenant.

The owner or the holder of the property is known as the *landlord* or *lessor*. The person who is given possession of the property is the *tenant* or *lessee*. The contract between the two parties is called a *lease*. The amount the landlord is to receive for the use of the property is the *rent*.

A tenant is distinguished from a lodger or roomer in that the former has the exclusive legal possession of the property, while the latter has merely the right to use the premises subject to the control and supervision of the owner.

The Lease. A lease is a contract creating the relation of landlord and tenant. The lease may be oral or written, express or implied, formal or simple, subject, however, to statutory requirements in some states that a lease of land for a term longer than one year must be in writing. Regardless of the form of the lease, the parties are bound by the terms of the contract. If a dispute arises between the tenant and the landlord over their rights and duties, the court will look to the contract to determine the correct decision. If, as so often happens, the contract is silent on the point in dispute, then the court falls back on the vast accumulation of judicial precedents covering the

LEASE CONTRACT FOR CITY PROPERTY. THE McGREGOR CO., PRINTERS, ATHENS, GA.

STATE OF GEORGIA, Clarke **County.**

THIS AGREEMENT, made the 6th day of January, 1957

between Paulson Realty Company

of the County of Clarke, hereinafter known as Lessor, and John Mitchell

of said county, hereinafter known as Lessee;

WITNESSETH: That the said Lessor has this day rented to said Lessee the following:

a residential dwelling

situated on the South side of Dobson Street

between ______ and ______ Street

in Clarke County, Georgia, and known as No. 254 for the purpose of identification and for no other purpose.

The duration of said rental shall be one year commencing on the 1st day of February, 1957, and ending on the 31st day of January, 1958

For the rental of said premises said Lessee is to pay the sum of $120 a month Dollars per month, payable in advance; and should said lessee fail to pay said rent promptly when due, or should sublet said premises or assign this lease without the consent of the lessor in writing, or should use said rented premises for any other purpose than that herein specified, or otherwise violate any of the terms of this contract, then the lessor may at its option, terminate this contract, cancel the same and take immediate possession of the rented premises, without waiving any rent that may have accrued at the time of cancellation, or any claim for damages for breach of the contract on the part of the lessee.

Said lessee hereby certifies that said premises have been examined by lessee and agrees to accept them as they now stand, and agrees that said lessor shall make only such repairs to said premises during the term of this contract as seem to the lessor advisable, but the lessor reserves the right to enter upon said premises for the purpose of making repairs or improvements upon the same or upon adjoining property of lessor.

The lessee agrees that no alterations shall be made in said rented premises, nor signs put up or painted on walls, windows or other portions of said premises without first having obtained written consent of the lessor and further that if the lessor requires, such alterations, signs, etc., shall at termination of contract be removed at the expense of the lessee and any damage caused by alterations or signs be paid for by lessee.

Lessee agrees to repair at his own expense any damage to the plumbing on said premises caused by freezing, and to pay the water, gas and electric rent on said premises, and to deliver said premises to the lessor at the expiration of the term of rental in as good order as when received, ordinary wear and tear with careful usage excepted. Said lessee further agrees to pay for all breakage or loss occurring to said premises.

Said lessor agrees that if the premises should be destroyed by fire or so damaged as to become untenantable, due not to the fault or neglect of lessee or his servants, employees or family or guests or other persons on said premises with lessee's consent or knowledge, the rent on said premises shall cease until the same are restored to tenantable condition, the lessor having the option to rebuild, repair or make any other disposition of said premises that he may deem proper.

This rent contract and the rights of lessee thereunder shall not be an asset of said lessee's estate to be sold either by administrators, executors, heirs, or by receivers or trustees in bankruptcy, or receiver in insolvency proceedings, but in the event of death or bankruptcy or insolvency of lessee, lessor may, if he so desires, immediately terminate this contract and resume possession of the premises. If through oversight or otherwise said lessee should hold such premises beyond the term herein limited then lessee shall become a lessee at will and shall surrender said property on sixty days notice from the lessor. It is expressly agreed that there shall be no extension or renewal of this lease or continued occupancy of said premises beyond the term of this lease unless there be an agreement in writing to that effect signed by the lessor.

Said lessee hereby promises to pay to lessor, or order, the sum herein stated at the times stated and interest on any past due and unpaid installments of rent at the rate of eight per cent. per annum from the time when due, and all costs of collection including ten per cent. as attorney's fees in case the matter is sued after the holder was given written notice of intention to sue and the term to which suit will be brought, mailing such notice to lessee at above address being sufficient compliance with these requirements and lessee waiving any other notice.

And for himself, his heirs and family said lessee hereby waives and renounces all benefits of homestead and exemption he may have under and by virtue of the Constitution and Laws of the State of Georgia and United States as against this debt.

No claims for damages shall be made by lessee nor delay in payment of rent for the want of repair in these premises or any other premises of lessor.

Lessor reserves the right to place a card "For Rent" or "For Sale" on said premises at any time within sixty days prior to the termination of this contract of rent.

It is agreed between the parties to this contract that neither shall be bound by any verbal statement or agreements or any subsequent contract relating to the above described property during the period covered by this contract unless endorsed hereon and signed by the parties thereto.

In WITNESS WHEREOF: Said lessor and lessee have hereunto set their hands and affixed their seals in duplicate the day and year first above written.

Paulson Realty Co. (L. S.)	John Mitchell (L. S.)
By John Paulson (L. S.)	(L. S.)
Lessor	Lessee

A Lease.

point. The judicial precedents may be supplemented by state statutes.

For the above reasons a lease should preferably be in writing and should be complete and cover all the terms of the contract. Such items as the time and place of payment of rent, the notice required to vacate, the duration or the nature of the tenancy, and any specific provision desired by either party, such as the right of the landlord to show the property to prospective purchasers should be included.

Types of Tenancies. One becomes a tenant by contract, either express or implied. The nature of the contract determines the class of tenancy created. There are four separate and distinct classes of tenancies, each having some rule of law governing it that does not apply to any other type of tenancy. The four classes of tenancies are:

1. Tenancy for years
2. Tenancy from year to year
3. Tenancy at will
4. Tenancy by sufferance

(1) TENANCY FOR YEARS. A *tenancy for years* is any tenancy for a definite period of time, whether it be one month, one year, or ninety-nine years. The termination date is fixed by the lease. The payment of the rent may be by the month even when the tenancy is for ten years. Some states hold that no notice to terminate the tenancy is required when the termination date is fixed by the lease. Other states fix by statute the number of days' notice which must be given.

(2) TENANCY FROM YEAR TO YEAR. When the tenancy is for an indefinite period of time with rent due at stated intervals, it is known as a *tenancy from year to year*. Under such a tenancy, a tenant merely pays the rent periodically and the lease lasts until the end of the period after proper notice of termination has been given. A

tenancy of this kind may be by the week, by the month, by the year, or any other period agreed upon.

Notice to terminate this type of tenancy must follow exactly the state law governing it. In a tenancy from month to month, notice is usually required thirty days before the rent-due date. In a tenancy from year to year, one group of states requires a ninety-day notice to terminate. Failure to give this notice at least ninety days before the end of the year automatically renews the lease for one more year on the same terms as those of the preceding year. Other states hold that failure to give notice of intention to terminate the lease merely creates a tenancy at will.

(3) TENANCY AT WILL. A *tenancy at will* exists when the tenant has possession of the property for an uncertain period. Either the tenant or the landlord can terminate the tenancy at will, although a reasonable notice to that effect is required, usually thirty days. Of all the types of tenancies this is the only one that is automatically terminated upon the death of the tenant.

(4) TENANCY BY SUFFERANCE. When a tenant holds over his tenancy after the expiration of the lease without permission of the landlord, a *tenancy by sufferance* exists until the landlord elects to treat the tenant as a trespasser or as a tenant. The landlord may treat the tenant as a trespasser, sue him for damages, and have him removed by legal proceedings; or, if the landlord prefers, he may accept payment of the rent due for another period and thus recognize the tenant's possession as rightful.

Rights of the Tenant. A lease gives the tenant certain rights, as follows:

1. Right to possession
2. Right to use the premises
3. Right to sublease

(1) Right to Possession. When the landlord signs the lease, he warrants that he has the right to lease the premises and that the tenant shall have quiet possession during the period of the lease. During the term of the lease, the tenant has the same right to exclusive possession of the premises as if he owned the property. If someone questions the owner's right to lease the property, the landlord must defend the tenant's right to exclusive possession. Failure of the landlord to give possession on time or to protect the tenant's rights subjects the landlord to liability for damages.

A particular cause of dispute between landlord and tenant is the existence of a nuisance that disturbs the tenant's quiet enjoyment of the property. If the nuisance existed at the time the tenant leased the property and he was aware of its existence, he will be deemed to have waived his right to complain. Also if the nuisance is one over which the landlord has no control, the tenant cannot avoid his contract even though the nuisance arose subsequent to the signing of the lease. If the landlord fails or refuses to abate a nuisance over which he has control, the tenant not only may terminate the lease but may sue for damages also. In other cases he may seek an injunction compelling the landlord to abate a nuisance. Failure to remove dead rats from the wall, failure to stop disorderly conduct on the part of other tenants, and frequent and unnecessary entrances upon the property by the landlord or his agents are examples of acts which the courts have held destroy the tenant's right to quiet enjoyment and constitute a breach of warranty on the part of the landlord.

(2) Right to Use the Premises. Unless this right is expressly restricted in the lease, the tenant has the right to use the premises in any way consistent with the nature of the property. He cannot convert a dwelling into a machine shop nor a clothing store into a restaurant. Damage to leased property other than that which

results from ordinary wear and tear is not permissible. The tenant may cut wood for his own use but not to sell.

(3) RIGHT TO SUBLEASE. A tenant, unless prohibited by the contract, has the right to sublease the premises, except in tenancies at will and by sufferance. Most business leases prohibit subleasing, and this provision of the contract must be scrupulously observed. The contract makes a distinction between subleasing and joint occupancy with another. The tenant may permit another to use the premises with him so long as he does not relinquish control over the premises.

Duties of the Tenant. Duties of the tenant are:

1. To pay rent
2. To protect and preserve the premises

(1) TO PAY RENT. The tenant's main duty is to pay the rent. This payment must be made in money unless the contract provides otherwise, such as a share of the crops. The rent is not due until the end of the term, but leases almost universally provide for the payment of rent in advance.

It is a common practice for the landlord to appoint an agent for the purpose of collecting the rent. The death of the principal automatically terminates the agency-principal relationship. If rent is paid to the agent after this termination and the agent does not remit to the proper party, the rent must be paid again.

If the rent is not paid on time, the landlord may terminate the lease and order the tenant to vacate, or he may permit the tenant to continue occupancy and sue for the rent. Under the common law the landlord could seize and hold any personal property found on the premises. This right has been either curtailed or abolished by statute. Most states permit the landlord to obtain a *distress warrant* and have the sheriff sell the property to pay the rent.

(2) To Protect and Preserve the Premises. The tenant must make all repairs necessary to prevent damage to or deterioration of the premises. He is not required to make repairs of a structural nature, however. If the roof blows off, the tenant need not put on a new roof unless he wishes to keep out the snow and rain. The landlord is under no obligation to put on a new roof either unless a state law requires the landlord to keep the property habitable. Damage to the leased property does not cancel the obligation to pay rent. The tenant may protect himself either by taking out insurance against damage to the property or by having a cancellation clause in the lease.

Under the common law the tenant had to restore property at his own expense if it was destroyed. There has been an almost uninterrupted trend to modify this rule either by statute or by judicial decision. A few states have gone so far as to release the tenant completely from all liability, including the further payment of rent, when the property has been rendered untenantable due to no fault of the tenant. The majority of states continue, however, to hold the tenant liable for the rent even though the property is no longer usable. The tenant may protect himself either by contract or by purchasing insurance to the extent of his possible loss.

Rights of the Landlord. The landlord has three definite rights under the lease:

1. To regain possession
2. To enter upon the property to preserve it
3. To assign his rights

(1) To Regain Possession. Upon the termination of the lease, the landlord has the right to regain peaceable possession of the premises. If this possession is refused, the most common remedy is to bring an *action of ejectment* in a court of law. Upon the successful completion of

this suit, the sheriff will forceably remove the tenant and his property.

When the landlord repossesses the property, he may also retain all permanent improvements and fixtures securely fastened to the property. The test is whether or not the improvements have become a part of the real estate. If they have, they cannot be removed.

(2) To Enter upon the Property to Preserve It. The landlord has a right to enter upon the property to preserve it. He cannot make extensive renovations that interfere with the tenant's peaceable occupancy. If the roof blows off or becomes leaky, the landlord may repair it or put on a new roof. He cannot use this occasion to add another story. If the landlord comes upon the property without permission, he may be treated as a stranger. He has no right to show the property to prospective purchasers or tenants. He may, of course, reserve this right in the lease itself.

(3) To Assign His Rights. The landlord has the right to assign his rights under the lease to a third party. The tenant cannot avoid any of his duties and obligations by reason of the assignment of the lease. Like all other assignments, the assignment does not release the assignor from the contract without the consent of the tenant. If, for example, the tenant was injured because of a concealed but defective water main cover, and the landlord knew of this defective condition, then the landlord would be liable even though he assigned his rights before the injury.

Duties of the Landlord. The lease also imposes upon the landlord certain dtuies. His chief duties are:

1. To pay taxes
2. To protect the tenant against latent defects

(1) TO PAY TAXES. Although the tenant occupies and uses the premises, the landlord must pay all taxes and special assessments. Sometimes the lease provides that the tenant shall pay the taxes. In such event, he is not liable for special assessments for sidewalks, street paving, and other improvements.

(2) TO PROTECT THE TENANT FROM LATENT DEFECTS. If the tenant is damaged because of latent defects, the principal is liable. Such defects might be contamination from contagious germs, unfilled wells that are concealed, and rotten timbers in the dwelling. Defects which can be seen by inspection are the tenant's responsibility. Most cities and many states have tenement laws that require the landlord to keep all rental property habitable and provided with adequate fire escapes. Any damage due to a failure to observe these laws may subject the landlord to liability for damages.

Termination of the Lease. A lease that is to exist for a fixed time automatically terminates upon the expiration of that period. The death of either party does not ordinarily affect the lease. If the leased property consists of rooms or apartments in a building and they are destroyed by fire or any other accidental cause, the lease is terminated without liability on the part of the tenant. The landlord may agree to the voluntary surrender of the possession of the premises before the lease expires. An abandonment of the premises without the consent of the landlord is not a surrender, however, but a breach of contract.

If the lease is to run from year to year or from month to month, the party wishing to terminate it must give the other party a written notice of his intention. Statutes prescribe the time and the manner of giving notice; they may also specify other particulars, such as the grounds for a termination of the tenancy.

If either party fails to give proper notice, the other party may continue the tenancy for another period.

NOTICE TO LEAVE THE PREMISES

To Mr. C. Harold Whitmore

You will please take notice that I *want you to leave the premises you now occupy, and which you have rented of* me, *situated and described as follows:*

Suite 4
Lakeview Apartment
Lake Shore Drive at Overview Street

in Cleveland, *County of* Cuyahoga *and State of* Ohio

Your compliance with this Notice by July 31

will prevent legal measures being taken by me *to obtain possession of the same, agreeably to law.*

Yours respectfully,

H. L. Simpson

May 1 19__.

A Landlord's Notice to Leave the Premises.

A tenant refusing to surrender possession of the property after the expiration of his lease may be liable in a summary action brought by the landlord to regain possession. This is called a *forcible entry and detainer action.* In this matter the statutes of the different states

To Mr. George A. Hardwick
1719 Glenview Road, St. Louis, Missouri

Take notice that I shall on the 31st *day of* March, *19*__, *quit the possession and remove from the premises located at*

1292 Clarendon Road, St. Louis, Missouri

which I now hold as your tenant. This 2nd *day of* January, *19*__.

John N. Richter

A Tenant's Notice That He Is Leaving the Premises.

have provided for the quick recovery of real property by the one legally entitled to it.

Improvements. Tenants frequently make improvements during the life of the lease. Many disputes arise as to the tenant's right to take these improvements with him. The test is whether an improvement is temporary or permanent. If a farm tenant builds a fence in the normal way, the fence is a permanent improvement and he has no right to remove it when he leaves. If the fence is loosely attached to temporary posts in such a manner as to indicate temporary usefulness, it is removable. In one case it was held that a poultry house built in the usual way was a permanent improvement and could not be removed. In a similar case the tenant built the poultry house on sled-like runners. When he was ready to leave, he hitched his team to the poultry house and hauled it away. The court held that he was within his rights because it was a temporary improvement.

It is well to remember that one may freely contract away his rights or he may waive them. In one case a tenant built a permanent frame house on leased property with the landlord's assurance that he could remove the house at the end of the lease. The landlord was bound by this contract.

Easements and Licenses. An *easement* is an interest in land, such as a right-of-way across another's land or the use of another's driveway. Strictly speaking, an easement is not a tenancy, but it is in the nature of an estate. Being an interest in land, the right must be created by a written contract or acquired by adverse possession by continued and uninterrupted use of the land.

A *license* is not an interest in land but a right to use in some minor way the real property of another. It may be acquired by an oral contract if the license is to run for one year or less.

Questions

1. (a) Who is a landlord?

(b) What characteristic distinguishes a tenant from a lodger?

2. If Healy leases a building for five years with the rent to be paid each year in advance, is this a tenancy for years or a tenancy from year to year?

3. If Mary and Howard rent an apartment for five months at $75 a month, what kind of tenancy is this?

4. If John rents a filling station "until it is sold," what kind of tenancy is this?

5. What rights does the tenant have when he leases property?

6. (a) If a hurricane breaks all the windows in a dwelling, must the tenant replace these windows at his own expense?

(b) If leased property is destroyed by fire, must the tenant continue to pay rent?

7. Who must pay the taxes on leased property, the landlord or the tenant?

8. Name three rights that a landlord has.

9. If a tenant builds a garage on the property, may he take the garage with him when he moves? Explain.

10. What is an easement?

Case Problems

1. A storm blew off the roof of a farm house. The tenant immediately at his own expense put on a new roof. The contract was silent about repairs. The tenant refused to pay any more rent until the rent equaled the cost of the roof. The landlord brought suit to evict the tenant for nonpayment of rent. Who was entitled to win the suit?

2. Davis leased a home from Hunnicutt for two years. The front steps were in bad condition at the time the lease was signed. Campbell, an insurance salesman, called at Davis' residence to sell him a comprehensive personal liability policy. The steps on which Campbell was standing collapsed and Campbell was seriously injured. He sued Davis for damages. Davis did not carry comprehensive personal liability insurance which would have protected him against this type of loss. Was Davis liable for damages?

3. Arnold leased a store for ten years to be used as a jewelry store. The lease prohibited subleasing, the penalty being cancellation of the lease. Arnold entered into a contract with Yates to operate a watch repair shop in a back room. Yates was to pay Arnold 20 per cent of his income from watch repairing as rent. The landlord attempted to cancel the lease. Did he have the right to do this?

4. A merchant leased a lot and a store building for a term of five years. The lease contained no covenant in respect to repairing or rebuilding the store in case it was damaged or destroyed. The building was accidentally destroyed by fire. The landlord refused to rebuild, and the tenant refused to pay rent for the unexpired period.

(a) Was the landlord entitled to collect rent for the period the lease had yet to run?

(b) Was the merchant under an obligation to rebuild?

5. On May 15 Pauly rented a house by oral agreement for one year; the occupancy was to begin on June 1. In the state where this property was located, when property is rented from month to month, a thirty-day notice of intention to vacate is required. If the rental contract is for one year or more, a ninety-day notice must be given. A failure to give the required notice renews the contract. On April 28 of the following year, Pauly gave written notice that he intended to vacate the house on June 1. The landlord contended that the lease ran for one more year. Was this correct?

6. Rex purchased the timber on Howington's farm. He could save considerable time and expense by crossing Brown's land. Brown agreed orally to let Rex cross his land upon the payment of $10. When the job was half completed, Brown attempted to prevent Rex from crossing his land. Did he have the right to stop him?

Chapter 45

Wills and Inheritances

Wills. Title to all property, both real and personal, may be transferred by a will. A will is not a contract, but it has the effect and force of a contract after the one who makes the will dies. A *will* is an instrument, prepared in the form prescribed by law, which provides for the disposition of a person's property to take effect after death.

Although a will is not a contract, practically the same rules that determine competency to contract apply to wills. Any person, other than a minor, of sound mind ordinarily is competent to make a will. In a few states minors can, under limited circumstances, make a will.

Limitations on Freedom to Dispose of Property by Will. The right to dispose of property by will is a highly prized right and but few restrictions are placed upon it. These restrictions are:

(1) One cannot deprive a spouse of his common-law right in the property unless this right has been abolished by statute. Under the common law, and the statutory law in many states, the wife is entitled to a life interest in one third of any real property that her husband owned at the time of his death. This right is termed *dower*. It does not extend to personal property. Dower is sometimes called the "widow's third." If the husband made a provision for his wife in his will, the wife may usually elect either to take the right of dower or to take under the will.

Curtesy is the right that a husband has in the real property of his wife after her death. The right of curtesy does not exist unless a lawful marriage was entered into and a child capable of inheriting was born. The fact that the child may have died immediately after birth does not affect the right. Many states have abolished the right of curtesy. In those states the husband takes a one-third interest in the property in the same manner as a widow.

Some states have changed or abolished both dower and curtesy. In such a case the surviving wife or husband inherits according to the statutory provision of the particular state.

(2) Confidential data cannot be bequeathed. A public official, such as the Secretary of State, cannot leave confidential data to a legatee.

(3) One cannot control by will the distribution of his property in perpetuity. The maximum time for the vesting of a devised estate under the rule against perpetuities is fixed as the duration of lives now in being, such as *A* and *B*, and until a third party, such as *C*, reaches twenty-one.

(4) In a few states, one cannot deprive a spouse, a child, or a parent of more than half his estate by leaving it to charity.

Terms Common to Wills. The person making the will is called a *testator*, if a man, and a *testatrix*, if a woman. If the gift is real estate, the one receiving the gift (the beneficiary) is called the *devisee;* if it is personal property, he is called the *legatee.* A *bequest* is a gift of personal property in general. A *legacy* is a gift of a sum of money. The person named in a will as the one to administer the estate is an *executor*, if a man, and an *executrix*, if a woman. One who dies without having made a will is said to die *intestate.* The person appointed by a court to settle the affairs of an intestate is an *administrator*, if a man, and an *administratrix*, if a woman.

Distinguishing Characteristics of a Will. A will has the following outstanding characteristics that distinguish it from many other legal instruments:

(1) A will is construed by the courts with less technical strictness than a deed or any other kind of written document.

(2) A will devising real property must be executed in conformity with the law of the state in which the property is situated. A will bequeathing personal property is governed by the law of the state in which the testator was domiciled at the time of his death.

(3) A will may be revoked at any time during the life of the testator, and at his pleasure.

Formalities. All states, either by legislative enactment or judicial decision, have prescribed the formalities for wills. These formalities vary from extreme simplicity to absurd complexity, but, simple or complex, the form must be strictly adhered to.

When property is left by will, title does not vest in the devisee until the will is probated, that is, until the court directs that the terms of the will be carried out. Naturally this division of property could not be accomplished if the will were not in writing. If a will is written in the testator's own handwriting and is dated, it need not be witnessed in more than a third of the states. In all other states the will must be witnessed by at least two, and in some states three, witnesses regardless of how it is written. The same rule applies in the other states if the will is typed or printed. Probably it is this requirement which has resulted in more wills being broken than any other requirement. The usual requirement is for the witnesses and the testator to sign in the presence of each other.

• In Georgia a man lay dying in a bed that was in the center of the room. When the witnesses to his will signed the will, they used a table six feet in back of the head of the bed; as a result, the testator did not see them sign the will. The court would not probate the will because the witnesses did not sign in the presence of the testator.

LAST WILL AND TESTAMENT OF F. J. ROSE

I, F. J. Rose, of the City of Chicago and State of Illinois, do make, publish, and declare this to be my last Will and Testament in manner following:

FIRST: I direct that all my just debts, funeral expenses, and the cost of administering my estate be paid by my executrix hereinafter named.

SECOND: I give, devise, and bequeath to my beloved daughter, Anna Rose Scott, now residing in Englewood, New Jersey, that certain piece of real estate, with all improvements thereon, situated in the same city and at the corner of Hudson Avenue and Tenafly Road.

THIRD: All the remainder and residue of my property, real, personal, and mixed, I give to my beloved wife, Mary Ellen Rose, for her use and forever.

FOURTH: I hereby nominate and appoint my wife, Mary Ellen Rose, executrix of this, my last Will and Testament, and I direct that she not be required to give bond or security for the performance of her duties as such.

LASTLY: I hereby revoke any and all former wills by me made.

In witness whereof I have hereunto set my hand this tenth day of October, in the year nineteen hundred .

F. J. Rose

Signed, published, and declared by the above-named F. J. Rose as and for his last Will and Testament, in the presence of us and each of us, who, in his presence, and at his request, and in the presence of one another, have hereunto subscribed our names as witnesses on the day and in the year above written.

C O Moore 4316 Cottage Grove Avenue, Chicago, Ill.
Sarah J King 1313 East 63 Street, Chicago, Ill.
S. S. Samuels 2611 Elm Street, Joliet, Ill.

A Will.

Usually the witnesses must testify when the will is probated that they signed the will as indicated by their signatures. Some typical pieces of testimony which have destroyed wills are: "He didn't say, 'This is my last will and testament' "; "After I signed it, the lawyer took it into another room for the boss to sign it"; "He told me he was making me his executor, but I didn't know this disqualified me as a witness"; "I knew I was a beneficiary, but I did not know this disqualified me as a witness."

These and many other instances testify to the extreme urgency of seeing that every technical requirement of the law is complied with. If a person's will is not drawn according to the legal requirements, the court may disregard it and the property may be disposed of in a manner entirely foreign to the testator's wishes.

Special Types of Wills. There are at least three special types of wills to meet special circumstances. First, there are *holographic wills,* which are written entirely in longhand by the testator. Many states will permit such wills to be probated even if there are no witnesses to the will. If its validity is questioned, a handwriting expert can prove whether or not the handwriting in the will is that of the testator's. Second, there are *nuncupative wills,* which are oral wills. An emergency, such as a serious injury in an automobile accident, may make it necessary to make an oral will. The testator, who may be conscious of imminent death, may summon two or more people and orally make his will. These witnesses must then reduce the will to writing within a specified number of days. Some states limit the use of nuncupative wills to members of the armed forces in time of war and mariners at sea. Third, most states make special provision for blind people. The reason for these laws is to excuse blind people from the requirement to see all witnesses sign.

The Wording of a Will. Any words that convey the intention of the testator are sufficient. No matter how inelegant and ungrammatical the language may be, if the intention of the testator can be ascertained, the court will order that the provisions of the will be carried out.

Poor wording in wills, however, is not confined to the illiterate. Since the court will order the terms of a will to be carried out exactly, the wording of the will should express the exact wishes of the testator.

- A well-to-do man, who had provided for his children previously, inserted into his will this provision: "To my brother, Kirby, I leave $8,000." By the time the testator died, his estate had shrunk from $80,000 to $10,000. He had intended to leave his brother one tenth of his estate; but, because of the wording used in the will, his brother received almost the entire estate after the expenses were paid. The testator should have written, "To my brother, Kirby, I leave one tenth of my estate, which sum in no event is to exceed $8,000."

- Two sisters drew wills, each leaving the other all her property. It was their intention that the survivor was to use the estate until her death, at which time she would devise it so that a worthless brother would not get any part of it. They both died at the same time in an automobile accident, and the brother inherited the entire estate. Their prime purpose in making a will had been to keep their property from going to "laughing heirs," those who are delighted when the testator dies. They could have prevented this by including a "common disaster" clause, stipulating how their estate should be distributed in the event both died simultaneously or even within thirty days of each other. Had they done this, the "laughing heir" would now be working instead of living on his inheritance.

The flaws in the wills described in the preceding paragraphs indicate clearly the danger of relying on "homemade" wills. The task of preparing a will which will meet all legal technicalities is clearly a job for an expert. This does not relieve the testator from all responsibility, however. A will may be expertly drawn, but later events may demand a modification.

- Another man left by his will everything he possessed to his wife. The language was clear and explicit. Soon after the will was drawn, a child was born; but no change was made in the will. In most states a man cannot entirely disinherit his children. He must at least recognize them in his will or the document will be void.

In this particular case after the man died, the will was disqualified; one third of the estate went to the wife, and two thirds to the child. The child's part could not be spent except under court order. Before the child became self-supporting, court costs and lawyer's fees consumed 60 per cent of the estate. The father's intentions were to enable his wife to use the money as she saw fit to provide for the child. He should have altered the will as soon as the child was born and left a nominal sum to the child and the bulk of the estate to his wife.

Title by Descent. When a person dies intestate, his property is distributed in accordance with the state law of descent. Every state in the union has such a law. Although these laws vary slightly, on the whole they provide as follows: The property of the intestate, especially his real estate, goes to his children subject to the dower (or curtesy) right of the surviving spouse. If there are no surviving children or grandchildren, the father and the mother, as the next of kin, receive the property. If they are not living, the brothers and sisters become the next of kin; and they are followed by grandparents, aunts and uncles, and so on. Some laws trace the kinship as far as third cousins; others let nieces and nephews precede grandparents. If there are no relatives in the range set out in the statute, the property belongs to the state.

If the owner of property makes no will but leaves his property to be distributed according to the law of descent in force in his state, he has no assurance that his property will be distributed in the manner he desires.

• A man gave his wife a $50,000 home which he had bought with money he had inherited from his parents. Shortly afterward, his wife died without leaving a will. A $20,000 share in the home thereupon went to the dead wife's brother.

Executors and Administrators. For the most part the duties and responsibilities of executors and administrators are similar, but there are three significant differences. (1) With but few exceptions anyone may be appointed an executor; but in the appointment of an administrator there is a clear order of priority in most states. The surviving spouse has first priority, followed by children, grandchildren, parents, and brothers or sisters. One's right to be an administrator is not absolute; certain minimum qualifications as to age, education, and residence are required. (2) An executor looks to the will to ascertain his duties and authority, while the administrator must look to the law governing administrators. (3) The executor may be excused by the testator from furnishing a bond, but an administrator must in all cases execute a bond guaranteeing his faithful performance of his duties. In rare cases the court may require a bond of an executor even when the will expressly exempts him.

The prime duty of an executor or an administrator is to preserve the estate and distribute it to the rightful parties. Any loss due to negligence, bad faith, or breach of trust subjects him to liability. He is required to act in good faith, with prudence, and within the powers conferred on him by will or by law. If any part of the estate is a going business, with but few exceptions the business must be dissolved. All existing contracts must be carried out, but no new commitments may be made except those necessary to preserve the estate or fulfill a contract. If a manufacturer, for example, has $10,000 worth of "goods in process," these may be carried on to finished goods so as to make them salable. A contract to purchase new raw materials to accomplish this purpose is binding on the estate. A will may expressly provide that the executor continue the business. But since neither an executor nor an administrator is an agent of the deceased, nor of the estate, he cannot bind the estate on contracts except those expressly authorized by will or those necessary for a proper administration of an estate. Third parties are charged with knowing these limitations upon the administrator's authority.

A will does not become effective until the death of the testator. If part of the property devised is sold before the will is in effect, the will is inoperative in regard to that particular piece of property.

In addition to an executor, many wills appoint a guardian for the minor children. If this is not done in a will, the court will do so. It is a question which is the wiser course. Probably the safest plan is for the testator to appoint some close relative in whom he has confidence and a bank or trust company to administer the estate as a trust. Most trust companies are reliable; but there are, of course, exceptions. Only a trust company with a reputation for fair dealing should be selected. There have been instances where banks through their trust departments have unloaded their worthless securities on the trust accounts. This practice is rare, but even its remote probability should be avoided so far as possible. Also, many of these banks through their trust agreement absolve themselves from all liability for mistakes and bad judgment. Like lawyers, doctors, and dentists, trust companies hold themselves out to the public as skilled in their profession. The trust agreement should not release them from this responsibility.

Revocation. A will may be changed, supplanted, or revoked at any time the testator chooses. It may be revoked by mutilation, cancellation, destruction, or execution of a new will. It must be destroyed, however, by the testator or by someone acting for him and in his presence. To prevent later disputes, the testator should insert in a new will a clause expressly revoking all prior wills. He should do this even though he may believe that he has never previously made a will, for he may have made one and forgotten about it.

Sometimes a will is mutilated or destroyed by mistake. This does not revoke the will. If the testator dies before he rewrites the will or if the will is mistakenly destroyed after the testator's death, it may be probated if its contents can be established to the satisfaction of the court. Marriage as a rule revokes a will, but a divorce does not revoke a will unless there has been a property settlement.

Codicil. A *codicil* is a postscript that is written below the main portion of the will, after the signature. It is considered a supplement or an addition to the will. The word "codicil" literally means a "little will." A codicil must be executed with all the formalities of the original will, and must be signed and witnessed in like manner.

Questions

1. What is a will?

2. What restrictions are there upon one's right to leave his property by will to anyone he chooses?

3. If one receives $5,000 by will, is this a bequest or a legacy?

4. How does one get actual title to property left to him by will?

5. (a) Do all states require all wills to be witnessed?

(b) How many witnesses are required to validate a will when witnesses are required?

6. Is it safe for one to draw one's own will?

7. If a man dies without leaving a will, how is his property distributed to the heirs?

8. What are the duties of the executor?

9. How may a will be revoked?

10. What is a codicil?

Case Problems

1. Kirkland, sales manager for the Langford Furniture Company, receivea an order for furniture amounting to $10,285 from the John Quarles Furniture Mart. The order was signed by John Knowles, executor for John Quarles. Kirkland shipped the merchandise promptly. When the account was long past due, it was found upon investigation that Quarles' will had never authorized Knowles to continue the business. The heirs of Quarles demanded that the bill

not be paid. Kirkland sued both the estate and John Knowles, executor. There were no bondsmen. Knowles was insolvent. Could Kirkland look to the estate for this debt?

2. Over the years Harvey and his wife, Lydia, accumulated an estate of $200,000. Harvey made a will leaving all his property, both personal and real, to Lydia. Two or three years later they were divorced, but no property settlement was made. Harvey remarried. Soon after his remarriage, he died without having changed or revoked his will. Sally, his second wife, demanded all his estate since there were no children. Lydia claimed that all the estate belonged to her. Who was entitled to the estate, Sally or Lydia?

3. McKay, who was seriously injured in an automobile accident, was convinced that he would die. He told two of his friends how he wanted his property distributed. The next day these two men wrote down what McKay told them and both signed it. McKay recovered in about three weeks but then died of a heart attack about two weeks later. There was no connection between his heart attack and his injury in the automobile accident. McKay did nothing before he died to change his oral will. One son, Todd, was dissatisfied with his share of the estate and took legal action to bar a probation of the oral will. Was the will valid?

4. At the time of his death Cohen lived in Georgia. He owned personal property worth over $1,000,000, most of which was kept in Virginia. The Georgia law requires three witnesses to a will, while the Virginia law requires only two witnesses. Cohen made a will just one month before his death and obtained two witnesses to his signature. He left $500,000 to a charitable organization. His two sons brought an action to invalidate the will because it did not meet the requirements of the Georgia law. Was this a valid will?

5. Welch, a single man, sold a patent for $50,000. He then married Evaline and gave her $25,000 in government E bonds as a wedding present. Shortly after their marriage Evaline died. They had no children and Evaline left no will. Welch's mother-in-law, demanded one half of the E bonds. Was she entitled to them?

Chapter 46

Bankruptcy

Purposes of Bankruptcy. *Bankruptcy* is a legal, not a financial status. No matter what the status of one's finances may be, he is not bankrupt until the court in a bankruptcy proceeding declares him a bankrupt. Insolvency is purely a financial status, that is, inability to pay one's debts. It may warrant a petition asking the court to declare the insolvent person a bankrupt; but mere insolvency is not bankruptcy. The Bankruptcy Act defines *insolvency* as insufficient assets to pay all debts outstanding, or an inability to pay one's debts when they come due.

The bankruptcy law has two very definite purposes:

1. To give the debtor a new start
2. To give creditors an equal chance in the collection of their claims

(1) TO GIVE DEBTOR A NEW START. If an honest debtor is hopelessly insolvent, he may be tempted to cease trying even to earn a living. Hope is the great stimulant to enterprise and honest endeavor. If hope vanishes, effort diminishes or may even vanish. By permitting an insolvent debtor to give up all his assets with a few minor exceptions and thereby get forgiveness of his debts, he can at least start anew with the hope of success. Frequently a debtor has assets considerably in excess of his debts, but the assets are "frozen" so that he cannot obtain enough cash to pay his current claims. The present Bankruptcy Act allows one to go into receivership without actually going all the way bankrupt. The court prescribes an equitable settlement under the

circumstances; and when these conditions are fully met, the debtor may resume full control of his business.

(2) To Give Creditors an Equal Chance. If one is bankrupt, it is unfair to permit some unsecured creditors to get paid in full while others receive nothing. By appointing a trustee to take over the bankrupt's property and to pay each creditor in proportion to his claim, a more equitable settlement is achieved. Not only is this arrangement more equitable, but it is less wasteful and less expensive than for each creditor to sue the debtor in separate suits.

Kinds of Bankruptcy. There are two kinds of bankruptcy:

1. Voluntary
2. Involuntary

(1) Voluntary Bankruptcy. Anyone, except a city, a railroad, an insurance company, or a bank, may file a voluntary petition to be adjudicated a bankrupt. It is not necessary that the petitioner be insolvent, but in practice only insolvent debtors ask to be declared bankrupt.

(2) Involuntary Bankruptcy. Under certain conditions one may be forced into involuntary bankruptcy. Three or more creditors, whose aggregate claims amount to $500 in excess of any collateral held as security, are necessary to file a petition to have an insolvent debtor declared a bankrupt if there are twelve or more creditors.

If the debtor is declared a bankrupt, the procedure in liquidating his estate is the same whether it is a voluntary bankruptcy proceeding or an involuntary one.

Acts of Bankruptcy. Before one may be declared an involuntary bankrupt he must have committed an act of bankruptcy. Any one of the following six acts is considered sufficient to warrant the court in declaring the debtor an involuntary bankrupt:

1. A fraudulent transfer
2. Giving preference to creditors
3. Permitting a lien to be obtained
4. Assignment of claims for the benefit of creditors
5. Appointing a receiver for assets
6. Admitting insolvency in writing

(1) A FRAUDULENT TRANSFER. The transfer by the debtor of some part of his property for the purpose of defrauding or hindering creditors may be by sale or by concealment. If one while insolvent gives a lien on his property to secure a loan and then uses the money to pay some creditors but not others, he has committed an act of bankruptcy. Also, selling merchandise and then concealing the money is an act of bankruptcy.

(2) GIVING PREFERENCE TO CREDITORS. If the assets of an insolvent debtor are transferred to one or more creditors for the purpose of preferring them over other creditors, the other creditors can petition the court to declare the debtor an involuntary bankrupt.

(3) PERMITTING A LIEN TO BE OBTAINED. If an insolvent debtor permits a lien to be obtained against him through a legal proceeding, he has committed an act of bankruptcy. The debtor may redeem himself, however, by paying the lien within thirty days, or at least five days before the enforcement of the lien.

- Spivak owed ten various creditors $75,000. He had assets of $30,000 in real property and $10,000 in personal property. One of the creditors obtained judgment for $5,000 and had the judgment recorded. He also attached two trucks worth $3,000. Both these liens are acts of bankruptcy. To avoid being declared an involuntary bankrupt, Spivak must pay them within thirty days or sooner if the property is to be sold at a sheriff's sale.

(4) ASSIGNMENT OF CLAIMS FOR THE BENEFIT OF CREDITORS. If an insolvent debtor makes an assignment of claims due him for the benefit of some of his creditors, he commits an act of bankruptcy.

(5) APPOINTING A RECEIVER FOR ASSETS. An insolvent debtor may have the court appoint a receiver for his estate. Also, under most state laws the creditors may have a receiver appointed. For either this voluntary or involuntary appointment of a receiver to be an act of bankruptcy, the debtor must be insolvent. Insolvency in this sense does not necessarily mean an excess of liabilities over assets. It means a mere inability to pay one's debts as they mature. The receiver, with the permission of the court, may permit the debtor to continue to operate his business under strict supervision of the trustee. If the operation of the business proves successful and all debts are paid, then the debtor is restored to full control.

(6) ADMITTING INSOLVENCY IN WRITING. The debtor may admit his insolvency in writing and express his willingness to be declared a bankrupt. In this event, none of the preceding acts need be committed in order for the creditors to have him declared a bankrupt. The chief difference between this type and a voluntary petition is that the creditors must employ the counsel and advance the necessary costs for bringing the action.

Procedure in a Bankruptcy Case. After the court declares a debtor bankrupt, the first step is to call a meeting of all creditors. These creditors then, with the approval of the Referee in Bankruptcy, elect a trustee to take over all the assets of the bankrupt. The trustee steps into the shoes of the bankrupt. He collects all debts due the bankrupt, preserves all physical assets, sues all delinquent creditors of the estate, and finally distributes all money realized according to a definite priority discussed later in this chapter.

Exempt Property. Each state has laws exempting certain property from seizure for the payment of debts. The most common types of property that are excluded are household effects, tools of the trade, such as a carpenter's tools, a dentist's equipment, and similar items within reasonable limits. Life insurance creates a problem because of the diversity of state laws on this subject. If the bankrupt is the insured and if he reserved the right to change the beneficiary, the general rule is that he owns the cash surrender value and this asset must be included in his assets which he turns over to the trustee. If he did not reserve the right to change the beneficiary, the cash surrender value does not belong to him. If the policy were bought, however, in contemplation of bankruptcy and for the purpose of defrauding creditors, the trustee may order the cash surrender value included.

Corporate Reorganization. In 1938 Congress passed a bankruptcy act designed especially for corporations. The usual result in a bankrupt case is for the bankrupt to turn over to a trustee in bankruptcy his entire business for the purpose of having it liquidated. Under this act, the corporate business is turned over in most cases to a trustee, not to liquidate it but to operate it in the hope that the business can be restored to solvency. When solvency is restored, the business is turned back to the absolute control of the stockholders. During the time the trustee in bankruptcy operates the business, he may and usually does employ the executives of the corporation to help him operate the business. They are the employees of the trustee, not of the corporation during this period. He fixes their salaries, defines their duties, and may discharge them at his discretion.

During this interval of operation, a reorganization plan is worked out. This plan is developed in cooperation with the creditors, the stockholders, and the Securities and Exchange Commission. The federal court in which the reorganization petition is filed must approve the reorganization plan before it becomes official. If all parties concerned are satisfied with the new plan, the trustee puts it into operation by relinquishing his authority and turning over control to the new directors. In the event no acceptable plan of reorganization can be worked out, the corporation is adjudged bankrupt and the business is liquidated like all other bankrupt firms.

Arrangements. If the insolvent debtor is not a corporation but a person, partnership, sole proprietorship, real property owner, or wage earner, he may work out an arrangement or composition of creditors that attempts to achieve for him the same advantages the corporate reorganization act gives to corporations. Under the common law, one recalcitrant creditor could prevent a composition among creditors of an insolvent debtor. Under the present law a majority of creditors can impose a settlement upon the rebellious minority. The debtor is as fully released from his debts as if he had been formally declared a bankrupt. The purpose of these arrangements or compositions is to reduce the expense and to enable the debtor to avoid the stigma of bankruptcy. The creditors receive as much or more than they would under a full bankrupt procedure.

Duties of the Bankrupt. The bankrupt must cooperate fully with the trustee. He must attend all creditors' meetings when requested and furnish all relevant evidence about debts due him. He must file with the trustee a schedule of all his assets and all his liabilities. This schedule must be in sufficient detail so that the trustee can list the secured creditors, the partially secured creditors, and the unsecured creditors. Failure of the bankrupt to cooperate with the trustee and to obey all orders of the referee not only may prevent his being discharged from bankruptcy, but may also subject him to criminal prosecution for contempt of court.

Proof of Claims. All creditors of the bankrupt must present proof of their claims to the trustee. A maximum of six months is allowed for presenting proof of claims, after which time all right to the claim is lost. This is true even though the creditor had no knowledge of the bankruptcy proceedings.

Reclamations. Frequently the bankrupt has in his possession at the time he is adjudicated a bankrupt, property that does not belong to him. This property takes the form of bailed goods or property held in trust for another, or as security for a loan. The true owner of the property is not technically a creditor of the bankrupt. He should file a reclamation claim for the specific property. If he files a proof of claim along with the other creditors, he forfeits his right to the specific property.

If one is in possession of a check drawn by the bankrupt, he may or may not lose depending on the circumstances. If the check is an uncertified check, the holder is a mere creditor of the bankrupt and is not entitled to have it cashed. This is the rule because of the fact that a check is not a true assignment of the funds in the bank. If the check is certified, however, the certification constitutes an assignment of funds sufficient to pay the check no longer belong to the bankrupt. The holder can apply for a specific claim upon the fund represented by the check.

Priority of Claims. All claims of a bankrupt may be classified as fully secured claims, partially secured claims, and unsecured claims. Bankruptcy does not disturb this order of priority, although the expenses of the bankruptcy proceedings take precedence even over fully secured claims.

Fully secured creditors may have their claims satisfied in full from the proceeds of the assets used for security. If these assets sell for more than enough to satisfy the secured debts, the remainder becomes available to general creditors.

Partially secured creditors are those with a first lien on some assets but not enough to satisfy the debts in full. The proceeds of the assets on which there are liens are used, with the exceptions set out below, to pay the partially secured creditors, and these creditors then become general creditors for the balance of their claims.

The priority of claims is as follows:

(1) The expenses of preserving and administering the estate

(2) Wage claims not exceeding $600 for any one wage earner provided the wages were earned not more than three months prior to the bankruptcy proceedings

(3) Tax claims

(4) Rent due and owing at the time the bankruptcy proceedings were instituted but not to exceed three months' rent

(5) Fully secured creditors

(6) Partially secured creditors

(7) Unsecured creditors

Debts not Discharged. Certain obligations cannot be avoided by bankruptcy. The most important of these claims are:

(1) Claims for alimony and child support

(2) All taxes—federal, state, and local

(3) Debts owed by reason of embezzlement or larceny

(4) Debts due on a judgment for malicious injury to others, such as a judgment obtained for assault and battery

(5) Wages earned within three months of the bankruptcy proceedings

(6) Deposits left with the bankrupt in a fiduciary capacity or as an employer who accepted a cash deposit from an employee as a fidelity bond

There are many circumstances under which certain debts are not discharged by bankruptcy, but the above list includes all the most usual ones.

Questions

1. Is bankruptcy a legal or a financial status?

2. State two purposes of the law permitting one to go bankrupt.

3. Who may be adjudicated a bankrupt?

4. What is the difference between a voluntary and an involuntary bankrupt?

5. What are some acts of bankruptcy?

6. If an insolvent debtor permits one of the creditors to obtain judgment against him, does this give the other creditors the right to have him declared an involuntary bankrupt?

7. What is the first step to be taken after the court declares a person bankrupt?

8. What are the duties of a bankrupt?

9. What claim has priority in bankrupt?

10. Name some obligations that cannot be avoided by bankruptcy?

Case Problems

1. Henderson held a check drawn by Sellers for $700. He held this check two weeks before presenting it to the bank for payment. When he did present it, he was told that Sellers had been declared a bankrupt two days before, and for that reason the check could not be paid although Sellers had ample funds in the bank to pay it. Henderson contended Sellers had assigned $700 to him before he became bankrupt and, therefore this $700 did not belong to him. Was this contention correct?

2. Rachels conducted a jewelry business. He put on a big sale and took in $25,000 in cash. About thirty days later he asked the court to declare him a voluntary bankrupt. He refused to tell the trustee what he did with the $25,000. Did he have to reveal this information?

3. The three Hill brothers were laborers for Mayberry, a bankrupt. Mayberry owed each of them $300 earned in the last two months. Mayberry's assets amounted to only $1,100 after all costs of the bankruptcy proceedings were paid. His debts amounted to $11,000. How much were the Hill brothers able to collect?

4. O'Hara was in extreme financial difficulties and realized he could not avoid eventual bankruptcy. He accumulated $50,000 in cash by selling much of his property at a large discount. He then purchased a ten-year endowment insurance policy on himself and made his wife the beneficiary. He did not reserve the right to change the beneficiary. He paid for the policy with a single premium payment of $50,000. The state law provided that the cash surrender value of a life insurance policy could not be levied on by creditors when the insured did not reserve the right to change the beneficiary. The creditors contended that this $50,000 belonged to them since the policy was purchased while insolvent and for the purpose of defrauding the creditors. Could the trustee demand that the cash surrender value of this policy be included in the bankrupt's assets?

5. Presley had assets valued at $18,000 and liabilities of $12,000. Most of his assets were "frozen" so that he could not meet his current liabilities. To persuade one creditor not to sue him, Presley gave the creditor a deed of trust on his stock of merchandise. The other creditors sought to have Presley declared a bankrupt. Was this an act of bankruptcy?

6. Short's wife divorced him and the court ordered Short to pay his wife $200 a month indefinitely as alimony. Short sought to avoid this claim by admitting bankruptcy. Could he do this?

7. Dr. McAlpin was declared an involuntary bankrupt. His offices were equipped with the most modern X-ray machines and other equipment, valued at $30,000. The state law stipulated that the tools of one's trade could not be attached by creditors, but the law was not specific as to what constituted tools of trade. Dr. McAlpin contended that none of his equipment need be turned over to the trustee in bankruptcy. The creditors contended that all but the bare minimum needed for general practice of medicine should be turned over. How much of this equipment could Dr. McAlpin keep?

Cases for Review of Part X

1. Blanchard was an employee in a hotel owned and operated by Hamaker. She found $60 in bills on the floor in the parlor of the hotel. She turned the money over to Hamaker on his assurance that he knew who the owner was. Later she learned that Hamaker did not know the owner and had kept the money. Blanchard brought suit to recover the $60. (Hamaker vs. Blanchard, 90 Pa. St. 377) Who was entitled to the $60?

2. Johnson set some bear traps on public land in Idaho. Black found one of the traps, removed it to a new location on the same public land, and caught a bear in the trap. Black was the first one to the trap, but Johnson later claimed the bear because the trap belonged to him. (Johnson vs. Black, 106 N. W. 434) To whom did the bear belong?

3. London owned an apartment house. He purchased from Williams some ice boxes and refrigerators to be placed in the kitchens of the apartments. Williams had retained a seller's lien on the equipment to secure the unpaid purchase price. To do this Williams had to prove that the ice boxes and refrigerators were fixtures and thus personal property, not real estate. (Williams vs. London, 115 N. Y. S. 574) Were they fixtures?

4. Whiting owned a farm from which he cut some trees preparatory to building some farm buildings. Before the logs were used for this purpose, Whiting sold the farm to Cook. The logs were lying on the ground at the time of the sale but nothing was said about who was to get the logs. After the sale of the farm, but before possession was given to Cook, Whiting sold the logs. Thereupon, Cook sued Whiting for the value of the logs, claiming they were a part of the real estate. (Cook vs. Whiting, 16 Ill. 480) Were the logs real estate or personal property?

5. Petz owned a restaurant building which he leased to the Voight Brewing Company. The lease contained no clause obligating the lessor to make repairs. The lessee occupied the building for several years during which time many essential repairs became necessary. Petz refused to make any repairs. The Voight Brewing Company made the necessary repairs and then refused to pay any more rent until the rent due exceeded the cost of the repairs. Petz then sued for the unpaid rent. (Petz vs. Voight Brewing Co., 16 Mich. 418) Was Petz entitled to recover?

6. Rosenberg was a voluntary bankrupt. When he applied for his discharge from bankruptcy, Bloom, a creditor, objected and alleged that the bankrupt had deliberately destroyed his records so that a satisfactory statement of his affairs could not be ascertained. Bloom had loaned Rosenberg large sums of money between 1920 and 1926. Records of all these loans and all other business transactions could not be produced when he went bankrupt in 1936. (Rosenberg vs. Bloom, et al., 99 Fed. [2nd] 249) Was Rosenburg entitled to discharge from bankruptcy?

7. Jacobs and Roth operated a shoe firm. This firm was adjudicated a bankrupt. During one of the meetings of creditors Jacobs was asked to identify a certain document which was handed to him. The document was a statement of credit given by the firm of Jacobs and Roth to the Fushonzeman Shoe Company. This shoe company was not now a creditor of the bankrupt, and Jacobs refused to explain the credit statement claiming that since that company was not a creditor, he did not have to supply any information relative to it. (In Re Jacobs & Roth, 154 Fed. 988) Did Jacobs have to supply whatever information the trustee in bankruptcy deemed relevant?

8. Poe was the mortgagor and Cockrell the mortgagee to the extent of $2,500 upon certain real estate. Poe, before the mortgage was paid, sold the mortgaged property to a corporation, and the corporation in turn conveyed the property to Burke who assumed the mortgage. When Burke defaulted on the mortgage, Corkrell brought suit to foreclose and also secure a deficiency judgment against both Poe and Burke. (Corkrell vs. Poe, 100 Wash. 625) Was Burke liable for the deficiency?

9. Baxter leased a house from Thompson with this provision: "for the full term of while he shall wish to live in Albert Lea." The rental was always paid promptly. Later Thompson desired to cancel the lease and served written notice on Baxter to vacate. Baxter refused and Thompson brought suit to recover the property. (Thompson vs. Baxter, 107 Minn. 102) Must Baxter vacate?

Glossary of Legal Terms

(Other legal terms are defined elsewhere in the text. Refer to the Index for them.)

Abrogate, to repeal; to annul or destroy; to abolish entirely.

Acceptance, an accepted draft; the assent by the person on whom a draft is drawn to pay it when due.

Acceptor, one who assents to an order or a draft.

Accord and satisfaction, an agreement made and executed in satisfaction of the rights one has acquired under a former contract.

Accused, a person charged with a criminal offense.

Acknowledgment, the admission of the execution of a writing made before a competent officer; the formal certificate made by an officer.

Acquittal, the action of a jury in a finding of not guilty.

Action, proceedings at law.

Adjudication, a judicial determination.

Administrator, a person appointed by a court to take charge of the estate of a deceased person.

Adult, one who has reached full legal age.

Affidavit, a voluntary sworn statement in writing.

Affirm, to declare to tell the truth under a penalty of perjury; to confirm.

Alias, Latin word meaning "another name"; an assumed name.

Alibi, a plea of having been in another place when a wrongful act was committed.

Alien, a citizen of one country residing in another.

Alienate, voluntarily to transfer the title to real property.

Alimony, an allowance made to a woman living apart from her husband.

Allegation, a statement of a fact in a legal proceeding.

Alteration, a change or a substitution of one thing for another.

Ambiguity, doubtfulness; the state of having two or more possible meanings.

Annuity, a sum payable yearly for a certain or an uncertain period.

Annulment, the act of making void.

Answer, a written statement of the defendant's claim, as to the facts in a suit in equity; response; reply.

Antedate, a date prior to the true one; an earlier date.

Arbitration, the trial and determination of a controversy by persons chosen by the parties to the dispute.

Arraign, to accuse; to impeach; to read the charge of an indictment.

Assault, to attempt to do hurt to another by physical violence.

Assent, to consent; to concur.

Assets, property available for the payment of debts.

Assign, to transfer property or a right to another.

Assignee, one to whom property has been assigned.

Attachment, the legal process by which a person or property is taken into custody.

Attest, to bear witness.

Attorney, one legally appointed to act for another.

Avoid, to make void; to annul.

Award, the decision of arbitrators.

Bail, security given for the appearance of a person in court.

Bankrupt, one who has been judicially discharged from the obligations of certain past claims.

Battery, the unlawful touching of another.

Beneficiary, the person named in an insurance policy as the one who is to receive the proceeds or benefits accruing thereunder.

Bequest, a gift of personal property by will.

Bilateral, a contract executory on both sides.

Bona fide, in good faith; without deceit or fraud; genuine.

Bond, an instrument under seal, in which a person binds himself to pay to another a sum of money.

Breach, in contracts, the violation of an agreement or obligation.

Brief, written or printed arguments or authorities furnished by a lawyer to a court.

Burglary, the breaking open and entering of a dwelling with the intent to commit a felony.

Case, an occurrence upon which an action in court is based.

Chattel, any article of personal property.

Client, one who employs a lawyer to represent him in legal matters.

Code, a compilation of laws by public authority.

Codicil, an addition of supplement to a will.

Collusion, a secret agreement between two or more persons, designed to obtain an object forbidden by law or to defraud another.

Competency, legal power; adequacy or ability.

Compromise, a settlement reached by mutual concessions.

Consanguinity, relationship by blood.

Consignee, one to whom goods are shipped.

Contract of record, name sometimes given to a judgment of a court.

Conveyance, an act by which the title to real property is transferred.

Corporeal, material; tangible; substantial.

Covenant, a promise contained in a sealed instrument; a solemn compact.

Coverture, the status or condition of a women during marriage.

Curator, a legally appointed custodian of property.

Custody, care, possession, or keeping of property.

Damages, compensation that the law awards for a wrong or an injury done.

Deceit, a device or false representation by which one person misleads another to the latter's injury.

Decree, the decision of a court of equity or admiralty.

Default, the nonperformance of a duty or an obligation.

Defendant, a person against whom a suit is brought.

Defense, that which is relied upon by a defendant to defeat an action; the resistance to an attack.

Demur, to raise an objection as to legal sufficiency.

Deposition, testimony taken down in writing under oath.

Descent, the hereditary succession to an estate.

Disability, incapacity for the performance of a legal act.

Disaffirm, to repudiate; to refuse to confirm.

Divorce, the dissolution of the marriage ties.

Domicile, the place where a person has his permanent home.

Duress, constraint or compulsion.

Easement, the right that one person has to use the land of another for a special purpose.

Embezzlement, the fraudulent appropriation of property by a person to whom it has been entrusted.

Emblements, growing crops that have been sown or planted.

Enact, to make into a law; to establish by a legal act.

Equitable, just; fair; right; reasonable.

Escrow, a written document held by a third person until the happening of a prescribed condition.

Estate, an interest in property.

Estoppel, that which precludes a man from denying or affirming certain facts in consequence of his previous conduct or admissions.

Eviction, the expulsion of an occupant of real property.

Evidence, testimony.

Ex parte, upon or from one side only.

Execution, a writ which authorizes an officer to carry into effect the judgment of the court.

Executor, the person named by the maker of a will to carry out its provisions.

Extradition, the surrender by one government to another of a person charged with a crime.

Factor, an agent appointed to sell goods on commission.

Fiduciary, involving a relation of trust or confidence.

Foreclosure, a proceeding by which the right of the mortgagor to redeem his property is extinguished.

Forfeiture, the loss of some right or privilege.

Franchise, a right or privilege conferred by law.

Garnishment, a process whereby property is attached.

Guardian, one who has the care of a person or property.

Heir, one who inherits by right of relationship.

Indemnity, compensation for loss sustained.

Indenture, a writing in two parts containing a seal.

Indictment, a formal charge preferred by a grand jury.

Infant, any person not of full legal age.

Injunction, a judicial order or decree forbidding the doing of a certain act.

Insolvency, the state of being unable to pay one's debts.

Instrument, a written document.

International law, law observed by independent nations in their intercourse with one another.

Intestate, one who dies without having made a valid will.

Invalid, void; of no legal effect.

Judgment, a decision of a court.

Legacy, a gift of personal property by will.

Legal, authorized or prescribed by law.

Legatee, one to whom a legacy is given.

Levy, to take possession of property to satisfy a judgment.

License, a permit to do an act which would otherwise be unlawful.

Lien, a right to control, hold and retain, or enforce a charge against another's property as security for a debt or claim.

Liquidated damages, the amount agreed upon in advance by the parties to a contract, to be paid in case of a breach.

Litigation, a suit at law; a judicial contest.

Malfeasance, the doing of some wrongful act.

Malice, ill-will towards some person.

Mandamus, a writ issued by a court directing the performance of certain acts.

Merger, an absorption; union or extinguishment of one contract or interest in another.

Minor, any person not of full legal age.

Misrepresentation, a false statement of fact.

Negligence, the omission to do what a reasonable, prudent person would do, or doing what such a person would not have done.

Nominal damages, a trifling sum given for the violation of a right where no actual loss has resulted.

Nuisance, something which wrongfully disturbs, annoys, or injures another.

Obligation, a duty.

Ordinance, a rule of law passed by the legislative body of a city.

Ouster, ejection; dispossession.

Parole, the promise of a prisoner that in return for conditional freedom he will follow certain requirements.

Per se, in itself.

Perjury, willful false testimony under oath in a judicial proceeding.

Plaintiff, one who brings an action in a court.

Precedent, authority followed in courts of justice; a previous decision in a similar case.

Probate, a court having jurisdiction over estates.

Prosecute, to proceed against by legal means.

Prima facie, at first view; apparently true; on the first appearance.

Proxy, a substitute; a person authorized to act for another.

Ratification, confirming an act which was executed without authority or an act which was voidable.

Realty, real property.

Receiver, a person appointed by a court to take charge of property pending litigation.

Release, the surrender or relinquishment to another of a right, claim, interest, or estate.

Remedy, means employed to enforce a duty or redress a wrong.

Replevin, an action to recover possession of property unlawfully detained.

Rescission, cancelling, annulling, avoiding.

Revocation, the annulment or cancellation of an instrument, act, or promise by one doing or making it.

Sentence, the penalty pronounced upon a person convicted of a crime.

SS. or ss., abbreviation for the Latin word scilicet, meaning, to wit; namely; that is to say.

Subpoena, a writ commanding a person to appear as a witness.

Suit, the prosecution of some claim in a court of justice.

Summons, a notice to a person to appear in court.

Testimony, statements of witnesses.

Trespass, an unwarranted invasion of another's right.

Trustee, one who holds property for the benefit of another.

Ultra vires, beyond the power, exceeding authority.

Unilateral, one-sided, applied to contracts where only one promise is still unperformed.

Usury, the taking of more than the legal rate of interest.

Venue, the place where the trial is held.

Verdict, a decision rendered by a jury.

Versus, against (abbreviated vs. and v.).

Waiver, the voluntary surrender or relinquishment of a right or privilege.

Waste, damage or destruction to property done or permitted by a tenant.

Witness, a person who gives testimony in court; one who sees a document executed and signs his name thereto.

Writ, a formal written command issued by a court of law.

Index

J

K

L

M

O

P

Q

R

S

T